Data Mining Cookbook

Data Mining Cookbook

Modeling Data for Marketing, Risk, and Customer Relationship Management

Olivia Parr Rud

Wiley Computer Publishing

John Wiley & Sons, Inc.

NEW YORK • CHICHESTER • WEINHEIM • BRISBANE • SINGAPORE • TORONTO

Publisher: Robert Ipsen

Editor: Robert M. Elliott

Assistant Editor: Emilie Herman

Managing Editor: John Atkins

Associate New Media Editor: Brian Snapp

Text Design & Composition: Argosy

Library of Congress Cataloging-in-Publication Data:

ISBN 0-471-38564-6

Printed in the United States of America.

10 9 8 7 6 5 4 3 2 1

What People Are Saying About Olivia Parr Rud's Data Mining Cookbook

In the *Data Mining Cookbook*, industry expert Olivia Parr Rud has done the impossible: She has made a very complex process easy for the novice to understand. In a step-by-step process, in plain English, Olivia tells us how we can benefit from modeling, and how to go about it. It's like an advanced graduate course boiled down to a very friendly, one-on-one conversation. The industry has long needed such a useful book.

Arthur Middleton Hughes
Vice President for Strategic Planning,
M\S Database Marketing

This book provides extraordinary organization to modeling customer behavior. Olivia Parr Rud has made the subject usable, practical, and fun. . . . *Data Mining Cookbook* is an essential resource for companies aspiring to the best strategy for success—customer intimacy.

William McKnight
President, McKnight Associates, Inc.

In today's digital environment, data flows at us as though through a fire hose. Olivia Parr Rud's *Data Mining Cookbook* satisfies the thirst for a user-friendly "cookbook" on data mining targeted at analysts and modelers responsible for serving up insightful analyses and reliable models.

Data Mining Cookbook includes all the ingredients to make it a valuable resource for the neophyte as well as the experienced modeler. *Data Mining Cookbook* starts with the basic ingredients, like the rudiments of data analysis, to ensure that the beginner can make sound interpretations of moderate-sized data sets. She finishes up with a closer look at the more complex statistical and artificial intelligence methods (with reduced emphasis on mathematical equations and jargon, and without computational formulas), which gives the advanced modeler an edge in developing the best possible models.

Bruce Ratner
Founder and President, DMStat1

To Betty for her strength and drive.
To Don for his intellect.

CONTENTS

ACKNOWLEDGMENTS

A few words of thanks seem inadequate to express my appreciation for those who have supported me over the last year.

I had expressed a desire to write a book on this subject for many years. When the opportunity became a reality, it required much sacrifice on the part of my family. And as those close to me know, there were other challenges to face. So it is a real feeling of accomplishment to present this material.

First of all, I'd like to thank my many data sources, all of which have chosen to remain anonymous. This would not have been possible without you.

During the course of writing this book, I had to continue to support my family. Thanks to Jim Sunderhauf and the team at Analytic Resources for helping me during the early phases of my writing. And special thanks to Devyani Sadh for believing in me and supporting me for a majority of the project.

My sincere appreciation goes to Alan Rinkus for proofing the entire manuscript under inhumane deadlines.

Thanks to Ruth Rowan and the team at Henry Stewart Conference Studies for giving me the opportunity to talk to modelers around the world and learn their interests and challenges.

Thanks to the Rowdy Mothers, many of whom are authors yourselves. Your encouragement and writing tips were invaluable.

Thanks to the editorial team at John Wiley & Sons, including Bob Elliott, Dawn Kamper, Emilie Herman, John Atkins, and Brian Snapp. Your gentle prodding and encouragement kept me on track most of the time.

Finally, thanks to Brandon, Adam, Vanessa, and Dean for tolerating my unavailability for the last year.

I am a data miner by vocation and home chef by avocation, so I was naturally intrigued when I heard about Olivia Parr Rud's *Data Mining Cookbook*. What sort of cookbook would it be, I wondered? My own extensive and eclectic cookery collection is comprised of many different styles. It includes lavishly illustrated coffee-table books filled with lush photographs of *haute cuisine* classics or edible sculptures from Japan's top sushi chefs. I love to feast my eyes on this sort of culinary erotica, but I do not fool myself that I could reproduce any of the featured dishes by following the skimpy recipes that accompany the photos! My collection also includes highly specialized books devoted to all the myriad uses for a particular ingredient such as mushrooms or tofu. There are books devoted to the cuisine of a particular country or region; books devoted to particular cooking methods like steaming or barbecue; books that comply with the dictates of various health, nutritional or religious regimens; even books devoted to the use of particular pieces of kitchen apparatus. Most of these books were gifts. Most of them never get used.

But, while scores of cookbooks sit unopened on the shelf, a few—*Joy of Cooking*, Julia Child—have torn jackets and colored Post-its stuck on many pages. These are practical books written by experienced practitioners who understand both their craft and how to explain it. In these favorite books, the important building blocks and basic techniques (cooking flour and fat to make a *roux*; simmering vegetables and bones to make a stock; encouraging yeast dough to rise and knowing when to punch it down, knead it, roll it, or let it rest) are described step by step with many illustrations. Often, there is a main recipe to illustrate the technique followed by enough variations to inspire the home chef to generalize still further.

I am pleased to report that Olivia Parr Rud has written just such a book. After explaining the role of predictive and descriptive modeling at different stages of the customer lifecycle, she provides case studies in modeling response, risk, cross-selling, retention, and overall profitability. The master recipe is a detailed, step-by-step exploration of a net present value model for a direct-mail life insurance marketing campaign. This is an excellent example because it requires combining estimates for response, risk, expense, and profitability, each of which is a model in its own right. By following the master recipe, the reader gets a thorough introduction to every step in the data mining process, from choosing an objective function to selecting appropriate data, transforming it into usable form, building a model set, deriving new predictive variables, modeling, evaluation, and testing. Along the way, even the most experienced data miner will benefit from many useful tips and insights that the author has gleaned from her many years of experience in the field.

At Data Miners, the analytic marketing consultancy I founded in 1997, we firmly believe that data mining projects succeed or fail on the basis of the quality of the data mining process and the suitability of the data used for mining. The choice of particular data mining techniques, algorithms, and software is of far less importance. It follows that the most important part of a data mining project is the careful selection and preparation of the data, and one of the most important skills for would-be data miners to develop is the ability to make connections between customer behavior and the tracks and traces that behavior leaves behind in the data. A good cook can turn out gourmet meals on a wood stove with a couple of cast iron skillets or on an electric burner in the kitchenette of a vacation condo, while a bad cook will turn out mediocre dishes in a fancy kitchen equipped with the best and most expensive restaurant-quality equipment. Olivia Parr Rud understands this. Although she provides a brief introduction to some of the trendier data mining techniques, such as neural networks and genetic algorithms, the modeling examples in this book are all built in the SAS programming language using its logistic regression procedure. These tools prove to be more than adequate for the task.

This book is not for the complete novice; there is no section offering new brides advice on how to boil water. The reader is assumed to have some knowledge of statistics and analytical modeling techniques and some familiarity with the SAS language, which is used for all examples. What is *not* assumed is familiarity with how to apply these tools in a data mining context in order to support database marketing and customer relationship management goals. If you are a statistician or marketing analyst who has been called upon to implement data mining models to increase response rates, increase profitability, increase customer loyalty or reduce risk through data mining, this book will have you cooking up great models in no time.

Michael J. A. Berry
Founder, Data Miners, Inc
Co-author, **Data Mining Techniques and Mastering Data Mining**

What Is Data Mining?

Data mining is a term that covers a broad range of techniques being used in a variety of industries. Due to increased competition for profits and market share in the marketing arena, data mining has become an essential practice for maintaining a competitive edge in every phase of the customer lifecycle.

Historically, one form of data mining was also known as "data dredging." This was considered beneath the standards of a good researcher. It implied that a researcher might actually search through data without any specific predetermined hypothesis. Recently, however, this practice has become much more acceptable, mainly because this form of data mining has led to the discovery of valuable nuggets of information. In corporate America, if a process uncovers information that increases profits, it quickly gains acceptance and respectability.

Another form of data mining began gaining popularity in the marketing arena in the late 1980s and early 1990s. A few cutting edge credit card banks saw a form of data mining, known as data modeling, as a way to enhance acquisition efforts and improve risk management. The high volume of activity and unprecedented growth provided a fertile ground for data modeling to flourish. The successful and profitable use of data modeling paved the way for other types of industries to embrace and leverage these techniques. Today, industries using data modeling techniques for marketing include insurance, retail and investment banking, utilities, telecommunications, catalog, energy, retail, resort, gaming, pharmaceuticals, and the list goes on and on.

What Is the Focus of This Book?

There are many books available on the statistical theories that underlie data modeling techniques. This is not one of them! This book focuses on the practical knowledge needed to use these techniques in the rapidly evolving world of marketing, risk, and customer relationship management (CRM).

Most companies are mystified by the variety and functionality of data mining software tools available today. Software vendors are touting "ease of use" or "no analytic skills necessary." However, those of us who have been working in this field for many years know the pitfalls inherent in these claims. We know that the success of any modeling project requires not only a good understanding of the methodologies but solid knowledge of the data, market, and overall business objectives. In fact, in relation to the entire process, the model processing is only a small piece.

The focus of this book is to detail clearly and exhaustively the entire model development process. The details include the necessary discussion from a business or marketing perspective as well as the intricate SAS code necessary for processing. The goal is to emphasize the importance of the steps that come before and after the actual model processing.

Who Should Read This Book?

As a result of the explosion in the use of data mining, there is an increasing demand for knowledgeable analysts or data miners to support these efforts. However, due to a short supply, companies are hiring talented statisticians and/or junior analysts who understand the techniques but lack the necessary business acumen. Or they are purchasing comprehensive data mining software tools that can deliver a solution with limited knowledge of the analytic techniques underlying it or the business issues relevant to the goal. In both cases, knowledge may be lacking in essential areas such as structuring the goal, obtaining and preparing the data, validating and applying the model, and measuring the results. Errors in any one of these areas can be disastrous and costly.

The purpose of this book is to serve as a handbook for analysts, data miners, and marketing managers at all levels. The comprehensive approach provides step-by-step instructions for the entire data modeling process, with special emphasis on the business knowledge necessary for effective results. For those who are new to data mining, this book serves as a comprehensive guide through the entire process. For the more experienced analyst, this book serves as a handy reference. And finally, managers who read this book gain a basic understanding of the skills and processes necessary to successfully use data models.

How This Book Is Organized

The book is organized in three parts. Part One lays the foundation. Chapter 1 discusses the importance of determining the goal or clearly defining the objective from a business perspective. Chapter 2 discusses and provides numerous cases for laying the foundation. This includes gathering the data or creating the modeling data set. Part Two details each step in the model development process through the use of a case study. Chapters 3 through 7 cover the steps for data cleanup, variable reduction and transformation, model processing, validation, and implementation. Part Three offers a series of case studies that detail the key steps in the data modeling process for a variety of objectives, including profiling, response, risk, churn, and lifetime value for the insurance, banking, telecommunications, and catalog industries.

As the book progresses through the steps of model development, I include suitable contributions from a few industry experts who I consider to be pioneers in the field of data mining. The contributions range from alternative perspectives on a subject such as multi-collinearity to additional approaches for building lifetime value models.

Tools You Will Need

To utilize this book as a solution provider, a basic understanding of statistics is recommended. If your goal is to generate ideas for uses of data modeling from a managerial level then good business judgement is all you need. All of the code samples are written in SAS. To implement them in SAS, you will need Base SAS and SAS/STAT. The spreadsheets are in Microsoft Excel. However, the basic logic and instruction are applicable to all software packages and modeling tools.

The Companion CD-ROM

Within chapters 3 through 12 of this book are blocks of SAS code used to develop, validate, and implement the data models. By adapting this code and using some common sense, it is possible to build a model from the data preparation phase through model development and validation. However, this could take a considerable amount of time and introduce the possibility of coding errors. To simplify this task and make the code easily accessible for a variety of model types, a companion CD-ROM is available for purchase separately.

The CD-ROM includes full examples of all the code necessary to develop a variety of models, including response, approval, attrition or churn, risk, and lifetime or net present value. Detailed code for developing the objective function includes examples from the credit cards, insurance, telecommunications, and catalog industries. The code is well documented and explains the goals and methodology for each step. The only software needed is Base SAS and SAS/STAT.

The spreadsheets used for creating gains tables and lift charts are also included. These can be used by plugging in the preliminary results from the analyses created in SAS.

While the steps before and after the model processing can be used in conjunction with any data modeling software package, the code can also serve as a stand-alone modeling template. The model processing steps focus on variable preparation for use in logistic regression. Additional efficiencies in the form of SAS macros for variable processing and validation are included.

What Is Not Covered in This Book

A book on data mining is really not complete without some mention of privacy. I believe it is a serious part of the work we do as data miners. The subject could fill an entire book. So I don't attempt to cover it in this book. But I do encourage all companies that use personal data for marketing purposes to develop a privacy policy. For more information and some simple guidelines, contact the Direct Marketing Association at (212) 790-1500 or visit their Web site at www.the-dma.org.

Summary

Effective data mining is a delicate blend of science and art. Every year, the number of tools available for data mining increases. Researchers develop new methods, software manufacturers automate existing methods, and talented analysts continue to push the envelope with standard techniques. Data mining and, more specifically, data modeling, is becoming a strategic necessity for companies to maintain profitability. My desire for this book serves as a handy reference and a seasoned guide as you pursue your data mining goals.

Olivia Parr Rud is executive vice president of Data Square, LLC. Olivia has over 20 years' experience in the financial services industry with a 10-year emphasis in data mining, modeling, and segmentation for the credit card, insurance, telecommunications, resort, retail, and catalog industries. Using a blend of her analytic skills and creative talents, she has provided analysis and developed solutions for her clients in the areas of acquisition, retention, risk, and overall profitability.

Prior to joining Data Square, Olivia held senior management positions at Fleet Credit Card Bank, Advanta Credit Card Bank, National Liberty Insurance, and Providian Bancorp. In these roles, Olivia helped to integrate analytic capabilities into every area of the business, including acquisition, campaign management, pricing, and customer service.

In addition to her work in data mining, Olivia leads seminars on effective communication and managing transition in the workplace. Her seminars focus on the personal challenges and opportunities of working in a highly volatile industry and provide tools to enhance communication and embrace change to create a "win-win" environment.

Olivia has a BA in Mathematics from Gettysburg College and an MS in Decision Science, with an emphasis in statistics, from Arizona State University. She is a frequent speaker at marketing conferences on data mining, database design, predictive modeling, Web modeling and marketing strategies.

Data Square is a premier database marketing consulting firm offering business intelligence solutions through the use of cutting-edge analytic services, database design and management, and e-business integration. As part of the total solution, Data Square offers Web-enabled data warehousing, data marting, data mining, and strategic consulting for both business-to-business and business-to-consumer marketers and e-marketers.

Data Square's team is comprised of highly skilled analysts, data specialists, and marketing experts who collaborate with clients to develop fully integrated CRM and eCRM strategies from acquisition and cross-sell/up-sell to retention, risk, and lifetime value. Through profiling, segmentation, modeling, tracking, and testing, the team at Data Square provides total business intelligence solutions for maximizing profitability. To find more about our *Marketing Solutions: Driven by Data, Powered by Strategy,* visit us at www.datasquare.com or call (203) 964-9733.

Jerry Bernhart is president of Bernhart Associates Executive Search, a nationally recognized search firm concentrating in the fields of database marketing and analysis. Jerry has placed hundreds of quantitative analysts since 1990. A well-known speaker and writer, Jerry is also a nominated member of The Pinnacle Society, an organization of high achievers in executive search. Jerry is a member DMA, ATA, NYDMC, MDMA, CADM, TMA, RON, IPA, DCA, US-Recruiters.com, and The Pinnacle Group (pending).

His company, Bernhart Associates Executive Search, concentrates exclusively in direct marketing, database marketing, quantitative analysis, and telemarketing management. You can find them on the Internet at www.bernhart.com. Jerry is also CEO of directmarketingcareers.com, the Internet's most complete employment site for the direct marketing industry. Visit http://www.directmarketingcareers.com.

William Burns has a Ph.D. in decision science and is currently teaching courses related to statistics and decision making at Cal State San Marcos. Formerly he was a marketing professor at UC-Davis and the University of Iowa. His research involves the computation of customer lifetime value as a means of making better marketing decisions. He also is authoring a book on how to apply decision-making principles in the selection of romantic relationships. He can be reached at WBVirtual@aol.com.

Mark Van Clieaf is managing director of MVC Associates International. He leads this North American consulting boutique that specializes in organization design and executive search in information-based marketing, direct marketing, and customer relationship management. Mark has led a number of research studies focused on best practices in CRM, e-commerce and the future of direct and interactive marketing. These studies and articles can be accessed at www.mvcinternational.com. He works with a number of leading Fortune 500 companies as part of their e-commerce and CRM strategies.

Allison Cornia is database marketing manager for the CRM/Home and Retail Division of Microsoft Corporation. Prior to joining Microsoft, Allison held the position of vice president of analytic services for Locus Direct Marketing Group, where she led a group of statisticians, programmers, and project managers in developing customer solutions for database marketing programs in a variety of industries. Her clients included many Fortune 1000 companies. Allison has been published in the *Association of Consumer Research Proceedings*, *DM News, Catalog Age*, and regularly speaks at the NCDM and DMA conferences. Creating actionable information and new ways of targeting consumers is her passion. Allison lives in the Seattle area with her husband, three sons, dog, guinea pig, and turtle.

Arthur Middleton Hughes, vice president for strategic planning of M\S Database Marketing in Los Angeles (www.msdbm.com), has spent the last 16 years designing and maintaining marketing databases for clients, including telephone companies, banks, pharmaceuticals, dot-coms, package goods, software and computer manufacturers, resorts, hotels, and automobiles. He is the author of *The Complete Database Marketer*, second edition (McGraw Hill, 1996), and *Strategic Database Marketing*, second edition (McGraw Hill, 2000). Arthur may be reached at ahughes@msdbm.com.

Drury Jenkins, an e-business strategy and technology director, has been a business analyst, solution provider, and IT generalist for 19 years, spanning multiple industries and solution areas and specializing in e-business initiatives and transformations, CRM, ERP, BPR, data mining, data warehousing, business intelligence, and e-analytics. Mr. Jenkins has spent the last few years helping the c-level of Fortune 500 and dot-com companies to generate and execute e-business/CRM blueprints to meet their strategic B-to-B and B-to-C objectives. He earned a computer science degree and an MBA from East Carolina University and is frequently an invited writer and speaker presenting on e-business, eCRM, business intelligence, business process reengineering, and technology architectures. Drury can be reached for consulting or speaking engagements at drury.jenkins@nc.rr.com.

Tom Kehler has over 20 years of entrepreneurial, technical, and general management experience in bringing marketing, e-commerce, and software development solutions to large corporations. His company, Recipio, delivers marketing solutions via technology that allows real time continuous dialogue between companies and their customers. Prior to Recipio, Mr. Kehler was CEO of Connect, Inc., which provides application software for Internet-based electronic commerce. Prior to that, Mr. Kehler was Chairman and CEO of IntelliCorp, which was the leading provider of knowledge management systems.

Recipio offers solutions that elicit customer insight and translate this information to actionable steps that enhance competitiveness through better, more customer-centric products; highly targeted, effective marketing campaigns; and ultimately, greatly enhanced customer loyalty. Learn more about Recipio at www.recipio.com.

Kent Leahy has been involved in segmentation modeling/data mining for the last 18 years, both as a private consultant and with various companies, including American Express, Citibank, Donnelley Marketing, and The Signature Group. Prior to his work in database marketing, he was a researcher with the Center for Health Services and Policy Research at Northwestern University. He has published articles in the *Journal of Interactive Marketing, AI Expert, Direct Marketing, DMA Research Council Newsletter, Research Council Journal, Direct Marketing*, and *DM News*. He has presented papers before the National Joint Meeting of the American Statistical Association, the Northeast Regional Meeting of the American Statistical Association, the DMA National Conference, and the NCDM. He holds a Masters degree in Quantitative Sociology from Illinois State University and an Advanced Certificate in Statistics/Operations Research from the Stern Graduate School of Business at New York University. He has also completed further postgraduate study in statistics at Northwestern University, DePaul University, and the University of Illinois-Chicago. He resides in New York City with his wife Bernadine.

Ronald Mazursky, president of Card Associates, has over 17 years of credit card marketing, business management, and consulting experience at Chase Manhattan Bank, MasterCard International, and Card Associates (CAI). His experience includes U.S. and international credit card and service marketing projects that involve product development and product management on both the bank level and the industry level. This enables CAI to offer valuable "inside" perspectives to the development and management of consumer financial products, services, and programs.

Ron's marketing experience encompasses new account acquisition and portfolio management. Ron relies on client-provided databases for purposes of segmentation and targeting. His experience includes market segmentation strategies based on lifestyle and lifecycle changes and geo-demographic variables. Ron has recently published a syndicated market research study in the bankcard industry called CobrandDynamics. It provides the first and only attitudinal and behavioral benchmarking and trending study by cobrand, affinity, and loyalty card industry segment. Ron can be contacted at Card Associates, Inc., (212) 684-2244, or via e-mail at RGMazursky@aol.com.

Jaya Kolhatkar is director of risk management at Amazon.com. Jaya manages all aspects of fraud control for Amazon.com globally. Prior to her current position, she oversaw risk management scoring and analysis function at a major financial institution for several years. She also has several years' experience in customer marketing scoring and analysis in a direct marketing environment. She has an MBA from Villanova University.

Bob McKim is president and CEO of MS Database Marketing, Inc., a technology-driven database marketing company focused on maximizing the value of their clients' databases. MS delivers CRM and prospect targeting solutions that are implemented via the Web and through traditional direct marketing programs. Their core competency is in delivering database solutions to marketing and sales organizations by mining data to identify strategic marketing opportunities. Through technology, database development, and a marketing focus, they deliver innovative strategic and tactical solutions to their clients. Visit their Web site at www.msdbm.com.

Shree Pragada is vice president of customer acquisitions for Fleet Financial Group, Credit Cards division in Horsham, Pennsylvania. Using a combination of his business, technical, and strategic experience, he provides an integrated perspective for customer acquisitions, customer relationship management, and optimization systems necessary for successful marketing. He is well versed in implementing direct marketing programs, designing test strategies, developing statistical models and scoring systems, and forecasting and tracking performance and profit.

Devyani Sadh, Ph.D., is CEO and founder of Data Square, a consulting company specializing in the custom design and development of marketing databases and analytical technologies to optimize Web-based and off-line customer relationship management. Devyani serves as lecturer at the University of Connecticut. In addition, she is the newsletter chair of the Direct Marketing Association's Research Council.

Prior to starting Data Square, Devyani founded Wunderman, Sadh and Associates, an information-based company that provided services to clients such as DMA's Ad Council, GE, IBM, MyPoints, Pantone, SmithKline Beecham, and Unilever. Devyani also served as head of statistical services at MIT, an Experian company. There she translated advanced theoretical practices into actionable marketing and communications solutions for clients such as America Online, Ameritech, American Express, Bell South, Disney, Kraft General Foods, Lotus Corporation, Seagram Americas, Sun Microsystems, Mitsubishi, Midas, Michelin, and Perrier. Devyani can be reached at devyani@datasquare.com.

PART ONE

Planning the Menu

Imagine you are someone who loves to cook! In fact, one of your favorite activities is preparing a gourmet dinner for an appreciative crowd! What is the first thing you do? Rush to the cupboards and start throwing any old ingredients into a bowl? Of course not! You carefully *plan* your meal. During the planning phase, there are many things to consider: What will you serve? Is there a central theme or purpose? Do you have the proper tools? Do you have the necessary ingredients? If not, can you buy them? How long will it take to prepare everything? How will you serve the food, sit-down or buffet style? All of these steps are important in the planning process.

Even though these considerations seem quite logical in planning a gourmet dinner, they also apply to the planning of almost any major project. Careful planning and preparation are essential to the success of any data mining project. And similar to planning a gourmet meal, you must first ask, "What do I want to create?" Or "What is my goal?" "Do I have the support of management?" "How will I reach my goal?" "What tools and resources will I need?" "How will I evaluate whether I have succeeded?" "How will I implement the result to ensure its success?"

The outcome and eventual success of any data modeling project or analysis depend heavily on how well the project objective is defined with respect to the specific business goal and how well the successful completion of the project will serve the overall goals of the company. For example, the specific business goal might be to learn about your customers, improve response rates, increase sales to current customers, decrease attrition, or optimize the efficiency of the next campaign. Each project may have different data requirements or may utilize different analytic methods, or both.

We begin our culinary data journey with a discussion of the building blocks necessary for effective data modeling. In chapter 1, I introduce the steps for building effective data models. I also provide a review of common data mining techniques used for marketing risk and customer relationship management. Throughout this chapter, I detail the importance of forming a clear objective and ensuring the necessary support within the organization. In chapter 2 I explore the many types and sources of data used for data mining. In the course of this chapter, I provide numerous case studies that detail data sources that are available for developing a data model.

CHAPTER 1

Setting the Objective

I n the years following World War II, the United States experienced an economic boom. Mass marketing swept the nation. Consumers wanted every new gadget and machine. They weren't choosy about colors and features. New products generated new markets. And companies sprang up or expanded to meet the demand.

Eventually, competition began to erode profit margins. Companies began offering multiple products, hoping to compete by appealing to different consumer tastes. Consumers became discriminating, which created a challenge for marketers. They wanted to get the right product to the right consumer. This created a need for target marketing—that is, directing an offer to a "target" audience. The growth of target marketing was facilitated by two factors: the availability of information and increased computer power.

We're all familiar with the data explosion. Beginning with credit bureaus tracking our debt behavior and warranty cards gathering demographics, we have become a nation of information. Supermarkets track our purchases, and Web sites capture our shopping behavior whether we purchase or not! As a result, it is essential for businesses to use data just to stay competitive in today's markets.

Targeting models, which are the focus of this book, assist marketers in targeting their best customers and prospects. They make use of the increase in available data as well as improved computer power. In fact, logistic regression, which is used for numerous models in this book, was quite impractical for general use before the advent of computers. One logistic model calculated by hand took several months to process. When I began building logistic models in 1991, I had a PC with 600 megabytes of disk space. Using SAS, it took 27 hours to process one model! And while the model was processing, my computer was unavailable for other work. I therefore had to use my time very efficiently. I would spend Monday through Friday carefully preparing and fitting the predictive variables. Finally, I would begin the model processing on Friday afternoon and allow it to run over the weekend. I would check the status from home to make sure there weren't any problems. I didn't want any unpleasant surprises on Monday morning.

In this chapter, I begin with an overview of the model-building process. This overview details the steps for a successful targeting model project, from conception to implementation. I begin with the most important step in developing a targeting model: establishing the goal or objective. Several sample applications of descriptive and predictive targeting models help to define the business objective of the project and its alignment with the overall goals of the company. Once the objective is established, the next step is to determine the best methodology. This chapter defines several methods for developing targeting models along with their advantages and disadvantages. The chapter wraps up with a discussion of the adaptive company culture needed to ensure a successful target modeling effort.

Defining the Goal

The use of targeting models has become very common in the marketing industry. (In some cases, managers know they should be using them but aren't quite sure how!) Many applications like those for response or approval are quite straightforward. But as companies attempt to model more complex issues, such as attrition and lifetime value, clearly and specifically defining the goal is of critical importance. Failure to correctly define the goal can result in wasted dollars and lost opportunity.

The first and most important step in any targeting-model project is to establish a clear goal and develop a process to achieve that goal. (I have broken the process into seven major steps; Figure 1.1 displays the steps and their companion chapters.)

In defining the goal, you must first decide what you are trying to measure or predict. Targeting models generally fall into two categories, predictive and descriptive. Predictive models calculate some value that represents future activity. It can be a continuous value, like a purchase amount or balance, or a

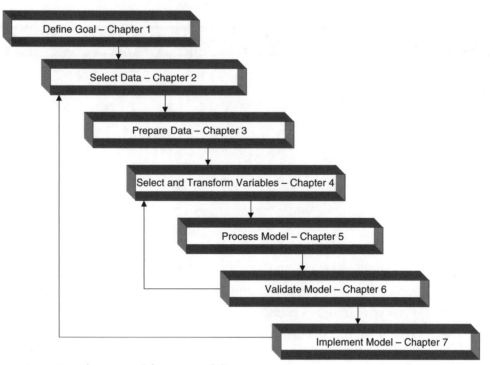

Figure 1.1   Steps for successful target modeling.

probability of likelihood for an action, such as response to an offer or default on a loan. A descriptive model is just as it sounds: It creates rules that are used to group subjects into descriptive categories.

Companies that engage in database marketing have multiple opportunities to embrace the use of predictive and descriptive models. In general, their goal is to attract and retain profitable customers. They use a variety of channels to promote their products or services, such as direct mail, telemarketing, direct sales, broadcasting, magazine and newspaper inserts, and the Internet. Each marketing effort has many components. Some are generic to all industries; others are unique to certain industries. Table 1.1 displays some key leverage points that provide targeting model development opportunities along with a list of industry types that might use them.

One effective way to determine the objective of the target modeling or profiling project is to ask such questions as these:

- Do you want to attract new customers?
- Do you want those new customers to be profitable?
- Do you want to avoid high-risk customers?

Table 1.1 Targeting Model Opportunities by Industry

INDUSTRY	RESPONSE	RISK	ATTRITION	CROSS-SELL & UP-SELL	NET PRESENT VALUE	LIFETIME VALUE
Banking	X	X	X	X	X	X
Insurance	X	X	X	X	X	X
Telco	X	X	X	X	X	X
Retail	X			X	X	X
Catalog	X			X	X	X
Resort	X		X	X	X	X
Utilities	X	X	X	X	X	X
Publishing	X		X	X	X	X

- Do you want to understand the characteristics of your current customers?
- Do you want to make your unprofitable customers more profitable?
- Do you want to retain your profitable customers?
- Do you want to win back your lost customers?
- Do you want to improve customer satisfaction?
- Do you want to increase sales?
- Do you want to reduce expenses?

These are all questions that can be addressed through the use of profiling, segmentation, and/or target modeling. Let's look at each question individually:

- *Do you want to attract new customers?* Targeted response modeling on new customer acquisition campaigns will bring in more customers for the same marketing cost.

- *Do you want those new customers to be profitable?* Lifetime value modeling will identify prospects with a high likelihood of being profitable customers in the long term.

- *Do you want to avoid high-risk customers?* Risk or approval models will identify customers or prospects that have a high likelihood of creating a loss for the company. In financial services, a typical loss comes from nonpayment on a loan. Insurance losses result from claims filed by the insured.

- *Do you want to understand the characteristics of your current customers?* This involves segmenting the customer base through profile analysis. It is a valuable exercise for many reasons. It allows you to see the characteristics of your most profitable customers. Once the segments are defined, you can match those characteristics to members of outside lists and build targeting models to attract more profitable customers. Another benefit of segmenting the most and least profitable customers is to offer varying levels of customer service.

- *Do you want to make your unprofitable customers more profitable?* Cross-sell and up-sell targeting models can be used to increase profits from current customers.

- *Do you want to retain your profitable customers?* Retention or churn models identify customers with a high likelihood of lowering or ceasing their current level of activity. By identifying these customers before they leave, you can take action to retain them. It is often less expensive to retain them than it is to win them back.

- *Do you want to win back your lost customers?* Win-back models are built to target former customers. They can target response or lifetime value depending on the objective.

- *Do you want to improve customer satisfaction?* In today's competitive market, customer satisfaction is key to success. Combining market research with customer profiling is an effective method of measuring customer satisfaction.

- *Do you want to increase sales?* Increased sales can be accomplished in several ways. A new customer acquisition model will grow the customer base, leading to increased sales. Cross-sell and up-sell models can also be used to increase sales.

- *Do you want to reduce expenses?* Better targeting through the use of models for new customer acquisition and customer relationship management will reduce expenses by improving the efficiency of your marketing efforts.

These questions help you express your goal in business terms. The next step is to translate your business goal into analytic terms. This next section defines some of the common analytic goals used today in marketing, risk, and customer relationship management.

Profile Analysis

An in-depth knowledge of your customers and prospects is essential to stay competitive in today's marketplace. Some of the benefits include improved targeting and product development. Profile analysis is an excellent way to get to know your customers or prospects. It involves measuring common characteristics within a population of interest. Demographics such as average age, gender (percent male), marital status (percent married, percent single, etc.), and average length of residence are typically included in a profile analysis. Other measures may be more business specific, such as age of customer relationship or average risk level. Others may cover a fixed time period and measure average dollars sales, average number of sales, or average net profits. Profiles are most useful when used within segments of the population of interest.

Segmentation

Targeting models are designed to improve the efficiency of actions based on marketing and/or risk. But before targeting models are developed, it is important to get a good understanding of your current customer base. Profile analysis is an effective technique for learning about your customers.

A common use of segmentation analysis is to segment customers by profitability and market potential. For example, a retail business divides its customer base into segments that describe their buying behavior in relation to their total buying behavior at all retail stores. Through this a retailer can assess which customers have the most potential. This is often called "Share of Wallet" analysis.

A profile analysis performed on a loan or credit card portfolio might be segmented into a two-dimensional matrix of risk and balances. This would provide a visual tool for assessing the different segments of the customer database for possible marketing and/or risk actions. For example, if one segment has high balances and high risk, you may want to increase the Annual Percentage Rate (APR). For low-risk segments, you may want to lower the APR in hopes of retaining or attracting balances of lower-risk customers.

Response

A response model is usually the first type of targeting model that a company seeks to develop. If no targeting has been done in the past, a response model can provide a huge boost to the efficiency of a marketing campaign by increasing responses and/or reducing mail expenses. The goal is to predict who will be responsive to an offer for a product or service. It can be based on past behavior of a similar population or some logical substitute.

A response can be received in several ways, depending on the offer channel. A mail offer can direct the responder to reply by mail, phone, or Internet. When compiling the results, it is important to monitor the response channel and manage duplicates. It is not unusual for a responder to mail a response and then respond by phone or Internet a few days later. There are even situations in which a company may receive more than one mail response from the same person. This is especially common if a prospect receives multiple or follow-up offers for the same product or service that are spaced several weeks apart. It is important to establish some rules for dealing with multiple responses in model development.

A phone offer has the benefit of instant results. A response can be measured instantly. But a nonresponse can be the result of several actions: The prospect said "no," or the prospect did not answer, or the phone number was incorrect.

Many companies are combining channels in an effort to improve service and save money. The Internet is an excellent channel for providing information and customer service. In the past, a direct mail offer had to contain all the information about the product or service. This mail piece could end up being quite expensive. Now, many companies are using a postcard or an inexpensive mail piece to direct people to a Web site. Once the customer is on the Web site, the company has a variety of available options to market products or services at a fraction of the cost of direct mail.

Risk

Approval or risk models are unique to certain industries that assume the potential for loss when offering a product or service. The most well-known types of risk occur in the banking and insurance industries.

Banks assume a financial risk when they grant loans. In general, these risk models attempt to predict the probability that a prospect will default or fail to pay back the borrowed amount. Many types of loans, such as mortgages or car loans, are secured. In this situation, the bank holds the title to the home or automobile for security. The risk is limited to the loan amount minus resale value of the home or car. Unsecured loans are loans for which the bank holds no security. The most common type of unsecured loan is the credit card. While predictive models are used for all types of loans, they are used extensively for credit cards. Some banks prefer to develop their own risk models. Others banks purchase standard or custom risk scores from any of the several companies that specialize in risk score development.

For the insurance industry, the risk is that of a customer filing a claim. The basic concept of insurance is to pool risk. Insurance companies have decades of experience in managing risk. Life, auto, health, accident, casualty, and liability are all types of insurance that use risk models to manage pricing and reserves. Due to heavy government regulation of pricing in the insurance industry, managing risk is a critical task for insurance companies to maintain profitability.

Many other industries incur risk by offering a product or service with the promise of future payment. This category includes telecommunications companies, energy providers, retailers, and many others. The type of risk is similar to that of the banking industry in that it reflects the probability of a customer defaulting on the payment for a good or service.

The risk of fraud is another area of concern for many companies but especially banks and insurance companies. If a credit card is lost or stolen, banks generally assume liability and absorb a portion of the charged amounts as a loss. Fraud detection models are assisting banks in reducing losses by learning the typical spending behavior of their customers. If a customer's spending habits change drastically, the approval process is halted or monitored until the situation can be evaluated.

Activation

Activation models are models that predict if a prospect will become a full-fledged customer. These models are most applicable in the financial services industry. For example, for a credit card prospect to become an active customer, the prospect must respond, be approved, and *use* the account. If the customer never uses the account, he or she actually ends up costing the bank more than a nonresponder. Most credit card banks offer incentives such as low-rate purchases or balance transfers to motivate new customers to activate. An insurance prospect can be viewed in much the same way. A prospect can respond and be approved, but if he or she does not pay the initial premium, the policy is never activated.

There are two ways to build an activation model. One method is to build a model that predicts response and a second model that predicts activation given response. The final probability of activation from the initial offer is the product of these two models. A second method is to use one-step modeling. This method predicts the probability of activation without separating the different phases. We will explore these two methodologies within our case study in part 2.

Cross-Sell and Up-Sell

Cross-sell models are used to predict the probability or value of a current customer buying a different product or service from the same company (cross-sell). Up-sell models predict the probability or value of a customer buying more of the same products or services.

As mentioned earlier, selling to current customers is quickly replacing new customer acquisition as one of the easiest way to increase profits. Testing offer sequences can help determine what and when to make the next offer. This allows companies to carefully manage offers to avoid over-soliciting and possibly alienating their customers.

Attrition

Attrition or churn is a growing problem in many industries. It is characterized by the act of customers switching companies, usually to take advantage of "a better deal." For years, credit card banks have lured customers from their competitors using low interest rates. Telecommunications companies continue to use strategic marketing tactics to lure customers away from their competitors. And a number of other industries spend a considerable amount of effort trying to retain customers and steal new ones from their competitors.

Over the last few years, the market for new credit card customers has shrunk considerably. This now means that credit card banks are forced to increase their customer base primarily by luring customers from other providers. Their tactic has been to offer low introductory interest rates for anywhere from three months to one year or more on either new purchases and/or balances transferred from another provider. Their hope is that customers will keep their balances with the bank after the interest converts to the normal rate. Many customers, though, are becoming quite adept at keeping their interest rates low by moving balances from one card to another near the time the rate returns to normal.

These activities introduce several modeling opportunities. One type of model predicts the act of reducing or ending the use of a product or service after an account has been activated. Attrition is defined as a decrease in the use of a product or service. For credit cards, attrition is the decrease in balances on which interest is being earned. Churn is defined as the closing of one account in conjunction with the opening of another account for the same product or service, usually at a reduced cost to the consumer. This is a major problem in the telecommunications industry.

Net Present Value

A net present value (NPV) model attempts to predict the overall profitability of a product for a predetermined length of time. The value is often calculated over a certain number of years and discounted to today's dollars. Although there are some standard methods for calculating net present value, many variations exist across products and industries.

In part 2, "The Cooking Demonstration," we will build a net present value model for direct mail life insurance. This NPV model improves targeting to new customers by assigning a net present value to a list of prospects. Each of the five chapters in part 2 provides step-by-step instructions for different phases of the model-building process.

Lifetime Value

A lifetime value model attempts to predict the overall profitability of a customer (person or business) for a predetermined length of time. Similar to the net present value, it is calculated over a certain number of years and discounted to today's dollars. The methods for calculating lifetime also vary across products and industries.

As markets shrink and competition increases, companies are looking for opportunities to profit from their existing customer base. As a result, many companies are expanding their product and/or service offerings in an effort to cross-sell or up-sell their existing customers. This approach is creating the need for a model that goes beyond the net present value of a product to one that defines the lifetime value of a customer or a customer lifetime value (LTV) model.

In chapter 12, we take the net present value model built in part 2 and expand it to a lifetime value model by including cross-sell and up-sell potential.

Choosing the Modeling Methodology

Today, there are numerous tools for developing predictive and descriptive models. Some use statistical methods such as linear regression and logistic regression. Others use nonstatistical or blended methods like neural networks, genetic algorithms, classification trees, and regression trees. Much has been written debating the best methodology. In my opinion, the steps surrounding the model processing are more critical to the overall success of the project than the technique used to build the model. That is why I focus primarily on logistic regression in this book. It is the most widely available technique. And, in my opinion, it performs as well as other methods, especially when put to the test of time. With the plethora of tools available, however, it is valuable to understand their similarities and differences.

My goal in this section is to explain, in everyday language, how these techniques work along with their strengths and weaknesses. If you want to know the underlying statistical or empirical theory, numerous papers and books are available. (See http://dataminingcookbook.wiley.com for references.)

Linear Regression

Simple linear regression analysis is a statistical technique that quantifies the relationship between two continuous variables: the dependent variable or the variable you are trying to predict and the independent or predictive variable. It works by finding a line through the data that minimizes the squared error from each point. Figure 1.2 shows a relationship between *sales* and *advertising* along with the regression equation. The goal is to be able to predict *sales* based on the amount spent on *advertising*. The graph shows a very linear relationship between *sales* and *advertising*. A key measure of the strength of the relation-

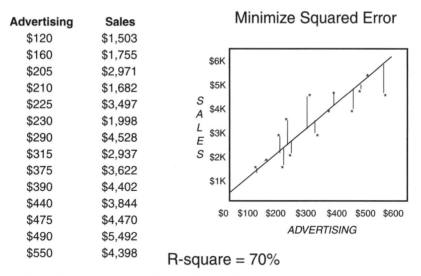

$$\text{Sales} = 17.813 + .0897 \text{*Advertising}$$

Advertising	Sales
$120	$1,503
$160	$1,755
$205	$2,971
$210	$1,682
$225	$3,497
$230	$1,998
$290	$4,528
$315	$2,937
$375	$3,622
$390	$4,402
$440	$3,844
$475	$4,470
$490	$5,492
$550	$4,398

R-square = 70%

Figure 1.2 Simple linear regression—linear relationship.

ship is the R-square. The R-square measures the amount of the overall variation in the data that is explained by the model. This regression analysis results in an R-square of 70%. This implies that 70% of the variation in sales can be explained by the variation in advertising.

Sometimes the relationship between the dependent and independent variables is not linear. In this situation, it may be necessary to transform the independent or predictive variable to allow for a better fit. Figure 1.3 shows a curvilinear relationship between *sales* and *advertising.* By using the square root of advertising we are able to find a better fit for the data.

When building targeting models for marketing, risk, and customer relationship management, it is common to have many predictive variables. Some analysts begin with literally thousands of variables. Using multiple predictive or independent continuous variables to predict a single continuous variable is called multiple linear regression. In Figure 1.4, *advertising dollars* and the *inflation rate* are linearly correlated with *sales.*

Targeting models created using linear regression are generally very robust. In marketing, they can be used alone or in combination with other models. In chapter 12 I demonstrate the use of linear regression as part of the lifetime value calculation.

$$\text{Sales} = -23.03 + 236.83 * \text{Advertising}^{1/2}$$

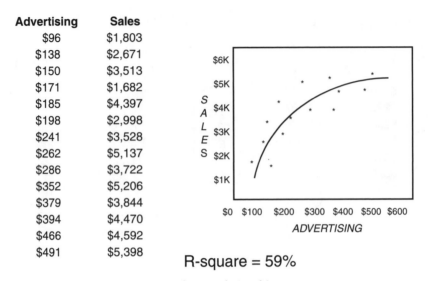

Advertising	Sales
$96	$1,803
$138	$2,671
$150	$3,513
$171	$1,682
$185	$4,397
$198	$2,998
$241	$3,528
$262	$5,137
$286	$3,722
$352	$5,206
$379	$3,844
$394	$4,470
$466	$4,592
$491	$5,398

R-square = 59%

Figure 1.3   Simple linear regression–curvilinear relationship.

$$\text{Sales} = 415.60 + 7.90 * \text{Advertising} + 12781 * \text{Inflation}$$

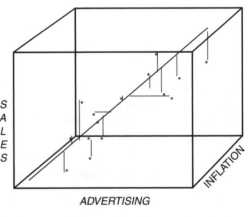

Advertising	Inflation	Sales
$120	3.4%	$1,503
$160	3.3%	$1,755
$205	3.6%	$2,971
$210	3.5%	$1,682
$225	3.4%	$3,497
$230	3.3%	$1,998
$290	3.2%	$4,528
$315	3.3%	$2,937
$375	3.3%	$3,622
$390	3.4%	$4,402
$440	3.2%	$3,844
$475	3.1%	$4,470
$490	3.2%	$5,492
$550	3.2%	$4,398

R-square = 70%

Figure 1.4   Multiple linear regression.

Logistic Regression

Logistic regression is very similar to linear regression. The key difference is that the dependent variable is not continuous; it is discrete or categorical. This makes it very useful in marketing because we are often trying to predict a discrete action such as a response to an offer or a default on a loan.

Technically, logistic regression can be used to predict outcomes for two or more levels. When building targeting models for marketing, however, the outcome usually has a two-level outcome. In order to use regression, the dependent variable is transformed into a continuous value that is a function of the probability of the event occurring.

My goal in this section is to avoid heavy statistical jargon. But because this is the primary method used in the book, I am including a thorough explanation of the methodology. Keep in mind that it is very similar to linear regression in the actual model processing.

In Figure 1.5, the graph displays a relationship between *response (0/1)* and *income* in dollars. The goal is to predict the probability of *response* to a catalog that sells high-end gifts using the prospect's *income*. Notice how the data points have a value of 0 or 1 for response. And on the *income* axis, the values of 0 for *response* are clustered around the lower values for *income*. Conversely, the values of 1 for *response* are clustered around the higher values for *income*. The sigmoidal function or s-curve is formed by averaging the 0s and 1s for each

$$\log(p/(1 - p)) = 4.900 + .0911 \times \text{Income}$$

- Predicts probability of event occurring using function of linear predictors

- p = probability of event occurring

- $p/(1 - p)$ is the odds of an event occurring

- Log of the odds: $\log(p/(1 - p))$ is linear function of predictors

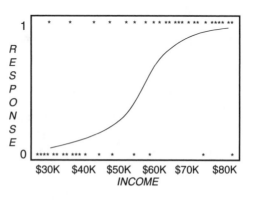

Uses sigmoidal function instead of linear function to fit the data.

Figure 1.5 Logistic regression.

value of *income*. It is simple to see that higher-income prospects respond at a higher rate than lower-income prospects.

The processing is as follows:

1. For each value of income, a probability (p) is calculated by averaging the values of response.
2. For each value of income, the odds are calculated using the formula $p/(1-p)$ where p is the probability.
3. The final transformation calculates the log of the odds: $\log(p/(1-p))$.

The model is derived by finding the linear relationship of income to the log of the odds using the equation:

$$\log(p/(1-p)) = \beta_0 + \beta_1 X_1 + \beta_2 X_2 + \ldots \beta_n X_n$$

where $\beta_0 \ldots \beta_n$ are the coefficients and $X_1 \ldots X_n$ are the predictive variables. Once the predictive coefficients or weights (βs) are derived, the final probability is calculated using the following formula:

$$P = \exp^{(\beta_0 + \beta_1 X_1 + \beta_2 X_2 + \ldots \beta_n X_n)} / \left(1 + \exp^{(\beta_0 + \beta_1 X_1 + \beta_2 X_2 + \ldots \beta_n X_n)}\right)$$

This formula can also be written in a simpler form as follows:

$$P = 1/(1 + e^{-(\beta_0 + \beta_1 X_1 + \beta_2 X_2 + \ldots \beta_n X_n)})$$

Similar to linear regression, logistic regression is based on a statistical distribution. Therefore it enjoys the same benefits as linear regression as a robust tool for developing targeting models.

Neural Networks

Neural network processing is very different from regression in that it does not follow any statistical distribution. It is modeled after the function of the human brain. The process is one of pattern recognition and error minimization. You can think of it as taking in information and learning from each experience.

Neural networks are made up of nodes that are arranged in layers. This construction varies depending on the type and complexity of the neural network. Figure 1.6 illustrates a simple neural network with one hidden layer. Before the process begins, the data is split into training and testing data sets. (A third group is held out for final validation.) Then weights or "inputs" are assigned to each of the nodes in the first layer. During each iteration, the inputs are processed through the system and compared to the actual value. The error is measured and fed back through the system to adjust the weights. In most cases,

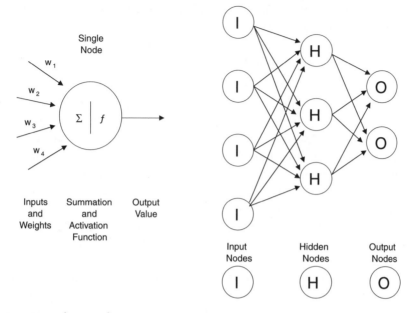

Single
Node

Inputs
and
Weights

Summation
and
Activation
Function

Value

Input
Nodes

Hidden
Nodes

Nodes

Figure 1.6 Neural network.

the weights get better at predicting the actual values. The process ends when a predetermined minimum error level is reached.

One specific type of neural network commonly used in marketing uses sigmoidal functions to fit each node. Recall that this is the same function that is used in logistic regression. You might think about this type of neural network as a series of "nested" logistic regressions. This technique is very powerful in fitting a binary or two-level outcome such as a response to an offer or a default on a loan.

One of the advantages of a neural network is its ability to pick up nonlinear relationships in the data. This can allow users to fit some types of data that would be difficult to fit using regression. One drawback, however, is its tendency to over-fit the data. This can cause the model to deteriorate more quickly when applied to new data. If this is the method of choice, be sure to validate carefully. Another disadvantage to consider is that the results of a neural network are often difficult to interpret.

Genetic Algorithms

Similar to neural networks, genetic algorithms do not have an underlying distribution. Their name stems from the fact that they follow the evolutionary process of "survival of the fittest." Simply put, many models are compared and adjusted over a series of iterations to find the best model for the task. There is some variation among methods. In general, though, the models are altered in each step using mating, mutation, and cloning.

As with all modeling methods, the first step is to determine the objective or goal of the model. Then a measure is selected to evaluate model fit. Let's say we want to find the best model for predicting balances. We use R-square to determine the model fit. In Figure 1.7 we have a group of models that represent the "first generation" of candidate models. These were selected at random or created using another technique. Each model is tested for its ability to predict balances. It is assigned a value or weight that reflects its ability to predict balances in comparison to its competitors. In the right-hand column, we see that the "% of Total" is calculated by dividing the individual R-square by the sum of the R-squares. This "% of Total" is treated like a weight that is then used to increase or decrease the model's chances to survive in the next generation of tests. In addition to the weights, the models are randomly subjected to other changes such as mating, mutation, and cloning. These involve randomly switching variables, signs, and functions. To control the process, it is necessary to establish rules for each process. After many iterations, or generations, a winning model will emerge. It does an excellent job of fitting a model. It, however, requires a lot of computer power. As computers continue to become more powerful, this method should gain popularity.

Model 1 $Y = x1*(b + X2)$
Model 2 $Y = b - \exp(x1)$
Model 3 $Y = x1 - X2$
Model 4 $Y = x1*x2$
Model 5 $Y = b + x1$

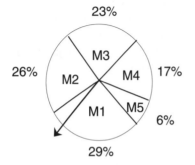

	Fitness Measure (r-square)	% of Total
Model 1	0.61	0.29
Model 2	0.55	0.26
Model 3	0.48	0.23
Model 4	0.36	0.17
Model 5	0.12	0.06
Total	2.12	1.00

Figure 1.7 Genetic algorithms.

Classification Trees

The goal of a classification tree is to sequentially partition the data to maximize the differences in the dependent variable. It is often referred to as a decision tree. The true purpose of a classification tree is to *classify* the data into distinct groups or branches that create the strongest separation in the values of the dependent variable.

Classification trees are very good at identifying segments with a desired behavior such as response or activation. This identification can be quite useful when a company is trying to understand what is driving market behavior. It also has an advantage over regression in its ability to detect nonlinear relationships. This can be very useful in identifying interactions for inputs into other modeling techniques. I demonstrate this in chapter 4.

Classification trees are "grown" through a series of steps and rules that offer great flexibility. In Figure 1.8, the tree differentiates between responders and nonresponders. The top node represents the performance of the overall campaign. Sales pieces were mailed to 10,000 names and yielded a response rate of 2.6%. The first split is on *gender*. This implies that the greatest difference between responders and nonresponders is *gender*. We see that *males* are much more responsive (3.2%) than *females* (2.1%). If we stop after one split, we would

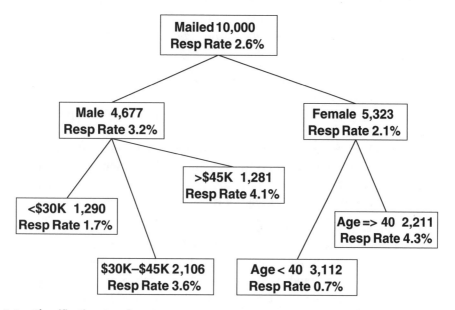

Figure 1.8 Classification tree for response.

consider *males* the better target group. Our goal, though, is to find groups within both genders that discriminate between responders and nonresponders. In the next split, these two groups or nodes are considered separately.

The second-level split from the *male* node is on *income*. This implies that income level varies the most between responders and nonresponders among the *males*. For females, the greatest difference is among *age* groups. It is very easy to identify the groups with the highest response rates. Let's say that management decides to mail only to groups where the response rate is more than 3.5%. The offers would be directed to males who make more than $30,000 a year and females over age 40.

A definite advantage of classification trees over other techniques is their ability to explain the results. I often develop complex logistic models for scoring and build a tree to explain the results to the marketers. Although the outcome is never identical, the tree does a good job of uncovering key drivers in the market. Due to their broad applicability, classification trees will continue to be a valuable tool for all types of target modeling.

The Adaptive Company

Every year more companies are embracing analytics to help them improve their marketing efforts. Doing so is no longer a luxury. The analytic approach to marketing is necessary for survival. There are many challenges in making a successful transition, however. One of the biggest challenges is being able to adapt quickly to change.

This is one situation in which smaller, leaner companies often have an advantage. Because adapting often requires total company realignment, some older, larger companies find it difficult to embrace the analytic approach for several reasons. First, their data systems don't support the information needs of the new paradigm. Second, the decision makers often don't understand the sophisticated technologies required to drive the business. This can make them resistant to using them. And third, the company personnel and compensation structures aren't designed to support the new approach.

The companies that are leading the pack are those that have managers and senior executives who support an analytic approach to marketing, risk, and customer relationship management. So many facets of the organizational structure need to be aligned to make it work. And all levels of management must agree to the goal and understand the ramifications. Consider the credit card bank whose management team was frustrated with their low approval rates. They asked the analytic group to build an acquisition model that targeted more approvable responders. The model was successfully developed with the caveat that response rates would decline slightly. But the overall number of accounts per piece mailed would be higher, leading to higher profits per piece mailed. Management approved the model-building project. When the model was implemented and response rates dropped, though, panic set in and the model was withdrawn from use.

To be successful, every area of the company must be willing to work toward the same goals. The finance department must be willing to work with other areas of the company to align revenue and profitability measures. The information technology group must support the hardware, software, and data needs of the analysts. The employees involved in the day-to-day production of goods and services must be willing to support the analytic approach by providing information and incorporating procedures to facilitate the flow of information. And finally, if the company has made a commitment to support an analytic approach, the rewards and incentives for all employees must be aligned with that commitment.

Hiring and Teamwork

Hiring talented analysts is key to the success of this approach. Human resources personnel must be trained to understand and identify the skills and education necessary to succeed in highly technical positions. Jerry Bernhart, of Bernhart and Associates, shares his insights in hiring a good market analyst:

> It has been my experience that in recruiting the best quantitative analysts it is not enough for them to know just the statistical tools. They must know how to apply them to real-world marketing problems. A hammer is a hammer, but the best carpenters know how to swing it. There is a big difference between the number cruncher who understands it from a textbook perspective and the true market analyst who can interpret it and apply it to the business.
>
> When interviewing junior-level candidates with little or no on-the-job experience in research or analysis you certainly can't expect them to give you a treatise on strategic marketing. However, you can use scenario-driven interviewing to reveal whether or not they have at least an intuitive understanding of what it means to solve a marketing problem.
>
> Once you hire them, keep them challenged. When you ask what motivates a market analyst, money is rarely at the top of the list. Rather, what you'll hear most often is that they want an opportunity where they can learn and apply new analytical methodologies. Good analysts tend to be highly creative, always looking for better ways to solve problems.

I totally concur with Jerry's views. The basic knowledge is important, but the breakthroughs come from the analyst's ability to creatively blend and adapt the latest tools and techniques.

Once you hire a good analyst, retaining him or her can be a challenge. The marketplace has many opportunities for this type of talent. As Jerry said, money is rarely a top motivator. So here are a few tips for managers: Give your analysts opportunities to learn and expand their skill base, supply them with leading-edge hardware and software, create opportunities for challenge and variety, and offer them flexible hours and workplace options. Jodi Barnes Nelson, Ph.D., a professor of Human Resources at North Carolina State University, comments on the organizational structure of the future:

> The virtual organization is quickly becoming a reality. We saw this in academia in the late 1980s with the wide acceptance of e-mail and listservs. Researchers in far-reaching places could now participate in joint projects with colleagues. As organizations downsize, rightsize, and globalize, the boundary-less organization becomes a reality.[*]

Finally, management must encourage teamwork and develop leadership incentives to meet the company goals. For example, if the company decides that attracting profitable customers is the primary goal, accountability and incentives need to be assigned to promote that goal. Consider the credit card bank that wanted to attract new profitable customers. The analyst developed a targeting model that attracted customers who were likely to build balances and retain those balances. When responses came in and it was time to approve the account, the risk department stepped in and declined the prospects with the greatest profit potential. Why? Because they had a risk level that was unacceptable. And the risk department was not striving for profitable customers; it was simply tasked with managing risk. So the risk department did not consider the fact that the higher-risk customers were much more likely to maintain balances at higher rates, thereby making them much more profitable.

Product Focus versus Customer Focus

As mentioned earlier, many companies are making the transition from a product focus to a customer focus. The reason for this transition is simple: In many industries it is becoming more difficult to attract new customers. It has become more efficient to broaden the company focus and develop new products for existing customers. This evolution from a product focus to a customer focus has been a gradual process. Mark Van Clieaf, Managing Director of MVC Associates International, details the history of this transition:

> Marketing decision sciences have played a role in each of "three waves" of becoming customer centric over the last 15 years. First came the loyalty/frequency wave. This started with many of the continuity clubs (books, music), airlines, and catalog companies. Initially good information-based marketing differentiated customers based on

[*] Barnes Nelson, J., Ph.D. 1997. "The Boundaryless Organization: Implications for Job Analysis, Recruitment and Selection." *Human Resources Planning* 20(4):39–49.

simple RFM metrics (recency, frequency, monetary value). Many loyalty programs were developed to attempt to recognize, differentiate, and reward tiers of better customers.

The second wave, customer value optimization, aimed for more precise matching of product to customer, with some level of tailoring products and services to smaller niches of customer segments. Where the first and second waves were essentially about products in search of customers, the third wave starts with customers and what can be done to meet their needs with products and services, whether individually or bundled. The third wave has seen a select few companies begin to use marketing decision sciences to create a single customer view across multiple product categories or lines of business. This customer view also includes the duration of the relationship beyond the one-year profit-and-loss statement and the financial implications for optimizing pricing and marketing spending over multiple years. This single view allows for the creation of new bundled value propositions.

One of the most difficult aspects of this transition has been from the "silo" structure where each manager owns a product to a market-based structure where each manager is responsible for a share of the market. If a company is expanding its products and services, the customer focus becomes critically important. Consider the company that relied heavily on its current customers for increased sales. Its new customer acquisition efforts were only marginally successful. So the company met its annual revenue goals by cross-selling and up-selling its current customers. Because each manager was responsible for a single product, all the managers were soliciting the same customers. Soon the customers started complaining about the number of telemarketing calls they were receiving. Many cancelled their accounts. One incident was reported where a customer had two solicitors from different divisions of the *same* company on the phone at the *same* time (using call waiting). On further analysis, it was determined that the customers deemed the most profitable were receiving as many as 30 calls a month. In essence, the company was abusing its best customers. The company was finally motivated to adopt a customer value approach to marketing that evaluated every offer based on a total customer value proposition.

Summary

As we move into the chapters ahead, we will become immersed in the intricate steps involved in developing targeting models. Remember to stay focused on the overall goal of the project. At every step, you should evaluate whether the process is continuing to meet your goals. And keep in mind that the successful company is able to adapt to the rapid changes in technology and market dynamics with ease. This success is made possible by a team of talented analysts who receive the respect and company support necessary to contribute creatively and effectively.

Once you have defined your objective and chosen the methodology, the next step is to determine the best source of data for the analysis. In the next chapter, I discuss the foundation of good analysis—the data. I will describe many types of data along with some typical sources and uses. I use multiple examples to describe some typical data sources for marketing, risk, and customer relationship management.

CHAPTER 2

Selecting the Data Sources

The world of data mining is experiencing an information explosion. The amount and complexity of data are expanding. And as companies embrace Web sites as a marketing and CRM tool, the amount of data is increasing exponentially.

To enhance their data mining efforts, many companies are diligently collecting, combining, and scrubbing data. Companies new to data mining are revamping their databases to allow for easier access and extractability. Companies whose primary business is to collect, enhance, and sell data are springing up every day. All of this can be a bit overwhelming. So, in this chapter, I start at the beginning. The first step in making the best use of any data source is to understand the nature of the data as well as how it is gathered and managed.

Chapter 2 begins with a discussion of various types of data along with the strengths and weakness of each type. The next section discusses some typical data sources with descriptions and cases from both internal and external repositories. The final section of the chapter offers some ideas for creating targeting model data sets; this section also includes numerous case studies. To create your own targeting model data set, you can use the definitions and case studies in this chapter as a template, creatively modifying these cases to develop a customized fit for your unique objective.

Types of Data

No matter where it comes from, data falls into three basic types: demographic, behavioral, and psychographic or attitudinal. Each type has its strengths and weaknesses.

Demographic data generally describes personal or household characteristics. It includes characteristics such as gender, age, marital status, income, home ownership, dwelling type, education level, ethnicity, and presence of children. Demographic data has a number of strengths. It is very stable, which makes it appealing for use in predictive modeling. Characteristics like marital status, home ownership, education level, and dwelling type aren't subject to change as frequently as behavioral data such as bank balances or attitudinal characteristics like favorite political candidate. And demographic data is usually less expensive than attitudinal and behavioral data, especially when purchased on a group level. One of the weaknesses of demographic data is that it is difficult to get on an individual basis with a high degree of accuracy. Unless it is required in return for a product or service, many people resist sharing this type of information or supply false information.

Behavioral data is a measurement of an action or behavior. Behavioral data is typically the most predictive type of data. Depending on the industry, this type of data may include elements like sales amounts, types and dates of purchase, payment dates and amounts, customer service activities, insurance claims or bankruptcy behavior, and more. Web site activity is another type of behavioral data. A Web site can be designed to capture sales as well as click stream behavior or the exact path of each Web site visitor.

Behavioral data usually does a better job of predicting future behavior than the other types of data. It is, however, generally the most difficult and expensive data to get from an outside source. This will be discussed in more detail in the next section.

Psychographic or attitudinal data is characterized by opinions, lifestyle characteristics, or personal values. Traditionally associated with market research, this type of data is mainly collected through surveys, opinion polls, and focus groups. It can also be inferred through magazine and purchase behavior. Due to increased competition, this type of data is being integrated into customer and prospect databases for improved target modeling and analysis.

Psychographic data brings an added dimension to predictive modeling. For companies that have squeezed all the predictive power out of their demographic and behavioral data, psychographic data can offer some improvement. It is also useful for determining the life stage of a customer or prospect. This creates many opportunities for developing products and services around life events such as marriage, childbirth, college, and retirement.

The biggest drawback to psychographic data is that it denotes intended behavior that may be highly, partly, or marginally correlated with actual behavior. Data may be collected through surveys or focus groups and then applied to a larger group of names using segmentation or another statistical technique. If data is applied using these methods, it is recommended that a test be constructed to validate the correlation.

Table 2.1 provides a quick reference and comparison of the three main types of data. The rating is based on individual-level data. If data is collected on a group and inferred on an individual level, it is generally less predictive and less expensive. The stability is about the same.

Table 2.1 Data Types and Characteristics

	PREDICTIVE POWER	STABILITY	COST
Demographic	Medium	High	Low
Behavioral	High	Low	High
Psychographic	Medium	Medium	High

Sources of Data

Data for modeling can be generated from a number of sources. Those sources fall into one of two categories: internal or external. Internal sources are those that are generated through company activity such as customer records, Web site, mail tapes from mail or phone campaigns, or databases and/or data warehouses that are specifically designed to house company data. External sources of data include companies such as the credit bureaus, list brokers and compilers, and corporations with large customer databases like publishers and catalogers.

Internal Sources

Internal sources are data sources that are housed within a company or establishment. They are often the most predictive data for modeling because they represent information that is specific to the company's product or service.

Some typical sources are the customer database, transaction database, offer history database, solicitation tapes, and data warehouses. The next section details the typical features and components of those databases.

Customer Database

A customer database is typically designed with one record per customer. In some organizations, it may be the only database. If that is the case, it may contain all the sales and/or activity records for every customer. It is more common, though, that the customer database contains the identifying information that can be linked to other databases such as a transaction database to obtain a current snapshot of a customer's performance. Even though there may be wide variation among companies and industries, the following list details some key elements in a typical customer database:

Customer ID. A unique numeric or alphanumeric code that identifies the customer throughout his or her entire lifecycle. Some companies may use an account number for this function, but this can be risky if the account numbers are subject to change. For example, credit card banks assign a new account number when a card is lost or stolen. The customer ID allows each account number to be linked to the unique customer, thereby preserving the entire customer history. It is essential in any database to effectively link and tract the behavior of and actions taken on an individual customer.

Household ID. A unique numeric or alphanumeric code that identifies the household of the customer through his or her entire lifecycle. This identifier is useful in some industries where more than one member of a household shares products or services.

Account number. A unique numeric or alphanumeric code that relates to a particular product or service. One customer can have several account numbers.

Customer name. The name of a person or a business. It is usually broken down into multiple fields: last name, first name, middle name or initial, salutation.

Address. The street address, typically broken into components such as number, street, suite or apartment number, city, state, and zip + 4. Some customer databases have a line for a P.O. Box. With population mobility about 10% per year, additional fields that contain former addresses are useful for tracking and matching customers to other files.

Phone number. Current and former numbers for home and work.

Demographics. Characteristics such as gender, age, and income may be stored for profiling and modeling.

Products or services. The list of products and product identification numbers that varies by company. An insurance company may list all the policies along with policy numbers. A bank may list all the products across different divisions of the bank including checking, savings, credit cards, investments, loans, and more. If the number of products and the product detail are extensive, this information may be stored in a separate database with a customer and household identifier.

Offer detail. The date, type of offer, creative, source code, pricing, distribution channel (mail, telemarketing, sales rep, e-mail), and any other details of an offer. Most companies look for opportunities to cross-sell or up-sell their current customers. There could be numerous "offer detail" fields in a customer record, each representing an offer for an additional product or service.

Model scores. Response, risk, attrition, profitability, scores, and/or any other scores that are created or purchased.

Transaction Database

The transaction database contains records of customer activity. It is often the richest and most predictive information, but it can be the most difficult to utilize. In most cases, each record represents a single transaction, so there may be multiple records for each customer. The transaction database can take on various forms depending on the type of business. In order to use this data for modeling, it must be summarized and aggregated to a customer level. Number of records per customer can differ. The following list is typical of what might be found in a transaction database:

Customer ID. A unique numeric or alphanumeric code that identifies the customer throughout his or her entire lifecycle. Some companies may use an account number for this function.

Account number. A unique numeric or alphanumeric code that relates to a particular product or service.

Sales activity. The amount of the transaction.

Date of activity. Date the transaction occurred.

A credit card transaction database will typically contain dates, charge amounts, returns, payments, and fee activity including late fees, overlimit fees, and/or annual fees. A useful summarization for modeling is monthly totals for each field. A catalog company's transaction database will typically contain dates, source codes that identify the specific catalog, sales, and returns.

Offer History Database

The offer history database contains details about offers made to prospects, customers, or both. The most useful format is a unique record for each customer or prospect. Variables created from this database are often the most predictive in response and activation targeting models. It seems logical that if you know someone has received your offer every month for six months, they are less likely to respond than someone who is seeing your offer for the first time. As competition intensifies, this type of information is becoming increasing important.

A customer offer history database would contain all cross-sell, up-sell, and retention offers. A prospect offer history database would contain all acquisition offers as well as any predictive information from outside sources. It is also useful to store former addresses on the prospect offer history database.

TIP It is common to purchase prospect data repeatedly from the same source. The goal may be to purchase new names or to get fresh information about existing names. In either case, it is useful to arrange with the data seller to assign a unique identifier to each prospect that is housed on the seller's database. Then when additional names are purchased or current names are refreshed, the match rate is much higher.

With an average amount of solicitation activity, this type of database can become very large. It is important to perform analysis to establish business rules that control the maintenance of this database. Fields like "date of first offer" are usually correlated with response behavior. The following list details some key elements in an offer history database:

Prospect ID/customer ID. A unique numeric or alphanumeric code that identifies the prospect for a specific length of time.

Household ID. A unique numeric or alphanumeric code that identifies the household of the customer through his or her entire lifecycle. This identifier is useful in some industries where more than one member of a household shares products or services.

Prospect name.* The name of a person or a business. It is usually broken down into multiple fields: last name, first name, middle name or initial, salutation.

Address.* The street address, typically broken into components such as number, street, suite or apartment number, city, state, zip + 4. As in the customer database, some prospect databases have a line for a P.O. Box.

---

* These elements appear only on a prospect offer history database. The customer database would support the customer offer history database with additional data.

Additional fields that contain former addresses are useful for matching prospects to outside files.

Phone number. Current and former numbers for home and work.

Offer detail. Includes the date, type of offer, creative, source code, pricing, distribution channel (mail, telemarketing, sales rep, e-mail), and any other details of the offer. There could be numerous groups of "offer detail" fields in a prospect or customer record, each representing an offer for an additional product or service.

Offer summary. Date of first offer (for each offer type), best offer (unique to product or service), etc.

Model scores.* Response, risk, attrition, profitability scores, and/or any other scores that are created or purchased.

Predictive data.* Includes any demographic, psychographic, or behavioral data.

Solicitation Mail and Phone Tapes

Solicitation tapes are created from either a customer database or a prospect list to provide pertinent information for a campaign. The tapes are usually shipped to a processor for mailing or a telemarketing shop for phone offers. If the goal is to eventually build a model from a specific campaign, the solicitation tape should contain the following information:

Customer or prospect ID. Described previously, this field can be used to match back to the customer or prospect database.

Predictive data. If data is purchased from an outside list company for the purpose of building a model, the predictive data for model development is included on the solicitation tape.

Data Warehouse

A data warehouse is a structure that links information from two or more databases. Using the data sources mentioned in the previous section, a data warehouse brings the data into a central repository, performs some data integration, clean-up, and summarization, and distributes the information data marts. Data marts are used to house subsets of the data from the central repository that has been selected and prepared for specific end users. (They are often called departmental data warehouses.) An analyst who wants to get data for a targeting model accesses the relevant data mart. The meta data provides a directory for the data marts. Figure 2.1 shows how the data gets from the various data sources, through the central repository to the data marts.

Figure 2.1 displays just one form of a data warehouse. Another business might choose an entirely different structure. The purpose of this section is to illustrate the importance of the data warehouse as it relates to accessing data for targeting model development.

Drury Jenkins, an expert in business intelligence systems, talks about the data warehouse and how it supports business intelligence with special emphasis on modeling and analytics:

> Business intelligence is the corporate ability to make better decisions faster. A customer-focused business intelligence environment provides the infrastructure that delivers information and decisions necessary to maximize the most critical of all corporate assets—the customer base. This infrastructure combines data, channels, and analytical techniques to enhance customer satisfaction and profitability through all major customer contact points. For marketers this means the ability to target the right customer, at the right time, in the right place, and with the right product. The channels include traditional as well as the fast-growing electronic inbound and outbound. The analytical techniques include behavior analysis, predictive modeling, time-series analysis, and other techniques.
>
> The key aspect to supplying the necessary data is the creation of a total view for each individual customer and their needs. Integration of customer data must provide a single, unified and accurate view of their customers across the entire organization. The

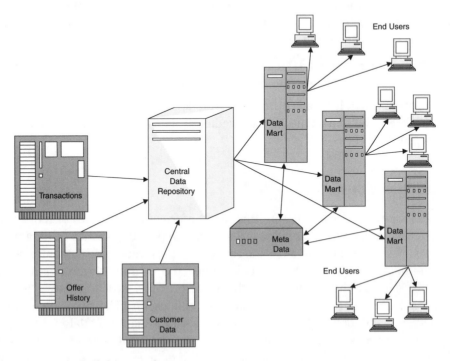

Figure 2.1 A typical data warehouse.

ultimate goal is to achieve a complete picture of a customer's interaction with the entire organization, only achieved by gathering and staging the appropriate data. In addition to pulling in demographics and other external data, numerous internal data are necessary.

Too often, obtainable data are fragmented and scattered over multiple computer sites and systems, hidden away in transaction database systems or personal productivity tools such as spreadsheets or micro databases. These disparate data were created in the most part by the explosive growth of client/server applications over the last decade, creating independent transaction-oriented databases. Implementing independent On Line Transaction Processing (OLTP) customer contact point systems, as opposed to an integrated Customer Relationship Management (CRM) approach, has also added to the disparate data problems. These customer service, sales force automation, call center, telesales, and marketing applications look at customers from different views, making it difficult to create a holistic view of the customer.

Identifying what data are needed for the customer-focused environment should begin with business drivers. It should end with innovative thinking about what information is needed and how it can be used to increase your customer base and loyalty. Once the data elements and usage are identified, a business intelligence architecture must exist that supports the necessary infrastructure. The most simplistic way to look at business intelligence architecture is by three segments:

- Gathering the important data

- Discovering and analyzing data while transforming to pertinent information

- Delivering the information

The second segment refers to analyzing data about customers and prospects through data mining and model development. The third segment also includes data analysis along with other information exploitation techniques that deliver information to employees, customers, and partners. The most misunderstood segment is probably the first, gathering the important data.

Numerous terms are used to describe the data gathering and storing aspect of a business intelligence environment. The primary term, *data warehousing*, has a metamorphosis of its own. Then we add in terms like data mart, central repository, meta data, and others. The most important data repository aspect is not its form, but instead the controls that exist. Business intelligence infrastructure should consist of the following control components:

- Extracting and staging data from sources

- Cleaning and aligning data/exception handling

- Transporting and loading data

- Summarizing data

- Refreshing process and procedures

- Employing meta data and business rules

The first five activities involve pulling, preparing, and loading data. These are important and must be a standard and repeatable process, but what is the role of meta data?

- Central control repository for all databases

- Repository for data hierarchies

- Repository for data rules, editing, transformations

- Repository for entity and dimension reference data

- Optimizes queries

- Common business definitions

- Hides complexity

- Links legacy systems to the warehouse repositories

- User and application profiling

There are two types of meta data—system and business. System meta data states the sources, refresh date, transformations, and other mechanical controls. Business meta data is used by analysts to understand where data is found as well as definitions, ownership, last update, calculations, and other rule-based controls. It is easy to see the importance of meta data to the business intelligence environment.

Data Warehousing: Mistakes and Best Practices

Drury also shares some common data warehousing mistakes, keys to success, and industry "best practices."

What are some of the common data warehousing mistakes?

- Not implementing a comprehensive meta data strategy
- Not deploying a centralized warehouse administration tool
- Not cleaning or intergrating transactional data
- Expecting the warehouse to stay static
- Underestimating refresh and update cycles
- Using a poor definition and approach
- Poor design and data modeling
- Using inexperienced personnel

There are a lot of data warehouse horror stories; however, there are also a lot of phenomenal success stories. What are the keys to a successful implementation?

- Executive sponsorship is a must.
- A full-time project team with experienced staff is necessary.
- Both IT and business units must be involved in the project.
- Business analysts who understand the business objective as well as the data warehouse and the data mining technology must be involved.
- The project's scope must be focused and achievable.
- Activities must support the business goals.
- An iterative approach must be used to build, test, and implement the solution.
- Proven technology components must be used.
- Data quality is a priority.
- Think globally. Act locally.
- Implement short term. Plan long term.

Now let's look at some data warehousing "Best Practices":

- Transactional systems flow up to a consolidating layer where cleansing, integration, and alignment occur. This Operational Data Store (ODS) layer feeds a dimensionally modeled data warehouse, which typically feeds application or departmentalized data marts.
- Data definitions are consistent, data is cleaned, and a clear understanding of a single system of record exists—"one version of the truth."
- Meta data standards and systems are deployed to ease the change process. All new systems are meta data driven for cost, speed, and flexibility.
- Technology complexity of databases is hidden by catalog structures. Clean interfaces to standard desktop productivity tools. Self-service is set up for end users with business meta data, so they can get their own data with easy-to-use tools.

As in data mining and model development, building and implementing a data warehouse require careful planning, dedicated personnel, and full company support. A well-designed data warehouse provides efficient access to multiple sources of internal data.

External Sources

The pressure is on for many companies to increase profits either through acquiring new customers or by increasing sales to existing customers. Both of these initiatives can be enhanced through the use of external sources.

External sources consist mainly of list sellers and compilers. As you would expect, list sellers are companies that sell lists. Few companies, however, have the sale of lists as their sole business. Many companies have a main business like magazine sales or catalog sales, with list sales as a secondary business. Depending on the type of business, they usually collect and sell names, addresses, and phone numbers, along with demographic, behavioral, and/or psychographic information. Sometimes they perform list "hygiene" or clean-up to improve the value of the list. Many of them sell their lists through list compilers and/or list brokers.

List compilers are companies that sell a variety of single and compiled lists. Some companies begin with a base like the phone book or driver's license registration data. Then they purchase lists, merge them together, and impute missing values. Many list compilers use survey research to enhance and validate their lists.

There are many companies that sell lists of names along with contact information and personal characteristics. Some specialize in certain types of data. The credit bureaus are well known for selling credit behavior data. They serve financial institutions by gathering and sharing credit behavior data among their members. There are literally hundreds of companies selling lists from very specific to nationwide coverage. (For information regarding specific companies, go to http://dataminingcookbook.wiley.com.)

Selecting Data for Modeling

Selecting the best data for targeting model development requires a thorough understanding of the market and the objective. Although the tools are important, the data serves as the frame or information base. The model is only as good and relevant as the underlying data.

Securing the data might involve extracting data from existing sources or developing your own. The appropriate selection of data for the development and validation of a targeting model is key to the model's success. This section describes some of the different sources and provides numerous cases from a variety of industries. These cases are typical of those used in the industry for building targeting models.

The first type of data discussed in this section is prospect data. This data is used for prospecting or acquiring new customers. For most companies this task is expensive, so an effective model can generate considerable savings. Next I discuss customer data. This data is used to cross-sell, up-sell, and retain existing customers. And finally, I discuss several types of risk data. This is appropriate for both prospects and customers.

Data for Prospecting

Data from a prior campaign is the best choice for target modeling. This is true whether or not the prior campaign matches the exact product or service you are modeling. Campaigns that have been generated from your company will be sensitive to factors like creative and brand identity. This may have a subtle effect on model performance.

If data from a prior campaign is not available, the next best thing to do is build a propensity model. This modeling technique takes data from an outside source to develop a model that targets a product or service similar to your primary targeting goal.

TIP

For best results in model development, strive to have the population from which the data is extracted be representative of the population to be scored.

More and more companies are forming affinity relationships with other companies to pool resources and increase profits. Credit card banks are forming partnerships with airlines, universities, clubs, retailers, and many others. Telecommunications companies are forming alliances with airlines, insurance companies, and others. One of the primary benefits is access to personal information that can be used to develop targeting models.

Modeling for New Customer Acquisition

Data from a prior campaign for the *same product* and to the *same group* is the optimal choice for data in any targeting model. This allows for the most accurate prediction of future behavior. The only factors that can't be captured in this scenario are seasonality, changes in the marketplace, and the effects of multiple offers. (Certain validation methods, discussed in chapter 6, are designed to help control for these time-related issues.)

As I mentioned earlier, there are a many ways to create a data set for modeling. But many of them have similar characteristics. The following cases are designed to provide you with ideas for creating your own modeling data sets.

Case 1: Same Product to the Same List Using a Prior Campaign

Last quarter, ABC Credit Card Bank purchased approximately 2 million names from Quality Credit Bureau for an acquisition campaign. The initial screening ensured that the names passed ABC's minimum risk criteria. Along with the names, ABC purchased more than 300 demographic and credit attributes. It mailed an offer of credit to the entire list of names with an annualized percentage rate (APR) of 11.9% and no annual fee. As long as all payments are received before the monthly due date, the rate is guaranteed not to change for one year. ABC captured the response from those campaigns over the next eight weeks. The response activity was appended to the original mail tape to create a modeling data set.

Over the next four weeks, ABC Credit Card Bank plans to build a response model using the 300+ variables that were purchased at the time of the original offer. Once the model is constructed and validated, ABC Credit Card Bank will have a robust tool for scoring a new set of names for credit card acquisition. For best results, the prospect should be sent the same offer (11.9% APR with no annual fee) using the same creative. In addition, they should be purchased from Quality Credit Bureau and undergo the same minimum risk screening.

Case 2: Same Product to the Same List with Selection Criteria Using Prior Campaign

Outside Outfitters is a company that sells clothing for the avid sports enthusiast. Six months ago, Outside Outfitters purchased a list of prospects from Power List Company. The list contained names, addresses, and 35 demographic and psychographic attributes. Outside Outfitters used criteria that selected only males, ages 30 to 55. They mailed a catalog that featured hunting gear. After three months of performance activity, response and sales amounts were appended to the original mail file to create a modeling data set.

Using the 35 demographic and psychographic attributes, Outside Outfitters plans to develop a predictive model to target responses with sales amounts that exceeded $20. Once the model is constructed and validated, Outside Outfitters will have a robust tool for scoring a new set of names for targeting $20+ purchases from their hunting gear catalog. For best results, the names should be purchased from Power List Company using the same selection criteria.

A targeting model that is developed for a *similar product* and/or to a *similar group* is often called a propensity model. Data from a prior campaign from a similar product or group works well for this type of model development. After you score the data and select the names for the campaign, be sure to take a random or stratified sample from the group of names that the model did not select. This will allow you to re-create the original group of names for model redevelopment. (This technique is explained later in the chapter.) It is advisable to adjust the performance forecasts when using a propensity model.

Case 3: Same Product to New List Using Prior Campaign

ABC Credit Card Bank from Case 1 wants to develop a response model for its standard 11.9% APR offer that can be used to score names on the MoreData Credit Bureau with the same minimum risk screening. All the other terms and conditions are the same as the prior campaign. The most cost-effective method of getting data for model development is to use the model that was developed for the Quality Credit Bureau. ABC plans to mail the top 50% of the names selected by the model. To ensure a data set for developing a robust response model that is more accurate for the MoreData Credit Bureau, ABC will take a random or stratified sample of the names not selected by the model.

Case 4: Similar Product to Same List Using Prior Campaign

XYZ Life Insurance Company is a direct mail insurance company. Its base product is term life insurance. The campaigns have an average response rate of about 1.2%. XYZ Life routinely buys lists from Value List Inc., a full-service list company that compiles data from numerous sources and provides list hygiene. Its selection criteria provide rules for selecting names from predetermined wealth and life-stage segments. XYZ Life wants to offer a whole life insurance policy to a similar list of prospects from Value List. It has a mail tape from a previous term life campaign with the buyers appended. It knows that the overall response rate for whole life insurance is typically 5% lower than the response rate for term life insurance. XYZ Life is able to build a propensity model on the term product to assist in targeting the whole life product. It will purchase a list with the same wealth and life-stage selection criteria from Value List. The overall expectations in performance will be reduced by a minimum of 5%. When the model is implemented, XYZ Life will sample the portion of names below the model cut-off to create a full modeling data set for refining the model to more effectively target the whole life buyers.

Case 5: Similar Product to Same List Using Prior Campaign

RST Cruise Company purchases lists from TLC Publishing Company on a regular basis for its seven-day Caribbean cruise. RST is interested in using the performance on this campaign to develop a model for an Alaskan cruise. It has a campaign mail tape from the Caribbean cruise campaign with cruise booking information appended. RST can build a propensity model to target the cruise population using the results from the Caribbean cruise campaign. Its knowledge of the industry tells RST that the popularity of the Alaskan cruise is about 60% of the popularity of the Caribbean cruise.

Case 6: Similar Product to New List with No Prior Campaign

Health Nut Corporation has developed a unique exercise machine. It is interested in selling it through the mail. It has identified a subset of 2,500 names from Lifestyle List Company that have purchased exercise equipment in the last three years. It is interested in developing a "look-alike" model to score the list using 35 demographic and lifestyle attributes that are available from most list sellers. To do this, it will use the full 2,500 names of past buyers of exercise equipment and a random sample of 20,000 names from the remainder of the list. Health Nut Corporation plans to build a purchase model using the 35 attributes purchased from Lifestyle List Company. Once the model is constructed and validated, Health Nut Corporation will have a robust tool for scoring the Lifestyle List Company and other lists with similar predictive variables.

Case 7: Same Product to Affinity Group List

RLI Long Distance is forming a partnership with Fly High Airlines. RLI plans to offer one frequent flier mile for every dollar spent on long distance calls. RLI would like to solicit Fly High Airlines frequent fliers to switch their long distance service to RLI. The frequent flier database has 155 demographic and behavioral attributes available for modeling. Because RLI has a captive audience and expects a high 25% activation rate, it decides to collect data for modeling with a random mailing to all the frequent flier members. After eight weeks, RLI plans to create a modeling data set by matching the new customers to the original offer data with the 155 attributes appended.

Data for Customer Models

As markets mature in many industries, attracting new customers is becoming increasingly difficult. This is especially true in the credit card industry, where banks are compelled to offer low rates to lure customers away from their competitors. The cost of acquiring a new customer has become so expensive that many companies are expanding their product lines to maximize the value of existing customer relationships. Credit card banks are offering insurance or investment products. Or they are merging with full-service banks and other financial institutions to offer a full suite of financial services. Telecommunications companies are expanding their product and service lines or merging with cable and Internet companies. Many companies in a variety of industries are viewing their customers as their key asset.

This creates many opportunities for target modeling. A customer who is already happy with your company's service is much more likely to purchase another product from you. This creates many opportunities for cross-sell and up-sell target modeling. Retention and renewal models are also critical to target customers who may be looking to terminate their relationship. Simple steps to retain a customer can be quite cost-effective.

Modeling for Cross-sell, Up-sell, Retention, and Renewal

Data from prior campaigns is also the best data for developing models for customer targeting. While most customer models are developed using internal data, overlay or external data is sometimes appended to customer data to enhance the predictive power of the targeting models. The following cases are designed to provide you with ideas for creating your own modeling data sets for cross-sell, up-sell, and retention.

TIP

Many list companies will allow you to test their overlay data at no charge. If a list company is interested in building a relationship, it usually is willing to provide its full list of attributes for testing. The best methodology is to take a past campaign and overlay the entire list of attributes. Next, develop a model to see which attributes are predictive for your product or service. If you find a few very powerful predictors, you can negotiate a price to purchase these attributes for future campaigns.

Case 8: Cross-sell

Sure Wire Communications has built a solid base of long distance customers over the past 10 years. It is now expanding into cable television and wants to cross-sell this service to its existing customer base. Through a phone survey to 200 customers, Sure Wire learned that approximately 25% are interested in signing up for cable service. To develop a model for targeting cable customers, it wants a campaign with a minimum of 5,000 responders. It is planning to mail an offer to a random sample of 25,000 customers. This will ensure that with as low as a 20% response rate, it will have enough responders to develop a model.

Case 9: Up-sell Using Life-Stage Segments

XYZ Life Insurance Company wants to develop a model to target customers who are most likely to increase their life insurance coverage. Based on past experience and common sense, it knows that customers who are just starting a family are good candidates for increased coverage. But it also knows that other life events can trigger the need for more life insurance. To enhance its customer file, XYZ is planning to test overlay data from Lifetime List Company. Lifetime specializes in *life-stage* segmentation. XYZ feels that this additional segmentation will increase the power of its model. To improve the results of the campaign, XYZ Life is planning to make the offer to all of its customers in Life Stage III. These are the customers who have a high probability of being in the process of beginning a family. XYZ Life will pull a random sample from the remainder of the names to complete the mailing. Once the results are final, it will have a full data set with *life-stage* enhancements for model development.

Case 10: Retention/Attrition/Churn

First Credit Card Bank wants to predict which customers are going to pay off their balances in the next three months. Once they are identified, First will perform a risk assessment to determine if it can lower their annualized percentage rate in an effort to keep their balances. Through analysis, First has determined that there is some seasonality in balance behavior. For example, balances usually increase in September and October due to school shopping. They also rise in November and December as a result of holiday shopping. Balances almost always drop in January as customers pay off their December balances. Another decrease is typical in April when customers receive their tax refunds. In order to capture the effects of seasonality, First decided to look at two years of data. It restricted the analysis to customers who were out of their introductory period by at least four months. The analysts at First structured the data so that they could use the month as a predictor along with all the behavioral and demographic characteristics on the account. The modeling data set was made up of all the attriters and a random sample of the nonattriters.

TIP

When purchasing attributes for modeling, it is important to get the attribute values that are valid at the time of name selection. Remember to account for processing time between the overlay and the actual rollout.

Data for Risk Models

Managing risk is a critical component to maintaining profitability in many industries. Most of us are familiar with the common risk inherent in the banking and insurance industries. The primary risk in banking is failure to repay a loan. In insurance, the primary risk lies in a customer filing a claim. Another major risk assumed by banks, insurance companies, and many other businesses is that of fraud. Stolen credit cards cost banks and retailers millions of dollars a year. Losses from fraudulent insurance claims are equally staggering.

Strong relationships have been identified between financial risk and some types of insurance risk. As a result, insurance companies are using financial risk models to support their insurance risk modeling efforts. One interesting demonstration of this is the fact that credit payment behavior is predictive of auto insurance claims. Even though they seem unrelated, the two behaviors are clearly linked and are used effectively in risk assessment.

Risk models are challenging to develop for a number of reasons. The performance window has to cover a period of several years to be effective, which makes them difficult to validate. Credit risk is sensitive to the health of the economy. And the risk of claims for insurance is vulnerable to population trends.

Credit data is easy to obtain. It's just expensive and can be used only for an offer of credit. Some insurance risk data, such as life and health, is relatively easy to obtain, but obtaining risk data for the automotive insurance industry can be difficult.

Modeling for Risk

Due to the availability of credit data from the credit bureaus, it is possible to build risk models on prospects. This creates quite an advantage to banks that are interested in developing their own proprietary risk scores. The following cases are designed to provide you with ideas for creating your own risk modeling data sets.

Case 11: Credit Risk for Prospects

High Street Bank has been very conservative in the past. Its product offerings were limited to checking accounts, savings accounts, and secured loans. As a way of attracting new customers, it is interested in offering unsecured loans. But first it wants to develop a predictive model to identify prospects that are likely to default. To create the modeling and development data set, it decides to purchase data from a credit bureau. High Street Bank is interested in predicting the risk of bankruptcy for a prospect for a three-year period. The risk department requests 12,000 archived credit files from four years ago, 6,000 that show a bankruptcy in the last three years and 6,000 with no bankruptcy. This will give it a snapshot of the customer at that point in time.

Case 12: Fraud Risk for Customers

First Credit Card Bank wants to develop a model to predict fraud. In the transaction database it captures purchase activity for each customer including the amount, date, and spending category. To develop a fraud model, it collects several weeks of purchase data for each customer. The average daily spending is calculated within each category. From this information, it can establish rules that trigger an inquiry if a customer's spending pattern changes.

Case 13: Insurance Risk for Customers

CCC Insurance Company wants to develop a model to predict comprehensive automobile claims for a one- to four-year period. Until now, it has been using simple segmentation based on demographic variables from the customer database. It wants to improve its prediction by building a model with overlay data from Sure Target List Company. Sure Target sells demographic, psychographic, and proprietary segments called Sure Hits that it developed using cluster analysis. To build the file for overlay, CCC randomly select 5,000 names from the customers with at least a five-year tenure who filed at least one claim in the last four years. It randomly selects another 5,000 customers with at least a five-year tenure who have never filed a claim. CCC sends the files to Sure Target List Company with a request that the customers be matched to an archive file from five years ago. The demographic, psychographic, and proprietary segments represent the customer profiles five years earlier. The data can be used to develop a predictive model that will target customers who are likely to file a claim in the next four years.

Constructing the Modeling Data Set

When designing a campaign for a mail or telephone offer with the goal of using the results to develop a model, it is important to have complete representation from the entire universe of names. If it is cost-prohibitive to mail the entire list, sampling is an effective alternative. It is critical, though, that the sample size is large enough to support both model development and validation. This can be determined using performance estimates and confidence intervals.

How Big Should My Sample Be?

This question is common among target modelers. Unfortunately, there is no exact answer. Sample size depends on many factors. What is the expected return rate on the target group? This could be performance based such as responders, approved accounts, or activated accounts, or risk based such as defaults or claims filed. How many variables are you planning to use in the model? The more variables you have, the more data you need. The goal is to have enough records in the target group to support all levels of the explanatory variables. One way to think about this is to consider that the significance is measured on the cross-section of every level of every variable.

Figure 2.2 displays a data set consisting of responders and nonresponders. The two characteristics or variables represented are *region* and *family size*. *Region* has four levels: East, South, Midwest, and West. *Family size* has values of 1 through 8. Each level of region is crossed with each level of family size. To use every level of these variables to predict response, each cross-section must have a minimum number of observations or values. And this is true among the responders and nonresponders. There is no exact minimum number, but a good rule of thumb is at least 25 observations. The more observations there are in the cell, the more likely it is that the value will have predictive power.

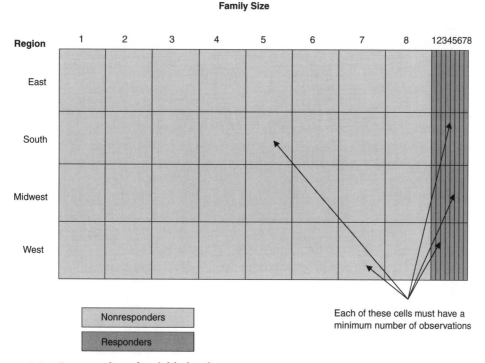

Figure 2.2 Cross-section of variable levels.

The optimal sample size also depends on the predictive power of the variables. It is more difficult to find predictive power with a small sample. But if you do, you will generally have a robust model. Keep in mind that if you have much smaller samples available for model development, it is still possible to build a model. It is just a little more difficult to find the strong predictive relationships.

Sampling Methods

In most situations a simple random sample will serve your modeling needs. If you plan to develop a model to replace a current model, it is important to capture the behavior of the prospects that your current model would not normally select. This can be accomplished by soliciting a randomly selected group of the names outside of the normal selects, as shown in Figure 2.3. The idea is to select an "nth" random sample. When constructing the modeling data set, use a weight equal to "n" for the random sample to re-create the entire universe. Be prepared for this to be a hard sell to management. This group of names does not perform as well as the group that the model selects. Consequently, or for this portion of the population, the company will probably lose money. Therefore, it is necessary to convince management of the value in this information.

Universe of Names

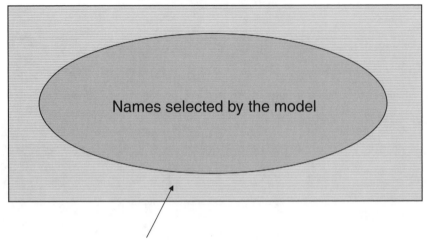

Pull a random sample from the names not selected by the model

Figure 2.3   Sampling for full representation.

Stratified sampling works well if you have a characteristic that you want to use as a predictor but the prevalence of that characteristic is very low. Stratified sampling simply means that you sample different segments of the population at different rates or "nths." For example, let's say you know that gender is a strong predictor for your product, but the list you are using to create your sample for model development is made up mostly of males. At some future date you plan to use the model to score a different list that is more evenly split on gender. When you select the names for your offer, pull a 1/1,000 sample from the males and a 1/100 sample from the females. This will pull in 10 times as many females as males.

To select different sample sizes within the population, you create separate random samples within each distinct group. The following SAS code details the steps:

```
data male(where=(ranuni(5555)<.001))
   female(where=(ranuni(5555)<.01));
 set.libname.list;
if gender = 'M' then output male;
else output female;
run;

data libname.sample;
 set male female;
if gender = 'M' then weight = 1000; else weight = 100;
run;
```

You may want to use weights in the modeling process to maintain the correct proportions. In the last section of the code, the data is joined together and weights are assigned to re-create the original sample proportions.

Developing Models from Modeled Data

Many analysts who are tasked with building a model have similar complaints. They are asked to build a model on data that was collected from a campaign where a model was used for the original name selection. In other words, they do not have a full representation of the universe of available names. Unfortunately, this is very often the case. When this occurs, you have a couple of choices. If the available sample represents greater than 80% of the total universe of names, you have a good chance of developing a model that will generalize to the entire universe. Depending on the strength of the new model and its ability to rank order the names, you might want to sample the nonselected names when you implement the model so you can perform additional validation.

If the available sample represents less than 80% of the total universe of names, you have two choices. You can mail a random sample of the entire population and wait for the results to build the model. Most companies would not tolerate this delay. Another choice is to include the names that were not solicited in the nontarget group. Because these names were not selected by the previous model they would presumably have a lower return rate. The resulting model would not be optimal, but it could provide improved targeting until a better model development sample is available.

Combining Data from Multiple Offers

Many campaigns consist of multiple offers to the same prospect or customer. For example, a bank mails a credit offer to a list of 100,000 prospects. Two weeks later the bank mails the same offer to the "best" 50,000 prospects from the same list. "Best" is defined by a score to rank the probability of response. And a third offer is mailed two weeks later to the "best" 25,000. In this situation, constructing the model development sample is not straightforward. You can't just look at the first mailing because a nonresponder in the first mailing might be a responder in a later mailing. If you combine all three mailings, though, you can have multiple records for the same person and the possibility of different outcomes for each.

One method for constructing the model development sample is to combine all three mailings. Then reduce the total mail file to one unique record per person. And finally, append the response activity to each record from any of the three mailings. This will allow you to take advantage of all the response activity. The model should be very robust; however, it will not accurately calculate probabilities. Therefore this model should be used only for ranking the names from most responsive to least responsive.

Summary

We've seen that data for developing targeting models comes in many forms and from many sources. In the course of business there are a myriad of ways to create and simulate model development data to target almost any goal. And finally, constructing the development data set leaves room for using your creativity. The most important point to remember is this: "Your model is only as good as your data!"

Now that we've planned the menu and gathered the ingredients, we are really ready to get cookin'. In part 2, we get into the nitty gritty. Beginning in chapter 3, we develop a model using a case study that takes us through chapter 7. So get your apron on and let's start cooking!

PART TWO

The Cooking Demonstration

Have you ever seen the commercials for a miracle food processor? It slices! It dices! It purees! It mixes, chops, and blends! This is where we begin our cooking demonstration! We start with raw data. We slice and dice the data and fill in where there are missing ingredients. We finally get the data ready for processing! Once the data ingredients are ready, we start cooking, testing, and evaluating our creation. Then we prepare to serve the finished product!

We begin our case study in part 2. Over the next five chapters, I develop a net present value model for a life insurance direct-mail campaign. Chapter 3 introduces the components of the model and discuss steps for preparing the data. Chapter 4 describes how the variables are selected and transformed to create the best fit. Chapter 5 is where the fun begins! We process the model and look at the initial results. Chapter 6 takes the model through some rigorous validation. And, finally, chapter 7 details the implementation, back-end validation, and maintenance.

As we delve into the details that take us through our case study, I include portions of the SAS code necessary to complete the task. As I explain the steps in the text, I refer to sections of the code that appear in **boldface.** These are the key steps for each data step or procedure and can be modified to fit data for numerous objectives over a variety of industries.

So don your aprons and let's start cooking!

CHAPTER 6

Preparing the Data for Modeling

D ata preparation is one of the most important steps in the model development process. From the simplest analysis to the most complex model, the quality of the data going in is key to the success of the project. The famous saying "Garbage in, garbage out" is quite fitting in this case. The ability of a model to produce robust results is as dependent on good data as it is on effective techniques.

Gaining access to the data and understanding its characteristics are the first steps to ensuring a good model. I begin chapter 3 with basic steps for reading in and combining data from multiple sources. Once the modeling data set is built, I begin the extremely boring but critically important task of cleaning the data. This involves looking for and handling data errors, outliers, and missing values. Once the data is accessed and cleaned, I create some routine variables through summarization, ratios, and date math. On completion of these steps, I have a data set worthy of modeling.

Accessing the Data

Before I begin the modeling process, I need to understand how data is classified and the various ways in which data is transported. Obtaining the data in a usable format is the first step in the data preparation process. Depending on the type of model you are developing, you may have to extract the data yourself or request it from an outside source. If you are developing a model using data on existing customers, you may be able to pull the desired records from a data warehouse. This data typically arrives in a usable format such as an SAS data set. If you are developing a model on an outside list or a prospect file, however, you may have some choices about the record format of the data.

If you are obtaining data for model development from an outside source or a separate internal source, request the data in ASCII (American Standard for Computer Information Interchange). An ASCII file is also known as a flat file or text file. The rows represent individual records or observations, and the columns or fields represent the characteristics or variables related to the records. An ASCII file comes in two basic record length formats, fixed and variable. (The format of the record should not be confused with the format of the data, which is discussed later.)

A *fixed* format is the easiest to read because it uses a fixed amount of space for each characteristic. Each row of data is the same length. The disadvantage of the fixed format is that it uses space for blank fields. Therefore, if many of the fields have missing values, it can be wasteful.

Figure 3.1 displays the first five records of a sample flat file in a fixed record format. The first nine spaces contain the prospect ID. The next space contains a geographic indicator. In the fifth record, the value for the geographic indicator is missing. Following the geographic indicator is the zip code. Notice that the zip code has nine digits. This is typically read in two separate fields. The last three fields are each one digit representing age group, gender, and marital status.

Notice the spaces in the first, second, and fifth rows. They will be read as missing values. They serve as placeholders to keep each field lined up with the proper field name. The following code reads in the fixed format data:

```
data libname.fixed;
infile 'C:\fixedfile.txt' missover recl=22;
input
pros_id      1-9           /*unique prospect identifier*/
region      $ 10           /*region of country*/
zip5        $ 11-15        /*five digit zipcode*/
zip4        $ 16-19        /*four digit zip extension*/
```

```
        0 -- 5 -- 10 -- 15 -- 20 --

        000000001S800143437B S
        000000002N19380      CFD
        000000003S008083522BMW
        000000004W945912441EMD
        000000005 696441001AFS
```

Figure 3.1 Fixed format.

```
age_grp   $ 20              /*age group*/
gender    $ 21              /*gender*/
marital   $ 22              /*marital status*/
;
run;
```

The code states exactly where each record begins and ends. It also uses a "$" before the variable to designate whether the *format of the data* is character or numeric. (Other data formats may be used for certain types of data. Contact your data source for guidance in reading alternate data formats.)

A *variable* format has the same structure for each row. The difference is in the column values or fields. If a column value is missing, no space is used for that field. A placeholder or *delimiter* is used to separate each value. Some examples of delimiters are commas, slashes, and spaces.

Figure 3.2 displays the first five records of a sample flat file in a variable format with a comma delimiter. The data is identical to the fixed format data; it is just separated using commas. There is one major advantage of this type of format. If there are a lot of missing values, the data takes up less space.

Notice how the spaces for missing values have two commas in a row. That tells the program to hold a space for the next variable in line. The "$" denotes a character variable. The following code reads in the variable format data:

```
data libname.variable;
infile 'C:\varfile.txt' delimiter=',';
input
pros_id                    /*unique prospect identifier*/
region $                   /*region of country*/
zip5 $                     /*five digit zipcode*/
zip4 $                     /*four digit zip extension*/
age_grp $                  /*age group*/
gender $                   /*gender*/
marital $                  /*marital status*/
;
run;
```

```
0 -- 5 -- 10 -- 15 -- 20 --

000000001,S,80014,3437,B,,S
000000002,N,19380,,C,F,D
000000003,S,00808,3522,B,M,W
000000004,W,94591,2441,E,M,D
000000005,,69644,1001,A,F,S
```

Figure 3.2   Variable format.

It is also important to request all supporting documentation such as a file layout and data dictionary. The file layout will tell you the variable names, the starting position of the data and length of field for each character, and the type of variable. The data dictionary will provide the format and a detailed description of each variable. It is also recommended to get a "data dump" or printout of the first 25–100 records. This is invaluable for seeing just what you are getting.

Classifying Data

There are two classes of data, qualitative and quantitative. *Qualitative data* use descriptive terms to differentiate values. For example, gender is generally classified into "M" or male and "F" or female. Qualitative data can be used for segmentation or classification. *Quantitative data* is characterized by numeric values. Gender could also be quantitative if prior rules are established. For example, you could say that the values for gender are 1 and 2 where 1 = "M" or male and 2 = "F" or female. Quantitative data is used for developing predictive models. There are four types of quantitative data.

Nominal data is numeric data that represents categories or attributes. The numeric values for gender (1 & 2) would be nominal data values. One important characteristic of nominal data is that it has no relative importance. For example, even though male = 1 and female = 2, the relative value of being female is not twice the value or a higher value than that of being male. For modeling purposes, a nominal variable with only two values would be coded with the values 0 and 1. This will be discussed in more detail in chapter 4.

Ordinal data is numeric data that represents categories that *have* relative importance. They can be used to rank strength or severity. For example, a list company assigns the values 1 through 5 to denote financial risk. The value 1, characterized by no late payments, is considered low risk. The value 5, characterized by a bankruptcy, is considered high risk. The values 2 through 4 are characterized by various previous delinquencies. A prospect with a risk ranking of 5 is definitely riskier than a prospect with a ranking of 1. But he or she is not five times as risky. And the difference in their ranks of $5 - 1 = 4$ has no meaning.

Interval data is numeric data that has relative importance and has no zero point. Also, addition and subtraction are meaningful operations. For example, many financial institutions use a risk score that has a much finer definition than the values 1 through 5, as in our previous example. A typical range is from 300 to 800. It is therefore possible to compare scores by measuring the difference.

Continuous data is the most common data used to develop predictive models. It can accommodate all basic arithmetic operations, including addition, subtraction, multiplication, and division. Most business data such as sales, balances, and minutes, is continuous data.

Reading Raw Data

Data formats are used to read each column or data field in its most useful form. The two most common formats are character and numeric. If you do not have a sample of the data to view and you are not sure of the type of data, it is advisable to read in the first 25–50 records with every field in character format. This takes very little time, allows you to test your code, and lets you print the first few records to get a good look at the data.

To create the modeling data set for our insurance case study I begin with two separate files:

The **original acquisition campaign offer file** has 729,228 records. It contains a prospect identifier along with 43 demographic, credit, and segmentation characteristics. It is a flat file with a fixed record length. It was a direct mail offer that was rolled out to the state of New York six months ago.

The **performance file** has 13,868 records and represents the responders to this campaign. It contains a prospect identifier and an activation flag. The activation flag indicates that the prospect passed the risk screening and paid the first premium. The file is a flat file with a fixed record length.

The input process begins with knowing the format of the data. The following code reads the entire campaign offer file and prints the first 25 records. The first line sets up the library, *acqmod*. The second line creates an SAS data set, *acqmod.campaign*. The infile statement identifies the flat file to read. The *missover* option tells the program to skip over missing values. And the recl=109 defines the length of each line so the program knows when to go to a new record. The "$" denotes a character or nonnumeric variable. The variable names are all held to seven characters to allow for numeric extensions later in the processing:

```
libname acqmod 'c:\insur\acquisit\modeldata';

data acqmod.campaign;
infile 'F:\insur\acquisit\camp.txt' missover recl=109;
input
pros_id       1-9                /*unique prospect identifier*/
pop_den     $ 13                 /*population density code*/
trav_cd     $ 14                 /*travel indicator*/
bankcrd     $ 15                 /*presence of bankcard*/
deptcrd     $ 16                 /*presence of dept store card*/
fin_co      $ 17                 /*pres of finance co. loan*/
premcrd     $ 18                 /*pres of premium bankcard*/
upsccrd     $ 19                 /*pres of upscale bankcard*/
apt_ind     $ 20                 /*apartment indicator*/
```

```
pob_ind      $ 21              /*P.O.Box indicator*/
clustr1      $ 22-23           /*statistical grouping*/
inc_est        24-27           /*estimated income in dollars*/
inc_grp      $ 28              /*income group*/
sgle_in      $ 29              /*marital status = single*/
opd_bcd      $ 30-35           /*bankcard open date*/
occu_cd      $ 36              /*occupation code*/
finl_id      $ 37              /*finance loan identifier*/
gender       $ 38              /*gender*/
ssn_ind      $ 39              /*presence of SOC SEC Number*/
driv_in      $ 40              /*driver indicator*/
mob_ind      $ 41              /*mail order buyer indicator*/
mortin1      $ 42              /*presence of first mortgage*/
mortin2      $ 43              /*presence of second mortgage*/
autoin1      $ 44              /*presence of one auto loan*/
autoin2      $ 45              /*presence of two auto loans*/
infd_ag        46-47           /*inferred age*/
age_ind      $ 48              /*indicator - how age derived*/
dob_yr       $ 49-52           /*year of birth*/
homeq_r      $ 53              /*home equity range*/
hom_equ      $ 54-61           /*home equity*/
childin      $ 62              /*presence of child indicator*/
homevlr      $ 63              /*home value range*/
clustr2      $ 64              /*statistical grouping*/
tot_acc        65-67           /*total credit accounts*/
actopl6        68-70           /*# accts open in last 6 mos*/
credlin        71-77           /*total credit lines*/
tot_bal        78-84           /*total credit card balances*/
inql6m         85-87           /*# credit inq. last 6 months*/
age_fil        88-90           /*age of file*/
totopac        91-93           /*total open credit accounts*/
no30day        94-96           /*number 30 day late ever*/
no90eve        97-99           /*number 90 day late ever*/
nobkrpt        100-102         /*number of bankruptcies*/
amtpdue        103-109         /*total currently past due*/
;
run;

options obs=25;
proc print;
title 'XYZ Life Insurance Campaign Data - 25 Records';
run;
```

The next code reads the performance data and prints the first 25 records. It also creates a variable *respond* that has the value of 1 for every record. Before I begin to read in the campaign data, I reset the *obs=max* option. This overwrites the options *obs=25* in the previous step.

```
options obs=max;
```

```
data acqmod.response;
infile 'F:\insur\acquisit\perform.txt' missover recl=10;
input
pros_id         1-9                /*unique prospect identifier*/
activate     $ 10                  /*activation indicator*/
;
respond = 1;
run;


options obs=25;
proc print;
title 'Life Insurance Performance Data - 25 Records';
run;
```

At this point, I have both the prospect file and responder file read into SAS data sets. In the next section, I combine them to make the modeling data set.

Creating the Modeling Data Set

In chapter 2, I described sources of data for model development. In many cases it is necessary to combine data from several sources. As explained earlier, I have two data sets that need to be combined to create the final data set: the original campaign data file and the performance data. The performance file contains only those prospects who responded and a flag to indicate whether they acti-vated. Both files contain a unique identifier, called a prospect ID (pros_id), for each record that can be used to match the policyholders back to the original campaign data. To combine files in a data step using SAS, it is necessary to sort the data by the field being used to combine the data. In our case study, I am using prospect ID. Before I create the modeling data set, I should consider whether I want to reduce the size of the modeling data set using sampling.

```
options obs=max;

proc sort data=acqmod.campaign;
by pros_id;
run;

proc sort data=acqmod.response;
by pros_id;
run;

data acqmod.both;
merge acqmod.campaign acqmod.response;
by pros_id;
run;
;
```

TIP

In many cases, you are asked to merge files that do not have a unique identifier for matching. In this situation, the most common method for merging is using name and address. There are an unlimited number of ways to configure the name and address for matching. The most cost-effective way to act on this is to use a proven software package. They make use of years of experience and offer great flexibility.

Sampling

Computer power has improved dramatically over the last few years. It might be argued that sampling isn't necessary for saving time and space, but it still makes good sense. It speeds up the process and generally produces the same results.

In target modeling, the target group is often a small percentage (< 10%) of the total population. In this situation, the best approach is to keep the entire target group and extract a random sample from the nontarget group. A sample of 50,000 to 75,000 for the nontarget group is usually optimal. You can always use less. It just becomes more difficult to develop a model with a high number of variables. If your results are significant, however, your model will be more robust.

In the case study, I have 13,868 responders and 715,360 nonresponders. My target group is actually a subset of the responders. I keep all of the responders and take a 1/10th random sample from the nonresponders. The following code creates the final data set. A frequency is run on the performance variables using weights for verification. The output from the frequency is seen in Figure 3.3. This exercise allows you to validate that the weights have been applied correctly. The final sample configuration is displayed in Table 3.1.

```
options obs=max;

data nonresp(where=(ranuni(5555)<.1));
set acqmod.both(where=(respond^=1));
run;

data acqmod.model;
set acqmod.both(where=(respond=1)) nonresps;
if respond = 1 then smp_wgt = 1;
else smp_wgt = 10;
respond = (respond = 1);
run;

proc freq;
weight smp_wgt;
table respond activate /missing;
run;
```

RESPOND	Frequency	Percent	Cumulative Frequency	Cumulative Percent
0	715360	98.1	715360	98.1
1	13868	1.9	729228	100.0

Number of responders (includes actives)

ACTIVATE	Frequency	Percent	Cumulative Frequency	Cumulative Percent
	715360	98.1	715360	98.1
0	12806	1.8	728166	99.9
1	1062	0.1	729228	100.0

Number of responders (excludes actives)

Number of actives

Figure 3.3 Sample frequences.

The sample frequencies show the number of records in the file and the sample. This is summarized in Table 3.1.

WARNING

It is important to match the responders to the file and determine who are the nonresponders before you take the sample. Otherwise, you might not get all the data for the responders.

Table 3.1 Modeling Sample Data Set

GROUP	CAMPAIGN	SAMPLE	WEIGHT
Actives	1,602	1,602	1
Responders/Nonactive	12,806	12,806	1
Nonresponders	715,360	71,536	10
Total	729,768	85,944	

Cleaning the Data

I now have the complete data set for modeling. The next step is to examine the data for errors, outliers, and missing values. This is the most time-consuming, least exciting, and most important step in the data preparation process. Luckily there are some effective techniques for managing this process.

First, I describe some techniques for cleaning and repairing data for continuous variables. Then I repeat the process for categorical variables.

Continuous Variables

To perform data hygiene on continuous variables, PROC UNIVARIATE is a useful procedure. It provides a great deal of information about the distribution of the variable including measures of central tendency, measures of spread, and the skewness or the degree of imbalance of the data.

For example, the following code will produce the output for examining the variable *estimated income* (inc_est).

```
proc univariate data=acqmod.model plot;
weight smp_wgt;
var inc_est;
run;
```

The results from PROC UNIVARIATE for estimated income (*inc_est*) are shown in Figure 3.4. The values are in thousands of dollars.

There is a lot of information in this univariate analysis. I just look for a few key things. Notice the measures in bold. In the *moments* section, the mean seems reasonable at $61.39224. But looking a little further I detect some data issues. Notice that the highest value in the extreme values is 660. In Figure 3.5, the histogram and box plot provide a good visual analysis of the overall distribution and the extreme value. I get another view of this one value. In the histogram, the bulk of the observations are near the bottom of the graph with the single high value near the top. The box plot also shows the limited range for the bulk of the data. The box area represents the central 50% of the data. The distance to the extreme value is very apparent. This point may be considered an outlier.

Outliers and Data Errors

An outlier is a single or low-frequency occurrence of the value of a variable that is far from the mean as well as the majority of the other values for that variable. Determining whether a value is an outlier or a data error is an art as well as a science. Having an intimate knowledge of your data is your best strength.

```
Variable=INC_EST
Weight=  SMP_WGT


              Moments                                                    Quantiles(Def=5)
N               85320  Sum Wgts     728478               100% Max       660        99%
Mean         61.39224  Sum        44722899                75% Q3         77        95%
Std Dev      81.05066  Variance    6569.21                50% Med        55        90%
Skewness           .   Kurtosis         .                25% Q1         38        10%
USS          3.3061E9  CSS         5.6048E8                0% Min        16         5%
CV            132.021  Std Mean   0.094962                                          1%
T:Mean=0      646.495  Pr>|T|       0.0001               Range         644
Num ^= 0        85320  Num > 0        85320               Q3-Q1          39
M(Sign)         42660  Pr>=|M|      0.0001               Mode           36
Sgn Rank     1.8199E9  Pr>=|S|      0.0001


                               Extremes
              Lowest     Obs      Highest      Obs
                 16(    43128)       251(    77863)
                 17(    80551)       253(     2246)
                 17(    35279)       256(    48800)
                 17(    34259)       321(    35915)
                 17(    24788)       660(    85206)


                        Missing Value         .
                        Count                84
                        % Count/Nobs        0.10
```

Figure 3.4   Initial univariate analysis of *estimated income*.

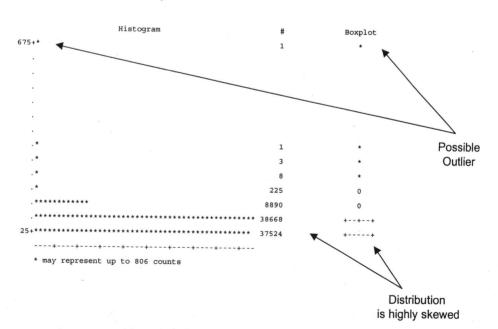

Figure 3.5   Histogram and box plot of *estimated income*.

Common sense and good logic will lead you to most of the problems. In our example, the one value that seems questionable is the maximum value (660). It could have an extra zero. One way to see if it is a data error is to look at some other values in the record. The variable *estimated income group* serves as a check for the value. The following code prints the record:

```
proc print data=acqmod.model(where=(inc_est=660));
var inc_grp;
run;
```

The following output shows the *estimated income group* is "K":

```
OBS     INC_GRP
85206       K
```

Based on the information provided with the data, I know the range of incomes in group K to be between $65,000 and $69,000. This leads us to believe that the value 660 should be 66. I can verify this by running a PROC MEANS for the remaining records in group K.

```
proc means data=acqmod.model maxdec = 2;
where inc_grp = 'K' and inc_est ^= 660;
var inc_est;
run;
```

The following SAS output validates our suspicion. All the other prospects with estimated income group = K have estimated income values between 65 and 69.

```
          Analysis Variable : INC_EST (K)

   N     Mean    Std Dev  Minimum  Maximum
  --------------------------------------------
  4948   66.98    1.41     65.00    69.00
  --------------------------------------------
```

Here I replace the value 660 with 66. When substituting a new value for a missing value, it is always a good idea to create a new variable name. This maintains the integrity of the original data.

```
data acqmod.model;
 set acqmod.model;
if inc_est = 660 then inc_est2 = 66;
else inc_est2 = inc_est;
run;
```

In Figure 3.6, we see the change in the histogram and the box plot as a result of correcting the outlier. The distribution is still centered near a lower range of values, but the skewness is greatly decreased.

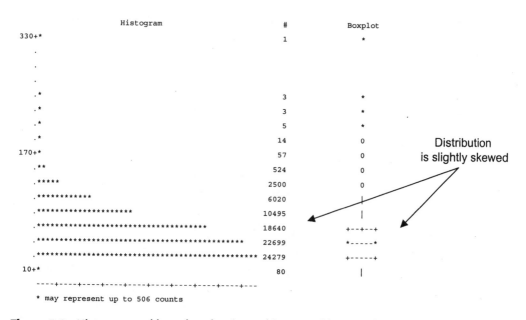

Figure 3.6   Histogram and box plot of *estimated income* with corrections.

If you have hundreds of variables, you may not want to spend a lot of time on each variable with missing or incorrect values. Time-consuming techniques for correction should be used sparingly. If you find an error and the fix is not obvious, you can treat it as a missing value.

Outliers are common in numeric data, especially when dealing with monetary variables. Another method for dealing with outliers is to develop a capping rule. This can be accomplished easily using some features in PROC UNIVARIATE. The following code produces an output data set with the standard deviation (*incstd*) and the 99th percentile value (*inc99*) for *estimated income* (inc_est).

```
proc univariate data=acqmod.model noprint;
weight smp_wgt;
var inc_est;
output out=incdata std=incstd pctlpts=99 pctlpre=inc;
run;

data acqmod.model;
 set acqmod.model;
if (_n_ eq 1) then set incdata(keep= incstd inc99);
if incstd > 2*inc99 then inc_est2 =
    min(inc_est,(4*inc99));
    else inc_est2 = inc_est;
run;
```

The code in bold is just one example of a rule for capping the values of a variable. It looks at the spread by seeing if the standard deviation is greater than twice the value at the 99th percentile. If it is, it caps the value at four times the 99th percentile. This still allows for generous spread without allowing in obvious outliers. This particular rule only works for variables with positive values. Depending on your data, you can vary the rules to suit your goals.

Missing Values

As information is gathered and combined, missing values are present in almost every data set. Many software packages ignore records with missing values, which makes them a nuisance. The fact that a value is missing, however, can be predictive. It is important to capture that information.

Consider the direct mail company that had its customer file appended with data from an outside list. Almost a third of its customers didn't match to the outside list. At first this was perceived as negative. But it turned out that these customers were much more responsive to offers for additional products. After further analysis, it was discovered that these customers were not on many outside lists. This made them more responsive because they were not receiving many direct mail offers from other companies. Capturing the fact that they had missing values improved the targeting model.

In our case study, we saw in the univariate analysis that we have 84 missing values for income. The first step is to create an indicator variable to capture the fact that the value is missing for certain records. The following code creates a variable to capture the information:

```
data acqmod.model;
 set acqmod.model;
if inc_est2 = . then inc_miss = 1;
else inc_miss = 0;
run;
```

The goal for replacing missing values is twofold: to fill the space with the most likely value and to maintain the overall distribution of the variable.

Single Value Substitution

Single value substitution is the simplest method for replacing missing values. There are three common choices: mean, median, and mode. The mean value is based on the statistical least-square-error calculation. This introduces the least variance into the distribution. If the distribution is highly skewed, the median may be a better choice. The following code substitutes the mean value for estimated income (*inc_est2*):

```
data acqmod.model;
 set acqmod.model;
if inc_est2 = . then inc_est3 = 61;
else inc_est3 = inc_est2;
run;
```

Class Mean Substitution

Class mean substitution uses the mean values within subgroups of other variables or combinations of variables. This method maintains more of the original distribution. The first step is to select one or two variables that may be highly correlated with income. Two values that would be highly correlated with income are home equity (*hom_equ*) and inferred age (*infd_ag*). The goal is to get the average estimated income for cross-sections of home equity ranges and age ranges for observations where estimated income is not missing. Because both variables are continuous, a data step is used to create the group variables, *age_grp* and *homeq_r*. PROC TABULATE is used to derive and display the values.

```
data acqmod.model;
 set acqmod.model;
 if 25 <= infd_ag <= 34 then age_grp = '25-34'; else
 if 35 <= infd_ag <= 44 then age_grp = '35-44'; else
 if 45 <= infd_ag <= 54 then age_grp = '45-54'; else
 if 55 <= infd_ag <= 65 then age_grp = '55-65';
 if 0   <= hom_equ<=100000 then homeq_r = '$0-$100K'; else
if 100000<hom_equ<=200000 then homeq_r = '$100-$200K'; else
if 200000<hom_equ<=300000 then homeq_r = '$200-$300K'; else
if 300000<hom_equ<=400000 then homeq_r = '$300-$400K'; else
if 400000<hom_equ<=500000 then homeq_r = '$400-$500K'; else
if 500000<hom_equ<=600000 then homeq_r = '$500-$600K'; else
if 600000<hom_equ<=700000 then homeq_r = '$600-$700K'; else
if 700000<hom_equ        then homeq_r = '$700K+';
run;


proc tabulate data=acqmod.model;
where inc_est2^=.;
weight smp_wgt;
class homeq_r age_grp;
var inc_est2;
table homeq_r ='Home Equity',age_grp='Age Group'*
       inc_est2=' '*mean=' '*f=dollar6.
/rts=13;
run;
```

The output in Figure 3.7 shows a strong variation in average income among the different combinations of home equity and age group. Using these values for missing value substitution will help to maintain the distribution of the data.

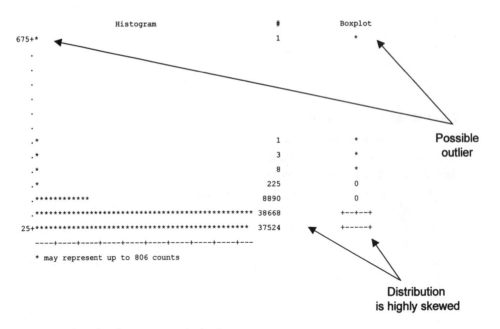

Figure 3.7 Values for class mean substitution.

The final step is to develop an algorithm that will create a new estimated income variable (*inc_est3*) that has no missing values.

```
data acqmod.model;
 set acqmod.model;
if inc_est2 = . then do;
if 25 <= infd_ag <= 34 then do;
      if 0    <= hom_equ<=100000 then inc_est3= 47; else
      if 100000<hom_equ<=200000 then inc_est3= 70; else
      if 200000<hom_equ<=300000 then inc_est3= 66; else
      if 300000<hom_equ<=400000 then inc_est3= 70; else
      if 400000<hom_equ<=500000 then inc_est3= 89; else
      if 500000<hom_equ<=600000 then inc_est3= 98; else
      if 600000<hom_equ<=700000 then inc_est3= 91; else
      if 700000<hom_equ         then inc_est3= 71;
      end; else
if 35 <= infd_ag <= 44 then do;
      if 0    <= hom_equ<=100000 then inc_est3= 55; else
      if 100000<hom_equ<=200000 then inc_est3= 73; else
            "              "          "          "
            "              "          "          "
      if 700000<hom_equ         then inc_est3= 101;
      end; else
if 45 <= infd_ag <= 54 then do;
      if 0    <= hom_equ<=100000 then inc_est3= 57; else
      if 100000<hom_equ<=200000 then inc_est3= 72; else
            "              "          "          "
            "              "          "          "
```

```
        if 700000<hom_equ        then inc_est3= 110;
        end; else
if 55 <= infd_ag <= 65 then do;
        if 0    <= hom_equ<=100000 then inc_est3= 55; else
        if 100000<hom_equ<=200000 then inc_est3= 68; else
              "              "       "         "
              "              "       "         "
        if 700000<hom_equ        then inc_est3= 107;
        end;
    end;
    run;
```

Regression Substitution

Similar to class mean substitution, regression substitution uses the means within subgroups of other variables. The advantage of regression is the ability to use continuous variables as well as look at many variables for a more precise measurement. The resulting regression score is used to impute the replacement value.

In our case study, I derive values for estimated income (*inc_est2*) using the continuous form of age (*infd_ag*), the mean for each category of home equity (*hom_equ*), total line of credit (*credlin*), and total credit balances (*tot_bal*). The following code performs a regression analysis and creates an output data set (*reg_out*) with the predictive coefficients.

```
proc reg data=acqmod.model outest=reg_out;
weight smp_wgt;
inc_reg: model inc_est2 = infd_ag hom_equ credlin tot_bal/ selection =
backward;
run;
```

Figure 3.8 shows a portion of the regression output. The parameter estimates are saved in the data set (*reg_out*) and used in PROC SCORE.

The following code is used to score the data to create *inc_reg*, the substitute value for income. A new data set is created called *acqmod.model2*. This creates a backup data set.

```
proc score data=acqmod.model score=reg_out out=acqmod.model2
      type=parms predict;
var infd_ag hom_equ credlin tot_bal;
run;
```

The following code creates inc_est3 using the regression value:

```
data acqmod.model2;
 set acqmod.model2;
if inc_est2 = . then inc_est3 = inc_reg;
else inc_est3 = inc_est2;
run;
```

Backward Elimination Procedure for Dependent Variable INC_EST2

Step 0   All Variables Entered   R-square = 0.66962678   C(p) = 5.00000000

	DF	Sum of Squares	Mean Square	F	Prob>F
Regression	4	372912001.28200	93228000.320499	43230.8	0.0001
Error	85315	183983294.99609	2156.51755255		
Total	85319	556895296.27809			

Variable	Parameter Estimate	Standard Error	Type II Sum of Squares	F	Prob>F
INTERCEP	36.87607683	0.25721498	44325117.661102	20554.0	0.0001
INFD_AG2	0.11445815	0.00602800	777500.06857066	360.54	0.0001
HOM_EQU2	-0.00000343	0.00000040	158246.95496857	73.38	0.0001
CREDLIN2	0.00011957	0.00000120	21410199.091371	9928.14	0.0001
TOT_BAL2	-0.00000670	0.00000136	52180.72203473	24.20	0.0001

Bounds on condition number: 19.28444,   161.5108

All variables left in the model are significant at the 0.1000 level.

Figure 3.8 Output for regression substitution.

One of the benefits of regression substitution is its ability to sustain the overall distribution of the data. To measure the effect on the spread of the data, I look at a PROC MEANS for the variable before (*inc_est2*) and after (*inc_est3*) the substitution:

```
proc means data=acqmod.model2 n nmiss mean std min max;
weight smp_wgt;
var inc_est2 inc_est3;
run;
```

I see in Figure 3.9 that the distribution is almost identical for both variables. The 84 values from the regression (*inc_reg*) that replaced the missing values in *inc_est2* are a good match for the distribution.

These actions can be performed on all of the continuous variables. See Appendix A for univariate analysis of remaining continuous variables. Now I must examine the quality of the categorical variables.

Variable	N	Nmiss	Mean	Std Dev	Minimum	Maximum
INC_EST2	85320	84	61.38	80.79	16.00	321.00
INC_EST3	85404	0	61.37	80.77	16.00	321.00

Figure 3.9 Means comparison of missing replacement..

Categorical Variables

As I described earlier, categorical variables are very different from continuous variables. It is still important to look at their distributions and handle any missing values.

Data Errors

A simple frequency is the best way to examine categorical variables for errors. Most categorical variables have a small enough number of levels to view individually.

```
proc freq data=acqmod.model2;
weight smp_wgt;
table pop_den trav_cd bankcrd apt_ind clustr1 inc_grp sgle_in opd_bcd
occu_cd finl_id hh_ind gender ssn_ind driv_in mob_ind mortin1 mortin2
autoin1 autoin2 infd_ag age_ind dob_yr homeq_r childin homevlr clustr2
/ missing;
run;
```

In Figure 3.10, I see that population density (*pop_den*) has four values, A, B, C, and P. I requested the missing option in our frequency, so I can see the number of missing values. The data dictionary states that the correct values for *pop_den* are A, B, and C. I presume that the value P is an error. I have a couple of choices to remedy the situation. I can delete it or replace it. For the purposes of this case study, I give it the value of the mode, which is C.

Missing Values

When modeling with nonnumeric (categorical) variables, the best way to handle missing values is to treat them as an additional category. This will be covered in greater detail in chapter 4.

See Appendix B for simple frequencies of the remaining categorical variables.

POP_DEN	Frequency	Percent	Cumulative Frequency	Cumulative Percent
	143889	19.73	143889	19.73
A	46934	6.44	190823	26.17
B	267947	36.74	458770	62.91
C	270458	37.09	729227	99.99
P	1	0.00	729228	100.00

Probable data entry error.

Figure 3.10 Frequency of population density.

Summary

In this chapter I demonstrated the process of getting data from its raw form to useful pieces of information. The process uses some techniques ranging from simple graphs to complex univariate outputs. But, in the end, it becomes obvious that with the typically large sample sizes used in marketing, it is necessary to use these techniques effectively. Why? Because the quality of the work from this point on is dependent on the accuracy and validity of the data.

Now that I have the ingredients, that is the data, I am ready to start preparing it for modeling. In chapter 4, I use some interesting techniques to select the final candidate variables. I also find the form or forms of each variable that maximizes the predictive power of the model.

Selecting and Transforming
the Variables

At this point in the process, the data has been carefully examined and refined for analysis. The next step is to define the goal in technical terms. For our case study, the objective is to build a net present value (NPV) model for a direct mail life insurance campaign. In this chapter, I will describe the components of NPV and detail the plan for developing the model.

Once the goal has been defined, the next step is to find a group of candidate variables that show potential for having strong predictive power. This is accomplished through variable reduction. To select the final candidate variables I use a combination of segmentation, transformation, and interaction detection.

Defining the Objective Function

In chapter 1, I stressed the importance of having a clear objective. In this chapter, I assign a technical definition—called the *objective function*—to the goal. Recall that the objective function is the technical definition of your business goal.

In our case study, the first goal is to predict net present value. I define the objective function as the value in today's dollars of future profits for a life insurance product. The NPV for this particular product consists of four major components: the probability of activation, the risk index, the product profitability, and the marketing expense. They are each defined as follows:

Probability of activation. A probability calculated by a model. The individual must respond, be approved by risk, and pay his or her first premium.

Risk index. Indices in matrix of gender by marital status by age group based on actuarial analysis. This value can also be calculated using a predictive model.

Product profitability. Present value of product-specific, three-year profit measure that is provided by the product manager.

Marketing expense. Cost of package, mailing, and processing (approval, fulfillment).

The final model is a combination of these four components:

Net Present Value = P(Activation) × Risk Index × Product Profitability – Marketing Expense

For our case study, I have specific methods and values for these measures.

Probability of Activation

To calculate the probability of activation, I have two options: build one model that predicts activation or build two models, one for response and one for activation, given response (model build on just responders to target actives). To determine which method works better, I will develop the model both ways.

Method 1: One model. When using one model, the goal is to target active accounts, that is, those responders who paid their first premium. To use the value "activate" in the analysis, it must be in a numeric form, preferably 0 or 1. We know from the frequency in chapter 3 that the values for the variable, *activate*, are as follows: activate = 1, respond but not activated = 0, no response = (missing). To model activation from the original offer, I must give nonresponders the value of 0. I create a new variable, *active*, and leave the original variable, *activate*, untouched.

```
data acqmod.model2;
set acqmod.model2;
if activate = . then active = 0;
else active = activate;
run;
```

We will now use the variable *active* as our dependent variable.

Method 2: Two models. When using two models, the goal is to build one model to target response and a second model to target activation, given response. The probability of activation, P(A), is the product of the probability of response, P(R), times the probability of activation, given response, P(A|R). For this method, I do not have to recode any of the dependent variables. The variables *respond* and *activate* are properly coded with the values of 0 and 1.

There are advantages and disadvantages to each method. Method 1 introduces less variance than the two-model approach in Method 2 simply because you are getting closer to your final goal with one model. The advantage of Method 2 is that it allows variables to enter the model that may have the opposite relationship between response and activation. For example, if *age* is positively correlated with response and negatively correlated with activation, it probably will not have any predictive power in Method 1. The opposite relationships will cancel each other out. Method 2, on the other hand, might have the variable *age* with a positive sign for response and a negative sign for activation. Another advantage to Method 2 is the ability to validate the models on the back end. In other words, if the model fails to perform as expected, it might be caused by a change in the market that is affecting response. In that situation, you could rebuild the response portion of the model. As we work through the case study, we track both methods to see which works better for our analysis.

Risk Index

The risk component of the NPV model is an index that was derived from a segmentation analysis on former customers. It represents an adjustment to the final NPV based on age group, gender, and marital status. As you can see in Table 4.1, young married females have a strong positive effect on profits. Conversely, single, elderly males have a negative effect on profits.

Product Profitability

For our case study, we received a value for the product profitability from the product manager of $811.30. This is based on the average profits on the whole life policy, discounted in today's dollars. I will cover the methodology for discounting in chapter 12.

Table 4.1 Risk Matrix

	MALE				FEMALE			
AGE	MARRIED	SINGLE	DIVORCED	WIDOWED	MARRIED	SINGLE	DIVORCED	WIDOWED
< 40	1.09	1.06	1.04	1.01	1.14	1.10	1.07	1.05
40–49	1.01	1.02	0.96	0.95	1.04	1.07	1.01	1.01
50–59	0.89	0.83	0.81	0.78	0.97	0.99	0.95	0.92
60+	0.75	0.65	0.72	0.70	0.94	0.89	0.84	0.78

Marketing Expense

The marketing expense for this product is $.78. This is a combination of the cost of the mail piece, $.45, postage of $.23 per piece, and $.10 for processing.

Deriving Variables

Once the data is deemed correct and missing values have been handled, the next step is to look for opportunities to derive new variables. This is a situation where knowledge of the data and the customer is critical. Combining variables through summarization or division can improve predictive power. Additional analysis of dates and the use of "date math" can assist in discovering new predictive variables.

Summarization

Summarization is an approach used to combine variables. This is done in certain cases where huge amounts of data are generated. Some common methods include addition, subtraction, and averaging.

Consider the amount of data in an active credit card transaction file. Daily processing includes purchases, returns, fees, and interchange income. Interchange income is the revenue that credit card banks collect from retailers for processing payments through their system. To make use of this information, it is typically aggregated to daily, weekly, monthly, or yearly totals and averages. For example, let's say you want to know the total monthly purchases for a group of customers. And you want to know if that total is changing from month to month. First, you summarize the daily purchases to get a monthly total. Then you subtract the months to get the difference.

The following code is not part of the case study, but it does represent an example of how to calculate the monthly totals, average daily purchases, and amount of monthly change:

```
data ccbank.dailyact;
 set ccbank.dailyact;

janpurch = sum(of pur0101-pur0131);  /* Summarize daily purchases */
febpurch = sum(of pur0201-pur0208);
 |    |    |    |    |    |
decpurch = sum(of pur1201-pur1231);

janavep = janpurch/31;               /* Average daily purchases */
febavep = febpurch/28;

change1 = janpurch - febpurch;       /* Calculate monthly change */
```

```
        change2 = febpurch - marpurch;
        run;
```

Ratios

Ratios are another variable form that is very useful for certain types of prediction. Many values have additional meaning when compared to some other factor. In this example, I have the variable credit line (*credlin2*). (Some variables now have a "2" on the end after having missing values replaced.) It represents the total credit line for all credit accounts. A total credit line is something people tend to build over time. To capture the value, I create a variable equal to the ratio of credit line to age of file (*age_fil2*). The following code creates the variable *crl_rat*.

```
        data acqmod.model2;
         set acqmod.model2;

        if age_fil2 > 0 then crl_rat=credlin2/age_fil2;
        else crl_rat = 0;
        run;
```

Dates

Dates are found in almost every data set. They can be very predictive as time measures or used in combination with other dates or different types of variables. In order to use them it is necessary to get them into a format that supports "date math." Date math is the ability to perform mathematical functions on dates. This includes addition, subtraction, multiplication, and division. SAS has numerous formats to capture date values. Once you put a date into an SAS format, it is stored as a whole number that represents the number of days since January 1, 1960. If you have two dates, you can compare them easily using this information.

In our case study, I have a date variable called *bankcard open date (opd_bcd)*. It contains six characters. The first four characters represent the year; the last two characters represent the month. The first step is to get the date into an SAS format. The **mdy** format takes the values inside the parentheses and assigns them to month, day, and year. For months, I use the **substr** command to pick the values. It begins in the fifth position and takes two characters in **substr(opd_bcd, 5,2)**. Year is pulled the same way, beginning in the first position and taking four characters.

Next, I create the variable **fix_dat**. This represents December 31, 1999. In the calculation, I use (fix_dat – opd_bcd2)/30 to represent the approximate number of months from the first bankcard open date to the end of 1999. Using date math, I create a variable that represents the ratio of the current balance to the age in months of the oldest bankcard. I call this variable *bal_rat*.

```
data acqmod.model2;
 set acqmod.model2;
opd_bcd2 = mdy(substr(opd_bcd,5,2),'01',substr(opd_bcd,1,4));
fix_dat = mdy('12','31','1999');

if opd_bcd ^= '000000' then
bal_rat = tot_bal2/((fix_dat - opd_bcd2)/30);
else bal_rat = 0;
run;
```

Variable Reduction

There are many opportunities to create variables through combinations and permutations of existing variables. This is one reason why familiarity with the data and the industry is so valuable. Once you've extracted, formatted, and created all eligible variables, it's time to narrow the field to a few strong contenders.

Continuous Variables

If you have fewer than 50 variables to start, you may not need to reduce the number of variables for final eligibility in the model. As the amount of data being collected continues to grow, the need for variable reduction increases. Some analysts, especially those using credit and transaction-level data, may be starting with 3,000+ eligible variables. Performing an in-depth analysis on each variable is not an efficient use of time. Many of the variables are correlated with each other. If you eliminate some that might have predictive power, usually some other ones will step in to do the job.

In the classic text *Applied Logistic Regression* [Hosmer and Lemshow, Wiley 1990], the authors recommend performing a univariate logistic regression on each variable. But with a large number of variables, this can be very time-consuming. It is simpler to use a procedure in SAS called PROC LOGISTIC. This is the same procedure that is used to build the final model, but it also works well as a variable reduction tool.

As an option in the model processing, choose **selection=stepwise maxstep=1** and **details**. (In chapter 5, I will cover the selection options in more detail.) This will run very quickly because you are running only one step in the modeling process.

Method 1: One Model

```
title1 "XYZ Insurance - Data Reduction";
proc logistic data=acqmod.model2 descending;
weight smp_wgt;
model active = inc_est3 inc_miss infd_ag2 hom_equ2 tot_acc2 actop162
tot_bal2 inql6m2 age_fil2 totopac2 credlin2 crl_rat bal_rat no30day2
nobkrpt amtpdue no90eve
/selection= stepwise maxstep=1 details;
run;
```

Part of the output will contain the table shown in Figure 4.1. From this table we can see the univariate predictive power of each continuous variable.

To select the final variables, look in the last column. A good rule of thumb is to keep all variables with a probability of chi-square of less than .5000. In our set of variables, all but NO30DAY and CRL_RAT remains in the candidate variable set. So I will eliminate those two variables from consideration.

Let's repeat this exercise for the models in Method 2. We want to keep all variables that are eligible for any of the models.

Analysis of Variables Not in the Model

Variable	Score Chi-Square	Pr > Chi-Square	
INC_EST3	80.5249	0.0001	
INC_MISS	1.0950	0.2954	
INFD_AG2	130.0832	0.0001	
HOM_EQU2	47.1153	0.0001	
TOT_ACC2	8.5238	0.0035	
ACTOPL62	22.9892	0.0001	These variables have low predictive power. The score chi-square is low, and the probability of significance by chance is > .5.
TOT_BAL2	52.3967	0.0001	
INQL6MO2	46.4617	0.0001	
AGE_FIL2	164.4868	0.0001	
TOTOPAC2	20.3280	0.0001	
CREDLIN2	63.7281	0.0001	
CRL_RAT	**0.0292**	**0.8644**	
BAL_RAT	20.3304	0.0001	
NO30DAY2	**0.0895**	**0.7649**	
NOBKRPT	1.9712	0.1603	
AMTPDUE	3.2699	0.0706	
NO90EVE	47.3837	0.0001	

Figure 4.1 Analysis of variables not in the model.

Chi-Square Statistic

In simple terms, the chi-square statistic measures the difference between what you expect to happen and what actually happens. The formula reads:

$$\text{Chi-square value } (\chi^2) = \frac{(\text{Expected} - \text{Actual})^2}{\text{Expected}}$$

If the chi-square value is large, then the p-value associated with the chi-square is small. The p-value represents the probability that the event occurred by chance. The chi-square statistic is the underlying test for many modeling procedures including logistic regression and certain classification trees.

Method 2: Two Models

```
title2 "Modeling Response";
proc logistic data=acqmod.model2 descending;
weight smp_wgt;
model respond = inc_est3 inc_miss infd_ag2 hom_equ2 tot_acc2 actopl62
tot_bal2 inql6m2 age_fil2 totopac2 credlin2 crl_rat bal_rat no30day2
nobkrpt amtpdue no90eve /selection= stepwise maxstep=1 details;
run;
```

Figure 4.2 shows the univariate or individual predictive power of each variable when modeling response. All variables have predictive power with estimated income (*inc_est3*) being the strongest predictor.

For predicting response, every variable is shown to be significant at the univariate level. I will allow all the variables to be candidates in the final model. If we were looking at hundreds of variables, one way to reduce the number is to select the 50 variables with the highest chi-square score.

```
title2 "Modeling Activiate";
proc logistic data=acqmod.model2 descending;
weight smp_wgt;
model activate = inc_est3 inc_miss infd_ag2 hom_equ2 tot_acc2 actopl62
tot_bal2 inql6m2 age_fil2 totopac2 credlin2 crl_rat bal_rat no30day2
nobkrpt amtpdue no90eve /selection= stepwise maxstep=1 details;
run;
```

In Figure 4.3, the univariate logistic regression results for *activation given response* shows three variables that are not significant at a level above Pr > .5000. These three variables will be dropped from consideration in the final model.

Variable	Score Chi-Square	Pr > Chi-Square
INC_EST3	**575.4842**	**0.0001**
INC_MISS	1.3002	0.2542
INFD_AG2	368.4335	0.0001
HOM_EQU2	253.5465	0.0001
TOT_ACC2	10.5224	0.0012
ACTOPL62	331.6257	0.0001
TOT_BAL2	400.1633	0.0001
INQL6MO2	384.7695	0.0001
AGE_FIL2	540.5628	0.0001
TOTOPAC2	3.9814	0.0460
CREDLIN2	380.6598	0.0001
CRL_RAT	4.8415	0.0278
BAL_RAT	118.2181	0.0001
NO30DAY2	1.4461	0.2292
NOBKRPT	77.8000	0.0001
AMTPDUE	80.3473	0.0001
NO90EVE	226.5162	0.0001

All these variables have high predictive power. The most predictive variable, INC_EST3, has the highest score chi-square.

Figure 4.2 Analysis of variables not in the model—respond.

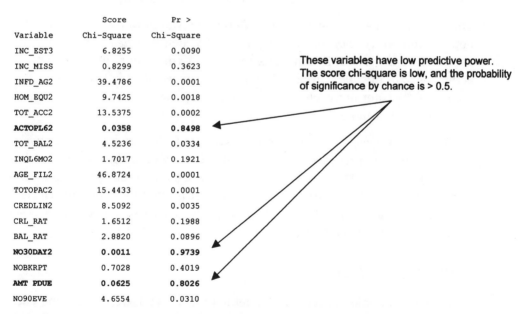

Variable	Score Chi-Square	Pr > Chi-Square
INC_EST3	6.8255	0.0090
INC_MISS	0.8299	0.3623
INFD_AG2	39.4786	0.0001
HOM_EQU2	9.7425	0.0018
TOT_ACC2	13.5375	0.0002
ACTOPL62	**0.0358**	**0.8498**
TOT_BAL2	4.5236	0.0334
INQL6MO2	1.7017	0.1921
AGE_FIL2	46.8724	0.0001
TOTOPAC2	15.4433	0.0001
CREDLIN2	8.5092	0.0035
CRL_RAT	1.6512	0.1988
BAL_RAT	2.8820	0.0896
NO30DAY2	**0.0011**	**0.9739**
NOBKRPT	0.7028	0.4019
AMT PDUE	**0.0625**	**0.8026**
NO90EVE	4.6554	0.0310

These variables have low predictive power. The score chi-square is low, and the probability of significance by chance is > 0.5.

Figure 4.3 Analysis of variables not in the model—activate|response.

Categorical Variables

As mentioned in chapter 2, categorical variables are those variables that have discrete values. An easy way to determine if they have predictive power is to perform a simple chi-square test using PROC FREQ. The missing option is included to see if the missing status has predictive power.

Method 1: One Model

```
proc freq data=acqmod.model2;
weight smp_wgt;
table active*(pop_den bankcrd)
/missing chisq;
run;
```

The frequency distribution in Figure 4.4 provides a lot of information. We can see that there are enough observations in each level of the variable for significance testing. A good rule of thumb is at least 25 observations in each cell. The chi-square statistic (24.817) shows high significance. There is a probability of .001 (significance level) that no significant relationship exists between activation and population density. To enter the final model, I want a significance level less than .5. This variable is a good candidate for the final model.

The column percent equates to the different activation rates for each level of population density (*pop_den*). The group for which *pop_den* is missing has a .09% activation rate. This compares to group A (densely populated) with an activation rate of .11%. Groups B and C are almost identical with activation rates of .07%. Later in the chapter, I will discuss how these values are used for collapsing the variable.

In Figure 4.5 we see that the chi-square statistic for the relationship between activation and the presence of a bankcard is 0.352 with a significance level of 0.553. This means that there is no statistically significant difference in activation rate between those prospects with bankcards and those without. The column percents are very close at 13% and 15%. This variable is not a good candidate for the final model processing.

Method 2: Two Models

To evaluate variables in the two-model approach, we have to examine each variable for response (model 1) and activation given response (model 2). The following code tests the predictive power of population density (*pop_den*) and presence of bankcard (*bankcrd*) in predicting response.

```
        ACTIVE      POP_DEN


        Frequency|
        Percent  |
        Row Pct  |
        Col Pct  |           |A       |B       |C       |  Total
                 +--------+--------+--------+--------+
              0 | 143643 |  46836 | 267591 | 270096 | 728166
                 |  19.70 |   6.42 |  36.70 |  37.04 |  99.85
                 |  19.73 |   6.43 |  36.75 |  37.09 |
                 |  99.83 |  99.79 |  99.87 |  99.87 |
                 +--------+--------+--------+--------+
              1 |    246 |     98 |    356 |    362 |   1062
                 |   0.03 |   0.01 |   0.05 |   0.05 |   0.15
                 |  23.16 |   9.23 |  33.52 |  34.09 |
                 |   0.17 |   0.21 |   0.13 |   0.13 |
                 +--------+--------+--------+--------+
        Total       143889    46934   267947   270458   729228
                     19.73     6.44    36.74    37.09   100.00
```

STATISTICS FOR TABLE OF ACTIVE BY POP_DEN

Statistic	DF	Value	Prob
Chi-Square	3	24.817	0.001
Likelihood Ratio Chi-Square	3	23.105	0.001
Mantel-Haenszel Chi-Square	1	14.004	0.001
Phi Coefficient		0.006	
Contingency Coefficient		0.006	
Cramer's V		0.006	

Sample Size = 729228

Figure 4.4 Table of active by population density.

```
proc freq data=acqmod.model2;
weight smp_wgt;
table respond*(pop_den bankcrd)
      /missing chisq;
run;
```

```
ACTIVE     BANKCRD

Frequency|
Percent  |
Row Pct  |
Col Pct  |N       |Y       | Total
         +--------+--------+
      0  | 40762  | 687404 | 728166
         | 5.59   | 94.26  | 99.85
         | 5.60   | 94.40  |
         | 99.87  | 99.85  |
         +--------+--------+
      1  |    55  |   1007 |  1062
         | 0.01   | 0.14   | 0.15
         | 5.18   | 94.82  |
         | 0.13   | 0.15   |
         +--------+--------+
Total      40817    688411   729228
           5.60     94.40    100.00
```

STATISTICS FOR TABLE OF ACTIVE BY BANKCRD

Statistic	DF	Value	Prob
Chi-Square	1	0.352	0.553
Likelihood Ratio Chi-Square	1	0.361	0.548
Continuity Adj. Chi-Square	1	0.277	0.598
Mantel-Haenszel Chi-Square	1	0.352	0.553
Fisher's Exact Test (Left)			0.742
(Right)			0.304
(2-Tail)			0.593
Phi Coefficient		0.001	
Contingency Coefficient		0.001	
Cramer's V		0.001	

Sample Size = 729228

Figure 4.5 Table of active by bankcard.

In Figure 4.6, the chi-square statistic of 85.859 shows a highly significant relationship between response and population density. The column percents also show great variation in response rate between the different levels of population density. This variable is a very good candidate for the final model.

```
RESPOND      POP_DEN


Frequency|
Percent  |
Row Pct  |
Col Pct  |        |A       |B       |C       |  Total
         +--------+--------+--------+--------+
      0  | 141100 | 45790  | 262910 | 265560 | 715360
         |  19.35 |  6.28  |  36.05 |  36.42 |  98.10
         |  19.72 |  6.40  |  36.75 |  37.12 |
         |  98.06 | 97.56  |  98.12 |  98.19 |

         +--------+--------+--------+--------+
      1  |  2789  |  1144  |  5037  |  4898  |  13868
         |  0.38  |  0.16  |  0.69  |  0.67  |  1.90
         |  20.11 |  8.25  |  36.32 |  35.32 |
         |  1.94  |  2.44  |  1.88  |  1.81  |

         +--------+--------+--------+--------+
Total     143889    46934    267947   270458   729228
           19.73     6.44     36.74    37.09   100.00
```

STATISTICS FOR TABLE OF RESPOND BY POP_DEN

Statistic	DF	Value	Prob
Chi-Square	3	85.859	0.001
Likelihood Ratio Chi-Square	3	80.201	0.001
Mantel-Haenszel Chi-Square	1	21.898	0.001
Phi Coefficient		0.011	
Contingency Coefficient		0.011	
Cramer's V		0.011	

Sample Size = 729228

Figure 4.6 Table of respond by population density.

In Figure 4.7, the chi-square statistic of .515 shows a marginally significant relationship between response and the presence of a bankcard. The column percents also show very little variation in response rate between the different

```
RESPOND        BANKCRD

Frequency|
Percent  |
Row Pct  |
Col Pct  |N        |Y        |  Total
         +---------+---------+
      0  |  40060  | 675300  |  715360
         |   5.49  |  92.60  |   98.10
         |   5.60  |  94.40  |
         |  98.15  |  98.10  |
         +---------+---------+
      1  |    757  |  13111  |   13868
         |   0.10  |   1.80  |    1.90
         |   5.46  |  94.54  |
         |   1.85  |   1.90  |
         +---------+---------+
Total       40817     688411     729228
             5.60      94.40     100.00
```

STATISTICS FOR TABLE OF RESPOND BY BANKCRD

Statistic	DF	Value	Prob
Chi-Square	1	0.515	0.473
Likelihood Ratio Chi-Square	1	0.519	0.471
Continuity Adj. Chi-Square	1	0.488	0.485
Mantel-Haenszel Chi-Square	1	0.515	0.473
Fisher's Exact Test (Left)			0.768
(Right)			0.243
(2-Tail)			0.490
Phi Coefficient		0.001	
Contingency Coefficient		0.001	
Cramer's V		0.001	

Sample Size = 729228

Figure 4.7 Table of respond by bankcard.

levels of population density. This variable is not a good candidate for the final model. Because the significance level is < .5, I will keep it for further analysis.

```
proc freq data=acqmod.model2;
where respond = 1;
weight smp_wgt;
table activate*(pop_den bankcrd)
/missing chisq;
run;
```

In Figure 4.8, the chi-square statistic of 9.640 shows a fairly significant relationship between activation given response and population density. The column percents also show some variation in response rate between the different levels of population density. This variable is a good candidate for the final model.

In Figure 4.9, the chi-square statistic of .174 shows a no statistically significant relationship between activation given response and presence of a bankcard. The column percents also show very little variation in activation rate between the different levels of population density (7.27 versus 7.68). With a significance level of .676, this variable is not a good candidate for the final model.

Developing Linear Predictors

As described in chapter 1, logistic regression is a powerful and robust statistical technique for predicting the probability of an event occurring. By robust, I mean that the model will perform well and hold up over time. Because the predictors are linear in the log of the odds (as defined in chapter 1), the trick is to get the predictors as linear as possible. There are several ways to accomplish this. In our case study, I will demonstrate some techniques that are rigorous and thorough. As a result, the predictors will be robust and have strong predictive power.

In our case study, we have a group of 20 variables that will be analyzed for final presentation in the model. Some are continuous, and some are categorical. Logistic regression sees all predictive variables as continuous. So for the non-continuous variables, I will use indicator variables to trick the model into thinking they are continuous.

Continuous Variables

A continuous variable with no missing values can be used "as is" as a predictor in a logistic model. To get the best model fit and predictive power, however, it is often useful to transform and/or segment the continuous variable to create a more linear relationship. One way to determine the best transformation or seg-

```
ACTIVATE      POP_DEN
```

Frequency Percent Row Pct Col Pct	A	B	C	Total
0	2543 18.34 19.86 91.18	1046 7.54 8.17 91.43	4681 33.75 36.55 92.93	4536 32.71 35.42 92.61	12806 92.34
1	246 1.77 23.16 8.82	98 0.71 9.23 8.57	356 2.57 33.52 7.07	362 2.61 34.09 7.39	1062 7.66
Total	2789 20.11	1144 8.25	5037 36.32	4898 35.32	13868 100.00

```
STATISTICS FOR TABLE OF ACTIVATE BY POP_DEN
```

Statistic	DF	Value	Prob
Chi-Square	3	9.640	0.022
Likelihood Ratio Chi-Square	3	9.431	0.024
Mantel-Haenszel Chi-Square	1	6.504	0.011
Phi Coefficient		0.026	
Contingency Coefficient		0.026	
Cramer's V		0.026	

```
Sample Size = 13868
```

Figure 4.8 Table of activate by population density.

mentation of a continuous variable is to create several variations and use a forward logistic regression to select the best fit. The first step is to break the continuous variable into segments.

```
        ACTIVATE        Bankcard

        Frequency|
        Percent  |
        Row Pct  |
        Col Pct  |N       |Y       | Total
        ---------+--------+--------+
        0        |    702 |  12104 |  12806
                 |   5.06 |  87.28 |  92.34
                 |   5.48 |  94.52 |
                 |  92.73 |  92.32 |
        ---------+--------+--------+
        1        |     55 |   1007 |   1062
                 |   0.40 |   7.26 |   7.66
                 |   5.18 |  94.82 |
                 |   7.27 |   7.68 |
        ---------+--------+--------+
        Total         757    13111    13868
                     5.46    94.54   100.00
```

STATISTICS FOR TABLE OF ACTIVATE BY BANKCRD

Statistic	DF	Value	Prob
Chi-Square	1	0.174	0.676
Likelihood Ratio Chi-Square	1	0.177	0.674
Continuity Adj. Chi-Square	1	0.121	0.728
Mantel-Haenszel Chi-Square	1	0.174	0.676
Fisher's Exact Test (Left)			0.682
(Right)			0.370
(2-Tail)			0.725
Phi Coefficient		0.004	
Contingency Coefficient		0.004	
Cramer's V		0.004	

Sample Size = 13868

Figure 4.9 Table of activate by bankcard.

Segmentation

Some analysts and modelers put all continuous variables into segments and treat them as categorical variables. This may work well to pick up nonlinear trends. The biggest drawback is that it loses the benefit of the relationship between the points in the curve that can be very robust over the long term. Another approach is to create segments for obviously discrete groups. Then test these segments against transformed continuous values and select the winners. Just how the winners are selected will be discussed later in the chapter. First I must create the segments for the continuous variables.

In our case study, I have the variable estimated income (*inc_est3*). To determine the best transformation and/or segmentation, I first segment the variable into 10 groups. Then I will look at a frequency of *est_inc3* crossed by the dependent variable to determine the best segmentation.

An easy way to divide into 10 groups with roughly the same number of observations in each group is to use PROC UNIVARIATE. Create an output data set containing values for the desired variable (*inc_est3*) at each tenth of the population. Use a NOPRINT option to suppress the output. The following code creates the values, appends them to the original data set, and produces the frequency table.

```
proc univariate data=acqmod.model2 noprint;
weight smp_wgt;
var inc_est3;
output out=incdata pctlpts= 10 20 30 40 50 60 70 80 90 100
pctlpre=inc;
run;

data acqmod.model2;
set acqmod.model2;
if (_n_ eq 1) then set incdata;
retain inc10 inc20 inc30 inc40 inc50 inc60 inc70 inc80 inc90 inc100;
run;

data acqmod.model2;
  set acqmod.model2;
if inc_est3 < inc10 then incgrp10 = 1; else
if inc_est3 < inc20 then incgrp10 = 2; else
if inc_est3 < inc30 then incgrp10 = 3; else
if inc_est3 < inc40 then incgrp10 = 4; else
if inc_est3 < inc50 then incgrp10 = 5; else
if inc_est3 < inc60 then incgrp10 = 6; else
if inc_est3 < inc70 then incgrp10 = 7; else
if inc_est3 < inc80 then incgrp10 = 8; else
if inc_est3 < inc90 then incgrp10 = 9; else
incgrp10 = 10;
run;
```

```
proc freq data=acqmod.model2;
weight smp_wgt;
table (activate respond active)*incgrp10;
run;
```

From the output, we can determine linearity and segmentation opportunities. First we look at *inc_est3* (in 10 groups) crossed by active (one model).

Method 1: One Model

In Figure 4.10 the column percent shows the *active* rate for each segment. The first four segments have a consistent active rate of around .20%. Beginning with segment 5, the rate drops steadily until it reaches segment 7 where it levels off at around .10%. To capture this effect with segments, I will create a variable that splits the values between 4 and 5. To create the variable I use the following code:

```
data acqmod.model2;
 set acqmod.model2;
if incgrp10 <= 4 then inc_low = 1; else inc_low = 0;
run;
```

At this point we have three variables that are forms of estimated income: *inc_miss*, *inc_est3*, and *inc_low*. Next, I will repeat the exercise for the two-model approach.

Method 2: Two Models

In Figure 4.11 the column percents for *response* follow a similar trend. The response rate decreases steadily down with a slight bump at segment 4. Because the trend downward is so consistent, I will not create a segmented variable

In Figure 4.12 we see that the trend for *activation given response* seems to mimic the trend for *activation* alone. The variable *inc_low*, which splits the values between 4 and 5, will work well for this model.

Transformations

Years ago, when computers were very slow, finding the best transforms for continuous variables was a laborious process. Today, the computer power allows us to test everything. The following methodology is limited only by your imagination.

In our case study, I am working with various forms of estimated income *(inc_est3)*. I have created three forms for each model: *inc_miss, inc_est3, and inc_low*. These represent the original form after data clean-up (inc_est3) and two segmented forms. Now I will test transformations to see if I can make

```
ACTIVE      INCGRP10

Frequency|
Percent  |
Row Pct  |
Col Pct  |      1|      2|      3|      4|      5| Total
         +-------+-------+-------+-------+-------+
      0  |  76860|  75034|  61711|  69063|  75415| 728166
         |  10.54|  10.29|   8.46|   9.47|  10.34|  99.85
         |  10.56|  10.30|   8.47|   9.48|  10.36|
         |  99.79|  99.80|  99.81|  99.80|  99.86|
         +-------+-------+-------+-------+-------+
      1  |    160|    151|    119|    138|    109|   1062
         |   0.02|   0.02|   0.02|   0.02|   0.01|   0.15
         |  15.07|  14.22|  11.21|  12.99|  10.26|
         |   0.21|   0.20|   0.19|   0.20|   0.14|
         +-------+-------+-------+-------+-------+
Total       77020   75185   61830   69201   75524  729228
            10.56   10.31    8.48    9.49   10.36  100.00


ACTIVE      INCGRP10

Frequency|
Percent  |
Row Pct  |
Col Pct  |      6|      7|      8|      9|     10| Total
         +-------+-------+-------+-------+-------+
      0  |  77224|  67559|  76373|  74245|  74682| 728166
         |  10.59|   9.26|  10.47|  10.18|  10.24|  99.85
         |  10.61|   9.28|  10.49|  10.20|  10.26|
         |  99.89|  99.90|  99.89|  99.89|  99.91|
         +-------+-------+-------+-------+-------+
      1  |     85|     66|     84|     81|     69|   1062
         |   0.01|   0.01|   0.01|   0.01|   0.01|   0.15
         |   8.00|   6.21|   7.91|   7.63|   6.50|
         |   0.11|   0.10|   0.11|   0.11|   0.09|
         +-------+-------+-------+-------+-------+
Total       77309   67625   76457   74326   74751  729228
            10.60    9.27   10.48   10.19   10.25  100.00
```

Figure 4.10 Active by income group.

```
RESPOND      INCGRP10
Frequency|
Percent  |
Row Pct  |
Col Pct  |       1|       2|       3|       4|       5| Total
         +--------+--------+--------+--------+--------+
       0 |  74970 |  73420 |  60460 |  67630 |  74060 | 715360
         |  10.28 |  10.07 |   8.29 |   9.27 |  10.16 |  98.10
         |  10.48 |  10.26 |   8.45 |   9.45 |  10.35 |
         |  97.34 |  97.65 |  97.78 |  97.73 |  98.06 |
         +--------+--------+--------+--------+--------+
       1 |   2050 |   1765 |   1370 |   1571 |   1464 |  13868
         |   0.28 |   0.24 |   0.19 |   0.22 |   0.20 |   1.90
         |  14.78 |  12.73 |   9.88 |  11.33 |  10.56 |
         |   2.66 |   2.35 |   2.22 |   2.27 |   1.94 |
         +--------+--------+--------+--------+--------+
Total       77020    75185    61830    69201    75524   729228
            10.56    10.31     8.48     9.49    10.36   100.00


RESPOND      INCGRP10
Frequency|
Percent  |
Row Pct  |
Col Pct  |       6|       7|       8|       9|      10| Total
         +--------+--------+--------+--------+--------+
       0 |  76040 |  66500 |  75310 |  73270 |  73700 | 715360
         |  10.43 |   9.12 |  10.33 |  10.05 |  10.11 |  98.10
         |  10.63 |   9.30 |  10.53 |  10.24 |  10.30 |
         |  98.36 |  98.34 |  98.50 |  98.58 |  98.59 |
         +--------+--------+--------+--------+--------+
       1 |   1269 |   1125 |   1147 |   1056 |   1051 |  13868
         |   0.17 |   0.15 |   0.16 |   0.14 |   0.14 |   1.90
         |   9.15 |   8.11 |   8.27 |   7.61 |   7.58 |
         |   1.64 |   1.66 |   1.50 |   1.42 |   1.41 |
         +--------+--------+--------+--------+--------+
Total       77309    67625    76457    74326    74751   729228
            10.60     9.27    10.48    10.19    10.25   100.00
```

Figure 4.11   Response by income group.

```
ACTIVATE      INCGRP10
Frequency|
Percent  |
Row Pct  |
Col Pct  |      1|      2|      3|      4|      5| Total
---------+------+------+------+------+------+
0        |  1890|  1614|  1251|  1433|  1355| 12806
         | 13.63| 11.64|  9.02| 10.33|  9.77| 92.34
         | 14.76| 12.60|  9.77| 11.19| 10.58|
         | 92.20| 91.44| 91.31| 91.22| 92.55|
---------+------+------+------+------+------+
1        |   160|   151|   119|   138|   109|  1062
         |  1.15|  1.09|  0.86|  1.00|  0.79|  7.66
         | 15.07| 14.22| 11.21| 12.99| 10.26|
         |  7.80|  8.56|  8.69|  8.78|  7.45|
---------+------+------+------+------+------+
Total       2050   1765   1370   1571   1464  13868
           14.78  12.73   9.88  11.33  10.56 100.00
```

```
ACTIVATE      INCGRP10
Frequency|
Percent  |
Row Pct  |
Col Pct  |      6|      7|      8|      9|     10| Total
---------+------+------+------+------+------+
0        |  1184|  1059|  1063|   975|   982| 12806
         |  8.54|  7.64|  7.67|  7.03|  7.08| 92.34
         |  9.25|  8.27|  8.30|  7.61|  7.67|
         | 93.30| 94.13| 92.68| 92.33| 93.43|
---------+------+------+------+------+------+
1        |    85|    66|    84|    81|    69|  1062
         |  0.61|  0.48|  0.61|  0.58|  0.50|  7.66
         |  8.00|  6.21|  7.91|  7.63|  6.50|
         |  6.70|  5.87|  7.32|  7.67|  6.57|
---------+------+------+------+------+------+
Total       1269   1125   1147   1056   1051  13868
            9.15   8.11   8.27   7.61   7.58 100.00
```

Figure 4.12 Activation by income group.

inc_est3 more linear. The first exercise is to create a series of transformed variables. The following code creates new variables that are continuous functions of income:

```
data acqmod.model2;
 set acqmod.model2;
inc_sq   = inc_est3**2;                        /*squared*/
inc_cu   = inc_est3**3;                        /*cubed*/
inc_sqrt = sqrt(inc_est3);                     /*square root*/
inc_curt = inc_est3**.3333;                    /*cube root*/
inc_log  = log(max(.0001,inc_est3));           /*log*/
inc_exp  = exp(max(.0001,inc_est3));           /*exponent*/

inc_tan  = tan(inc_est3);                      /*tangent*/
inc_sin  = sin(inc_est3);                      /*sine*/
inc_cos  = cos(inc_est3);                      /*cosine*/

inc_inv  = 1/max(.0001,inc_est3);              /*inverse*/
inc_sqi  = 1/max(.0001,inc_est3**2);           /*squared inverse*/
inc_cui  = 1/max(.0001,inc_est3**3);           /*cubed inverse*/
inc_sqri = 1/max(.0001,sqrt(inc_est3));        /*square root inv*/
inc_curi = 1/max(.0001,inc_est3**.3333);       /*cube root inverse*/

inc_logi = 1/max(.0001,log(max(.0001,inc_est3))); /*log inverse*/
inc_expi = 1/max(.0001,exp(max(.0001,inc_est3))); /*exponent inv*/

inc_tani = 1/max(.0001,tan(inc_est3));         /*tangent inverse*/
inc_sini = 1/max(.0001,sin(inc_est3));         /*sine inverse*/
inc_cosi = 1/max(.0001,cos(inc_est3));         /*cosine inverse*/
run;
```

Now I have 22 forms of the variable estimated income. I have 20 continuous forms and 2 categorical forms. I will use logistic regression to find the best form or forms of the variable for the final model.

Method 1: One Model

The following code runs a logistic regression on every eligible form of the variable estimated income. I use the maxstep = 2 option to get the two best-fitting forms (working together) of estimated income.

```
proc logistic data=acqmod.model2 descending;
weight smp_wgt;
model active = inc_est3 inc_miss inc_low
inc_sq inc_cu inc_sqrt inc_curt inc_log inc_exp
inc_tan inc_sin inc_cos inc_inv inc_sqi inc_cui inc_sqri inc_curi
inc_logi inc_expi inc_tani inc_sini inc_cosi
/selection = stepwise maxstep = 2 details;
```

The result of the stepwise logistic shows that the binary variable, *inc_low*, has the strongest predictive power. The only other form of estimated income that works with *inc_low* to predict *active* is the transformation (*inc_sqrt*). I will introduce these two variables into the final model for Method 1.

```
Summary of Stepwise Procedure
```

Step	Variable Entered	Number In	Score Chi-Square	Wald Chi-Square	Pr > Chi-Square
1	INC_LOW	1	96.0055	.	0.0001
2	INC_SQRT	2	8.1273	.	0.0044

Method 2: Two Models

The following code repeats the process of finding the best forms of income. But this time I am predicting response.

```
proc logistic data=acqmod.model2 descending;
weight smp_wgt;
model respond =  inc_est3 inc_miss inc_low
inc_sq inc_cu inc_sqrt inc_curt inc_log inc_exp
inc_tan inc_sin inc_cos inc_inv inc_sqi inc_cui inc_sqri inc_curi
inc_logi inc_expi inc_tani inc_sini inc_cosi
/ selection = stepwise maxstep = 2 details;

run;
```

When predicting response *(respond)*, the result of the stepwise logistic shows that the inverse of estimated income, *inc_inv*, has the strongest predictive power. Notice the extremely high chi-square value of 722.3. This variable does a very good job of fitting the data. The next strongest predictor, the inverse of the square root *(inc_sqri)*, is also predictive. I will introduce both forms into the final model.

```
Summary of Forward Procedure
```

Step	Variable Entered	Number In	Score Chi-Square	Wald Chi-Square	Pr > Chi-Square
1	INC_INV	1	722.3	.	0.0001
2	INC_SQRI	2	10.9754	.	0.0009

And finally, the following code determines the best fit of estimated income for predicting actives, given that the prospect responded. (Recall that activate is missing for nonresponders, so they will be eliminated from processing automatically.)

```
proc logistic data=acqmod.model2 descending;
weight smp_wgt;
```

```
model activate = inc_est3 inc_miss inc_low
inc_sq inc_cu inc_sqrt inc_curt inc_log inc_exp
inc_tan inc_sin inc_cos inc_inv inc_sqi inc_cui inc_sqri inc_curi
inc_logi inc_expi inc_tani inc_sini inc_cosi
/ selection = stepwise maxstep = 2 details;

run;
```

When predicting activation given response *(activation|respond)*, the only variable with predictive power is *inc_low*. I will introduce that form into the final model.

```
Summary of Stepwise Procedure
```

Step	Variable Entered	Number In	Score Chi-Square	Wald Chi-Square	Pr > Chi-Square
1	INC_LOW	1	10.4630	.	0.0012

At this point, we have all the forms of estimated income for introduction into the final model. I will repeat this process for all continuous variables that were deemed eligible for final consideration.

Categorical Variables

Many categorical variables are powerful predictors. They, however, are often in a form that is not useful for regression modeling. Because logistic regression sees all predictors as continuous, I must redesign the variables to suit this form. The best technique is to create *indicator variables*. Indicator variables are variables that have a value of 1 if a condition is true and 0 otherwise.

Method 1: One Model

Earlier in the chapter, I tested the predictive power of *pop_den*. The frequency table shows the activation rate by class of *pop_den*.

In Figure 4.13, we see that the values B and C have identical activation rates of .13%. I will collapse them into the same group and create indicator variables to define membership in each class or group of classes.

```
data acqmod.model2;
 set acqmod.model2;
if pop_den = 'A' then popdnsA = 1; else popdensA = 0;
if pop_den in ('B','C') then popdnsBC = 1; else popdnsBC = 0;
run;
```

Notice that I didn't define the class of *pop_den* that contains the missing values. This group's activation rate is significantly different from A and "B & C."

```
ACTIVE        POP_DEN


Frequency|
Percent  |
Row Pct  |
Col Pct  |        |A       |B       |C       |   Total
         +--------+--------+--------+--------+
       0 | 143643 |  46836 | 267591 | 270096 |  728166
         |  19.70 |   6.42 |  36.70 |  37.04 |   99.85
         |  19.73 |   6.43 |  36.75 |  37.09 |
         |  99.83 |  99.79 |  99.87 |  99.87 |
         +--------+--------+--------+--------+
       1 |    246 |     98 |    356 |    362 |    1062
         |   0.03 |   0.01 |   0.05 |   0.05 |    0.15
         |  23.16 |   9.23 |  33.52 |  34.09 |
         |   0.17 |   0.21 |   0.13 |   0.13 |
         +--------+--------+--------+--------+
   Total    143889    46934   267947   270458   729228
             19.73     6.44    36.74    37.09   100.00
```

Figure 4.13   Active by population density.

But I don't have to create a separate variable to define it because it will be the default value when both *popdnsA* and *popdnsBC* are equal to 0. When creating indicator variables, you will always need one less variable than the number of categories.

Method 2: Two Models

I will go through the same exercise for predicting *response* and *activation given response*.

In Figure 4.14, we see that the difference in response rate for these groups seems to be most dramatic between class A versus the rest. Our variable *popdnsA* will work for this model.

Figure 4.15 shows that when modeling activation given response, we have little variation between the classes. The biggest difference is between "B & C" versus "A and Missing." The variable *popdnsBC* will work for this model.

At this point, we have all the forms of *population density* for introduction into the final model. I will repeat this process for all categorical variables that were deemed eligible for final consideration.

```
RESPOND      POP_DEN

Frequency|
Percent  |
Row Pct  |
Col Pct  |         |A       |B       |C       |   Total
         -----------------------------------------------
       0 | 141100  |  45790 | 262910 | 265560 |  715360
         |  19.35  |   6.28 |  36.05 |  36.42 |   98.10
         |  19.72  |   6.40 |  36.75 |  37.12 |
         |  98.06  |  97.56 |  98.12 |  98.19 |
         -----------------------------------------------
       1 |   2789  |   1144 |   5037 |   4898 |   13868
         |   0.38  |   0.16 |   0.69 |   0.67 |    1.90
         |  20.11  |   8.25 |  36.32 |  35.32 |
         |   1.94  |   2.44 |   1.88 |   1.81 |
         -----------------------------------------------
   Total   143889     46934   267947   270458    729228
            19.73       6.44    36.74    37.09    100.00
```

Figure 4.14 Response by population density.

```
ACTIVATE     POP_DEN

Frequency|
Percent  |
Row Pct  |
Col Pct  |         |A       |B       |C       |   Total
         -----------------------------------------------
       0 |   2543  |   1046 |   4681 |   4536 |   12806
         |  18.34  |   7.54 |  33.75 |  32.71 |   92.34
         |  19.86  |   8.17 |  36.55 |  35.42 |
         |  91.18  |  91.43 |  92.93 |  92.61 |
         -----------------------------------------------
       1 |    246  |     98 |    356 |    362 |    1062
         |   1.77  |   0.71 |   2.57 |   2.61 |    7.66
         |  23.16  |   9.23 |  33.52 |  34.09 |
         |   8.82  |   8.57 |   7.07 |   7.39 |
         -----------------------------------------------
   Total     2789      1144     5037     4898     13868
            20.11      8.25    36.32    35.32    100.00
```

Figure 4.15 Activation by population density.

Interactions Detection

An interaction between variables is said to be present if the relationship of one predictor varies for different levels of another predictor. One way to find interactions between variables is to create combinations and test them for significance. If you are starting out with hundreds of variables, this may not be a good use of time. In addition, if you have even as many as 50 variables with univariate predictive power, you may not add much benefit by finding interactions.

Many of the data mining software packages have a module for building classification trees. They offer a quick way to discover interactions. In Figure 4.16, a simple tree shows interactions between *mortin1, mortin2, autoin1, and age_ind*.

The following code creates three variables from the information in the classification tree. Because these branches of the tree show strong predictive power, these three indicator variables are used in the final model processing.

```
data acqmod.model2;
 set acqmod.model2;
if mortin1 = 'M' and mortin2 = 'N' then mortal1 = 1;
      else mortal1 = 0;
if mortin1 in ('N', ' ') and autoind1 = ' ' and infd_ag => 40)
        then mortal2 = 1; else mortal2 = 0;
```

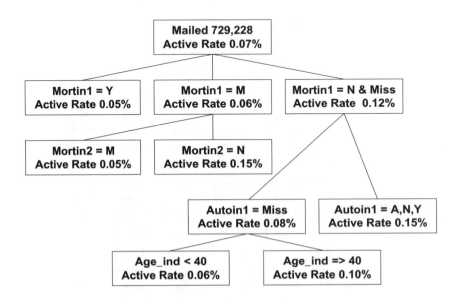

Figure 4.16 Interaction detection using classification trees.

```
if mortin1 in ('N', ' ')and autoin1 ^= ' ' then mortal3 = 1;
    else mortal3 = 0;
run;
```

Summary

The emphasis of this chapter was on reducing the number of eligible variables. I did a lot of work ahead of time so that I could have a clear goal and clean, accurate data. I started out with the development of some new variables that provide added predictive power. In preparation for the final model processing, I used some simple techniques to reduce the number of variables. These techniques eliminated variables that were marginal and unpredictive. They are especially useful when you start out with hundreds of variables.

Next, through the use of some clever coding, I molded the remaining variables into strong predictors. And every step of the way, I worked through the one-model and two-model approaches. We are now ready to take our final candidate variables and create the winning model. In chapter 5, I perform the final model processing and initial validation.

CHAPTER **5**

Processing and Evaluating the Model

Have you ever watched a cooking show? It always looks so easy, doesn't it? The chef has all the ingredients prepared and stored in various containers on the countertop. By this time the hard work is done! All the chef has to do is determine the best method for blending and preparing the ingredients to create the final product. We've also reached that stage. Now we're going to have some fun! The hard work in the model development process is done. Now it's time to begin baking and enjoy the fruits of our labor.

There are many options of methodologies for model processing. In chapter 1, I discussed several traditional and some cutting-edge techniques. As we have seen in the previous chapters, there is much more to model development than just the model processing. And within the model processing itself, there are many choices.

In the case study, I have been preparing to build a logistic model. In this chapter, I begin by splitting the data into the model development and model validation data sets. Beginning with the one-model approach, I use several variable selection techniques to find the best variables for predicting our target group. I then repeat the same steps with the two-model approach. Finally, I create a *decile analysis* to evaluate and compare the models.

Processing the Model

As I stated in chapter 3, I am using logistic regression as my modeling technique. While many other techniques are available, I prefer logistic regression because (1) when done correctly it is very powerful, (2) it is straightforward, and (3) it has a lower risk of over-fitting the data. Logistic regression is an excellent technique for finding a linear path through the data that minimizes the error. All of the variable preparation work I have done up to this point has been to fit a function of our dependent variable, active, with a linear combination of the predictors.

As described in chapter 1, logistic regression uses continuous values to predict a categorical outcome. In our case study, I am using two methods to target active accounts. Recall that *active* has a value of 1 if the prospect responded, was approved, and paid the first premium. Otherwise, *active* has a value of 0. Method 1 uses one model to predict the probability of a prospect responding, being approved, and paying the first premium, thus making the prospect an "active." Method 2 uses two models: one to predict the probability of responding; and the second uses only responders to predict the probability of being approved and activating the account by paying the first premium. The overall probability of becoming active is derived by combining the two model scores.

Following the variable reduction and creation processes in chapter 4, I have roughly 70 variables for evaluation in the final model. Some of the variables were created for the model in Method 1 and others for the two models in Method 2. Because there was a large overlap in variables between the models in Method 1 and Method 2, I will use the entire list for all models. The processing might take slightly longer, but it saves time in writing and tracking code.

The sidebar on page 104 describes several selection methods that are available in SAS's PROC LOGISTIC. In our final processing stage, I take advantage of three of those methods, *Stepwise*, *Backward*, and *Score*. By using several methods, I can take advantage of some variable reduction techniques while creating the best fitting model. The steps are as follows:

Why Use Logistic Regression?

Every year a new technique is developed and/or automated to improve the targeting model development process. Each new technique promises to improve the lift and save you money. In my experience, if you take the time to carefully prepare and transform the variables, the resulting model will be equally powerful and will outlast the competition.

Stepwise. The first step will be to run a stepwise regression with an artificially high level of significance. This will further reduce the number of candidate variables by selecting the variables in order of predictive power. I will use a significance level of .30.

Backward. Next, I will run a backward regression with the same artificially high level of significance. Recall that this method fits all the variables into a model and then removes variables with low predictive power. The benefit of this method is that it might keep a variable that has low individual predictive power but in combination with other variables has high predictive power. It is possible to get an entirely different set of variables from this method than with the stepwise method.

Score. This step evaluates models for all possible subsets of variables. I will request the two best models for each number of variables by using the BEST=2 option. Once I select the final variables, I will run a logistic regression without any selection options to derive the final coefficients and create an output data set.

I am now ready to process my candidate variables in the final model for both Method 1 (one-step model) and Method 2 (two-step model). I can see from my candidate list that I have many variables that were created from base variables. For example, for Method 1 I have four different forms of *infd_age: age_cui*, *age_cos*, *age_sqi*, and *age_low*. You might ask, "What about multicollinearity?" To some degree, my selection criteria will not select (forward and stepwise) and eliminate (backward) variables that are explaining the same variation in the data. But it is possible for two or more forms of the same variable to enter the model. Or other variables that are correlated with each other might end up in the model together. The truth is, multicollinearity is not a problem for us. Large data sets and the goal of prediction make it a nonissue, as Kent Leahy explains in the sidebar on page 106.

Splitting the Data

One of the cardinal rules of model development is, "Always validate your model on data that was not used in model development." This rule allows you to test the robustness of the model. In other words, you would expect the model to do well on the data used to develop it. If the model performs well on a similar data set, then you know you haven't modeled the variation that is unique to your development data set.

This brings us to the final step before the model processing—splitting the file into the modeling and validation data sets.

TIP

If you are dealing with sparse data in your target group, splitting the data can leave you with too few in the target group for modeling. One remedy is split the nontarget group as usual. Then use the entire target group for both the modeling and development data sets. Extra validation measures, described in chapter 6, are advisable to avoid over-fitting.

Rather than actually creating separate data sets, I assign a weight that has a value equal to "missing." This technique maintains the entire data set through the model while using only the "nonmissing" data for model development.

Selection Methods

SAS's PROC LOGISTIC provides several options for the selection method that designate the order in which the variables are entered into or removed from the model.

Forward. This method begins by calculating and examining the univariate chi-square or individual predictive power of each variable. It looks for the predictive variable that has the most variation or greatest differences between its levels when compared to the different levels of the target variable. Once it has selected the most predictive variable from the candidate variable list, it recalculates the univariate chi-square for each remaining candidate variable using a conditional probability. In other words, it now considers the individual incremental predictive power of the remaining candidate variables, given that the first variable has been selected and is explaining some of the variation in the data. If two variables are highly correlated and one enters the model, the chi-square or individual incremental predictive power of the other variable (not in the model) will drop in relation to the degree of the correlation.

Next, it selects the second most predictive variable and repeats the process of calculating the univariate chi-square or the individual incremental predictive power of the remaining variables not in the model. It also recalculates the chi-square of the two variables now in the model. But this time it calculates the multivariate chi-square or predictive power of each variable, given that the other variable is now explaining some of the variation in the data.

Again, it selects the next most predictive variable, repeats the process of calculating the univariate chi-square power of the remaining variables not in the model, and recalculates the multivariate chi-square of the three variables now in the model. The process repeats until there are no significant variables in the remaining candidate variables not in the model.

The actual split can be 50/50, 60/40, 70/30, etc. I typically use 50/50. The following code is used to create a weight value (splitwgt). I also create a variable, *records*, with the value of 1 for each prospect. This is used in the final validation tables:

```
data acqmod.model2;
set acqmod.model2;
if ranuni(5555) < .5 then splitwgt = smp_wgt;
else splitwgt = .;
records = 1;
run;
```

Stepwise. This method is very similar to *forward* selection. Each time a new variable enters the model, the univariate chi-square of the remaining variables not in the model is recalculated. Also, the multivariate chi-square or incremental predictive power of each predictive variable in the model is recalculated. The main difference is that if any variable, newly entered or already in the model, becomes insignificant after it or another variable enters, it will be removed.

This method offers some additional power over selection in finding the best set of predictors. Its main disadvantage is slower processing time because each step considers every variable for entry or removal.

Backward. This method begins with all the variables in the model. Each variable begins the process with a multivariate chi-square or a measure of predictive power when considered in conjunction with all other variables. It then removes any variable whose predictive power is insignificant, beginning with the most insignificant variable. After each variable is removed, the multivariate chi-square for all variables still in the model is recalculated with one less variable. This continues until all remaining variables have multivariate significance.

This method has one distinct benefit over forward and stepwise. It allows variables of lower significance to be considered in combination that might never enter the model under the forward and stepwise methods. Therefore, the resulting model may depend on more equal contributions of many variables instead of the dominance of one or two very powerful variables.

Score. This method constructs models using all possible subsets of variables within the list of candidate variables using the highest likelihood score (chi-square) statistic. It does not derive the model coefficients. It simply lists the best variables for each model along with the overall chi-square.

Multicollinearity: When the Solution Is the Problem

Kent Leahy, discusses the benefits of multicollinearity in data analysis.

As every student of Statistics 101 knows, highly correlated predictors can cause problems in a regression or regression-like model (e.g., logit). These problems are principally ones of reliability and interpretability of the model coefficient estimates. A common solution, therefore, has been to delete one or more of the offending collinear model variables or to use factor or principal components analysis to reduce the amount of redundant variation present in the data.

Multicollinearity (MC), however, is not always harmful, and deleting a variable or variables under such circumstances can be the real problem. Unfortunately, this is not well understood by many in the industry, even among those with substantial statistical backgrounds.

Before discussing MC, it should be acknowledged that without any correlation between predictors, multiple regression (MR) analysis would merely be a more convenient method of processing a series of bivariate regressions. Relationships between variables then actually give life to MR, and indeed to all multivariate statistical techniques.

If the correlation between two predictors (or a linear combination of predictors) is inordinately high, however, then conditions can arise that are deemed problematic. A distinction is thus routinely made between correlated predictors and MC. Although no universally acceptable definition of MC has been established, correlations of .70 and above are frequently mentioned as benchmarks.

The most egregious aspect of MC is that it increases the standard error of the sampling distribution of the coefficients of highly collinear variables. This manifests itself in parameter estimates that may vary substantially from sample-to-sample. For example, if two samples are obtained from a given population, and the same partial regression coefficient is estimated from each, then it is considerably more likely that they will differ in the presence of high collinearity. And the higher the intercorrelation, the greater the likelihood of sample-to-sample divergence.

MC, however, does not violate any of the assumptions of ordinary least-squares (OLS) regression, and thus the OLS parameter estimator under such circumstances is still BLUE (Best Linear Unbiased Estimator). MC can, however, cause a substantial decrease in "statistical power," because the amount of variation held in common between two variables and the dependent variable can leave little remaining data to reliably estimate the separate effects of each. MC is thus a lack of data condition necessitating a larger sample size to achieve the same level of statistical significance. The analogy between an inadequate sample and MC is cogently and clearly articulated by Achen [1982]:

> "Beginning students of methodology occasionally worry that their independent variables are correlated with the so-called multicollinearity problem. But multicollinearity violates no regression assumptions. Unbiased, consistent estimates will occur, and the standard errors will be correctly estimated. The only effect of multicollinearity is to make it harder to get coefficient estimates with small standard errors. But having a small number of observations also has that effect. Thus, "What should I do about multicollinearity?" is a question like "What should I do if I don't have many observations?" *

If the coefficient estimates of highly related predictors are statistically significant, however, then the parameter estimates are every bit as reliable as any other predictor. As it turns out, even if they are not significant, prediction is still unlikely to be affected, the reason being that although the estimates of the separate effects of collinear variables have large variances, the sum of the regression coefficient values tends to remain stable, and thus prediction is unlikely to be affected.

If MC is not a problem, then why do so many statistics texts say that it is? And why do so many people believe it is? The answer has to do with the purpose for which the model is developed. Authors of statistical texts in applied areas such as medicine, business, and economics assume that the model is to be used to "explain" some type of behavior rather that merely "predict" it. In this context, the model is assumed to be based on a set of theory-relevant predictors constituting what is referred to as a properly "specified" model. The goal here is to allocate unbiased explanatory power to each variable, and because highly correlated variables can make it difficult to separate out their unique or independent effects, MC can be problematic. And this is why statistics texts typically inveigh against MC.

If the goal is prediction, however, and not explanation, then the primary concern is not so much in knowing how or why each variable impacts on the dependent variable, but rather on the efficacy of the model as a predictive instrument. This does not imply that explanatory information is not useful or important, but merely recognizes that it is not feasible to develop a properly or reasonably specified model by using stepwise procedures with hundreds of variables that happen to be available for use. In fact, rarely is a model developed in direct response applications that can be considered reasonably specified to the point that parameter bias is not a real threat from an interpretive standpoint.

The important point is that the inability of a model to provide interpretive insight doesn't necessarily mean that it can't predict well or otherwise assign

continues

---

*Achen, C. H . (1982). Interpreting and Using Regression. Beverly Hills, CA: SAGE.

(Continued)

hierarchical probabilities to an outcome measure in an actionable manner. This is patently obvious from the results obtained from typical predictive segmentation models in the industry.

Establishing that MC does not have any adverse effects on a model, however, is not a sufficient rationale for retaining a highly correlated variable in a model. The question then becomes "Why keep them if they are at best only innocuous?"

The answer is that not all variation between two predictors is redundant. By deleting a highly correlated variable we run the risk of throwing away additional useful predictive information, such as the independent or unique variation accounted for by the discarded predictor or that variation above and beyond that accounted by the two variables jointly.

In addition, there are also variables or variable effects that operate by removing non-criterion-related variation in other model predictors that are correlated with it, thereby enhancing the predictive ability of those variables in the model. By deleting a highly correlated variable or variables, we thus may well be compromising or lessening the effectiveness of our model as a predictive tool.

In summary, an erroneous impression currently exists both within and outside the industry that highly but imperfectly correlated predictors have a deleterious effect on predictive segmentation models. As pointed out here, however, not only are highly correlated variables not harmful in the context of models generated for predictive purposes, but deleting them can actually result in poorer predictive instruments. As a matter of sound statistical modeling procedures, highly but imperfectly correlated predictors (i.e., those that are not sample specific) should be retained in a predictive segmentation model, providing (1) they sufficiently enhance the predictive ability of the model and (2) adequate attention has been paid to the usual reliability concerns, including parsimony.

Now I have a data set that is ready for modeling complete with eligible variables and weights. The first model I process utilizes Method 1, the one model approach.

Method 1: One Model

The following code creates a model with variables that are significant at the .3 or less level. I use a `keep=` option in the model statement to reduce the number of variables that will be carried along in the model processing. This will reduce the processing time. I do keep a few extra variables (*shown in italics*) that will be used in the validation tables. The `descending` option instructs the model to target the highest value of the dependent variable. Because the values for active are 0 and 1, the model will create a score that targets the probability of the value being 1: an *active* account. I stipulate the model sensitivity with the **sle=**, which stands for sensitivity level entering, and **sls=,** which stands for sensitivity level staying. These are the sensitivity levels for variables entering and remaining in the model.

```
proc logistic data=acqmod.model2(keep=active age_cui age_cos age_sqi
age_low inc_sqrt inc_sqri inc_inv inc_low mortal1 mortal2 mortal3
hom_log hom_cui hom_curt hom_med sgle_in infd_ag2 gender
toa_low toa_tan toa_cu toa_curt tob_med tob_sqrt tob_log tob_low
inq_sqrt top_logi top_cu top_med top_cui top_low crl_med crl_tan crl_low
rat_log rat_tan rat_med rat_low brt_med brt_logi brt_low popdnsA
popdnsBC trav_cdd apt_indd clus1_1 clus1_2 sgle_ind occ_miss finl_idd
hh_ind_d gender_d driv_ind mortin1n mort1mis mort2mis auto2mis childind
occ_G finl_idm gender_f driv_ino mob_indd mortin1y auto1mis auto2_n
clu2miss no90de_d actopl6d no30dayd splitwgt records smp_wgt respond
activate pros_id) descending;
weight splitwgt;
model active = age_cui age_cos age_sqi age_low inc_sqrt inc_sqri inc_inv
inc_low mortal1 mortal2 mortal3 hom_log hom_cui hom_curt hom_med toa_low
toa_tan toa_cu toa_curt tob_med tob_sqrt tob_log tob_low inq_sqrt
top_logi top_cu top_med top_cui top_low crl_med crl_tan crl_low rat_log
rat_tan rat_med rat_low brt_med brt_logi brt_low popdnsA popdnsBC
trav_cdd apt_indd clus1_1 clus1_2 sgle_ind occ_miss finl_idd hh_ind_d
gender_d driv_ind mortin1n mort1mis mort2mis auto2mis childind  occ_G
finl_idm gender_f driv_ino mob_indd mortin1y auto1mis auto2_n clu2miss
no90de_d actopl6d no30dayd
/selection = stepwise sle=.3 sls=.3;
run;
```

In Figure 5.1, we see the beginning of the output for the stepwise selection. Notice how 42,675 observations were deleted from the model processing. These are the observations that have missing weights. By including them in the data set with missing weights, they will be scored with a probability that can be used for model validation.

My stepwise logistic regression selected 28 variables that had a level of significance <= .3. The list appears in Figure 5.2. These will be combined with the results of the backward logistic regression to create a final list of variables for the *score* selection process.

I now run a backward regression to see if the list of candidate variables includes variables not captured in the stepwise selection.

```
proc logistic data=acqmod.model2(keep=active age_cui age_cos age_sqi
age_low inc_sqrt inc_sqri inc_inv inc_low mortal1 mortal2 mortal3
hom_log hom_cui hom_curt hom_med sgle_in infd_ag2 gender
toa_low toa_tan toa_cu toa_curt tob_med tob_sqrt tob_log tob_low
inq_sqrt top_logi top_cu top_med top_cui top_low crl_med crl_tan crl_low
```

```
rat_log rat_tan rat_med rat_low brt_med brt_logi brt_low popdnsA
popdnsBC trav_cdd apt_indd clus1_1 clus1_2 sgle_ind occ_miss finl_idd
hh_ind_d gender_d driv_ind mortin1n mort1mis mort2mis auto2mis childind
occ_G finl_idm gender_f driv_ino mob_indd mortin1y auto1mis auto2_n
clu2miss no90de_d actop16d no30dayd splitwgt records smp_wgt respond
activate pros_id) descending;
weight splitwgt;
model active = age_cui age_cos age_sqi age_low inc_sqrt inc_sqri inc_inv
inc_low mortal1 mortal2 mortal3 hom_log hom_cui hom_curt hom_med toa_low
toa_tan toa_cu toa_curt tob_med tob_sqrt tob_log tob_low inq_sqrt
top_logi top_cu top_med top_cui top_low crl_med crl_tan crl_low rat_log
rat_tan rat_med rat_low brt_med brt_logi brt_low popdnsA popdnsBC
trav_cdd apt_indd clus1_1 clus1_2 sgle_ind occ_miss finl_idd hh_ind_d
gender_d driv_ind mortin1n mort1mis mort2mis auto2mis childind occ_G
finl_idm gender_f driv_ino mob_indd mortin1y auto1mis auto2_n clu2miss
no90de_d actop16d no30dayd
/selection = backward sls=.3;
run;
```

In Figure 5.3, the list of variables from the backward selection is slightly different from the stepwise selection.

Next, I take the combination of variables and put them into PROC LOGISTIC
with a *score* selection method. (The variables appear in caps because they were
cut and pasted from the stepwise and backward selection output.) The only
coding difference is the **selection = score best=2.**

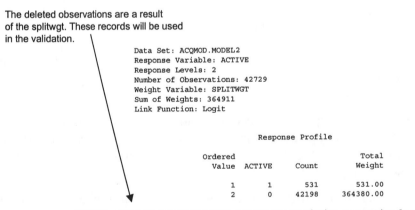

The deleted observations are a result
of the splitwgt. These records will be used
in the validation.

```
                    Data Set: ACQMOD.MODEL2
                    Response Variable: ACTIVE
                    Response Levels: 2
                    Number of Observations: 42729
                    Weight Variable: SPLITWGT
                    Sum of Weights: 364911
                    Link Function: Logit


                           Response Profile

                 Ordered                          Total
                 Value   ACTIVE      Count        Weight

                   1        1         531         531.00
                   2        0       42198      364380.00

WARNING: 42675 observation(s) were deleted due to missing or negative frequencies or weights.



                        Stepwise Selection Procedure


    Step  0. Intercept entered:
```

Figure 5.1 Logistic output: first page using stepwise method.

```
proc logistic data=acqmod.model2(keep= HOM_CUI BRT_LOGI AGE_COS AGE_SQI
AGE_LOW INC_SQRT MORTAL1 MORTAL3 HOM_LOG HOM_MED TOA_TAN TOA_CU TOB_SQRT
TOB_LOG INQ_SQRT TOP_LOGI TOP_CU TOP_CUI CRL_LOW RAT_LOG RAT_TAN RAT_MED
BRT_MED POPDNSBC APT_INDD SGLE_IND GENDER_D CHILDIND OCC_G NO90DE_D
ACTOPL6D
respond activate pros_id active splitwgt records smp_wgt) descending;
weight splitwgt;
model active =HOM_CUI BRT_LOGI AGE_COS AGE_SQI AGE_LOW INC_SQRT MORTAL1
MORTAL3 HOM_LOG HOM_MED TOA_TAN TOA_CU TOB_SQRT TOB_LOG INQ_SQRT
TOP_LOGI TOP_CU TOP_CUI CRL_LOW RAT_LOG RAT_TAN RAT_MED BRT_MED POPDNSBC
APT_INDD SGLE_IND GENDER_D CHILDIND OCC_G NO90DE_D ACTOPL6D
/selection=score best=2;
run;
```

Activation Model - One Step
Stepwise Selection

The LOGISTIC Procedure

Analysis of Maximum Likelihood Estimates

Variable	DF	Parameter Estimate	Standard Error	Wald Chi-Square	Pr > Chi-Square	Standardized Estimate	Odds Ratio
INTERCPT	1	-7.5813	0.7726	96.3012	0.0001	.	.
AGE_COS	1	-0.1985	0.0625	10.0797	0.0015	-0.226958	0.820
AGE_SQI	1	609.9	226.9	7.2284	0.0072	0.302531	999.000
AGE_LOW	1	-0.2491	0.1986	1.5731	0.2098	-0.120876	0.780
INC_SQRT	1	-0.1704	0.0758	5.0613	0.0245	-0.473939	0.843
MORTAL1	1	0.3175	0.1479	4.6045	0.0319	0.173862	1.374
MORTAL3	1	0.6299	0.1373	21.0587	0.0001	0.394044	1.878
HOM_CUI	1	-0.00004	0.000022	2.8398	0.0920	-0.277887	1.000
HOM_MED	1	0.2998	0.1438	4.3431	0.0372	0.241400	1.350
TOA_TAN	1	0.00228	0.00126	3.2632	0.0709	0.148184	1.002
TOA_CU	1	9.446E-6	2.416E-6	15.2871	0.0001	0.432069	1.000
TOB_SQRT	1	-0.00077	0.000733	1.1099	0.2921	-0.264038	0.999
TOB_LOG	1	0.0504	0.0278	3.2912	0.0697	0.290415	1.052
INQ_SQRT	1	0.1297	0.0630	4.2344	0.0396	0.150654	1.138
TOP_CU	1	-0.00002	0.000011	4.5633	0.0327	-0.305483	1.000
CRL_LOW	1	0.5817	0.1872	9.6555	0.0019	0.456406	1.789
RAT_LOG	1	0.1179	0.0543	4.7142	0.0299	0.263988	1.125
RAT_TAN	1	-0.0004	0.00017	5.5949	0.0180	-0.570110	1.000
RAT_MED	1	-0.1963	0.1479	1.7611	0.1845	-0.146270	0.822
BRT_MED	1	-0.3111	0.1666	3.4856	0.0619	-0.250528	0.733
BRT_LOGI	1	-0.00003	0.00002	1.8491	0.1739	-0.118643	1.000
POPDNSBC	1	-0.2617	0.0958	7.4596	0.0063	-0.185961	0.770
APT_INDD	1	0.1415	0.1042	1.8444	0.1744	0.087090	1.152
SGLE_IND	1	0.4741	0.1081	19.2251	0.0001	0.264578	1.607
GENDER_D	1	0.3894	0.0879	19.6308	0.0001	0.310016	1.476
CHILDIND	1	-0.4735	0.1422	11.0894	0.0009	-0.310557	0.623
OCC_G	1	0.5832	0.3373	2.9891	0.0838	0.177099	1.792
NO90DE_D	1	0.6703	0.1796	13.9310	0.0002	0.183863	1.955
ACTOPL6D	1	-0.1739	0.0982	3.1387	0.0765	-0.127940	0.840

Association of Predicted Probabilities and Observed Responses

```
Concordant = 42.8%        Somers' D = 0.295
Discordant = 13.3%        Gamma     = 0.525
Tied       = 43.9%        Tau-a     = 0.007
(22407138 pairs)          c         = 0.647
```

Figure 5.2 Logistic output: final page using stepwise method.

The results from the Score selection method are seen in Figure 5.4. This selection method gives us 63 variable lists, 2 for each model with 1 through 30 variables and 1 for a model with 31 variables. It also lists the overall score for the model fit. There are a number of issues to consider when selecting the model from the list of Score. If management wants a simple model with 10 or fewer variables, then the decision is easy. I usually start looking at about 20 variables. I examine the change in the overall score to see where adding 1 more variable can make a big difference. For this model I select 25 variables.

```
                    Activation Model - One Step

                        Backward Selection

                      The LOGISTIC Procedure

                      The LOGISTIC Procedure

                  Analysis of Maximum Likelihood Estimates
```

Variable	DF	Parameter Estimate	Standard Error	Wald Chi-Square	Pr > Chi-Square	Standardized Estimate	Odds Ratio
INTERCPT	1	-7.7175	0.7841	96.8714	0.0001	.	.
AGE_COS	1	-0.1974	0.0625	9.9774	0.0016	-0.225801	0.821
AGE_SQI	1	600.7	226.8	7.0139	0.0081	0.297937	999.000
AGE_LOW	1	-0.2475	0.1984	1.5566	0.2122	-0.120131	0.781
INC_SQRT	1	-0.1747	0.0758	5.3140	0.0212	-0.485857	0.840
MORTAL1	1	0.3136	0.1479	4.4969	0.0340	0.171770	1.368
MORTAL3	1	0.6239	0.1368	20.8036	0.0001	0.390260	1.866
HOM_LOG	1	0.0176	0.0109	2.5870	0.1077	0.277613	1.018
HOM_MED	1	0.3217	0.1533	4.4010	0.0359	0.259045	1.379
TOA_TAN	1	0.00235	0.00126	3.4675	0.0626	0.152657	1.002
TOA_CU	1	9.487E-6	2.415E-6	15.4359	0.0001	0.433932	1.000
TOB_SQRT	1	-0.00088	0.000722	1.4761	0.2244	-0.299798	0.999
TOB_LOG	1	0.0559	0.0260	4.6291	0.0314	0.321971	1.057
INQ_SQRT	1	0.1291	0.0630	4.2003	0.0404	0.150042	1.138
TOP_LOGI	1	0.000346	0.000234	2.1861	0.1393	0.545665	1.000
TOP_CU	1	-0.00002	0.000011	4.6795	0.0305	-0.310806	1.000
TOP_CUI	1	-3.7787	2.3316	2.6264	0.1051	-0.604665	0.023
CRL_LOW	1	0.5862	0.1856	9.9710	0.0016	0.459929	1.797
RAT_LOG	1	0.1104	0.0554	3.9682	0.0464	0.247384	1.117
RAT_TAN	1	-0.0004	0.000174	5.2592	0.0218	-0.563325	1.000
RAT_MED	1	-0.2283	0.1498	2.3240	0.1274	-0.170101	0.796
BRT_MED	1	-0.3446	0.1631	4.4668	0.0346	-0.277544	0.708
POPDNSBC	1	-0.2616	0.0958	7.4548	0.0063	-0.185884	0.770
APT_INDD	1	0.1371	0.1042	1.7305	0.1884	0.084361	1.147
SGLE_IND	1	0.4911	0.1084	20.5398	0.0001	0.274067	1.634
GENDER_D	1	0.3941	0.0880	20.0773	0.0001	0.313795	1.483
CHILDIND	1	-0.4744	0.1422	11.1323	0.0008	-0.311106	0.622
OCC_G	1	0.5972	0.3373	3.1342	0.0767	0.181350	1.817
NO90DE_D	1	0.6796	0.1797	14.3042	0.0002	0.186415	1.973
ACTOPL6D	1	-0.1591	0.0986	2.6035	0.1066	-0.117033	0.853

```
       Association of Predicted Probabilities and Observed Responses

              Concordant = 41.9%       Somers' D = 0.285
              Discordant = 13.4%       Gamma     = 0.515
              Tied       = 44.6%       Tau-a     = 0.007
              (22407138 pairs)         c         = 0.643
```

Figure 5.3 Backward selection variable list.

The first step in evaluating the results of the model is to look at a decile analysis. To create a decile analysis, I first sort the records by descending model score. Then I divide the records into 10 equal groups. The statistics you choose in your table can provide a lot of information about the predictive power of the model. The following code creates a preliminary decile analysis in SAS's PROC TABULATE. It allows us to examine how well the model sorts our target group, the *actives*. I create one table using the data on which the model was built and a second one using the validation data. But before I create the tables, I must rerun the model with the selected subset and create an output data set. The following code reruns the model to get the estimates for the 25-variable model. It creates an output data set called *acqmod.out_act1*. The output data set contains a value, *pred*. It is the predicted probability for each record. This will be used in the validation tables.

```
                        Activation Model - One Step
                          Best Subsets Selection

        Data Set: ACQMOD.MODEL1A
        Response Variable: ACTIVE
        Response Levels: 2
        Number of Observations: 42729
        Weight Variable: SPLITWGT
        Sum of Weights: 364911
        Link Function: Logit

                            Response Profile

                 Ordered                            Total
                 Value   ACTIVE      Count           Weight

                   1        1         531           531.00
                   2        0       42198        364380.00

   WARNING: 42675 observation(s) were deleted due to missing or negative frequencies or weights.

   Regression Models Selected by Score Criterion

        Number of       Score
        Variables       Value    Variables Included in Model

            1         150.8714   MORTAL3
            1         101.1803   HOM_LOG
        ----------------------------------------------------
            2         195.7452   MORTAL3 SGLE_IND
            2         183.1325   AGE_SQI MORTAL3
        ----------------------------------------------------
```

```
   -------------------------------------------------------------------------------------------------
           25        374.0805   HOM_CUI AGE_COS AGE_SQI INC_SQRT MORTAL1 MORTAL3 HOM_MED TOA_TAN
                                TOA_CU TOB_LOG INQ_SQRT TOP_LOGI TOP_CU TOP_CUI CRL_LOW RAT_LOG
                                BRT_MED POPDNSBC APT_INDD SGLE_IND GENDER_D CHILDIND OCC_G NO90DE_D
                                ACTOPL6D
           25        374.0785   AGE_COS AGE_SQI INC_SQRT MORTAL1 MORTAL3 HOM_LOG HOM_MED TOA_TAN
                                TOA_CU TOB_LOG INQ_SQRT TOP_LOGI TOP_CU TOP_CUI CRL_LOW RAT_LOG
                                BRT_MED POPDNSBC APT_INDD SGLE_IND GENDER_D CHILDIND OCC_G NO90DE_D
                                ACTOPL6D
   -------------------------------------------------------------------------------------------------

   -------------------------------------------------------------------------------------------------
           31        377.8114   HOM_CUI AVB_LOGI AGE_COS AGE_SQI AGE_LOW INC_SQRT MORTAL1 MORTAL3
                                HOM_LOG HOM_MED TOA_TAN TOA_CU TOB_SQRT TOB_LOG INQ_SQRT TOP_LOGI
                                TOP_CU TOP_CUI CRL_LOW RAT_LOG RAT_TAN RAT_MED BRT_MED POPDNSBC
                                APT_INDD SGLE_IND GENDER_D CHILDIND OCC_G NO90DE_D ACTOPL6D
   -------------------------------------------------------------------------------------------------
```

Variable listing for the 25 variable model with the highest score.

Figure 5.4 Output from best subsets.

```
proc logistic data=acqmod.model2(keep=
HOM_CUI AGE_COS AGE_SQI INC_SQRT MORTAL1 MORTAL3 HOM_MED TOA_TAN TOA_CU
TOB_LOG INQ_SQRT TOP_LOGI TOP_CU TOP_CUI CRL_LOW RAT_LOG BRT_MED
POPDNSBC APT_INDD SGLE_IND GENDER_D CHILDIND OCC_G NO90DE_D ACTOPL6D
respond activate pros_id active splitwgt records smp_wgt) descending;
weight splitwgt;
model active =
HOM_CUI AGE_COS AGE_SQI INC_SQRT MORTAL1 MORTAL3 HOM_MED TOA_TAN TOA_CU
TOB_LOG INQ_SQRT TOP_LOGI TOP_CU TOP_CUI CRL_LOW BRT_LOG BRT_MED
POPDNSBC APT_INDD SGLE_IND GENDER_D CHILDIND OCC_G NO90DE_D ACTOPL6D;
output out=acqmod.out_act1 pred=pred;
run;
```

The following code sorts the data by the predicted value *pred*. The descending option brings the highest predicted probabilities to the beginning of the data set.

```
proc sort data=acqmod.out_act1;
by descending pred;
run;
```

What Is the Right Number of Variables?

I'm often asked this question! There is no right answer. I've seen models with as few as 5 variables and as many as 100. In the case study, I looked for a point where the increased predictive power for each new variable was tapering off. This is a good rule of thumb when you are just considering model efficiency.

In considering model performance, I think there are a few basic considerations. One argument for a specific number of variables could be robustness. It's not clear whether a model with a large number of variables is more robust than a model with a small number of variables. It depends on the market. With a large number of variables, the model will be less sensitive to changes to the inputs from any one variable. If your market is very stable, you might be better off with a large number of variables. On the other hand, if your market behavior reflects changing trends, you might want fewer variables that capture those changes more dynamically.

Another consideration might be processing simplicity. Unless the processing is totally automated, models with large numbers of variables are more prone to errors in scoring.

And finally, business issues can determine the best number of variables. If companies want to avoid biased selections based on certain demographics, a higher number of variables would spread the effect. On the other hand, some managers are more comfortable with fewer variables because they can understand the components that are driving the model. Business knowledge and experience are your best guide.

The following code calculates the total sum of the weights, *sumwgt*, in the data set. The goal is to divide the data set into 10 equal groups or deciles. By creating deciles of the file, sorted by probabilities of becoming active, we can evaluate how well the model score pulls the true actives (active = 1) to the best decile (decile 0).

There are several other methods for creating deciles within the SAS system. PROC RANK is a procedure designed for that purpose. Another technique is to use the decile identifiers available from PROC UNIVARIATE. Both PROC RANK and PROC UNIVARIATE use values to identify the decile cutoffs. Because I am using a sample with weights, there are many groups that have the same exact probability. And using those techniques everyone with the same probability goes into the same decile. Therefore, it is difficult to create deciles of equal size.

```
proc univariate data=acqmod.out_act1
        (where=( splitwgt =.)) noprint;
weight smp_wgt;
var pred active;
output out=preddata sumwgt=sumwgt;
run;
```

The following code appends the *sumwgt* or the weighted total number of records to the file and creates a new data set with only the model data (where splitwgt =1). Next, a variable is created called *number* that assigns a unique value to each observation in order of predicted probability to become active. The deciles are created using cutoffs at each tenth of the file. And finally, a variable, *activ_r*, is created that represents a numeric form of activate. This is used in the table below.

```
/* DECILE CREATION */
data acqmod.mod_dec;
 set acqmod.out_act1(where=( splitwgt =.));
if (_n_ = 1) then set preddata;
retain sumwgt;
number+smp_wgt;
if number < .1*sumwgt then mod_dec = 0; else
if number < .2*sumwgt then mod_dec = 1; else
if number < .3*sumwgt then mod_dec = 2; else
if number < .4*sumwgt then mod_dec = 3; else
if number < .5*sumwgt then mod_dec = 4; else
if number < .6*sumwgt then mod_dec = 5; else
if number < .7*sumwgt then mod_dec = 6; else
if number < .8*sumwgt then mod_dec = 7; else
if number < .9*sumwgt then mod_dec = 8; else
mod_dec = 9;
activ_r = (activate = '1');
run;
```

The following code uses PROC TABULATE to create the decile analysis, a table that calculates the number of observations (records) in each decile, the average predicted probability per decile, the percent active per responders (target of Method 2, model 2), the response rate (target of Method 2, model 1), and the active rate (target of Method 1).

```
title1 "Decile Analysis - Activation Model - One Step";
title2 "Model Data - Score Selection";
proc tabulate data=acqmod.mod_dec;
weight smp_wgt;
class mod_dec;
var respond active pred records activ_r;
table mod_dec='Decile' all='Total',
        records='Prospects'*sum=' '*f=comma10.
        pred='Predicted Probability'*(mean=' '*f=11.5)
        activ_r='Percent Active of Responders'*(mean=' '*f=11.5)
        respond='Percent Respond'*(mean=' '*f=11.5)
        active='Percent Active'*(mean=' '*f=11.5)
/rts = 9 row=float;
run;
```

In Figure 5.5, the decile analysis shows the model's ability to *rank order* the prospects by their *active* behavior. To clarify, each prospect's probability of becoming active is considered its rank. The goal of the model is to rank order the prospects so as to bring the true actives to the lowest decile. At first glance we can see that the best decile (0) has 17.5 as many actives as the worst decile

Decile Analysis - Activation Model- One Step

Model Data - Score Selection

This model is targeting activation. On the **model** data, the best decile (0) is 17.5 times better (.00436) than the worst decile (.00025) in targeting *actives*.

Decile	Prospects	Predicted Probability	Percent Active of Responders	Percent Respond	Percent Active
0	36,483	0.00467	0.11174	0.03900	0.00436
1	36,499	0.00245	0.10010	0.02655	0.00266
2	36,488	0.00176	0.08858	0.02351	0.00208
3	36,486	0.00137	0.06516	0.01935	0.00126
4	36,498	0.00111	0.05401	0.01775	0.00096
5	36,484	0.00093	0.05923	0.01573	0.00093
6	36,498	0.00077	0.06439	0.01447	0.00093
7	36,485	0.00064	0.05051	0.01357	0.00069
8	36,496	0.00051	0.04145	0.01058	0.00044
9	36,494	0.00034	0.02616	0.00943	0.00025
Total	364,911	0.00146	0.07661	0.01899	0.00146

Figure 5.5 Decile analysis using model data.

(9). And as we go from decile 0 to decile 9, the percent active value is monotonically decreasing with a strong decrease in the first three deciles. The only exception is the two deciles in the middle with the same percent active rate. This is not unusual since the model is most powerful in deciles 0 and 9, where it gets the best separation. Overall, the model score does a good job of targeting active accounts. Because the model was built on the data used in Figure 5.5, a better test will be on the validation data set.

Another consideration is how closely the "Percent Active" matches the "Predicted Probability." The values in these columns for each decile are not as close as they could be. If my sample had been larger, they would probably be more equal. I will look for similar behavior in the decile analysis for the validation data set.

Preliminary Evaluation

Because I carried the validation data through the model using the missing weights, each time the model is processed, the validation data set is scored along with the model data. By creating a decile analysis on the validation data set we can evaluate how well the model will transfer the results to similar data. As mentioned earlier, a model that works well on alternate data is said to be *robust*. In chapter 6, I will discuss additional methods for validation that go beyond simple decile analysis.

The next code listing creates the same table for the validation data set. This provides our first analysis of the ability of the model to rank order data other than the model development data. It is a good test of the robustness of the model or its ability to perform on other prospect data. The code is the same as for the model data decile analysis except for the **(where=(splitwgt = .))** option. This accesses the "hold out" sample or validation data set.

```
proc univariate data=acqmod.out_act1
        (where=( splitwgt = .)) noprint;
weight smp_wgt;
var pred active;
output out=preddata sumwgt=sumwgt;
run;

data acqmod.val_dec;
  set acqmod.out_act1(where=( splitwgt = .));
if (_n_ eq 1) then set preddata;
retain sumwgt;
number+smp_wgt;
if number < .1*sumwgt then val_dec = 0; else
if number < .2*sumwgt then val_dec = 1; else
if number < .3*sumwgt then val_dec = 2; else
if number < .4*sumwgt then val_dec = 3; else
```

```
if number < .5*sumwgt then val_dec = 4; else
if number < .6*sumwgt then val_dec = 5; else
if number < .7*sumwgt then val_dec = 6; else
if number < .8*sumwgt then val_dec = 7; else
if number < .9*sumwgt then val_dec = 8; else
val_dec = 9;
activ_r = (activate = '1');
run;

title1 "Decile Analysis - Activation Model - One Step";
title2 "Validation Data - Score Selection";
PROC tabulate data=acqmod.val_dec;
weight smp_wgt;
class val_dec;
var respond active pred records activ_r;
table val_dec='Decile' all='Total',
        records='Prospects'*sum=' '*f=comma10.
        pred='Predicted Probability'*(mean=' '*f=11.5)
        activ_r='Percent Active of Responders'*(mean=' '*f=11.5)
        respond='Percent Respond'*(mean=' '*f=11.5)
        active='Percent Active'*(mean=' '*f=11.5)
/rts = 9 row=float;
run;
```

The validation decile analysis seen in Figure 5.6 shows slight degradation from the original model. This is to be expected. But the rank ordering is still strong

Decile Analysis - Activation Model- One Step

Validation Data - Score Selection

Decile	Prospects	Predicted Probability	Percent Active of Responders	Percent Respond	Percent Active
0	36,429	0.00463	0.10583	0.03813	0.00404
1	36,425	0.00244	0.08377	0.02622	0.00220
2	36,441	0.00175	0.07946	0.02418	0.00192
3	36,424	0.00137	0.07044	0.01988	0.00140
4	36,439	0.00111	0.06897	0.01671	0.00115
5	36,431	0.00092	0.05704	0.01540	0.00088
6	36,424	0.00077	0.07634	0.01439	0.00110
7	36,434	0.00064	0.05603	0.01274	0.00071
8	36,431	0.00051	0.04762	0.01211	0.00058
9	36,439	0.00034	0.05656	0.01068	0.00060
Total	364,317	0.00145	0.07655	0.01904	0.00146

• This model is targeting activation. On the **validation** data, the best decile (0) is almost 7 times better (.00404) than the worst decile (.00060) in targeting *actives*.

• Deciles 5, 6, and 9 are not perfectly rank ordered, but the values are close enough

Figure 5.6 Decile analysis using validation data.

with the best decile attracting almost seven times as many actives as the worst decile. We see the same degree of difference between the "Predicted Probability" and the actual "Percent Active" as we saw in the decile analysis of the model data in Figure 5.5. Decile 0 shows the most dramatic difference, but the other deciles follow a similar pattern to the model data. There is also a little flip-flop going on in deciles 5 and 6, but the degree is minor and probably reflects nuances in the data. In chapter 6, I will perform some more general types of validation, which will determine if this is a real problem.

Method 2: Two Models—Response

The process for two models is similar to the process for the single model. The only difference is that the response and activation models are processed separately through the stepwise, backward, and Score selection methods. The code differences are highlighted here:

```
proc logistic data=acqmod.model2(keep=variables) descending;
weight splitwgt;
model respond = variables
/selection = stepwise sle=.3 sls=.3;
run;
proc logistic data=acqmod.model2(keep=variables) descending;
weight splitwgt;
model respond = variables
/selection = backward sls=.3;
run;

proc logistic data=acqmod.model2(keep=variables) descending;
weight splitwgt;
model respond = variables
/selection = score best=2;
run;
```

The output from the Method 2 response models is similar to the Method 1 approach. Figure 5.7 shows the decile analysis for the response model calculated on the validation data set. It shows strong rank ordering for response. The rank ordering for activation is a little weaker, which is to be expected. There are different drivers for response and activation. Because activation is strongly driven by response, the ranking for activation is strong.

Method 2: Two Models—Activation

As I process the model for predicting activation given response (active|response), recall that I can use the value activate because it has a value of missing for nonresponders. This means that the nonresponders will be eliminated from the model processing. The following code processes the model:

Decile Analysis - Response Model - Two Step
Validation Data - Score Selection

Decile	Prospects	Predicted Probability	Percent Active of Responders	Percent Respond	Percent Active	
--------	-----------	----------------------	------------------------------	-----------------	----------------	
0	36,431	0.04396	0.09353	0.04285	0.00401	This model is targeting response. On the validation data, the best decile (0) is almost 6 times better (.04285) than the worst decile (.00730) in targeting *responders*.
1	36,424	0.02872	0.07221	0.03004	0.00217	
2	36,433	0.02323	0.07223	0.02204	0.00159	
3	36,429	0.01977	0.07172	0.02029	0.00145	
4	36,441	0.01714	0.08169	0.01814	0.00148	
5	36,428	0.01505	0.06204	0.01504	0.00093	
6	36,433	0.01324	0.07064	0.01243	0.00088	This model also does a good job of targeting activation. This is because activation is so strongly driven by response.
7	36,430	0.01155	0.07209	0.01180	0.00085	
8	36,432	0.00981	0.07330	0.01049	0.00077	
9	36,436	0.00728	0.06015	0.00730	0.00044	
Total	364,317	0.01897	0.07655	0.01904	0.00146	

Figure 5.7 Method 2 response model decile analysis.

```
proc logistic data=acqmod.model2(keep=variables) descending;
weight splitwgt;
model activate = variables
/selection = stepwise sle=.3 sls=.3;
run;

proc logistic data=acqmod.model2(keep=variables) descending;
weight splitwgt;
model activate = variables
/selection = backward sls=.3;
run;

proc logistic data=acqmod.model2(keep=variables) descending;
weight splitwgt;
model activate = variables
/selection = score best=2;
run;
```

The output from the Method 2 activation models is similar to the Method 1 approach. Figure 5.8 shows the decile analysis for the activation model calculated on the validation data set. It shows strong rank ordering for activation given response. As expected, it is weak when predicting activation for the entire file. Our next step is to compare the results of the two methods.

Decile Analysis - Activation Model - Two Step
Validation Data - Score Selection

Decile	Prospects	Predicted Probability	Percent Active of Responders	Percent Respond	Percent Active
0	36,428	0.14591	0.10321	0.02740	0.00283
1	36,428	0.10254	0.09010	0.02163	0.00195
2	36,438	0.08758	0.09599	0.01916	0.00184
3	36,425	0.07715	0.08271	0.01826	0.00151
4	36,436	0.06890	0.07357	0.01828	0.00134
5	36,430	0.06163	0.08182	0.01812	0.00148
6	36,435	0.05467	0.05455	0.01660	0.00091
7	36,428	0.04783	0.05686	0.01642	0.00093
8	36,431	0.04046	0.04910	0.01677	0.00082
9	36,438	0.02967	0.05401	0.01778	0.00096
Total	364,317	0.07163	0.07655	0.01904	0.00146

This model is targeting activation given response. On the validation data, the best decile (0) is about 50% better (.10321) than the worst decile (.05401) in targeting *actives given response.*

The ability of this model to predict activation straight from the prospect list is weak.

Figure 5.8 Method 2 activation model decile analysis.

Comparing Method 1 and Method 2

At this point, I have several options for the final model. I have a single model that predicts the probability of an active account that was created using Method 1, the single-model approach. And I have two models from Method 2, one that predicts the probability of response and the other that predicts the probability of an active account, given response (active|response).

To compare the performance between the two methods, I must combine the models developed in Method 2. To do this, I use a simplified form of Bayes' Theorem. Let's say:

P(R) = the probability of response (model 1 in Method 2)

P(A|R) = the probability of becoming active given response (model 2 in Method 2)

P(A and R) = the probability of responding and becoming active

Then:

$$P(A \text{ and } R) = P(R) * P(A|R)$$

Therefore, to get the probability of responding and becoming active, I multiply the probabilities created in model 1 and model 2.

Following the processing of the score selection for each of the two models in Method 2, I reran the models with the final variables and created two output data sets that contained the predicted scores, *acqmod.out_rsp2* and *acqmod.out_act2*. The following code takes the output data sets from the Method 2 models built using the score option. The **where=(splitwgt = .)** option designates both probabilities are taken from the validation data set. Because the same sample was used to build both models in Method 2, when merged together by *pros_id* the names should match up exactly. The **rename=(pred=predrsp)** creates different names for the predictors for each model.

```
proc sort data=acqmod.out_rsp2 out=acqmod.validrsp
      (where=( splitwgt = .) rename=(pred=predrsp));
      by pros_id;
run;

proc sort data=acqmod.out_act2 out=acqmod.validact
      (where=( splitwgt = .) rename=(pred=predact));
      by pros_id;
run;

data acqmod.blend;
merge acqmod.validrsp acqmod.validact;
by pros_id;
run;

data acqmod.blend;
 set acqmod.blend;
predact2 = predrsp*predact;
run;
```

To compare the models, I create a decile analysis for the probability of becoming active derived using Method 2 (**predact2**) with the following code:

```
proc sort data=acqmod.blend;
by descending predact2;
run;

proc univariate data=acqmod.blend noprint;
weight smp_wgt;
var predact2;
output out=preddata sumwgt=sumwgt;
run;

data acqmod.blend;
 set acqmod.blend;
if (_n_ eq 1) then set preddata;
retain sumwgt;
number+smp_wgt;
if number < .1*sumwgt then act2dec = 0; else
```

```
if number < .2*sumwgt then act2dec = 1; else
if number < .3*sumwgt then act2dec = 2; else
if number < .4*sumwgt then act2dec = 3; else
if number < .5*sumwgt then act2dec = 4; else
if number < .6*sumwgt then act2dec = 5; else
if number < .7*sumwgt then act2dec = 6; else
if number < .8*sumwgt then act2dec = 7; else
if number < .9*sumwgt then act2dec = 8; else
act2dec = 9;
run;


title1 "Decile Analysis - Model Comparison";
title2 "Validation Data - Two Step Model";
PROC tabulate data=acqmod.blend;
weight smp_wgt;
class act2dec;
var active predact2 records;
table act2dec='Decile' all='Total',
      records='Prospects'*sum=' '*f=comma10.
      predact2='Predicted Probability'*(mean=' '*f=11.5)
      active='Percent Active'*(mean=' '*f=11.5)
/rts = 9 row=float;
run;
```

In Figure 5.9, the decile analysis of the combined scores on the validation data for the two-model approach shows a slightly better performance than the one-model approach in Figure 5.6. This provides confidence in our results. At first glance, it's difficult to pick the winner.

Decile Analysis - Model Comparison
Validation Data - Two Step Model

Decile	Prospects	Predicted Probability	Percent Active
0	36,429	0.00469	0.00406
1	36,425	0.00245	0.00242
2	36,435	0.00175	0.00156
3	36,428	0.00136	0.00156
4	36,438	0.00111	0.00110
5	36,426	0.00091	0.00113
6	36,434	0.00076	0.00121
7	36,434	0.00063	0.00041
8	36,431	0.00050	0.00058
9	36,437	0.00034	0.00055
Total	364,317	0.00145	0.00146

This model is targeting actives. On the validation data, the best decile (0) is over 7 times better (.00406) than the worst decile (.00055) in targeting *actives*.

These results are very similar to the results of the one model approach.

Figure 5.9 Combined model decile analysis.

Summary

This chapter allowed us to enjoy the fruits of our labor. I built several models with strong power to rank order the prospects by their propensity to become active. We saw that many of the segmented and transformed variables dominated the models. And we explored several methods for finding the best-fitting model using two distinct methodologies. In the next chapter, I will measure the robustness of our models and select a winner.

Validating the Model

T he masterpiece is out of the oven! Now we want to ensure that it was cooked to perfection. It's time for the taste test!

Validating the model is a critical step in the process. It allows us to determine if we've successfully performed all the prior steps. If a model does not validate well, it can be due to data problems, poorly fitting variables, or problematic techniques. There are several methods for validating models. In this chapter, I begin with the basic tools for validating the model, gains tables and gains charts. Marketers and managers love them because they take the modeling results right to the bottom line. Next, I test the results of the model algorithm on an alternate data set. A major section of the chapter focuses on the steps for creating confidence intervals around the model estimates using resampling. This is gaining popularity as an excellent method for determining the robustness of a model. In the final section I discuss ways to validate the model by measuring its effect on key market drivers.

Gains Tables and Charts

A gains table is an excellent tool for evaluating the performance of a model. It contains actionable information that can be easily understood and used by non-technical marketers and managers. Using our case study, I will demonstrate the power of a gains table for Method 1.

Method 1: One Model

Recall that in Method 1 I developed a score for targeting actives using the one-model approach. To further validate the results of the model, I put the information from the decile analysis in Figure 5.6 into a spreadsheet; now I can create the gains table in Figure 6.1.

Column A mirrors the decile analysis in Figure 5.6. It shows each decile containing 10% of the total mail file.

Column B is cumulative percent of file for validation portion of the prospect data set.

Column C, as in Figure 5.6, is the average *Probability of Activation* for each decile as defined by the model.

Column D, as in Figure 5.6, is the average *Percent Actives* in the validation data set for each decile. This represents the number of true actives in the validation data set divided by the total prospects for each decile.

Column E is a cumulative calculation of column D or *Cumulative Percent Actives*. At each decile you can estimate the number of true actives for a given "Depth of File" or from decile 0 to a designated decile. If we consider the value for decile 4, we can say that the average Percent Active for deciles 0 through 4 is 0.214%.

Column F is the number of true actives in the decile (Col. A * Col. D).

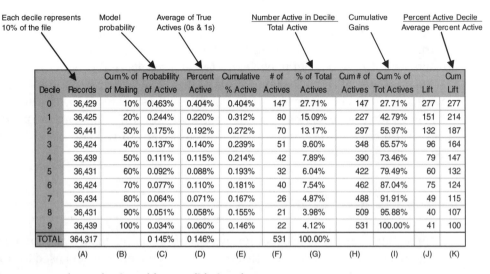

			Each decile represents 10% of the file (A)	Model probability (B)	Average of True Actives (0s & 1s) (C)		Number Active in Decile Total Active (D)	Cumulative Gains (E)	Percent Active Decile Average Percent Active	
Decile	Records	Cum % of Mailing	Probability of Active	Percent Active	Cumulative % Active	# of Actives	% of Total Actives	Cum # of Actives	Cum % of Tot Actives	Lift	Cum Lift
0	36,429	10%	0.463%	0.404%	0.404%	147	27.71%	147	27.71%	277	277
1	36,425	20%	0.244%	0.220%	0.312%	80	15.09%	227	42.79%	151	214
2	36,441	30%	0.175%	0.192%	0.272%	70	13.17%	297	55.97%	132	187
3	36,424	40%	0.137%	0.140%	0.239%	51	9.60%	348	65.57%	96	164
4	36,439	50%	0.111%	0.115%	0.214%	42	7.89%	390	73.46%	79	147
5	36,431	60%	0.092%	0.088%	0.193%	32	6.04%	422	79.49%	60	132
6	36,424	70%	0.077%	0.110%	0.181%	40	7.54%	462	87.04%	75	124
7	36,434	80%	0.064%	0.071%	0.167%	26	4.87%	488	91.91%	49	115
8	36,431	90%	0.051%	0.058%	0.155%	21	3.98%	509	95.88%	40	107
9	36,439	100%	0.034%	0.060%	0.146%	22	4.12%	531	100.00%	41	100
TOTAL	364,317		0.145%	0.146%		531	100.00%				
	(A)	(B)	(C)	(D)	(E)	(F)	(G)	(H)	(I)	(J)	(K)

Figure 6.1 Enhanced gains table on validation data.

Column G is column F divided by the sum of column F. This represents the percent *Actives* of the *Total Actives* that are contained in each decile. If we consider the value in Decile 1, we can say that 27.71% of all *Actives* in the validation data set were put into decile 1 by the model.

Column H is a cumulative of column F. This represents the total *Number of Actives* for a given "Depth of File" or from decile 0 to a designated decile.

Column I is column H divided by the number of total actives. At each decile you can determine the *Cumulative Percent of Total Actives* that are contained in decile 0 through a given decile. If we consider the value in decile 1, we can say that 42.79% of all *Actives* are in deciles 0 and 1.

Column J is the "lift" of each decile. The lift is calculated by dividing the decile percent active by the overall percent active in column D. The value of 277 in decile 0 means that the prospects in decile 0 are 277% more likely to activate than the overall average.

Column K is the cumulative Lift through a specific decile. It is calculated by dividing a decile value in column E by the overall percent active.

The *lift* measurement is a favorite among marketers for evaluating and comparing models. At each decile it demonstrates the model's power to beat the random approach or average performance. In Figure 6.1, we see that decile 0 is 2.77 times the average. Up to and including decile 3, the model performs better than average. Another way to use *lift* is in *cumulative lift*. This means to a given "Depth of File": the model performs better than random. If we go through decile 3, we can say that for the first four deciles, the model performs 64% better than average. Figure 6.2, a *validation gains chart*, provides a visual interpretation of the concept of Lift.

The *gains chart* is an excellent visual tool for understanding the power of a model. It is designed to compare the percent of the target group to the percent of the prospect file through the rank ordered data set. At 50% of the file we can capture 74% of the active accounts—a 47% increase in *Actives*. (This will be discussed in more detail in chapter 7.)

Method 2: Two Models

Recall that in Method 2, I built a model to target *Response* and a second model to target *Actives* given response.

In Figure 6.3 we see the ability of the Method 2 model to rank order the data. When comparing the active rate for the deciles, the power of the model is slightly better than the Method 1 model in distinguishing actives from nonresponders and nonactive responders. The *lift measures* imitate the similarity.

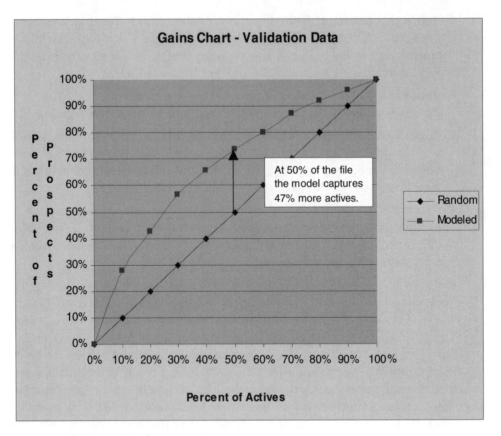

Figure 6.2 Validation gains chart.

Recall that the response model in the two-model approach did a good job of predicting actives overall. The gains chart in Figure 6.4 compares the activation model from the one-model approach to the response and combination models developed using the two-model approach. The response model seems to do almost as well as the active models. Again, this supports our theory that the probability of being active is strongly driven by response.

In conclusion, Method 1 and Method 2 produce very similar results when modeling the probability of an account being *active*. This may not always be the case. It is worth exploring both methods to determine the best method for each situation. In the next sections, I will compare the stability of the models through further validation. In chapter 7, I will discuss alternate ways to use the Method 2 models in the implementation process.

This model is targeting activation using the two-model approach. On the **validation** data, the best decile (0) is a little over seven times (.00406) better than the worst decile (.0005) in targeting *actives*.

Decile	Records	Cum % of Mailing	Probability of Active	Percent Active	Cumulative % Active	# of Actives	% of Total Actives	Cum # of Actives	Cum % of Tot Actives	Lift	Cum Lift
0	36,429	10%	0.469%	0.406%	0.406%	148	27.85%	148	27.85%	278	278
1	36,425	20%	0.245%	0.242%	0.324%	88	16.60%	236	44.44%	166	222
2	36,435	30%	0.175%	0.156%	0.268%	57	10.70%	293	55.14%	107	184
3	36,428	40%	0.136%	0.156%	0.240%	57	10.70%	350	65.84%	107	165
4	36,438	50%	0.111%	0.110%	0.214%	40	7.55%	390	73.39%	75	147
5	36,426	60%	0.091%	0.113%	0.197%	41	7.75%	431	81.14%	77	135
6	36,434	70%	0.076%	0.121%	0.186%	44	8.30%	475	89.44%	83	128
7	36,434	80%	0.063%	0.041%	0.168%	15	2.81%	490	92.25%	28	115
8	36,431	90%	0.050%	0.058%	0.156%	21	3.98%	511	96.23%	40	107
9	36,437	100%	0.034%	0.055%	0.146%	20	3.77%	531	100.00%	38	100
TOTAL	364,317		0.145%	0.146%		531	100.00%				

The lift is also similar to the lift in Method 1.

Figure 6.3   Enhanced gains table on validation data.

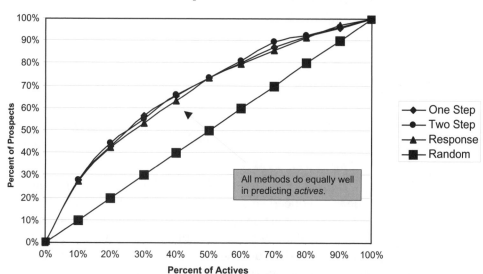

Model Comparison Gains Chart

All methods do equally well in predicting *actives*.

Legend:
- One Step
- Two Step
- Response
- Random

x-axis: Percent of Actives
y-axis: Percent of Prospects

Figure 6.4   Gains chart comparing models from Method 1 and Method 2.

Scoring Alternate Data Sets

In business, the typical purpose of developing a targeting model is to predict behavior on a data set other than that on which the model was developed. In our case study, I have our "hold out" sample that I used for validation. But because it was randomly sampled from the same data set as the model development data, I expect it to deliver a performance very similar to that of the model development data. The best way to test the robustness of the model is to score a campaign that more closely reflects the intended use. For example, a similar campaign from a different time period is optimal because most models are designed for future use in the same general market. Other options include campaigns from different geographic regions or for a slightly different product.

Our case study deals with the insurance industry, which is highly regulated. Therefore, it is quite common to begin marketing in just one or two states. Expansion typically happens on a state-by-state basis. For our case study, the goal is to use the model for name selection in a new state with the hope of improving on random selection. Our model was developed on a campaign in the state of New York. Now I will validate the scoring algorithm on the results from the state of Colorado.

I will concentrate on the Method 1 approach for this validation because the mechanics and results should be similar. The same processing will be performed on the Method 2 combined model for comparison. The first step is to read in the data from the Colorado campaign. The input statement is modified to read in only the necessary variables.

```
data acqmod.colorado;
infile 'F:\insur\acquisit\camp3.txt' missover recl=99;
input
prosp_id      1-9              /*unique prospect identifier*/
pop_den     $ 13              /*population density code*/
        |            |            |            |            |
        |            |            |            |            |
no90eve     97-99            /*number of payments over 90 days */
;
run;
```

The next step is to create the variable transformations needed for the model scoring. The code is a reduced version of the code used in chapter 4 to create the original variables so it won't be repeated here. I rerun the logistic model on the original (New York) data to create a data set with one observation using **outest=acqmod.nyscore**. This data set contains the coefficients of the model. The output from **acqmod.nyscore** is seen in Figure 6.5.

OBS	_LINK_	_TYPE_	_NAME_	INTERCEP	HOM_CUI	AGE_COS	AGE_SQI	INC_SQRT	MORTAL1	MORTAL3	HOM_MED
1	LOGIT	PARMS	ESTIMATE	-7.65976	-.000034026	-0.18209	372.299	-0.20938	0.32729	0.62568	0.30335

OBS	TOA_TAN	TOA_CU	TOB_LOG	INQ_SQRT	TOP_LOGI	TOP_CU	TOP_CUI	CRL_LOW	RAT_LOG	RAT_MED
1	.0023379	.0000096308	0.040987	0.11823	.00031204	-.000024588	-3.41194	0.63959	0.14747	-0.30808

OBS	POPDNSBC	APT_INDD	SGLE_IND	GENDER_D	CHILDIND	OCC_G	NO90DE_D	ACTOPL6D	_LNLIKE_
1	-0.25937	0.13769	0.48900	0.39401	-0.47305	0.60437	0.68165	-0.16514	-3832.99

Figure 6.5 Coefficient data set.

```
proc logistic data=acqmod.colorado descending
        outest=acqmod.nyscore;
weight splitwgt;
model active =
HOM_CUI AGE_COS AGE_SQI INC_SQRT MORTAL1 MORTAL3 HOM_MED TOA_TAN TOA_CU
TOB_LOG INQ_SQRT TOP_LOGI TOP_CU TOP_CUI CRL_LOW RAT_LOG BRT_MED
POPDNSBC APT_INDD SGLE_IND GENDER_D CHILDIND OCC_G NO90DE_D ACTOPL6D;
run;


proc print data = acqmod.nyscore;
run;
```

The final scoring is carried out using PROC SCORE. The procedure multiplies the coefficients in the model from (*acqmod.nyscore*) times the variable values in the data set to be scored (*acqmod.colorado*) and creates a new data set (*acqmod.validco*), which contains the estimates or betas for each observation. The line beginning with 'id' brings additional variables into the scored data set.

```
proc score data=acqmod.colorado
        out=acqmod.validco predict score=acqmod.nyscore type=parms;
id respond activate pros_id activ_r activate splitwgt records smp_wgt;
VAR HOM_CUI AGE_COS AGE_SQI INC_SQRT MORTAL1 MORTAL3 HOM_MED TOA_TAN
TOA_CU TOB_LOG INQ_SQRT TOP_LOGI TOP_CU TOP_CUI CRL_LOW RAT_LOG BRT_MED
POPDNSBC APT_INDD SGLE_IND GENDER_D CHILDIND OCC_G NO90DE_D ACTOPL6D;
run;
```

The output for PROC SCORE gives us the sum of the betas. Recall from chapter 1 that we use it in the following equation to calculate the probability:

$$P = \exp^{\left(\beta_0 + \beta_1 X_1 + \beta_2 X_2 + \ldots \beta_n X_n\right)} / \left(1 + \exp^{\left(\beta_0 + \beta_1 X_1 + \beta_2 X_2 + \ldots \beta_n X_n\right)}\right)$$

The rank ordering for the **estimate** and the predicted probability (**pred**) are the same. I sort the file by descending estimate and find the sum of the weights (sumwgt) to create a decile analysis.

```
proc sort data=acqmod.validco;
by descending estimate;
run;

proc univariate data=acqmod.validco noprint;
weight smp_wgt;
var estimate;
output out=preddata sumwgt=sumwgt;
run;


data acqmod.validco;
 set acqmod.validco;
active = (activate='1');
pred = exp(estimate)/(1+exp(estimate));
if (_n_ eq 1) then set preddata;
retain sumwgt;
number+smp_wgt;
if number < .1*sumwgt then val_dec = 0; else
if number < .2*sumwgt then val_dec = 1; else
if number < .3*sumwgt then val_dec = 2; else
if number < .4*sumwgt then val_dec = 3; else
if number < .5*sumwgt then val_dec = 4; else
if number < .6*sumwgt then val_dec = 5; else
if number < .7*sumwgt then val_dec = 6; else
if number < .8*sumwgt then val_dec = 7; else
if number < .9*sumwgt then val_dec = 8; else
val_dec = 9;
records = 1;
run;

title1 "Gains Table - Colorado";
title2 "Validation Data";
PROC tabulate data=acqmod.validco;
weight smp_wgt;
class val_dec;
var respond active pred records activ_r;
table val_dec='Decile' all='Total',
      records='Prospects'*sum=' '*f=comma10.
      pred='Predicted Probability'*(mean=' '*f=11.5)
      active='Percent Active'*(mean=' '*f=11.5)
/rts = 9 row=float;
run;
```

In Figure 6.6, we see that the Method 1 model does show a loss of power when scored on the campaign from another state. This is probably due to some population differences between states. Figure 6.7 shows similar results from the Method 2 model. In any case, the performance is still much better than random with the best decile showing three times the active rate of the worst decile.

Validation Gains Table for Colorado
Method 1

Decile	Records	Cum % of Mailing	Probablility of Active	Percent Active	Cumulative % Active	# of Actives	% of Total Actives	Cum # of Actives	Cum % of Tot Actives	Lift	Cum Lift
0	75,522	10%	0.492%	0.163%	0.163%	123	14.68%	123	14.68%	147	147
1	75,528	20%	0.265%	0.144%	0.153%	109	12.97%	232	27.66%	130	138
2	75,529	30%	0.198%	0.136%	0.148%	103	12.25%	335	39.91%	123	133
3	75,518	40%	0.159%	0.135%	0.144%	102	12.16%	437	52.07%	122	130
4	75,530	50%	0.132%	0.099%	0.135%	75	8.92%	511	60.99%	89	122
5	75,527	60%	0.111%	0.107%	0.131%	81	9.64%	592	70.63%	96	118
6	75,530	70%	0.093%	0.097%	0.126%	73	8.74%	665	79.37%	87	113
7	75,525	80%	0.077%	0.107%	0.123%	81	9.64%	746	89.01%	96	111
8	75,522	90%	0.062%	0.070%	0.118%	53	6.31%	799	95.31%	63	106
9	75,534	100%	0.041%	0.052%	0.111%	39	4.69%	838	100.00%	47	100
TOTAL	755,265		0.163%	0.111%		838	100.00%				

A campaign from the state of Colorado is scored using the model. The performance is much better than random. The best decile (0) is 3 times better (.163%) than the worst decile (.052%) in targeting *actives*.

The lift in the upper deciles is also much lower than in the data from Pennsylvania.

Figure 6.6   Alternate state gains table—Method 1.

Validation Gains Table for Colorado
Method 2

Decile	Records	Cum % of Mailing	Probablility of Active	Percent Active	Cumulative % Active	# of Actives	% of Total Actives	Cum # of Actives	Cum % of Tot Actives	Lift	Cum Lift
0	75,517	10%	0.498%	0.162%	0.162%	122	14.57%	122	14.57%	146	146
1	75,531	20%	0.266%	0.147%	0.154%	111	13.22%	233	27.79%	132	139
2	75,522	30%	0.197%	0.138%	0.149%	104	12.41%	338	40.20%	124	134
3	75,531	40%	0.157%	0.130%	0.144%	98	11.69%	436	51.89%	117	130
4	75,525	50%	0.130%	0.106%	0.137%	80	9.53%	516	61.42%	95	123
5	75,528	60%	0.108%	0.106%	0.131%	80	9.53%	596	70.95%	95	118
6	75,525	70%	0.091%	0.102%	0.127%	77	9.17%	673	80.13%	92	114
7	75,530	80%	0.075%	0.097%	0.123%	73	8.72%	746	88.85%	87	111
8	75,521	90%	0.059%	0.070%	0.118%	53	6.29%	799	95.14%	63	106
9	75,535	100%	0.038%	0.054%	0.111%	41	4.86%	840	100.00%	49	100
TOTAL	755,265		0.162%	0.111%		840	100.00%				

A campaign from the state of Colorado is scored using the model. The performance is much better than random. The best decile (0) is 3 times better (.162%) than the worst decile (.054%) in targeting *actives*.

The gains look much like the results from Method 1.

Figure 6.7   Alternate state gains table—Method 2.

Therefore, in the typical application this type of model would be very efficient in reducing the costs related to entering a new state. The model could be used to score the new state data. The best approach is to mail the top two or three deciles and sample the remaining deciles. Then develop a new model with the results of the campaign.

At this point the Method 1 model and the Method 2 model are running neck and neck. The next section will describe some powerful tools to test the robustness of the models and select a winner.

Resampling

Resampling is a common-sense, nonstatistical technique for estimating and validating models. It provides an empirical estimation (based on experience and observation) instead of a parametric estimation (based on a system or distribution). Consider the basic premise that over-fitting is fitting a model so well that it is picking up irregularities in the data that may be unique to that particular data set. In model development, resampling is commonly used in two ways: (1) it avoids over-fitting by calculating model coefficients or estimates based on repeated sampling; or (2) it detects over-fitting by using repeated samples to validate the results of a model. Because our modeling technique is not prone to over-fitting the data, I will focus on the use of resampling as a validation technique. This allows us to calculate confidence intervals around our estimates.

Two main types of resampling techniques are used in database marketing: jackknifing and bootstrapping. The following discussion and examples highlight and compare the power of these two techniques.

Jackknifing

In its purest form, jackknifing is a resampling technique based on the "leave-one-out" principle. So, if N is the total number of observations in the data set, jackknifing calculates the estimates on $N - 1$ different samples each having $N - 1$ observations. This works well for small data sets. In model development, though, we are dealing with large data sets that can be cumbersome to process. A variation of the jackknifing procedure works well on large data sets. It works on the same principle as leave-one-out. Instead of just one record, it leaves out a group of records. Overall, it gives equal opportunity to every observation in the data set.

In our case study, the model was developed on a 50% random sample, presumed to be representative of the entire campaign data set. A 50% random sample was held out for validation. In this section, I use jackknifing to estimate the predicted probability of active, the actual active rate, and the lift for each decile using 100–99% samples. I will show the code for this process for the Method 1 model. The process will be repeated for the Method 2 model, and the results will be compared.

The program begins with the logistic regression to create an output file (*acqmod.resamp*) that contains only the validation data and a few key variables. Each record is scored with a predicted value (*pred*).

```
proc logistic data=acqmod.model2 descending;
weight splitwgt;
model active =HOM_CUI AGE_COS AGE_SQI INC_SQRT MORTAL1 MORTAL3 HOM_MED
TOA_TAN TOA_CU TOB_LOG INQ_SQRT TOP_LOGI TOP_CU TOP_CUI CRL_LOW RAT_LOG
BRT_MED POPDNSBC APT_INDD SGLE_IND GENDER_D CHILDIND OCC_G NO90DE_D
ACTOPL6D;
output out=acqmod.resamp(where=(splitwgt=.) keep=pred active records
smp_wgt splitwgt) pred=pred;
run;
```

The following code begins a macro that creates 100 jackknife samples. Using a *do* loop, each iteration eliminates 1% of the data. This is repeated 100 times. The ranuni (5555) function with the positive seed (5555) ensures the same random number assignment for each iteration of the *do* loop. The resulting samples each have a different 1% eliminated.

```
%macro jackknif;
%do prcnt = 1 %to 100;
        data acqmod.outk&prcnt;
         set acqmod.resamp;
         if .01*(&prcnt-1) <  ranuni(5555) < .01*(&prcnt) then delete;
    run;
```

The following code is similar to that in chapter 5 for creating deciles. In this case, this process is repeated 100 times to create 100 decile values. The value *&prcnt* increments by 1 during each iteration.

```
proc sort data=acqmod.outk&prcnt;
by descending pred;
run;

proc univariate data=acqmod.outk&prcnt noprint;
weight smp_wgt;
var pred;
output out=preddata sumwgt=sumwgt;
run;

data acqmod.outk&prcnt;
 set acqmod.outk&prcnt;
if (_n_ eq 1) then set preddata;
```

```
retain sumwgt;
number+smp_wgt;
if number < .1*sumwgt then val_dec = 0; else
if number < .2*sumwgt then val_dec = 1; else
if number < .3*sumwgt then val_dec = 2; else
if number < .4*sumwgt then val_dec = 3; else
if number < .5*sumwgt then val_dec = 4; else
if number < .6*sumwgt then val_dec = 5; else
if number < .7*sumwgt then val_dec = 6; else
if number < .8*sumwgt then val_dec = 7; else
if number < .9*sumwgt then val_dec = 8; else
                              val_dec = 9;
run;
```

In proc summary, the average values for active rate (*actmn&samp*) and predicted probability (*prdmn&samp*) are calculated for each decile. This is repeated and incremented 100 times; 100 output data sets (*jkmns&prcnt*) are created with the average values.

```
proc summary data=acqmod.outk&prcnt;
var active pred;
class val_dec;
weight smp_wgt;
output out=acqmod.jkmns&prcnt mean=actmn&prcnt prdmn&prcnt;
run;
```

To calculate the lift for each decile, the value for the overall predicted probability of active and the actual active rate are needed. These are extracted from the output file from proc summary. There is one observation in the output data set where the decile value (*val_dec*) is missing (.). That represents the overall means for each requested variable.

```
data actomean(rename=(actmn&prcnt=actom&prcnt) drop=val_dec);
  set acqmod.jkmns&prcnt(where=(val_dec=.) keep=actmn&prcnt val_dec);
run;
```

The overall values are appended to the data sets and the lifts are calculated.

```
data acqmod.jkmns&prcnt;
  set acqmod.jkmns&prcnt;
if (_n_ eq 1) then set actomean;
retain actom&prcnt;
liftd&prcnt = 100*actmn&prcnt/actom&prcnt;
```

After this process is repeated 100 times, the macro is terminated.

```
%end;
%mend;

%jackknif;
```

The 100 output files are merged together by decile. The values for the mean and standard deviation are calculated for the predicted probability of active, the actual active rate, and the lift. The corresponding confidence intervals are also calculated.

```
data acqmod.jk_sum(keep = prdmjk lci_p uci_p
actmjk lci_a uci_a lftmjk lci_l uci_l val_dec);
 merge
 acqmod.jkmns1 acqmod.jkmns2 acqmod.jkmns3 ............acqmod.jkmns99
acqmod.jkmns100;
by val_dec;
prdmjk  = mean(of prdmn1-prdmn100); /* predicted probability */
prdsdjk =  std(of prdmn1-prdmn100);

actmjk  = mean(of actmn1-actmn100); /* active rate */
actsdjk =  std(of actmn1-actmn100);

lftmjk  = mean(of liftd1-liftd100); /* lift on active rate */
lftsdjk =  std(of liftd1-liftd100);

lci_p   = prdmjk - 1.96*actsdjk; /* confidence itnerval on predicted */
uci_p   = prdmjk + 1.96*actsdjk;

lci_a   = actmjk - 1.96*actsdjk; /* confidence itnerval on actual */
uci_a   = actmjk + 1.96*actsdjk;

lci_l   = lftmjk - 1.96*lftsdjk; /* confidence itnerval on lift */
uci_l   = lftmjk + 1.96*lftsdjk;
run;
```

Proc format and proc tabulate create the gains table for validating the model. Figure 6.8 shows the jackknife estimates, along with the confidence intervals for the predicted probability of active, the actual active rate, and the lift.

```
proc format;
picture perc
        low-high = '009.999%' (mult=1000000);

proc tabulate data=acqmod.jk_sum;
var  prdmjk lci_p uci_p
actmjk lci_a uci_a lftmjk lci_l uci_l;
class val_dec;
table (val_dec='Decile' all='Total'),
(prdmjk='JK Est Prob'*mean=' '*f=perc.
lci_p  ='JK Lower CI Prob'*mean=' '*f=perc.
uci_p  ='JK Upper CI Prob'*mean=' '*f=perc.

actmjk='JK Est % Active'*mean=' '*f=perc.
lci_a  ='JK Lower CI % Active'*mean=' '*f=perc.
uci_a  ='JK Upper CI % Active'*mean=' '*f=perc.
```

Decile	JK Est Prob	JK Lower CI Prob	JK Upper CI Prob	JK Est % Active	JK Lower CI % Active	JK Upper CI % Active	JK Est Lift	JK Lower CI Lift	JK Upper CI Lift
0	4.630%	4.561%	4.700%	4.035%	3.965%	4.105%	277	273	281
1	2.436%	2.384%	2.488%	2.195%	2.143%	2.247%	151	148	154
2	1.748%	1.697%	1.799%	1.930%	1.878%	1.981%	132	129	136
3	1.367%	1.320%	1.415%	1.393%	1.346%	1.440%	96	93	99
4	1.113%	1.069%	1.157%	1.164%	1.120%	1.208%	80	77	83
5	0.923%	0.882%	0.964%	0.865%	0.824%	0.906%	59	57	62
6	0.774%	0.732%	0.817%	1.096%	1.053%	1.138%	75	72	78
7	0.640%	0.613%	0.667%	0.713%	0.686%	0.741%	49	47	51
8	0.511%	0.484%	0.538%	0.576%	0.549%	0.603%	40	38	41
9	0.344%	0.319%	0.369%	0.603%	0.578%	0.628%	41	40	43
Total	1.449%	1.406%	1.491%	1.457%	1.414%	1.500%	100	97	103

The confidence intervals for all the deciles are pretty tight, implying a robust model.

Figure 6.8 Jackknife confidence interval gains table—Method 1.

```
lftmjk='JK Est Lift'*mean=' '*f=6.
lci_l ='JK Lower CI Lift'*mean=' '*f=6.
uci_l ='JK Upper CI Lift'*mean=' '*f=6.)
/rts=6 row=float;
run;
```

Similar processing was performed to create jackknife estimates for the Method 2 model. Figure 6.9 shows very similar results to Method 1. Figure 6.10 compares the upper and lower bounds of the confidence intervals to judge stability. Method 1 appears to provide a smoother lift curve.

Bootstrapping

Similar to jackknifing, bootstrapping is an empirical technique for finding confidence intervals around an estimate. The major difference is that bootstrapping uses full samples of the data that are pulled from the original full sample *with replacement*. In other words, with a sample size of N, N random samples are drawn from the original sample. Because the bootstrap sample is pulled with replacement, it is possible for one observation to be represented several

	JK Est Prob	JK Lower CI Prob	JK Upper CI Prob	JK Est % Active	JK Lower CI % Active	JK Upper CI % Active	JK Est Lift	JK Lower CI Lift	JK Upper CI Lift
Decile									
0	4.689%	4.593%	4.786%	4.082%	3.985%	4.178%	280	274	286
1	2.447%	2.373%	2.522%	2.396%	2.321%	2.470%	164	160	169
2	1.751%	1.708%	1.793%	1.564%	1.522%	1.607%	107	105	110
3	1.358%	1.319%	1.397%	1.564%	1.525%	1.603%	107	105	110
4	1.105%	1.066%	1.144%	1.096%	1.057%	1.135%	75	73	78
5	0.914%	0.871%	0.956%	1.122%	1.079%	1.165%	77	74	80
6	0.760%	0.716%	0.803%	1.212%	1.168%	1.255%	83	80	86
7	0.625%	0.602%	0.647%	0.412%	0.389%	0.434%	28	27	30
8	0.497%	0.472%	0.523%	0.575%	0.550%	0.601%	40	38	41
9	0.336%	0.314%	0.358%	0.548%	0.527%	0.570%	38	36	39
Total	1.448%	1.403%	1.493%	1.457%	1.412%	1.502%	100	97	103

The confidence intervals for all the deciles are slightly larger than the Method 1 model.

Figure 6.9 Jackknife confidence interval gains table—Method 2.

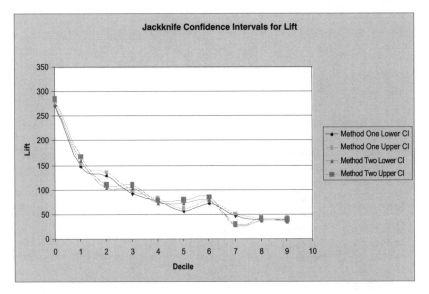

Figure 6.10 Jackknife confidence interval model comparison graph.

times and another observation to be missed completely. This process is repeated many times. Many industry experts consider it a better tool for validation; however, it is more rigorous to perform.

To calculate a bootstrap confidence interval, I must first calculate the bootstrap estimate using the following formula:

$BS_{est} = 2*Sample_{est} - mean(BS_i)$ where BSi = the set of bootstrap estimates from the sample.

In order to calculate a confidence interval, I must derive a standard error for the bootstrap. I use the standard deviation of the set of bootstrap estimates (BSi). A 95% bootstrap confidence intervals is derived using the following formula:

$UCI = BS_{est} + |Z_{.025}| * SE_{BSi}$ $LCI = BS_{est} - |Z_{.025}| * SE_{BSi}$

Due to the large samples in marketing data, it is often impractical and unnecessary to pull the number of samples equal to the number of observations used in the analysis. As I did in the jackknifing example, I will modify the technique. I begin with the same output sample that I used in the jackknifing example (**acq-mod.resamp**). The first few steps create decile values on the whole validation data set. This is similar to the decile analysis I created in chapter 5.

```
proc sort data=acqmod.resamp;
by descending pred;
run;

proc univariate data=acqmod.resamp noprint;
weight smp_wgt;
var pred active;
output out=preddata sumwgt=sumwgt mean= predmean actmean;
run;

data acqmod.resamp;
 set acqmod.resamp;
if (_n_ eq 1) then set preddata;
retain sumwgt predmean actmean;
number+smp_wgt;
if number < .1*sumwgt then val_dec = 0; else
if number < .2*sumwgt then val_dec = 1; else
if number < .3*sumwgt then val_dec = 2; else
if number < .4*sumwgt then val_dec = 3; else
if number < .5*sumwgt then val_dec = 4; else
if number < .6*sumwgt then val_dec = 5; else
if number < .7*sumwgt then val_dec = 6; else
if number < .8*sumwgt then val_dec = 7; else
if number < .9*sumwgt then val_dec = 8; else
val_dec = 9;
run;
```

Using the decile values as class values, proc summary calculates the overall mean for the active rate and the predicted probability for each decile. These values are used in the final bootstrap calculation.

```
proc summary data=acqmod.resamp;
var active  pred smp_wgt;
class val_dec;
weight smp_wgt;
output out=acqmod.fullmean mean=actmnf prdmnf;
run;
```

The next two steps grab the overall mean from the data set *acqmod.fullmean* and attach it to every record in *acmod.fullmean*. This will be used in the final lift calculation.

```
data actfmean(rename=(actmnf=actomn_g) drop=val_dec);
 set acqmod.fullmean(where=(val_dec=.) keep=actmnf val_dec);
run;

data acqmod.fullmean;
 set acqmod.fullmean;
if (_n_ eq 1) then set actfmean;
retain actomn_g;
run;
```

Now I begin the bootstrap resampling process. This program is designed to pull 1/100th of the file and repeat this process 100 times *with replacement.* This creates one bootstrap sample. This can be repeated hundreds of times. In practice, though, it is unusual to find value in pulling more than 25 bootstrap samples.

The program is designed to have one macro that repeats the entire process 25 times. This process will be described in detail as we go through the code. The second macro is embedded in the beginning of the first macro. This embedded macro pulls the 1/100th samples using a ranuni (–1) function. The negative seed (-1) uses the time of day to assign the random values to each observation. This ensures that each sample is independent of the prior sample or samples that have been pulled. Each of the 100 iterations is pulled from **acqmod.resamp**, implying full replacement of the prior sample.

```
%macro bootst25;
%do samp = 1 %to 25;

%macro bootstrp;
%do prcnt = 1 %to 100;
        data acqmod.modbs&prcnt;
         set acqmod.resamp;
        if .01*(&prcnt-1) <  ranuni(-1) < .01*(&prcnt) then output
         acqmod.modbs&prcnt;
run;
```

```
%end;
%mend;

%bootstrp
```

The next step combines the 100 - 1/100th samples to create the first bootstrap sample.

```
data acqmod.allbs&samp;
set
  acqmod.modbs1 acqmod.modbs2 acqmod.modbs3 ... acqmod.modbs100;
run;
```

The next few steps create the deciles (*val_dec*) for each of the 25 bootstrap samples.

```
proc sort data=acqmod.allbs&samp;
by descending pred;
run;

proc univariate data=acqmod.allbs&samp noprint;
weight smp_wgt;
var pred;
output out=preddata sumwgt=sumwgt;
run;

data acqmod.allbs&samp;
 set acqmod.allbs&samp;
if (_n_ eq 1) then set preddata;
retain sumwgt;
number+smp_wgt;
if number < .1*sumwgt then val_dec = 0; else
if number < .2*sumwgt then val_dec = 1; else
if number < .3*sumwgt then val_dec = 2; else
if number < .4*sumwgt then val_dec = 3; else
if number < .5*sumwgt then val_dec = 4; else
if number < .6*sumwgt then val_dec = 5; else
if number < .7*sumwgt then val_dec = 6; else
if number < .8*sumwgt then val_dec = 7; else
if number < .9*sumwgt then val_dec = 8; else
                          val_dec = 9;
run;
```

As in the jackknife example, the average values for the active rate (*actmn&samp*) and predicted probability (*prdmn&samp*) are calculated using proc summary.

```
proc summary data=acqmod.allbs&samp;
var active  pred smp_wgt;
class val_dec;
```

```
weight smp_wgt;
output out=acqmod.bsmns&samp mean=actmn&samp prdmn&samp;
run;
```

The following code pulls the overall mean for each sample *(where= (val_dec=.))* and renames it *(actomn&samp)* to designate that it is the overall mean for the sample.

```
data actomean(rename=(actmn&samp=actomn&samp) drop=val_dec);
 set acqmod.bsmns&samp(where=(val_dec=.) keep=actmn&samp val_dec);
run;
```

The overall mean is then appended to each bootstrap sample to create the lift value *(liftd&samp)* for each bootstrap sample. At this point, I have created all the values for which I want confidence intervals. The *bootst25* macro iterates 25 times to create the 25 bootstrap samples.

```
data acqmod.bsmns&samp;
 set acqmod.bsmns&samp;
if (_n_ eq 1) then set actomean;
retain actomn&samp;
liftd&samp = 100*actmn&samp/actomn&samp;
run;

%end;
%mend;

%bootst25
```

At this point, the macro processing is finished, and we have our 25 bootstrap samples. The following code combines the 25 bootstrap samples with the data set containing the values for the original validation sample (acqmod.fullmean) using the decile value. It then calculates the mean and standard deviation for each estimate: active rate, predicted probability, and lift. Following the formula for bootstrap coefficients, it concludes with calculations for the bootstrap estimates and confidence intervals for the three estimates.

```
data acqmod.bs_sum(keep = liftf bsest_p prdmnf lci_p uci_p bsest_a
actmnf
lci_a uci_a bsest_l lftmbs lci_l uci_l val_dec actomn_g);
 merge  acqmod.bsmns1 acqmod.bsmns2 acqmod.bsmns3
.............................acqmod.bsmns24
        acqmod.bsmns25 acqmod.fullmean;
by val_dec;
prdmbs  = mean(of prdmn1-prdmn25);
prdsdbs =  std(of prdmn1-prdmn25);

actmbs  = mean(of actmn1-actmn25);
actsdbs =  std(of actmn1-actmn25);
```

```
lftmbs  = mean(of liftd1-liftd25);
lftsdbs =  std(of liftd1-liftd25);


liftf   = 100*actmnf/actomn_g;

bsest_p = 2*prdmnf - prdmbs;
lci_p   = bsest_p - 1.96*actsdbs;
uci_p   = bsest_p + 1.96*actsdbs;


bsest_a = 2*actmnf - actmbs;
lci_a   = bsest_a - 1.96*actsdbs;
uci_a   = bsest_a + 1.96*actsdbs;


bsest_l = 2*liftf - lftmbs;
lci_l   = bsest_l - 1.96*lftsdbs;
uci_l   = bsest_l + 1.96*lftsdbs;
run;
```

Finally, the code that follows produces the gains table seen in Figure 6.11. The results are very similar to the results seen using the jackknifing technique. The range of values around all the estimates are fairly close, indicating a robust model.

```
proc format;
picture perc
        low-high = '09.999%' (mult=1000000);

proc tabulate data=acqmod.bs_sum;
var liftf bsest_p prdmnf lci_p uci_p bsest_a actmnf
lci_a uci_a bsest_l lftmbs lci_l uci_l;
class val_dec;
table (val_dec='Decile' all='Total'),
(prdmnf='Actual Prob'*mean=' '*f=perc.
bsest_p='BS Est Prob'*mean=' '*f=perc.
lci_p  ='BS Lower CI Prob'*mean=' '*f=perc.
uci_p  ='BS Upper CI Prob'*mean=' '*f=perc.

actmnf ='Percent Active'*mean=' '*f=perc.
bsest_a='BS Est % Active'*mean=' '*f=perc.
lci_a  ='BS Lower CI % Active'*mean=' '*f=perc.
uci_a  ='BS Upper CI % Active'*mean=' '*f=perc.

liftf ='Lift'*mean=' '*f=4.
bsest_l='BS Est Lift'*mean=' '*f=4.
lci_l  ='BS Lower CI Lift'*mean=' '*f=4.
uci_l  ='BS Upper CI Lift'*mean=' '*f=4.)
/rts=6 row=float;
run;
```

These confidence intervals appear to be much looser than the jackknife intervals.

Decile	Actual Prob	BS Est Prob	BS Lower CI Prob	BS Upper CI Prob	Percent Active	BS Est % Active	BS Lower CI % Active	BS Upper CI % Active	Lift	BS Est Lift	BS Lower CI Lift	BS Upper CI Lift
0	4.631%	4.641%	3.934%	5.347%	4.036%	4.101%	3.395%	4.807%	277	280	244	316
1	2.436%	2.435%	2.065%	2.806%	2.196%	2.182%	1.812%	2.552%	151	149	124	174
2	1.748%	1.748%	1.326%	2.171%	1.920%	1.977%	1.554%	2.400%	132	135	108	161
3	1.367%	1.367%	1.066%	1.668%	1.399%	1.395%	1.094%	1.696%	96	95	73	117
4	1.113%	1.113%	0.827%	1.398%	1.152%	1.177%	0.892%	1.462%	79	80	60	100
5	0.923%	0.923%	0.648%	1.199%	0.878%	0.897%	0.621%	1.173%	60	61	43	79
6	0.774%	0.774%	0.482%	1.066%	1.098%	1.067%	0.775%	1.360%	75	73	53	92
7	0.640%	0.640%	0.338%	0.942%	0.713%	0.717%	0.415%	1.019%	49	49	30	68
8	0.511%	0.511%	0.326%	0.695%	0.576%	0.565%	0.381%	0.749%	40	38	25	52
9	0.344%	0.343%	0.137%	0.550%	0.603%	0.590%	0.383%	0.796%	41	40	25	55
Total	1.449%	1.450%	1.115%	1.784%	1.457%	1.467%	1.132%	1.801%	100	100	79	121

Figure 6.11 Bootstrap confidence interval gains table—Method 1.

In Figure 6.12, the bootstrapping gains table on the Method 2 model shows the same irregularities as the jackknifing showed. In Figure 6.13, the instability of the Method 2 model is very visible. As we continue with our case study, I select the Method 1 model as the winner and proceed with further validation.

Adjusting the Bootstrap Sample for a Larger File

Confidence intervals will vary by sample size. If you are planning to calculate estimates and confidence intervals for evaluation on a file larger than your current sample, this can be accomplished by adjusting the size of the bootstrap. For example, if you have a sample of 50,000 names and you are interested in finding confidence intervals for a file with 75,000 names, you can pull 150 – 1/100th samples. This would give you a bootstrap sample of 75,000. Repeat this 25+ times for a robust estimate on the larger file.

Decile Analysis on Key Variables

The modeling techniques discussed up till now are great for selecting the best names to offer. But this is not always enough. In many industries there is a need for managers to know what factors are driving the models. Hence, many of these techniques are given the label "black box." This is a fair criticism. It probably would have succeeded in suppressing the use of models if not for one reason—they work! Their success lies in their ability to quantify and balance so many factors simultaneously.

We are still, however, stuck with a model that is difficult to interpret. First of all, a unit change in the coefficient is interpreted in the log of the odds. That might be meaningful if the model had only a couple of variables. Today's models, however, are not designed to interpret the coefficients; they are designed to predict behavior to assist in marketing selections. So I need to employ other techniques to uncover key drivers.

Because many marketers know the key drivers in their markets, one way to show that the model is attracting the usual crowd is to do a decile analysis on key variables. The following code creates a gains table on some key variables. (Each variable is in numeric form.)

```
proc tabulate data=acqmod.var_anal;
weight smp_wgt;
class val_dec ;
var infd_ag2 mortin1n mortin2n gender_d apt_indn credlin2
```

Decile	Actual Prob	BS Est Prob	BS Lower CI Prob	BS Upper CI Prob	Percent Active	BS Est % Active	BS Lower CI % Active	BS Upper CI % Active	Lift	BS Est Lift	BS Lower CI Lift	BS Upper CI Lift
0	4.689%	4.757%	4.051%	5.464%	4.062%	4.154%	3.447%	4.860%	279	284	248	319
1	2.447%	2.458%	2.088%	2.828%	2.415%	2.621%	2.251%	2.992%	166	179	154	204
2	1.751%	1.753%	1.330%	2.176%	1.564%	1.264%	0.841%	1.687%	107	86	59	113
3	1.358%	1.349%	1.048%	1.650%	1.564%	1.725%	1.423%	2.026%	107	118	96	139
4	1.105%	1.097%	0.812%	1.383%	1.097%	1.067%	0.781%	1.352%	75	73	53	93
5	0.914%	0.904%	0.629%	1.180%	1.125%	1.391%	1.116%	1.667%	77	95	77	113
6	0.760%	0.745%	0.453%	1.037%	1.207%	1.286%	0.994%	1.578%	83	88	68	107
7	0.625%	0.609%	0.307%	0.911%	0.411%	0.113%	0.188%	0.415%	28	8	-11	27
8	0.497%	0.484%	0.299%	0.668%	0.576%	0.565%	0.381%	0.749%	40	38	25	52
9	0.336%	0.328%	0.122%	0.535%	0.548%	0.480%	0.274%	0.687%	38	33	18	48
Total	1.448%	1.448%	1.114%	1.783%	1.457%	1.467%	1.132%	1.801%	100	100	79	121

The confidence intervals for Method 2 appear to be as loose as those in Method 1. They are not monotonically decreasing.

Figure 6.12 Bootstrap confidence interval gains table—Method 2.

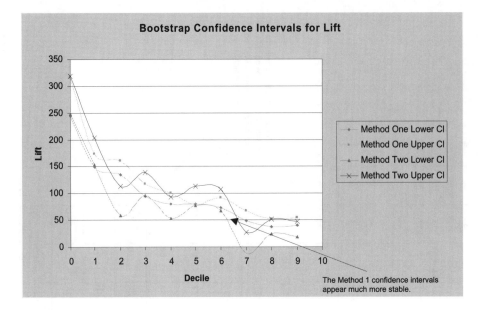

Figure 6.13 Bootstrap confidence interval model comparison graph.

```
inc_est2 tot_bal2 tot_acc2 amtpdue sgle_ind
table val_dec=' ' all='Total',
        infd_ag2='Infrd Age'*mean=' '*f=6.1
        inc_est3='Est Income (000)'*mean=' '*f=dollar6.1
        amtpdue='Amount Past Due'*mean=' '*f=dollar6.1
        credlin2='Average Credit Line'*mean=' '*f=dollar10.1
        tot_bal2='Average Total Balance'*mean=' '*f=dollar10.1
        tot_acc2='Average Total Accounts'*mean=' '*f=9.1
        mortin1n='% 1st Mort'*pctsum<val_dec all>=' '*f=7.2
        mortin2n='% 2nd Mort'*pctsum<val_dec all>=' '*f=7.2
        sgle_ind='% Single'*pctsum<val_dec all>=' '*f=7.2
        gender_d='% Male'*pctsum<val_dec all>=' '*f=7.2
        apt_indn='% in  Apart  -ment'*pctsum<val_dec all>=' '*f=7.2
/rts = 10 row=float box='    Decile';
run;
```

The resulting gains table in Figure 6.14 displays the trends for key variables across deciles. Inferred age is displayed as an average value per decile. It is clear that the younger prospects have a higher likelihood of becoming active. Financial trends can be seen in the next four columns. The remaining variables show the percentages of a given condition. For first mortgage indicator, the percent with a first mortgage is higher in the lower deciles. This is also true for the second mortgage indicator. The final three columns show the percentage of males, singles, and apartment dwellers. Each of these characteristics is positively correlated with response. By creating this type of table with key model

Decile	Infrd Age	Est Income (000)	Amount Past Due	Average Credit Line	Average Total Balance	Average Total Accounts	% 1st Mort	% 2nd Mort	% Single	% Male	% in Apartment
0	35.5	$40	$27	$53,579	$33,767	15.7	38.99	20.83	34.46	14.30	25.27
1	38.5	$46	$36	$84,213	$58,105	17.3	24.33	17.13	21.90	12.17	17.95
2	40.8	$52	$9	$118,895	$86,452	18.7	15.02	14.48	13.57	12.21	13.72
3	42.2	$57	$7	$151,606	$113,043	20.3	8.38	11.74	9.43	11.72	10.82
4	43.3	$61	$7	$171,098	$128,245	20.6	5.31	9.41	6.89	10.89	8.48
5	44.1	$66	$10	$202,013	$154,062	21.3	3.37	8.19	4.56	10.33	7.50
6	45.1	$68	$11	$211,646	$159,034	21.3	1.97	6.58	3.63	9.22	5.47
7	45.9	$72	$7	$228,706	$172,163	21.7	1.57	5.38	2.69	8.40	4.50
8	46.3	$74	$4	$241,922	$180,883	21.5	0.69	3.89	1.61	6.61	3.71
9	46.4	$77	$5	$259,638	$194,982	21.3	0.37	2.36	1.26	4.14	2.58
Total	42.8	$61	$12	$172,334	$128,076	20.0	100.00	100.00	100.00	100.00	100.00

Figure 6.14 Key variable validation gains table.

drivers, you can verify that the prospects in the best deciles resemble your typical best prospects.

Summary

In this chapter, we learned some common-sense methods for validating a model. The reason for their success is simple. Rather than explain a relationship, the models assign probabilities and rank prospects, customers, or any other group on their likelihood of taking a specific action. The best validation techniques simply attempt to simulate the rigors of actual implementation through the use of alternate data sets, resampling, and variable decile analysis. Through these methods, we've concluded that Method 1 produced a more stable model. Now that we're satisfied with the finished product, let's explore ways to put the models in practice.

CHAPTER 7

Implementing and Maintaining the Model

O ur masterpiece survived the taste tests! Now we must make sure it is served in style.

Even though I have worked diligently to create the best possible model, the results can be disastrous if the model is not implemented correctly. In this chapter, I discuss the steps for automated and manual scoring, including auditing techniques. Next, I describe a variety of name selection scenarios that are geared toward specific goals like maximizing profits, optimizing marketing efficiency or capturing market share. And finally, I describe some methods for model tracking and troubleshooting. These are all designed to keep your data kitchen in good order!

Scoring a New File

A model is generally designed to score a new data set with the goal of improving the name selection for a new campaign. This is typically done in one of two ways: The data set is brought in-house to be scored, or the scoring algorithm is sent out for scoring by the data vendor or service bureau. In either case, you need to ensure that the data being scored is similar to the data on which the model was developed by performing prescoring validation. If the new data is from the same source as the model development data, the characteristics should be very similar. If the new names are from a different source, it may be necessary to factor in those differences when projecting the model performance. They both, however, warrant scrutiny to ensure the best results.

Scoring In-house

As I demonstrated in chapter 6, the PROC LOGISTIC technique in SAS provides an option that creates a data set containing the coefficients and other critical information for scoring a new data set. Using PROC SCORE, it simply matches the file containing the scoring algorithm to the file needing to be scored. This can be done only after the new data set is read into SAS and processed to create the final variables to be scored.

Data Validation

Recall how I scored data from an alternate state using the one-step model developed in our case study. Because the data was from the same campaign, I knew the variables were created from the same source. We therefore knew that any differences in characteristics were due to geography.

Similarly, a model implemented on data from the same source as the model development data should have similar characteristics and produce similar scores. These differences are quantified using descriptive statistics, as shown in the alternate state case in chapter 6. Although it is not usually the intention, it is not uncommon for a model to be developed on data from one source and to be used to score data from another source. In either case, key drivers can be identified and quantified to manage model performance expectations:

Population or market changes. These are the most common causes of shifting characteristic values and scores. These changes affect all types and sources of data. The fast-growing industries are most vulnerable due to rapid market changes. This has been apparent in the credit card industry over the last 10 years, with huge shifts in average debt and risk profiles. Newer competitive industries like telecom and utilities will experience rapid shifts in market characteristics and behavior.

Different selection criteria. As I discussed in chapter 2, model development data typically is extracted from a prior campaign. The selection criteria for this prior campaign may or may not have been designed for future model development. In either case, there is often a set of selection criteria that is business-based. In other words, certain rules, perhaps unrelated to the goal of the model, are used for name selection and extraction. For example, a life insurance product may not be approved for someone under age 18. Or a certain product may be appropriate only for adults with children. Banks often have rules about not offering loan products to anyone who has a bankruptcy on his or her credit report. In each of these cases, certain groups would be excluded from the file and by default be ineligible for model development. Therefore, it is important to either match the selection criteria in scoring or account for the differences.

Variation in data creation. This is an issue only when scoring data from a different source than that of the model development data. For example, let's say a model is developed using one list source, and the main characteristics used in the model are *age* and *gender*. You might think that another file with the same characteristics and selection criteria would produce similar scores, but this is often not the case because the way the characteristic values are gathered may vary greatly. Let's look at *age*. It can be self-reported. You can just imagine the bias that might come from that. Or it can be taken from motor vehicle records, which are pretty accurate sources. But it's not available in all states. Age is also estimated using other age-sensitive characteristics such as graduation year or age of credit bureau file. These estimates make certain assumptions that may or may not be accurate. Finally, many sources provide data cleansing. The missing value substitution methodology alone can create great variation in the values.

Market or Population Changes

Now we've seen some ways in which changes can occur in data. In chapter 6, I scored data from an alternate state and saw a considerable degradation in the model performance. A simple way to determine what is causing the difference is to do some exploratory data analysis on the model variables. We will look at a numeric form of the base values rather than the transformed values to see where the differences lie. The base variables in the model are home equity (*hom_equ*), inferred age (*infd_age*), credit line (*credlin*), estimated income (*inc_est*), first mortgage indicator (*mortin1n*), second mortgage indicator (*mortin2n*), total open credit accounts (*totopac*), total credit accounts (*tot_acc*), total credit balances (*tot_bal*), population density (*popdensbc*), apartment indicator (*apt_indd*), single indicator (*sgle_ind*), gender (*gender_d*), child indicator, (*childind*), occupational group (*occu_g*), number of 90-day delinquencies (*no90de_e*), and accounts open in the last six months (*actopl6d*). (For some categorical variables, I analyze the binary form that went into the model.) The following code creates a comparative nonweighted means for the New York campaign (the data on which the model was developed) and the more recent Colorado campaign:

```
proc means data=acqmod.model2 maxdec=2;
VAR INFD_AG CREDLIN HOM_EQU INC_EST MORTIN1N MORTIN2N TOTOPAC TOT_ACC
TOT_BAL POPDNSBC APT_INDD SGLE_IND GENDER_D CHILDIND OCC_G NO90DE_D
ACTOPL6D;
run;
```

```
proc means data=acqmod.colorad2 maxdec=2;
VAR INFD_AG CREDLIN HOM_EQU INC_EST MORTIN1N MORTIN2N TOTOPAC TOT_ACC
TOT_BAL POPDNSBC APT_INDD SGLE_IND GENDER_D CHILDIND OCC_G NO90DE_D
ACTOPL6D;
run;
```

In Figures 7.1 and 7.2, we compare the values for each variable. We see that there are some large variations in mean values and maximum values. The *average credit line* is almost 50% higher in New York. The *home equity values* are over 300% higher for New York. And *total credit balances* are twice as high in New York. These differences would account for the differences in the model scores.

Different Selection Criteria

To determine if name selects have been done properly, it would be necessary to look at a similar analysis and check ranges. For example, if we knew that the name selects for Colorado should have been between 25 and 65, it is easy to check this on the means analysis.

Variable	N	Mean	Std Dev	Minimum	Maximum
INFD_AG	85404	42.62	9.35	25.00	65.00
CREDLIN	85404	169154.91	197662.57	0.00	9250120.00
HOM_EQU	85404	149520.96	2005772.10	0.00	73741824.00
INC_EST	85320	60.57	27.53	16.00	321.00
MORTIN1N	85404	0.12	0.33	0.00	1.00
MORTIN2N	85404	0.25	0.44	0.00	1.00
TOTOPAC	85404	12.55	7.01	1.00	63.00
TOT_ACC	85404	20.01	11.21	1.00	87.00
TOT_BAL	85404	125243.88	169626.22	0.00	5544774.00
POPDNSBC	85404	0.74	0.44	0.00	1.00
APT_INDD	85404	0.19	0.39	0.00	1.00
SGLE_IND	85404	0.15	0.36	0.00	1.00
GENDER_D	85404	0.44	0.50	0.00	1.00
CHILDIND	85404	0.20	0.40	0.00	1.00
OCC_G	85404	0.97	0.18	0.00	1.00
NO90DE_D	85404	0.03	0.18	0.00	1.00
ACTOPL6D	85404	0.70	0.46	0.00	1.00

Figure 7.1 Means analysis of model variables for New York.

Variable	N	Mean	Std Dev	Minimum	Maximum
INFD_AG	80265	44.85	10.48	25.00	65.00
CREDLIN	80265	102739.26	110578.06	0.00	5029397.00
HOM_EQU	80265	35034.41	49402.53	0.00	2010880.00
INC_EST	80265	50.50	19.73	0.00	251.00
MORTIN1N	80265	0.31	0.46	0.00	1.00
MORTIN2N	80265	0.73	0.45	0.00	1.00
TOTOPAC	80265	11.65	7.12	1.00	94.00
TOT_ACC	80265	18.90	11.61	1.00	131.00
TOT_BAL	80265	68715.99	91276.83	0.00	4695637.00
POPDNSBC	80265	0.92	0.28	0.00	1.00
APT_INDD	80265	0.13	0.34	0.00	1.00
SGLE_IND	80265	0.12	0.33	0.00	1.00
GENDER_D	80265	0.43	0.50	0.00	1.00
CHILDIND	80265	0.20	0.40	0.00	1.00
OCC_G	80265	0.96	0.20	0.00	1.00
NO90DE_D	80265	0.05	0.22	0.00	1.00
ACTOPL6D	80265	0.76	0.43	0.00	1.00

Figure 7.2 Means analysis of model variables for Colorado.

Variation in Data Sources

This is the toughest type of discrepancy to uncover. It requires researching the source of each variable or characteristic and understanding how it is created. If you are combining data from many sources on an ongoing basis, doing this research is worthwhile. You need to make sure the measurements are consistent. For example, let's say the variable, presence of children, turns out to be predictive from one data source. When you get the same variable from another data source, though, it has no predictive power. If may be a function of how that variable was derived. One source may use census data, and another source may use files from a publishing house that sells children's magazines. There will always be some variations from different sources. The key is to know how much and plan accordingly.

Outside Scoring and Auditing

It is often the case that a model is developed in-house and sent to the data vendor or service bureau for scoring. This requires that the data processing code (including all the variable transformations) be processed off-site. In this situation, it is advisable to get some distribution analysis from the data provider. This will give you an idea of how well the data fits the model. In some cases, the data processing and scoring algorithm may have to be translated into a different language. This is when a score audit is essential.

A score audit is a simple exercise to validate that the scores have been applied correctly. Let's say that I am sending the data processing code and scoring algorithm to a service bureau. And I know that once it gets there it is translated into another language to run on a mainframe. Our goal is to make sure the coding translation has been done correctly. First I rewrite the code so that it does not contain any extraneous information. The following code highlights what I send:

```
******* CAPPING OUTLIERS ******;
%macro cap(var, svar);
proc univariate data=acqmod.audit noprint;
var &var;
output out=&svar.data std=&svar.std pctlpts= 99 pctlpre=&svar;
run;

data acqmod.audit;
 set acqmod.audit;
if (_n_ eq 1) then set &svar.data(keep= &svar.std &svar.99);
if &svar.std > 2*&svar.99 then &var.2 = min(&var,(4*&svar.99)); else
&var.2 = &var;
run;

%mend;
%cap(infd_ag, age)
%cap(tot_acc, toa)
%cap(hom_equ, hom)
%cap(actop16, acp)
%cap(tot_bal, tob)
%cap(inq16m,  inq)
%cap(totopac, top)
%cap(credlin, crl)
%cap(age_fil, aof)
```

This capping rule works only for variables with nonnegative values. With a slight adjustment, it can work for all values. Also, please note that as a result of the capping macro, each continuous variable has a '2' at the end of the variable name.

```
********* DATES *********;
data acqmod.audit;
 set acqmod.audit;
opd_bcd3 = mdy(substr(opd_bcd2,5,2),'01',substr(opd_bcd2,1,4));
fix_dat = mdy('12','01','1999');
```

```
if opd_bcd3 => '190000' then
bal_rat = tot_bal2/((fix_dat - opd_bcd3)/30);
else bal_rat = 0;
run;
```

The following code creates the variable transformations for *inferred age (infd_ag)*. This step is repeated for all continuous variables in the model. PROC UNIVARIATE creates the decile value (age10) needed for the binary form of age. *Age_cos* and *age_sqi* are also created. They are output into a data set called **acqmod.agedset**;

```
************* INFERRED AGE *************;

data acqmod.agedset;
set acqmod.audit(keep=pros_id infd_ag2);
age_cos  = cos(infd_ag2);
age_sqi  = 1/max(.0001,infd_ag2**2);
run;
```

Now I sort each data set containing each continuous variable and its transformations.

```
%macro srt(svar);
proc sort data = acqmod.&svar.dset;
by pros_id;
run;
%mend;
%srt(age)
%srt(inc)
%srt(hom)
%srt(toa)
%srt(tob)
%srt(inq)
%srt(top)
%srt(crl)
%srt(brt)

proc sort data = acqmod.audit;
by pros_id;
run;
```

Finally, I merge each data set containing the transformations back together with the original data set (*acqmod.audit*) to create **acqmod.audit2**:

```
data acqmod.audit2;
merge
acqmod.audit
acqmod.agedset(keep = pros_id age_cos age_sqi)
acqmod.incdset(keep = pros_id inc_sqrt)
acqmod.homdset(keep = pros_id hom_cui hom_med)
```

```
acqmod.toadset(keep = pros_id toa_tan toa_cu)
acqmod.tobdset(keep = pros_id tob_log)
acqmod.inqdset(keep = pros_id inq_sqrt)
acqmod.topdset(keep = pros_id top_logi top_cu top_cui)
acqmod.crldset(keep = pros_id crl_low)
acqmod.brtdset(keep = pros_id brt_med brt_log);
by pros_id;
run;
```

The final portion of the code is the scoring algorithm that calculates the predicted values (pres_scr). It begins by calculating the sum of the estimates (sum_est). It is then put into the logistic equation to calculate the probability:

```
data acqmod.audit2;
  set acqmod.audit2;
estimate = -7.65976
        -    0.000034026 * hom_cui
        -        0.18209 * age_cos
        +        372.299 * age_sqi
        -        0.20938 * inc_sqrt
        +        0.32729 * mortal1
        +        0.62568 * mortal3
        +        0.30335 * hom_med
        +      0.0023379 * toa_tan
        +  0.0000096308 * toa_cu
        +       0.040987 * tob_log
        +        0.11823 * inq_sqrt
        +     0.00031204 * top_logi
        -    0.000024588 * top_cu
        -        3.41194 * top_cui
        +        0.63959 * crl_low
        +        0.14747 * brt_log
        -        0.30808 * brt_med
        -        0.25937 * popdnsbc
        +        0.13769 * apt_indd
        +         0.4890 * sgle_ind
        +        0.39401 * gender_d
        -        0.47305 * childind
        +        0.60437 * occ_g
        +        0.68165 * no90de_d
        -        0.16514 * actopl6d;
pred_scr = exp(estimate)/(1+exp(estimate));
smp_wgt = 1;
run;
```

Once the service bureau has scored the file, your task is to make sure it was scored correctly. The first step is to request from the service bureau a random sample of the scored names along with the scores they calculated and all of the necessary attributes or variable values. I usually request about 5,000 records. This allows for some analysis of expected performance. It is important to get a random sample instead of the first 5,000 records. There is usually some order in the way a file is arranged, so a random sample removes the chance of any bias.

Once the file arrives, the first task is to read the file and calculate your own scores. Then for each record you must compare the score that you calculate to the score that the service bureau sent you. The following code reads in the data:

```
libname acqmod 'c:\insur\acquisit\modeldata';


data acqmod.test;
infile 'F:\insur\acquisit\audit.txt' missover recl=72;
input
pop_den    $ 1               /*population density*/
apt_ind    $ 2               /*apartment indicator*/
inc_est      3-6             /*estimated income in dollars*/
sngl_in    $ 7               /*marital status = single*/
opd_bcd    $ 8-13            /*bankcard open date*/
occu_cd    $ 14              /*occupation code*/
gender     $ 15              /*gender*/
mortin1    $ 16              /*presence of first mortgage*/
mortin2    $ 17              /*presence of second mortgage*/
infd_ag      18-19           /*inferred age*/
homeq_r    $ 21              /*home equity range*/
hom_equ    $ 22-29           /*home equity*/
childin    $ 30              /*presence of child indicator*/
tot_acc      31-33           /*total credit accounts*/
actopl6      34-36           /*# accts open in last 6 mos*/
credlin      37-43           /*total credit lines*/
tot_bal      44-50           /*total credit card balances*/
inql6mo      51-53           /*# credit inquiry last 6 months*/
age_fil      54-56           /*age of file*/
totopac      57-59           /*total open credit accounts*/
no90eve      60-62           /*number 90 day late ever*/
sumbetas     63-67           /*sum of betas*/
score        68-72           /*predicted value*/
;
run;
```

The code to create the variable transformations and score the file is identical to the previous code and won't be repeated here. One additional variable is created that compares the difference in scores (*error*). Once I have read in the data and scored the new file, I test the accuracy using proc means:

```
data acqmod.test;
 set acqmod.test;
estimate =  -7.65976
       -  0.000034026 * hom_cui
                 |     |     |
                 |     |     |
       -       0.16514 * actopl6d
;
```

```
pred_scr = exp(estimate)/(1+exp(estimate));
error = score - pred_scr;
run;

proc means data = acqmod.test;
var error;
run;
```

Figure 7.3 shows the average amount of error or difference in the scores calculated at the service bureau and the scores calculated in our code. Because the error is greater than .0001, I know the error is not due to rounding. A simple way to figure out the source of the error is to create a variable that identifies those records with the large error. Then I can run a regression and see which variables are correlated with the error.

In Figure 7.3 we see that the maximum error is .3549141. This indicates that there is a problem with the code. One simple way to determine which variable or variables are the culprits is to run a regression with the error as the dependent variable. The following code runs a stepwise regression with one step.

```
proc reg data= acqmod.test;
model error=  hom_cui age_cos age_sqi inq_sqrt mortal1 mortal3 hom_med
toa_tan toa_cu tob_log top_logi top_cu top_cui crl_low rat_log
brt_med popdnsbc apt_indd sgle_ind gender_d childind occ_g no90de_d
actopl6d/
selection = maxr stop=1;
run;
```

We see from the output in Figure 7.4 that the variable *gender_d* is highly correlated with the error. After a discussion with the service bureau, I discover that the coefficient for the variable, *gender_d* had been coded incorrectly. This error is corrected, another sample file is provided, and the process is repeated until

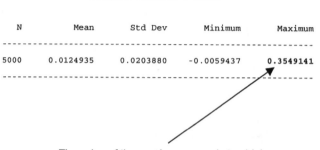

```
                Analysis Variable : ERROR

        N        Mean       Std Dev      Minimum      Maximum
     --------------------------------------------------------------
       5000    0.0124935    0.0203880   -0.0059437    0.3549141
     --------------------------------------------------------------
```

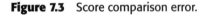

The value of the maximum error is too high.

Figure 7.3 Score comparison error.

```
                  Maximum R-square Improvement for Dependent Variable ERROR


Step 1   Variable GENDER_D Entered  R-square = 0.41341192   C(p) =2718.0450781


                         DF      Sum of Squares      Mean Square         F   Prob>F


          Regression      1          0.85904726       0.85904726   3522.46   0.0001
          Error        4998          1.21889781       0.00024388
          Total        4999          2.07794507


                     Parameter         Standard          Type II
          Variable    Estimate            Error   Sum of Squares         F   Prob>F


          INTERCEP  -0.00057222       0.00031183       0.00082120      3.37   0.0666
          GENDER_D   0.02621536       0.00044171       0.85904726   3522.46   0.0001
Bounds on condition number:            1,            1
------------------------------------------------------------------------------------------


The above model is the best  1-variable model found.
```

Figure 7.4   Regression on error.

the maximum error rate is less than .0001. (The minimum error rate must also be greater than -.0001.)

Implementing the Model

We have done a lot of work to get to this point. Now we have an opportunity to see the financial impact of our efforts. This stage is very rewarding because we can relate the results of our work to the bottom line. And management will definitely notice!

Calculating the Financials

Recall that in chapter 4 I defined net present value (NPV) as the value in today's dollars of future profits for a life insurance campaign. When averaged over a group of prospects, it might also be considered the lifetime value. However, we are not considering future sales at this stage. That model is developed in chapter 12. So I will use the term average net present value to differentiate it from the lifetime value model in chapter 12.

 The average NPV consists of four major components: the probability of activation, the risk index, the net present value of the product profitability, and the marketing expense. (These are defined in detail in chapter 4.) They are combined as follows::

Average Net Present Value = P(Activation) × Risk Index × NPV of Product Profitability – Marketing Expense

The probability of activation comes directly from our model. The risk index uses the values from Table 4.1. Table 7.1 shows how the NPV of the 3-year product profitability is derived. Gross profit is revenues minus costs. Net present value of profits is gross profit divided by the discount rate. This is discussed in more detail in chapter 12. The sum of the net present value over 3 years divided by the number of initial customers equals $811.30. This is called the average net present value or lifetime value for each customer for a single product.

The first step is to assign a risk score to each prospect based on a combination of gender, marital status, and inferred age group from Table 4.1:

```
data acqmod.test;
 set acqmod.test;
if gender = 'M' then do;
      if marital = 'M' then do;
                 if infd_ag2 < 40 then risk_adj = 1.09;
            else if infd_ag2 < 50 then risk_adj = 1.01;
            else if infd_ag2 < 60 then risk_adj = 0.89;
            else                       risk_adj = 0.75;
      end;
      else if marital = 'S' then do;
                 if infd_ag2 < 40 then risk_adj = 1.06;
          |          |          |          |          |
          |          |          |          |          |
      else if marital = 'W' then do;
```

Table 7.1 Average Net Present Value Calculation for Single Product

	INITIAL SALE 1ST YEAR	RENEWAL 2ND YEAR	RENEWAL 3RD YEAR
Initial customers	50,000	35,500	28,045
Renewal rate	71%	79%	85%
Total revenue	$30,710,500	$21,804,455	$17,225,519
Policy maintenance & claims	$9,738,150	$8,004,309	$7,184,680
Gross profit	$20,972,350	$13,800,146	$10,040,839
Discount rate	1.00	1.15	1.32
Net present value	$20,972,350	$12,000,127	$7,592,317
Cumulative net present value	$20,972,350	$32,972,477	$40,564,794
Average net present value	$ 419.45	$ 659.45	$ 811.30

```
                     if infd_ag2 < 40 then risk_adj = 1.05;
                else if infd_ag2 < 50 then risk_adj = 1.01;
                else if infd_ag2 < 60 then risk_adj = 0.92;
                else                      risk_adj = 0.78;
         end;
  end;
```

The next step assigns the average net present value of the product profitability, *prodprof*. And finally the average net present value (*npv_3yr*) is derived by multiplying the probability of becoming active (*pred_scr*) times the risk adjustment index (*risk_adj*) times the sum of the discounted profits from the initial policy (*prodprof*) minus the initial marketing expense:

```
prodprof = 811.30;
npv_3yr= pred_scr*risk_adj*prodprof - .78;
run;
proc sort data=acqmod.test;
by descending npv_3yr;
run;

data acqmod.test;
 set acqmod.test;
smp_wgt=1;
sumwgt=5000;
number+smp_wgt;
if number < .1*sumwgt then val_dec = 0; else
if number < .2*sumwgt then val_dec = 1; else
if number < .3*sumwgt then val_dec = 2; else
if number < .4*sumwgt then val_dec = 3; else
if number < .5*sumwgt then val_dec = 4; else
if number < .6*sumwgt then val_dec = 5; else
if number < .7*sumwgt then val_dec = 6; else
if number < .8*sumwgt then val_dec = 7; else
if number < .9*sumwgt then val_dec = 8; else
val_dec = 9;
run;

proc tabulate data=acqmod.test;
weight smp_wgt;
class val_dec;
var records pred_scr risk_adj npv_3yr;
table val_dec='Decile' all='Total',
        records='Prospects'*sum=' '*f=comma10.
        pred_scr='Predicted Probability'*(mean=' '*f=11.5)
        risk_adj = 'Risk Index'*(mean=' '*f=6.2)
        npv_3yr = 'Total   3-Year Net Present Value'
            *(mean=' '*f=dollar8.2)
        /rts = 9 row=float;
run;
```

TIP

If you have a very large file and you want more choices for determining where to make a cut-off, you can create more groups. For example, if you wanted to look at 20 groups (sometimes called twentiles), just divide the file into 20 equal parts and display the results.

A model is a powerful tool for ranking customers or prospects. Figure 7.5 shows the expected active rate, average risk index, and three-year present

	Prospects	Predicted Probability	Risk Index	3-Year Net Present Value
Decile				
0	2,500	0.00427	1.04	$2.82
1	2,500	0.00222	1.02	$1.06
2	2,500	0.00168	0.99	$0.57
3	2,500	0.00134	1.01	$0.32
4	2,500	0.00112	1.02	$0.15
5	2,500	0.00095	0.99	$-0.02
6	2,500	0.00081	0.98	$-0.02
7	2,500	0.00067	0.97	$-0.14
8	2,500	0.00054	1.00	$-0.25
9	2,500	0.00035	0.98	$-0.34
Total	25,000	0.00139	1.00	$0.38

Figure 7.5 Decile analysis of scored file.

value by decile for the new file based on the sample that was scored. The model, however, does not provide the rules for making the final name selections. The decision about how deep to go into a file is purely a business decision.

In Figure 7.6, I plug the expected active rate for each decile into the NPV formula. The columns in the table are used to calculate the NPV projections necessary to make an intelligent business decision:

Prospects. The number of prospects in the scored file.

Predicted active rate. The rate per decile from Figure 7.5.

Risk index. The average risk based on a matrix provided by actuarial (see Table 4.1).

Product profitability. The expected profit from the initial policy discounted in today's dollars. The values are the same for every prospect because the model targets only one product. The calculation for discounting will be explained in chapter 12.

Average NPV. The average three-year profit from the one product offered, discounted in today's dollars.

Average cumulative NPV. The cumulative of average NPV.

Sum of cumulative NPV. The cumulative total dollars of NPV.

Decile	Prospects	Predicted Active Rate	Risk Index	Product Profitability	Marketing Expense	Average NPV	Average Cum NPV	Sum Cum NPV
1	147,692	0.427%	1.04	$811.30	$0.78	$2.82	$2.82	$416,908
2	147,692	0.222%	1.02	$811.30	$0.78	$1.06	$1.94	$573,034
3	147,692	0.168%	0.99	$811.30	$0.78	$0.57	$1.48	$657,123
4	147,692	0.134%	1.01	$811.30	$0.78	$0.32	$1.19	$704,092
5	147,692	0.112%	1.02	$811.30	$0.78	$0.15	$0.98	$725,777
6	147,692	0.095%	0.99	$811.30	$0.78	-$0.02	$0.82	$723,270
7	147,692	0.081%	0.98	$811.30	$0.78	-$0.14	$0.68	$703,186
8	147,692	0.067%	0.97	$811.30	$0.78	-$0.25	$0.56	$665,859
9	147,692	0.054%	1.00	$811.30	$0.78	-$0.34	$0.46	$615,363
10	147,692	0.035%	0.98	$811.30	$0.78	-$0.50	$0.37	$541,262

Decile-level financial estimates allow managers and marketers to manage campaigns to meet company goals.

Figure 7.6 NPV model gains table.

Determining the File Cut-off

Once the file has been scored and the financials have been calculated, it's time to decide how many names to select or how much of the file to solicit. This is typically called the file cut-off. Figure 7.6 does an excellent job of providing the information needed for name selection. It, however, doesn't *give* the answer. There are a number of considerations when trying to decide how many deciles to solicit. For example, at first glance you might decide to cut the file at the fifth decile. The reason is rather obvious: This is last decile in which the NPV is positive. There are a number of other good choices, however, depending on your business goals.

Let's say you're a young company going after market share. Management might decide that you are willing to spend $0.25 to bring in a new customer. Then you can cross-sell and up-sell additional products. This is a very reasonable approach that would allow you to solicit eight deciles. (In chapter 12, I will develop a lifetime value model that incorporates cross-sell and up-sell potential.)

Perhaps your company decides that it must make a minimum of $0.30 on each customer to cover fixed expenses like salaries and building costs. In this situation, you would solicit the first four deciles. Another choice could be made based on model efficiency. If you look at the drop in NPV, the model seems to lose its high discrimination power after the third decile.

It's important to note that any decision to cut the file at a certain dollar (or cents) amount does not have to be made using deciles. The decile analysis can provide guidance while the actual cut-off could be at mid-decile based on a fixed amount. In our previous example, the average for decile 4 is $0.30. But at some point within that decile, the NPV drops below $0.30, so you might want to cut the file at an NPV of $0.30. The main point to remember is that selecting the file cut-off is a *business decision*. The decile analysis can provide guidance, but the decision must be clear and aligned with the goals of the business.

Champion versus Challenger

In many situations, a model is developed to replace an existing model. It may be that the old model is not performing. Or perhaps some new predictive information is available that can be incorporated into a new model. Whatever the reason, it is important to compare the new model, or the "Challenger," to the existing model, or "Champion." Again, depending on your goals, there are a number of ways to do this.

In Figure 7.7, we see the entire file represented by the rectangle. The ovals represent the names selected by each model. If your "Champion" is doing well, you

This area represents
the worst prospects.

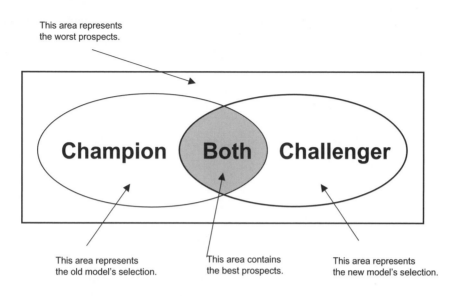

This area represents
the old model's selection.

This area contains
the best prospects.

This area represents
the new model's selection.

Figure 7.7 Champion versus Challenger.

might decide to mail the entire file selected by the "Champion" and mail a sample from the portion of the "Challenger" oval that was *not* selected by the "Champion." This allows you to weight the names from the sample so you can track and compare both models' performance.

At this point, I have calculated an expected net present value for a single product. This is an excellent tool for estimating the long-term profitability of a customer based on the sale of a single product. We know that one of our company goals is to leverage the customer relationship by selling additional products and services to our current customer base. As mentioned previously, in chapter 12 I expand our case study to the level of long-term customer profitability by considering the present value of future potential sales. I will integrate that into our prospect model to calculate lifetime value.

The Two-Model Matrix

I decided against using the two-model approach because of instability. However, it may be preferred in certain situations because of its flexibility. Because the models have been built separately, it is possible to manage the components separately. This may be very useful for certain business strategies. It can also make the model performance easier to track. In other words, you can monitor response and activation separately.

The code is similar to the one-model code. The difference is that the decile values have to be calculated and blended together. The first step is to sort the validation data by the response score (*predrsp*), create deciles called *rsp_dec*, and output a new data set. The steps are repeated to create deciles in a new data set based on activation called *act_dec*.

```
proc sort data=acqmod.out_rsp2(rename=(pred=predrsp));
by descending predrsp;
run;

proc univariate data=acqmod.out_rsp2(where=( splitwgt = .)) noprint;
weight smp_wgt;
var predrsp;
output out=preddata sumwgt=sumwgt;
run;

data acqmod.validrsp;
  set acqmod.out_rsp2(where=( splitwgt = .));
if (_n_ eq 1) then set preddata;
retain sumwgt;
number+smp_wgt;
if number < .1*sumwgt then rsp_dec = 0; else
if number < .2*sumwgt then rsp_dec = 1; else
if number < .3*sumwgt then rsp_dec = 2; else
if number < .4*sumwgt then rsp_dec = 3; else
if number < .5*sumwgt then rsp_dec = 4; else
if number < .6*sumwgt then rsp_dec = 5; else
if number < .7*sumwgt then rsp_dec = 6; else
if number < .8*sumwgt then rsp_dec = 7; else
if number < .9*sumwgt then rsp_dec = 8; else
rsp_dec = 9;
run;

proc sort data=acqmod.out_act2(rename=(pred=predact));
by descending predact;
run;

proc univariate data=acqmod.out_act2(where=(splitwgt = .)) noprint;
weight smp_wgt;
var predact active;
output out=preddata sumwgt=sumwgt;
run;

data acqmod.validact;
  set acqmod.out_act2(where=( splitwgt = .));
if (_n_ eq 1) then set preddata;
retain sumwgt;
number+smp_wgt;
if number < .1*sumwgt then act_dec = 0; else
if number < .2*sumwgt then act_dec = 1; else
```

```
if number < .3*sumwgt then act_dec = 2; else
if number < .4*sumwgt then act_dec = 3; else
if number < .5*sumwgt then act_dec = 4; else
if number < .6*sumwgt then act_dec = 5; else
if number < .7*sumwgt then act_dec = 6; else
if number < .8*sumwgt then act_dec = 7; else
if number < .9*sumwgt then act_dec = 8; else
act_dec = 9;
activ_r = 0; activ_r = activate;
run;
```

Next, the two data sets are sorted and merged by *pros_id*. PROC TABULATE is used create a cross-matrix of values.

```
proc sort data=acqmod.validrsp;
by pros_id;
run;

proc sort data=acqmod.validact;
by pros_id;
run;

data acqmod.blend;
merge acqmod.validrsp acqmod.validact;
by pros_id;
run;

proc tabulate data=acqmod.blend;
weight smp_wgt;
class rsp_dec act_dec;
var respond active records activ_r;
table (rsp_dec='Response Decile' all='Total')*
        (records='Count'*sum=' '*f=comma7.
        activ_r='Actv Rate'*(mean=' '*f=percent5.2)
        respond='Resp Rate'*(mean=' '*f=percent5.2)),
        (act_dec='Active Decile' all='Total') /rts = 21 row=float;
run;
```

The resulting table is very busy and uninteresting, but the values are transferred to a spreadsheet and graph. In Figure 7.8, we see a three-dimensional graph that shows the frequency of each response decile crossed with each active|response decile. This could be used to determine cut-offs that meet certain minimum response rates as well as minimum approval rates. As mentioned previously, it is also useful if you want to track model performance separately. For example, the response model could stop performing while the approval model continues to do well. In this case, you would have to rebuild only the response model.

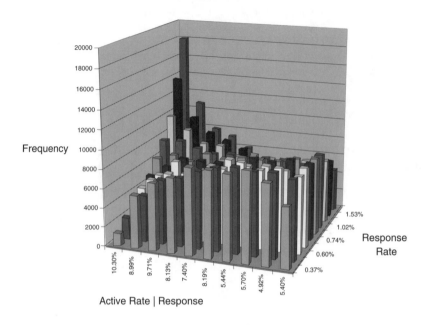

Figure 7.8   Two Model Approach.

Model Tracking

Throughout this book, I have stressed that the steps surrounding model development are key to the success of a model. At this point, if things don't go as expected it may be necessary to figure out what went wrong. In the accompanying sidebar, Allison Cornia presents her top 10 list for sleuthing out the problem.

When Good Models Go Bad

Allison Cornia, Vice President at Microsoft Corporation, discusses her top 10 list of techniques for tracking problems in models.

Building a good model isn't just about sound analytic work. A good targeted-marketing campaign is like a precisely engineered motor. Every part of the process depends on another for success. And every once in a while, a target-marketing campaign doesn't work as planned. "Response wasn't very high." "The customers didn't materialize." "Sales barely even moved enough for a rounding error." Knowing that something is not working is easy. Figuring out where the campaign went wrong is the difficult part. As a modeler, you may be surprised at what happens to your work when you are finished. With so many steps to the process, how do you know where things went wrong? What do you do when you have a proven offer and creative but the campaign flops? The following list is my top 10 troubleshooting tips when it appears that your arrow has not hit its target.

1. **Check the phones.** This sounds really obvious, but if the phones aren't ringing within days (for direct mail) or minutes (for e-mail and direct TV) after the offer has hit, check your inbound call system. I had one customer call me and say, "The phones aren't ringing. The models (the data) are bad!" I furiously checked the data processing and reviewed the analytical procedures looking for why response was so far off. Later I learned that the Vice President of Marketing for the marketing company was terminated for a faulty phone system.

   It seems really elementary. But the stories abound where the phone number was printed incorrectly or pointed to the wrong department, or the system just plain didn't work. It is crucial to make sure the inbound path is configured properly as well. I recently had an experience as a consumer in which, when I followed the automated attendant's instructions, it dead-ended me every time. And as result, the company did not get my business. So the message here is to test the system. And not just from your phone at the office, but have people in different parts of the country call at different times prior to launch.

   And in this day of dot-commerce, the same applies with a slight twist. Check the Web site. If you are sending people to a specific URL, make sure they get there without receiving an error message. Make sure they can click through to suggested sites, make real sure they can click on the "BUY NOW" button, and be absolutely sure they can complete their transaction. In these early days of e-commerce, those that give purchasers an effortless and secure transaction experience are going to be winning now and dominating in the future.

2. **Track the mail.** With first-class mail, it is reasonably easy to predict delivery times. However, it is not entirely infallible. If you have shipped mail to other parts of the country, make sure you know what day the mail actually dropped. The USPS is beta testing a new bar code on mail that allows people to track first-class mail much like overnight deliveries. Once this software is released and becomes more widely available, it will be easier to judge when the calls/clicks should start arriving. I always lose sleep after a mail drop because I know that until the phones start to ring, people are apt to get anxious and point fingers at the data. Timing on the mail drop should also be evaluated to avoid the "dead seasons" in direct response (i.e., the week of Christmas).

continues

(Continued)

3. **Listen in on your call center.** If response seems high and/or acceptable but conversion rates are low, listen in on customer calls. Are your customers getting through in acceptable amounts of time? Or are they spending lots of time on hold? Is the Web site up to the traffic load, or are people unable to access the site? Listen to the call reps. Are they courteous and helpful? Are they answering questions correctly about the products they are selling? This can be helpful in a number of ways. First and foremost, you will be able to tell what kind of experience your customers are having and how well that meets expectations. Second, if there is a bad fit between the data and the creative, the call center representatives will tell you with their comments or lack of sales. In one example from the financial services sector, a large well-known dot.com mortgager sent out a great offer. However, it was a new product, and the target data was difficult to define based on the product definition. While response was phenomenal, the conversion rates were low as many responders were not qualified for the product. By talking to the call center reps, we could tell many of the problems with the targeting, and adjustments could be made before the next wave of mail went out.

4. **Check the implementation of the model/targeting.** Whether you are using an algorithm or a segmentation schema, make sure that the "scoring" or implementation has gone correctly. Most people will perform a validation of the coding on a small sample that is usually held out from the modeling process. In today's environment of "big data," it is difficult and sometimes impossible to validate scores on entire databases. Most of the time, the culprit is not an error in the coding or scoring but the underlying data in the database. Because of the size of most data marts, not every field may have been "vetted" properly. While the sample may have had "clean" data in it, the database to which you are applying it may have values that are widely skewed, corrupt, dirty, or not there at all. One way to counteract this is to take several samples from the database and apply the scores/schema. Look at the underlying data. Does it mirror what you would expect to find? If you are lucky enough to be able to vet your entire database, do it. Anything other than being able to validate in the entire environment pales in comparison.

5. **Was the right group pulled?** Again, this might seem elementary but I have seen many examples where the model/schema was applied properly, but the data extracted for the fulfillment house was incorrect. Make sure that your programmers understand that "1" is the top decile and "10" is really not the group you are after. Most of us in the industry have heard horror stories about score reversals. A direct marketing agency had to credit its customer a half million dollars in mailings because a programmer inverted a decile score.

How can you tell this has happened to you? If response rates seem extremely low but still have somewhat of a pulse, and if the offer is a proven offer, this may be an area that you want to investigate further. How can you confirm it? First, take the mail file and have this group's data (that would have been used to score them) appended. Score the model or apply the schema. Are they in the correct deciles/groups? If the answer is yes, you may need to look elsewhere for the source of your problem. If the answer is no, perform one other check. Go back to the main file/database where these persons' scores are stored. Pull out those names that were mailed and confirm that they belong to the deciles/groups they should. This two-part validation will answer two issues: Was the data scored properly to begin with, and was the model inverted? In the example of the direct marketing agency, the problem lay with having two data-bases in two different IT environments. The mainframe held the main database and was where the models were scored. A copy of these scores and deciles was extracted and given to an IT group in a relational setting. The scores were added to the relational environment and in doing so, the programmers ignored the decile codes and redeciled with the highest scores being assigned to decile 10 instead of 1. In revalidating and investigating all the efforts, if we had just compared the individual scores on the file in the relational setting without comparing back to the mainframe, we would have missed the problem. The cautionary tale here is that it can happen, so be careful not to let it.

6. **Like a good farmer, check your crop rotation.** This is another elementary point in database management, but again it can be overlooked. I was once asked if "list fatigue" existed, and I believe it does but can be avoided/mini-mized. One tactic is to develop some sound business rules that allow you to systematically rotate your lists. In direct marketing, the rule of thumb is usu-ally 90-day intervals. There are some exceptions, though. With in-house files/databases, in-depth profiling will tell you what your frequency should be for talking to the customer. Some customers love constant communications (frequent purchasers, heavy users), while others would prefer you never talk to them (the opt-outs). E-mail solicitations have become very popular, mainly due to the low costs associated with producing them, but caution should be exercised in how often you fill up someone's inbox with offers. Even though we have all become somewhat numb to the amount of mailbox stuffers we receive, e-mail solicitations have a slightly more invasive feel than direct mail, similar to telemarketing calls. I often wonder how businesses that I haven't bought from get my e-mail address. If we as direct marketers can appreciate this distinction with e-mail and refrain from spamming our hearts out, we can probably assure ourselves that we won't be regulated in how often we can e-mail people and preserve a low-cost alternative for talking to our customers.

continues

(Continued)

How can you tell if list fatigue is setting in? Are response and conversion rates gradually declining in a nice steady curve? Can you tell me the average number of times a person is mailed and with what frequency? Do you have business rules that prevent you from over-communicating to customers? If the answers to these questions are yes, no, and no, chances are you aren't rotating your crops enough.

7. **Does your model/schema have external validity?** This is a question that sometimes is forgotten. You have great analysts who build technically perfect models. But can anyone interpret them in the context of the business? If the answer is no, your models/schemas do not have external validity. External validity to modeling is analogous to common sense. For example, let's take a look at a financial services model that finds that one of the factors in a model to predict demand for a high-interest-rate mortgage is someone's FICO score. FICO is weighted positively, which would be interpreted to mean that someone with a really high FICO score is more likely to convert. Well, any mortgage banker in the crowd will tell you that goes against what really happens. People with high FICO scores are people with excellent credit and therefore would most likely not be interested in, or likely to borrow at, high interest rates. Try evaluating and interpreting analytical work with a marketing manager's perspective. It will help you to evaluate whether your model/schema has external validity.

8. **Does your model have good internal validity?** When I refer to internal validity, I am referring to the validity of the model/schema building process itself. There are many ways to prevent a badly built model/schema from ever seeing the light of day. One good approach is to have the model/schema building process formalized with validation checks and reviews built into the process. Good modelers always keep a "hold-out" sample for validating their work. Documentation at every step of the process is good so in the case that something goes wrong, one can follow the model-building process much like a story. Not every modeler is very thorough. Having a formalized documentation/process can help to avoid errors. Having modelers review each other's work is also helpful. Often, I am asked to decipher whether a model is "good" or not by just looking at the algorithm. That in itself is not enough to determine the quality of the model. Understanding the underlying data, as well as the process by which the modeler built the algorithm, is crucial. In one such case, the model seemed to be valid. On reviewing the data, however, I found the culprit. The algorithm included an occupation code variable. However, when I looked at the data, this variable was an alphanumeric code that would have had to be transformed to be of any use in a model. And that hadn't happened. This example brings up another related issue. With the explosion in the importance and demand for dataminers, there are many groups/people operating out there who are less than thorough when building models/schemas. If someone builds you a model, ask him or her to detail the process by which he

or she built it and by what standards he or she evaluated it. If you aren't sure how to evaluate his or her work, hire or find someone who can.

9. **Bad ingredients make bad models.** Nothing will ruin a model or campaign faster than bad data. Model-building software has become so automated that anyone can build a model with a point and click. But the real service that an experienced analyst brings is being able to detect bad data early on. EDA, or exploratory data analysis, is the first step toward building a good model/schema and avoiding the bad data experience. If you are the analyst, don't take someone's word that the data is what it is; check it out for yourself. Know your data inside and out. I once had an experience where the client gave me all the nonresponders but told me they were responders. Only when I got to the part where I checked my external validity did I find the problem and correct it. If you work in database marketing, don't assume that others understand data the same way. Confirm how samples are pulled, confirm data content, and examine files very closely. If you are working with appended data, make sure that the data is clean. This is more difficult because you may not be as familiar with it. Ask for ranges of values for each field and for the mean scores/frequencies for the entire database that the data came from. A related issue with appended data is that it should make sense with what you are trying to predict. Financial data is a very powerful ingredient in a model/schema to predict demand for financial services, but as a predictor for toothpaste purchase behavior, it is not. Choose your ingredients wisely.

10. **Sometimes good models, like good horses, need to be put out to pasture.** Good models, built on well-chosen data, will perform over time. But like all good things, models do have a life cycle. Because not every market is the same and consumers tend to change over time, it almost ensures that the process of prediction will not be an event. How can you tell if it is time to refresh/rebuild your model? Have you seen a complete drop-off in response/conversion without a change in your creative/offer or the market at large? If yes, it's time to rebuild. But nobody wants to wait until that happens; you would prefer to be proactive about rebuilding models. So, that said, how do you know when it's time? The first clue is to look at the market itself. Is it volatile and unpredictable? Or is it staid and flat? Has something changed in the marketplace recently (i.e., legislation, new competitors, new product improvements, new usage) that has changed overall demand? Are you communicating/distributing through new channels (i.e., the Internet)? Have you changed the offer/creative? All of the preceding questions will help you to determine how often and when new models should be built. If you are proactive by watching the market, the customers, and the campaigns you will know when it is time. One suggestion is to always be testing a "challenger" to the "established champ." When the challenger starts to out-perform the champ consistently, it's time to retire the champ.

Back-end Validation

In my opinion, the most exciting and stressful part of the modeling process is waiting for the results to come in. I usually set up a daily monitoring program to track the results. That approach can be dangerous, though, because you can't determine the true performance until you have a decent sample size. My advice is to set up a tracking program and then be patient. Wait until you have at least a couple hundred responders before you celebrate.

In the case study, I am predicting the probability of a prospect becoming an active account. This presumes that the prospect responds. I can multiply the number of early responders times the expected active rate, given response, to get a rough idea of how the campaign is performing.

Once all of the results are in, it is critical to document the campaign performance. It is good to have a standard report. This becomes part of a model log (described in the next section). For the case study, the company mailed deciles 1 through 5 and sampled deciles 6 through 10. In Figure 7.9, the model results are compared with the expected performance shown in Figure 7.6. Each component within each decile is compared.

We notice a slight difference in the expected performance and the actual performance. But overall, model performance is good. For both the "active rate"

Comparison of Percent Active

Decile	Prospects	Predicted Active Rate	Actual Active Rate	% Diff
1	147,692	0.427%	0.389%	-8.90%
2	147,692	0.222%	0.219%	-1.35%
3	147,692	0.168%	0.159%	-5.36%
4	147,692	0.134%	0.133%	-0.75%
5	147,692	0.112%	0.109%	-2.68%
6	5,000	0.095%	0.089%	-6.32%
7	5,000	0.081%	0.082%	1.23%
8	5,000	0.067%	0.071%	5.97%
9	5,000	0.054%	0.057%	5.56%
10	5,000	0.035%	0.037%	4.86%

Comparison of Net Present Value

Decile	Prospects	Average NPV	Average NPV	% Diff
1	147,692	$2.82	$2.52	-10.73%
2	147,692	$1.06	$1.03	-2.56%
3	147,692	$0.57	$0.51	-10.42%
4	147,692	$0.32	$0.30	-5.66%
5	147,692	$0.15	$0.14	-4.65%
6	5,000	-$0.02	-$0.02	4.27%
7	5,000	-$0.14	-$0.13	-2.02%
8	5,000	-$0.25	-$0.25	0.22%
9	5,000	-$0.34	-$0.32	-5.88%
10	5,000	-$0.50	-$0.48	-4.57%

The last column in each table calculates the percent difference between the expected and the actual.

Figure 7.9 Back-end validation report.

and the "average NPV," the rank ordering is strong and the variation from expected performance is at or below 10%.

Model Maintenance

I have worked with modelers, marketers, and managers for many years. And I am always amazed at how little is known about what models exist within the corporation, how they were built, and how they have been used to date. After all the time and effort spent developing and validating a model, it is worth the extra effort to document and track the model's origin and utilization. The first step is to determine the expected life of the model.

Model Life

The life of a model depends on a couple of factors. One of the main factors is the target. If you are modeling response, it is possible to redevelop the model within a few months. If the target is risk, it is difficult to know how the model performs for a couple of years. If the model has an expected life of several years, it is always possible to track the performance along the way.

Benchmarking

As in our case study, most predictive models are developed on data with performance appended. If the performance window is three years, it should contain all the activity for the three-year period. In other words, let's say you want to predict bankruptcy over a three-year period. You would take all names that are current for time T. The performance is then measured in the time period between T + 6 to T + 36 months. So when the model is implemented on a new file, the performance can be measured or benchmarked at each six-month period.

If the model is not performing as expected, then the choice has to be made whether to continue use, rebuild, or refresh.

Rebuild or Refresh?

When a model begins to degrade, the decision must be made to rebuild or refresh the model. To rebuild means to start from scratch, as I did in chapter 3. I would use new data, build new variables, and rework the entire process. To refresh means that you keep the current variables and rerun the model on new data.

It usually makes sense to refresh the model unless there is an opportunity to introduce new predictive information. For example, if a new data source becomes available it might make sense to incorporate that information into a new model. If a model is very old, it is often advisable to test building a new one. And finally, if there are strong shifts in the marketplace, a full-scale model redevelopment may be warranted. This happened in the credit card industry when low introductory rates were launched. The key drivers for response and balance transfers were changing with the drop in rates.

Model Log

A model log is a register that contains information about each model such as development details, key features, and an implementation log. Table 7.2 is an example of a model log for our case study.

A model log saves hours of time and effort as it serves as a quick reference for managers, marketers, and analysts to see what's available, how models were

Table 7.2 Sample Model Log

NAME OF MODEL	LIFEA2000
Dates of development	3/00–4/00
Model developer	O. Parr Rud
Overall objective	Increase NPV
Specific target	Accounts with premium amount > 0
Model development data (date)	NewLife600 (6/99)
First campaign implementation	NewLife750 (6/00)
Implementation date	6/15/00
Score distribution (validation)	Mean = .037, St Dev = .00059, Min = .00001, Max=.683
Score distribution (implementation)	Mean = .034, St Dev = .00085, Min = .00001, Max=.462
Selection criteria	Decile 5
Selection business logic	$> \$.05$ NPV
Preselects	Age 25–65; minimum risk screening
Expected performance	$726M NPV
Actual performance	$703M NPV
Model details	Sampled lower deciles for model validation and redevelopment
Key drivers	Population density, life stage variables

developed, who's the target audience, and more. It tracks models over the long term with details such as the following:

Model name or number. Select a name that reflects the objective or product. Combining it with a number allows for tracking redevelopment models.

Date of model development. Range of development time.

Model developer. Name of person who developed model.

Model development data. Campaign used for model development.

Overall objective. Reason for model development.

Specific target. Specific group of interest or value estimated.

Development data. Campaign used for development.

Initial campaign. Initial implementation campaign.

Implementation date. First use date.

Score distribution (validation). Mean, standard deviation, minimum and maximum values of score on validation sample.

Score distribution (implementation). Mean, standard deviation, minimum and maximum values of score on implementation sample.

Selection criteria. Score cut-off or depth of file.

Selection business logic. Reason for selection criteria.

Preselects. Cuts prior to scoring.

Expected performance. Expected rate of target variable; response, approval, active, etc.

Actual performance. Actual rate of target variable; response, approval, active, etc.

Model details. Characteristics about the model development that might be unique or unusual.

Key drivers. Key predictors in the model.

I recommend a spreadsheet with separate pages for each model. One page might look something like the page in Table 7.2. A new page should be added each time a model is used. This should include the target population, date of score, date of mailing, score distribution parameters, preselects, cut-off score, product code or codes, and results.

Summary

In this chapter, I estimated the financial impact of the model by calculating net present value. This allowed me to assess the model's impact on the company's bottom line. Using decile analysis, the marketers and managers are able to select the number of names to solicit to best meet their business goals.

As with any great meal, there is also the clean-up! In our case, tracking results and recording model development are critical to the long-term efficiency of using targeting models.

PART THREE

Recipes for
Every Occasion

Do you like holiday dinners? Are you a vegetarian? Do you have special dietary restrictions? When deciding what to cook, you have many choices!

Targeting models also serve a variety of marketing tastes. Determining who will respond, who is low risk, who will be active, loyal, and above all, profitable— these are all activities for which segmentation and targeting can be valuable. In this part of the book, I cover a variety of modeling objectives for several industries. In chapter 8, I begin with profiling and segmentation, a prudent first step in any customer analysis project. I provide examples for both the catalog and financial services industry using both data-driven and market-driven techniques. In chapter 9 I detail the steps for developing a response model for a business-to-business application. In chapter 10 I develop a risk model for the telecommunication industry. And in chapter 11, I develop a churn or attrition model for the credit card industry. Chapter 12 continues the case study from chapters 3 through 7 with the development of a lifetime value model for the direct-mail life insurance industry.

If your work schedule is anything like mine, you must eat fast food once in a while. Well, that's how I like to describe modeling on the Web. It's designed to handle large amounts of data very quickly and can't really be done by hand. In chapter 13, I discuss how the Web is changing the world of marketing. With the help of some contributions from leading thinkers in the field, I discuss how modeling, both traditional and interactive, can be used on a Web site for marketing, risk, and customer relationship management.

Understanding Your Customer: Profiling and Segmentation

The methodologies discussed in this chapter could have easily been included at the beginning of this book, but because they don't really fit into the realm of predictive modeling, I decided to write a separate chapter. The cases in this chapter describe several techniques and applications for understanding your customer. Common sense tells us that it's a good first step to successful customer relationship management. It is also an important step for effective prospecting. In other words, once you know what customer attributes and behaviors are currently driving your profitability, you can use these to direct your prospecting efforts as well. (In fact, when I decided on a title for this chapter, I was hesitant to limit it to just "customer.") The first step in effective prospecting is learning how to find prospects that look like your customers. It is also useful to segment and profile your prospect base to assist acquisition efforts. The goal in both cases is to identify what drives customer profitability.

This chapter begins by defining profiling and segmentation and discussing some of the types and uses of these techniques. Some typical applications are discussed with references to the data types mentioned in chapter 2. The second half of the chapter details the process using three case studies. The first is from the catalog industry, in which I perform some simple profile and penetration analyses. Next, I develop a customer value matrix for a credit card customer database. The final case study illustrates the use of cluster analysis to discover segments.

What Is the Importance of Understanding Your Customer?

This sounds like a dumb question, doesn't it? You would be amazed, though, at how many companies operate for years—pumping out offers for products and services—without a clue of what their best customer looks like. For every company in every industry, this is the most important first step to profitable marketing.

Similar to modeling, before you begin any profiling or segmentation project, it is important to establish your objective. This is crucial because it will affect the way you approach the task. The objective can be explained by reviewing the definitions of *profiling* and *segmentation*.

Profiling is exactly what it implies: the act of using data to describe or *profile* a group of customers or prospects. It can be performed on an entire database or distinct sections of the database. The distinct sections are known as segments. Typically they are mutually exclusive, which means no one can be a member of more than one segment.

Segmentation is the act of splitting a database into distinct sections or segments. There are two basic approaches to segmentation: market driven and data driven. Market-driven approaches allow you to use characteristics that you determine to be important drivers of your business. In other words, you preselect the characteristics that define the segments. This is why defining your objective is so critical. The ultimate plans for using the segments will determine the best method for creating them. On the other hand, data-driven approaches use techniques such as cluster analysis or factor analysis to find homogenous groups. This might be useful if you are working with data about which you have little knowledge.

Types of Profiling and Segmentation

If you've never done any segmentation or modeling, your customer base may seem like a big blob that behaves a certain way, depending on the latest stimulus. If you do a little digging, you will find a variety of demographic and psychographic characteristics as well as a multitude of buying behaviors, risk patterns, and levels of profitability among the members of your database. This is the beauty of segmentation and profiling. Once you understand the distinct groups within the database, you can use this knowledge for product development, customer service customization, media and channel selection, and targeting selection.

RFM: Recency, Frequency, Monetary Value

One of the most common types of profiling originated in the catalog industry. Commonly called RFM, it is a method of segmenting customers on their buying behavior. Its use is primarily for improving the efficiency of marketing efforts to existing customers. It is a very powerful tool that involves little more than creating segments from the three groups.

Recency. This value is the number of months since the last purchase. It is typically the most powerful of the three characteristics for predicting response to a subsequent offer. This seems quite logical. It says that if you've recently purchased something from a company, you are more likely to make another purchase than someone who did not recently make a purchase.

Frequency. This value is the number of purchases. It can be the total of purchases within a specific time frame or include all purchases. This characteristic is second to *recency* in predictive power for response. Again, it is quite intuitive as to why it relates to future purchases.

Monetary value. This value is the total dollar amount. Similar to frequency, it can be within a specific time frame or include all purchases. Of the three, this characteristic is the least powerful when it comes to predicting response. But when used in combination, it can add another dimension of understanding.

These three characteristics can be used alone or in combination with other characteristics to assist in CRM efforts. Arthur M. Hughes, in his book *Strategic Database Marketing* (Probus, 1994), describes a number of excellent applications for RFM analysis. In the second half of the chapter, I will work through a case study in which I calculate RFM for a catalog company.

Demographic

Have you ever seen the ad that shows a 60's flower child living in a conservative neighborhood? The emphasis is on finding the individual who may not fit the local demographic profile. In reality, though, many people who live in the same area behave in a similar fashion.

As I mentioned in chapter 2, there are many sources of demographic data. Many sources are collected at the individual level with enhancements from the demographics of the surrounding geographic area. Segmenting by values such as age, gender, income, and marital status can assist in product development, creative design, and targeting.

There are several methods for using demographics to segment your database and/or build customer profiles. Later on in the chapter, I will create a customer value matrix using a combination of demographic and performance measures for a database of credit card customers.

Life Stage

Whether we like it or not, we are all aging! And with few exceptions, our lives follow patterns that change over time to meet our needs. These patterns are clustered into groups defined by demographics like age, gender, marital status, and presence of children to form life stage segments.

Life stage segments are typically broken into young singles; couples or families; middle-aged singles, couples, or families; and older singles or couples. Additional enhancements can be achieved by overlaying financial, behavioral, and psychographic data to create well-defined homogeneous segments. Understanding these segments provides opportunities for businesses to develop relevant products and fine-tune their marketing strategies.

At this point, I've spent quite a bit of time explaining and stressing the importance of profiling and segmentation. You can see that the methodologies vary depending on the application. Before I get into our case studies, it is worthwhile to stress the importance of setting an objective and developing a plan. See the accompanying sidebar for a discussion from Ron Mazursky on the keys to market segmentation.

Ten Keys to Market Segmentation

Ron Mazursky, a consultant with many years' experience in segmentation for the credit card industry and president of Card Associates, Inc., shares his wisdom on market segmentation. Notice the many parallels to basic data modeling best practices.

Pat was in the office early to develop the budget and plans for the coming year when Sal came in.

"Good morning, Pat. Remember the meeting we had last week? Well, I need you to make up for the shortfall in income we discussed. Come up with a plan to make this happen. Let's discuss it on Friday." Sal left the office after a few pleasantries. Pat thought to himself, "Not much more to say. Lots to think about. Where do I start?"

If this hasn't happened to you yet, it will. Senior management tends to oversee *corporate* goals and objectives. Unfortunately, more often than not, clear and precise business objectives are not agreed to and managed carefully. As a result, business lines may end up with contradictory goals and strategies, leading to unintended outcomes.

We need to manage business lines by specific objectives. These objectives should be targeted and measurable. By targeted, we mean well defined by identifying criteria, such as demographic, geographic, psychographic, profitability, or behavioral. By measurable, we mean that all objectives should have a quantitative component, such as dollars, percents, or other numbers-based measures.

In determining our strategy to improve performance, we typically need to identify a process for segmenting our customer or prospect universe to focus our efforts. Market segmentation frequently involves classifying a population into identifiable units based on similarities in variables. If we look at the credit card universe (where Sal and Pat work), we can identify segments based on behavioral tendencies (such as spending, credit revolving, credit score), profitability tendencies (such as high, medium, low), psychographic tendencies (such as value-added drivers like rewards, discounts, insurance components—core features and benefit drivers like lower rates, lower or no fees, balance transfer offers, Internet access—and affinity drivers like membership in clubs, alumni organizations, charities), and more.

The process of market segmentation can be pursued through various models. We will present but one approach. Modify it as you develop your segmentation skills. You can be assured that this approach is not "cast in stone." With different clients and in different scenarios, I always adjust my approach as I evaluate a specific situation.

Ten Keys to Market Segmentation

1. **Define your business objectives.** At the start of any segmentation process, agree on and clearly state your goals using language that reflects targeting and measurement. Business objectives can be (1) new account, sales, or usage driven; (2) new product driven; (3) profitability driven; or (4) product or service positioning driven.

2. **Assemble your market segmentation team.** Staff this team from within your organization and supplement it, as necessary, with outside vendors. The key areas of your organization ought to be included, such as marketing, sales, market research, database analysis, information systems, financial analysis, operations, and risk management. This will vary by organization and industry.

3. **Review and evaluate your data requirements.** Make sure you have considered all necessary data elements for analysis and segmentation purposes. Remember to view internal as well as external data overlays. Types of data could include survey, geo-demographic overlays, and transactional behavior. Data

continues

(Continued)

must be relevant to your business objectives. You are reviewing all data to determine only the necessary elements because collecting and analyzing data on all customers or prospects is very time-consuming and expensive.

4. Select the appropriate basis of analysis. Data is collected on different bases—at different times you might use individual-specific, account-level, or household-level data. First understand what data is available. Then remember what is relevant to your business objective.

5. Identify a sample from the population for analysis. Who do you want to analyze for segmentation purposes? Very often the population is too large (and too expensive) to analyze as a whole. A representative sample should be chosen based on the business objective.

6. Obtain data from the various sources you've identified for the sample you've selected. The analytical database may contain transactional data, survey data, and geo-demographic data. Data will likely be delivered to you in different formats and will need to be reformatted to populate a common analytical database.

7. "Clean" the data where necessary. In some cases, records can contain data that might not be representative of the sample. These "outliers" might need to be excluded from the analysis or replaced with a representative (minimum, maximum, or average) value.

8. Select a segmentation method that is appropriate for the situation. There are three segmentation methods that could be employed: predefined segmentation, statistical segmentation, or hybrid segmentation. The predefined segmentation method allows the analyst to create the segment definitions based on prior experience and analysis. In this case, you know the data, you work with a limited number of variables, and you determine a limited number of segments. For example, in Sal and Pat's business, we've had experience working with purchase inactive segments, potential attriter segments, and potential credit usage segments. The appropriate segments will be defined and selected based on the business objective and your knowledge of the customer base.

9. The statistical method should be employed when there are many segments involved and you have little or no experience with the population being investigated. In this case, through statistical techniques (i.e., cluster analysis), you create a limited number of segments (try to keep it under 15 segments). This method could be employed if you were working on a new customer base or a

list source where you had no prior experience. Hybrid segmentation allows you to combine predefined segmentation with statistical segmentation, in any order, based on your success in deriving segments. The combination of methods will yield a greater penetration of the customer base, but it will likely cost significantly more than applying only one approach.

10. Determine how well the segmentation worked. Now that we've applied the segmentation method appropriate for the situation, we need to evaluate how well the segmentation method performed. This evaluation analysis can be conducted via quantitative and qualitative steps. The analysis should determine whether all individuals within each segment are similar (profile, frequency distributions), whether each segment is different from the other segments, and whether each segment allows for a clear strategy that will meet the business objective.

Segments should pass the following **RULEs** in order to be tested:

- Relevant to the business objective
- Understandable and easy to characterize
- Large enough to warrant a special offering
- Easy to develop unique offerings

Apply the segmentations that have passed the above **RULEs** to various list sources and test the appropriate tactics. After testing, evaluate the results behaviorally and financially to determine which segmentations and offerings should be expanded to the target population. How did they perform against the business objectives?

By the time you've reached this last step, you may have what you think are a number of winning segmentations and tactics. We often fail to remember the business objectives until it is too late. It is critical that you have designed the segmentations to satisfy a business objective and that you have evaluated the market tests based on those same business objectives.

It feels great having actionable, well-defined segments, but do they achieve your original set of business objectives? If not, the fall-out could be costly on other fronts, such as lower profitability, reduced product usage, or negative changes in attitude or expectations.

By keeping your business objectives in mind throughout the development, testing, and analysis stages, you are more assured of meeting your goals, maximizing your profitability and improving your customers' long-term behavior.

Profiling and Penetration Analysis of a Catalog Company's Customers

Southern Area Merchants (SAM) is a catalog company specializing in gifts and tools for the home and garden. It has been running a successful business for more than 10 years and now has a database of 35,610 customers. But SAMs noticed that its response rates have been dropping, and so it is interested in learning some of the key drivers of response. It is also interested in expanding its customer base. It is therefore looking for ways to identify good prospects from outside list sources. The first step is to perform RFM analysis.

RFM Analysis

As mentioned earlier, recency, frequency, and monetary value are typically the strongest drivers of response for a catalog company. To discover the effects of these measures on SAM's database, I identify the variables in the database:

lstpurch. Months since last purchase or *recency*.

numpurch. Number of purchases in the last 36 months or *frequency*.

totpurch. Total dollar amount of purchases in the last 36 months or *monetary value*.

The first step is to get a distribution of the customers' general patterns. I use PROC FREQ to calculate the number customers in each subgroup of recency, frequency, and monetary value. To make it more useful, I begin by creating formats to collapse the subgroups. PROC FORMAT creates templates that can be used in various summary procedures. The following code creates the formats and produces the frequencies:

```
proc format;
value recency
low-1 = '0-1 Months'
2-3 = '2-3 Months'
4-7 = '4-7 Months'
8-12 = '8-12 Months'
13-high = '13+ Months'
;
value count
.     = 'Unknown'
0-1 = '0-1'
2-4   = '2-4'
5-10  = '5-10'
11-<21 = '11-20'
21-high = '21-30'
;
```

```
value sales
low-<100 = '< $100'
101-200 = '$100-$200'
201-300 = '$200-$300'
301-400 = '$300-$400'
401-500 = '$400-$500'
500-high = '$500+'
;
run;

proc freq data=ch08.customer;
format lstpurch recency. numpurch count. totpurch sales.;
table lstpurch numpurch totpurch/missing;
run;
```

Figure 8.1 provides a good overview of customer buying habits for SAMs. I can see that the majority of customers haven't purchased anything for at least four

Recency of Purchases

LSTPURCH	Frequency	Percent	Cumulative Frequency	Cumulative Percent
0-1 Months	5090	14.3	5090	14.3
2-3 Months	5570	15.6	10660	29.9
4-7 Months	13125	36.9	23785	66.8
8-12 Months	11825	33.2	35610	100.0

Number of Purchases

NUMPURCH	Frequency	Percent	Cumulative Frequency	Cumulative Percent
0-1	12945	36.4	12945	36.4
2-4	17115	48.1	30060	84.4
5-10	4820	13.5	34880	98.0
11-20	730	2.0	35610	100.0

Total Purchases

TOTPURCH	Frequency	Percent	Cumulative Frequency	Cumulative Percent
< $100	14815	41.6	14815	41.6
$100-$200	10135	28.5	24950	70.1
$200-$300	4715	13.2	29665	83.3
$300-$400	2450	6.9	32115	90.2
$400-$500	1155	3.2	33270	93.4
$500+	2340	6.6	35610	100.0

Figure 8.1 RFM analysis.

months. A large percentage of customers made between two and four purchases in the last year with 85% making fewer than five purchases. The total
dollar value of yearly total purchases is mainly below $100, with almost 85%
below $300.

The next step is to look at the response rate from a recent catalog mailing to see
how these three drivers affect response. The following code sorts the customer
file by *recency* and creates quintiles (equal fifths of the file). By calculating the
response rate for each decile, I can determine the relationship between *recency*
and *response*.

```
proc sort data=ch08.customer;
by lstpurch;
run;

data ch08.customer;
  set ch08.customer;
rec_ord = _n_;
run;

proc univariate data=ch08.customer noprint;
var rec_ord;
output out=ch08.rec_dec pctlpts= 20 40 60 80 100 pctlpre=rec;
run;

data freqs;
set ch08.customer;
if (_n_ eq 1) then set ch08.rec_dec;
retain rec20 rec40 rec60 rec80 rec100;
run;

data freqs;
  set freqs;
if rec_ord <= rec20 then Quantile = 'Q1'; else
if rec_ord <= rec40 then Quantile = 'Q2'; else
if rec_ord <= rec60 then Quantile = 'Q3'; else
if rec_ord <= rec80 then Quantile = 'Q4'; else
                         Quantile = 'Q5';
label Quantile='Recency Quantile';
run;

proc tabulate data=freqs;
class quantile;
var respond;
table quantile='Quantile'*respond=' '*mean=' '*f=10.3, all='Response
Rate'/rts=12 row=float box='Recency';
run;
```

This process is repeated for frequency and monetary value. PROC TABULATE
displays the response rate for each quintile. The results for all three measures

are shown in Figure 8.2. We can see that the measure with the strongest relationship to *response* is recency.

Figure 8.3 compares recency, frequency, and monetary value as they relate to response. Again, we can see that the recency of purchase is the strongest driver. This is a valuable piece of information and can be used to target the next catalog. In fact, many catalog companies include a new catalog in every order. This is a very inexpensive way to take advantage of recent purchase activity.

Penetration Analysis

As I said earlier, SAM wants to explore cost-effective techniques for acquiring new customers. Penetration analysis is an effective method for comparing the distribution of the customer base to the general population. As I mentioned in chapter 2, many companies sell lists that cover a broad base of the population.

The methodology is simple. You begin with a frequency distribution of some basic demographic variables. In our case, I select age, gender, length of residence, income, population density, education level, homeowner status, family size, child indicator.

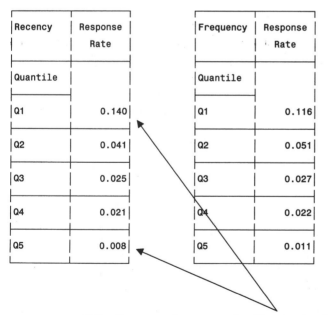

Recency Quantile	Response Rate
Q1	0.140
Q2	0.041
Q3	0.025
Q4	0.021
Q5	0.008

Frequency Quantile	Response Rate
Q1	0.116
Q2	0.051
Q3	0.027
Q4	0.022
Q5	0.011

Monetary Quantile	Response Rate
Q1	0.089
Q2	0.055
Q3	0.037
Q4	0.026
Q5	0.018

Notice the range of response rates. **Recency** has the highest discrimination between the top and bottom decile.

Figure 8.2   RFM quintiles by response.

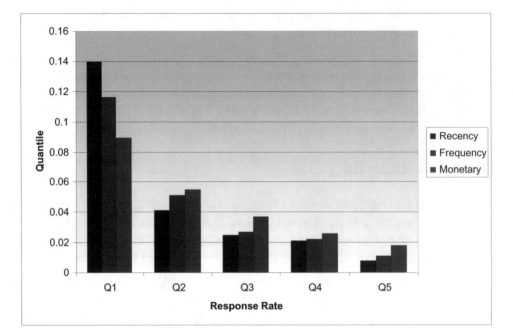

Figure 8.3 Histogram of RFM quintiles by response.

```
proc format;
value age
0-29 = ' < 30'
30-34 = '30-34'
35-39 = '35-39'
40-44 = '40-44'
45-49 = '45-49'
50-54 = '50-54'
55-64 = '55-64'
65-high = '65+'
;
value $gender
' ' = 'Unknown'
'M' = 'Male'
'F' = 'Female'
value count
.      = 'Unknown'
0-2 = '0-2'
3-5   = '3-5'
6-10  = '6-10'
11-<21 = '11-20'
21-high = '21-30'
;
run;
```

```
proc freq data=ch08.customer;
format age age. length count.;
table age length /missing;
run;
```

Figure 8.4 shows the output from PROC FREQ for the first two variables. This gives us information about the distribution of our customers. Notice how 33% of the customers are between the ages of 45 and 50. In order to make use of this information for new acquisition marketing, we need to compare this finding to the general population. The next PROC FREQ creates similar profiles for the general population:

```
proc freq data=ch08.pop;
format age age. length count.;
table age length /missing;
run;
```

Age

AGE	Frequency	Percent	Cumulative Frequency	Cumulative Percent
< 30	5	0.0	5	0.0
30-34	720	2.0	725	2.0
35-39	3445	9.7	4170	11.7
40-44	10440	29.3	14610	41.0
45-49	11795	33.1	26405	74.2
50-54	5005	14.1	31410	88.2
55-64	3435	9.6	34845	97.9
65+	765	2.1	35610	100.0

Length of Residence

LENGTH	Frequency	Percent	Cumulative Frequency	Cumulative Percent
Unknown	75	0.2	75	0.2
0-2	10135	28.5	10210	28.7
3-5	9090	25.5	19300	54.2
6-10	9785	27.5	29085	81.7
11-20	6035	16.9	35120	98.6
21-30	490	1.4	35610	100.0

Figure 8.4   Customer profiles.

Age

AGE	Frequency	Percent	Cumulative Frequency	Cumulative Percent
< 30	11220	0.2	11220	0.2
30-34	105842	1.9	117062	2.1
35-39	387464	6.8	504526	8.9
40-44	1341725	23.6	1846251	32.4
45-49	2084676	36.6	3930927	69.1
50-54	900779	15.8	4831706	84.9
55-64	726869	12.8	5558575	97.7
65+	131835	2.3	5690410	100.0

Length of Residence

LENGTH	Frequency	Percent	Cumulative Frequency	Cumulative Percent
Unknown	69938	1.2	69938	1.2
0-2	1071136	18.8	1141074	20.1
3-5	900779	15.8	2041853	35.9
6-10	1027565	18.1	3069418	53.9
11-20	1308626	23.0	4378044	76.9
21-30	1312366	23.1	5690410	100.0

Figure 8.5 Market profiles.

Notice how Figure 8.5 displays the same distributions as Figure 8.4 except this time they are on the general population. Figure 8.6 shows a market comparison graph of age. Table 8.1 brings the information from the two analyses together and creates a measure called a penetration index. This is derived by dividing the customer percentage by the market percentage for each group and multiplying by 100.

Figure 8.6 provides a graphical display of the differences in distribution for the various age groupings. SAM would be wise to see new customers in the 35–44 age group. This age range is more prominent in its customer base than in the general population.

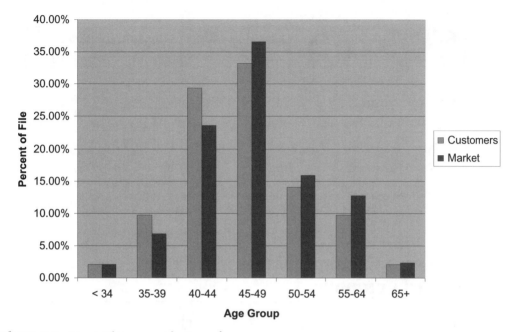

Figure 8.6 Penetration comparison graph on age.

Table 8.1 Penetration Analysis

AGE	CUSTOMERS	PERCENT OF CUSTOMERS	MARKET	PERCENT OF MARKET	PENETRATION INDEX
< 34	725	2.04%	117,062	2.06%	99
35–39	3,445	9.67%	387,464	6.81%	142
40–44	10,440	29.32%	1,341,725	23.58%	124
45–49	11,795	33.12%	2,084,676	36.63%	90
50–54	5,005	14.06%	900,779	15.83%	89
55–64	3,435	9.65%	726,869	12.77%	76
65+	765	2.15%	131,835	2.32%	93
Total	**35,610**		**5,690,410**		

continues

(Continued)

LENGTH	CUSTOMERS	PERCENT OF CUSTOMERS	MARKET	PERCENT OF MARKET	PENETRATION INDEX
Unknown	75	0.21%	69,938	1.23%	17
0–2	10,135	28.46%	1,071,136	18.82%	151
3–5	9,090	25.53%	900,779	15.83%	161
6–10	9,785	27.48%	1,027,565	18.06%	152
11–20	6,035	16.95%	1,308,626	23.00%	74
21–30	490	1.38%	1,312,366	23.06%	6
Total	35,610		5,690,410		

Developing a Customer Value Matrix for a Credit Card Company

Our second case study expands the use of profiling and segmentation to a customer view that reflects behavior as well as demographics. Risk is a form of behavior that has implications in many industries. As we saw in our life insurance case study in chapters 3 through 7, the risk of claims is a strong profit driver in the insurance industry. Credit card banks are also vulnerable to the effect of risk. A slight increase in bankruptcies and charge-offs can quickly erode small profit margins.

To understand our customer base with respect to revenue and risk, I perform a customer value analysis. This allows me to segment the customer base with respect to profitability leading to improved customer relationship management.

Customer Value Analysis

Credit card profitability is achieved by balancing revenue (less costs) and risk. An effective way to segment the market is by a combination of risk and net revenue. The first step is to determine the splitting values for risk and revenue. In this case, I use $150 for revenue and 650 for risk. These values are not cast in stone. The revenue value of $150 represents some revolving activity or high transaction activity. Accounts with revenues higher than $150 are worth considering for more marketing efforts. The risk score of 650 corresponds to an average charge-off rate that the bank considers tolerable. Accounts with scores below 650 are considered high risk.

The following code uses PROC FORMAT to split the population into two groups by both revenue and risk:

```
proc format;
value revenue
low-<151 = 'Low Revenue'
151-high = 'High Revenue'
;
value risk
low-<651 = 'High Risk'
651-high = 'Low Risk'
;
run;
```

Next, I use PROC TABULATE to create a customer value matrix. The procedure uses the previous formats to split the groups. The table statement crosses revenue (acctrev) by risk score (riskscr) with the number and percent of customers (records):

```
proc tabulate data=ch08.profit;
format acctrev revenue. riskscr risk.;
class acctrev riskscr;
var records;
table (acctrev=' ' all='Total'),(riskscr=' ' all='Total')
        *(records='#'*sum=' '*f=comma8. records='%'*pctsum=' '*f=8.2)
/rts=15 box='Customer Value Matrix';
run;
```

The results of the analysis are displayed in Figure 8.7. This matrix gives us an instant view of the customer database with respect to revenue and risk. We see that over 66% are considered high revenue and almost 53% are low risk. Our best customers, low risk and high revenue, make up 33% of our customer base.

Customer Value Matrix	High Risk		Low Risk		Total	
	#	%	#	%	#	%
Low Revenue	21,775	13.97	30,446	19.54	52,221	33.51
High Revenue	51,775	33.23	51,829	33.26	103,604	66.49
Total	73,550	47.20	82,275	52.80	155,825	100.00

Figure 8.7 Customer value matrix.

The next step is to see what they look like. I will profile the customers within each segment.

The following data step creates a new variable called *segment*. This variable has a value for each of our four segments. Following the data step, I format the segment values for use in our profile table:

```
data ch08.profit;
 set ch08.profit;
if riskscr < 651 then do;
        if acctrev < 151 then segment = '1';
        else segment = '2';
end;
else do;
        if acctrev < 151 then segment = '3';
        else segment = '4';
end;
run;

proc format;
value $ segment
 '1' = 'High Risk Low Revenue'
 '2' = 'High Risk High Revenue'
 '3' = 'Low Risk Low Revenue'
 '4' = 'Low Risk High Revenue'
 ;
run;
```

Using PROC TABULATE, I profile each segment by finding the average values of selected demographic and behavioral variables within each segment. The following code calculates the mean, minimum, and maximum for each selected variable:

```
proc tabulate data=ch08.profit;
format segment $segment.;
class segment;
var records age length numkids income male riskscr acctrev;
table records='Total Customers'*sum=' '*f=comma9.
    riskscr='Risk Score'*(mean='Mean'*f=comma5. min='Min'
     *f=comma4. max='Max'*f=comma4.)
    acctrev='Account Revenues'*(mean='Mean'*f=dollar6. min='Min'
     *f=dollar5. max='Max'*f=dollar5.)
    age='Age'*(mean='Mean'*f=comma5. min='Min'
     *f=comma4. max='Max'*f=comma4.)
    length='Length of Residence'*(mean='Mean'*f=comma5. min='Min'
     *f=comma4. max='Max'*f=comma5.)
    numkids='Number of Children'*(mean='Mean'*f=comma6.2 min='Min'
     *f=comma4. max='Max'*f=comma4.)
```

```
      income='Income (000)'*(mean='Mean'*f=dollar6. min='Min'
        *f=dollar5. max='Max'*f=dollar5.)
      male='Percent Male'*(mean='Mean'*f=percent6.2 min='Min'
        *f=percent4. max='Max'*f=percent4.),
     (segment=' ' all='Total')
 /rts=30 box='Customer Profiles';
 run;
```

In Figure 8.8, we see the variables across the rows and the segments in columns. This facilitates easy comparison of different values within the groups. I like to check the extreme values (min and max) for irregularities.

Once I am comfortable with the range of the variables, I display the mean values only in a table that is useful for developing marketing strategies. In Figure 8.9, the averages for each variable are displayed, and each segment is named for its overall character.

Managers and marketers find this type of analysis very useful for developing marketing strategies. Let's look at each segment separately:

Consummate consumers. These are the most profitable customers. They are low risk and generate high revenues. Banks can use this knowledge to offer extra services and proactively offer lower rates in the face of steep competition.

Risky revenue. These are also profitable customers. Their main liability is that they are high risk. Many banks see this as a reason to reduce balances. With higher pricing, though, these customers can be the most profitable because they are less likely to attrite.

Business builders. These are the most challenging customers. They would be profitable if they carried balances, but they tend to pay their full balance every month. Some in the industry call them the "dreaded transactors." These customers can sometimes be lured to revolve (carry balances) with low rates, but this can be a losing proposition for the bank. Another option is to charge an annual fee. Some banks are successful with a creative blending of purchase incentives and temporary low rates.

Balance bombs. No one wants these customers. They are risky and do not revolve balances. Some banks identify these customers so they can reduce their credit lines and raise their interest rates to dissuade them from continuing the relationship.

Every industry has drivers that can be effectively segmented. This simple exercise can provide direction and generate ideas for improved customer profitability.

Customer Profiles		High Risk Low Revenue	High Risk High Revenue	Low Risk Low Revenue	Low Risk High Revenue	Total
Total Customers		21,775	51,775	30,446	51,829	155,825
Risk Score	Mean	570	570	739	718	652
	Min	408	393	651	651	393
	Max	650	650	831	824	831
Account Revenues	Mean	$59	$643	$49	$652	$448
	Min	$0	$151	$0	$151	$0
	Max	$151	$1,514	$151	$1,514	$1,514
Age	Mean	32	34	48	43	34
	Min	18	18	18	18	18
	Max	92	92	92	92	92
Length of Residence	Mean	40	55	78	87	68
	Min	1	1	1	1	1
	Max	387	415	473	846	846
Number of Children	Mean	2.13	2.11	1.97	1.95	2.03
	Min	0	0	0	0	0
	Max	6	6	6	6	6
Income (000)	Mean	$41	$45	$53	$52	$48
	Min	$20	$20	$20	$20	$20
	Max	$315	$380	$383	$846	$846
Percent Male	Mean	45.69%	48.91%	51.60%	54.82%	50.95%
	Min	0%	0%	0%	0%	0%
	Max	100%	100%	100%	100%	100%

Figure 8.8 Customer profiles by segment.

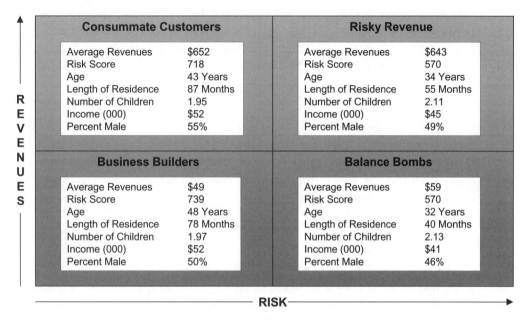

Figure 8.9 Customer profiles by segment, simplified.

Performing Cluster Analysis to Discover Customer Segments

Cluster analysis is a family of mathematical and statistical techniques that divides data into groups with similar characteristics. Recall that in chapter 4, I used frequencies to find similar groups within variable ranges. Clustering performs a similar process but in the multivariate sense. It uses Euclidean distance to group observations together that are similar across several characteristics, while attempting to separate observations that are dissimilar across those same characteristics.

It is a process with many opportunities for guidance and interpretation. Several algorithms are used in clustering. In our case study, I use PROC FASTCLUS. This is designed for use on large data sets. It begins by randomly assigning cluster seeds or centers. The number of seeds is equal to the number of clusters requested. Each observation is assigned to the nearest seed. The seed is then reassigned to the mean in each cluster. The process is repeated until the change in the seed becomes sufficiently small.

To illustrate the methodology, I use two variables from the catalog data in our earlier case study. Before I run the cluster analysis I must standardize the variables. Because the clustering algorithm I am using depends on distance between variable values, the scales of the variables must be similar. Otherwise, the variable with the largest scale will dominate the clustering procedure. The following code standardizes the variables using PROC STANDARD:

```
proc standard mean=0 std=1 out=stan;
var age income;
run;
```

The programming to create the clusters is very simple. I designate three clusters with random seeds (random=5555). Replace=full directs the program to replace all the seeds with the cluster means at each step. I want to plot the results, so I create an output dataset call *outclus*.

```
proc fastclus data=stan maxclusters=3 random=5555 replace=full
 out=outclus;
    var age income;
run;
```

In Figure 8.10, the output displays the distance from the seeds to the farthest point as well as the distances between clusters. The cluster means do show a notable difference in values for age and income. For an even better view of the clusters, I create a plot of the clusters using the following code:

```
proc plot;
    plot age*income=cluster;
run;
```

The plot in Figure 8.11 shows three distinct groups. We can now tailor our marketing campaigns to each group separately. Similar to the profile analysis, understanding the segments can improve targeting and provide insights for marketers to create relevant offers.

Summary

In any industry, the first step to finding and creating profitable customers is determining what drives profitability. This leads to better prospecting and more successful customer relationship management. You can segment and profile your customer base to uncover those profit drivers using your knowledge of your customers, products, and markets. Or you can use data-driven techniques to find natural clusters in your customer or prospect base. Whatever the method, the process will lead to knowledge and understanding that is critical to maintaining a competitive edge.

Be on the lookout for new opportunities in the use of segmentation and profiling on the Internet. In chapter 13, I will discuss some powerful uses for profiling, segmentation, and scoring on demand.

Cluster Summary

Cluster	Frequency	RMS Std Deviation	Maximum Distance from Seed to Observation	Nearest Cluster	Distance Between Cluster Centroids
1	26885	0.6916	3.5728	2	1.7570
2	9279	0.7201	3.6684	1	1.7570
3	1388	0.9554	3.9711	1	3.4607

Distance between cluster centroids.

Distance from centroid to outermost point.

Statistics for Variables

Variable	Total STD	Within STD	R-Squared	RSQ/(1-RSQ)
AGE	1.000000	0.667176	0.554899	1.246683
INCOME	1.000000	0.750598	0.436632	0.775039
OVER-ALL	1.000000	0.710113	0.495766	0.983205

Statistics for Variables

Pseudo F Statistic = 18459.19

Approximate Expected Over-All R-Squared = 0.66670

Cubic Clustering Criterion = -130.262

WARNING: The two above values are invalid for correlated variables.

Cluster Means

Cluster	AGE	INCOME
1	-0.46095	-0.03887
2	1.26275	-0.37944
3	0.48676	3.28951

Cluster Standard Deviations

Cluster	AGE	INCOME
1	0.63827	0.74105
2	0.73973	0.69985
3	0.70255	1.15407

Figure 8.10 Cluster analysis on age and income.

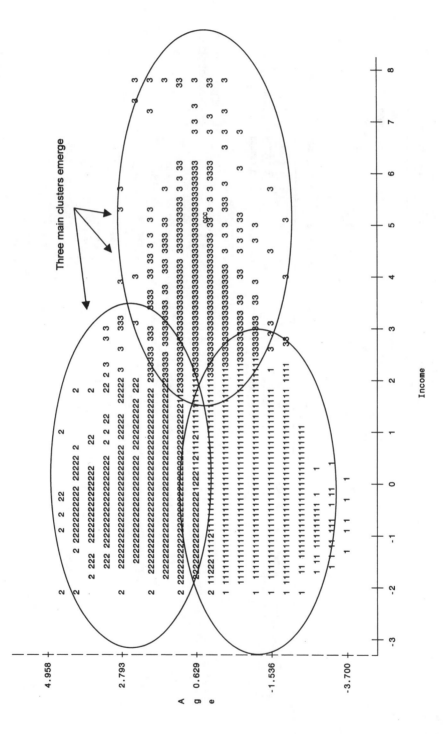

Figure 8.11 Plot of clusters on age and income.

CHAPTER 9

Targeting New Prospects: Modeling Response

The first type of predictive model that most companies endeavor to use is the response model. Recall from chapter 1 that a response model simply estimates the probability of response to an offer. Response is one of the easiest dynamics to model and can be validated very quickly. In part 2, our case study predicted activation. But in the two-model approach, I developed a model to predict response and another to predict activation given response. In this chapter, I will perform a similar exercise. To provide a slightly different perspective, I will use a business-to-business example. Our case study for this chapter involves predicting the propensity to respond to an offer to buy office supplies from an office supply retail chain. I will use some predictive variables that are familiar. And I will introduce another group of variables that are unique to business-to-business modeling. In addition, I will demonstrate how weights can be used to improve the results. The actual modeling process will follow the same steps as were demonstrated in part 2.

Defining the Objective

Downing Office Products contracts with large companies to sell office supplies, office furniture, and technical equipment. It also has many retails stores through which it collects information about its customers. It is interested in increasing sales to new and existing customers through a combination of direct mail and telemarketing. Downing's marketing director decided to purchase business names and other company information to develop a response model. The company also purchased census information with local demographic data for each business on the list.

To build a response model, the data set needs to contain responders and nonresponders along with predictive information about both groups. To get a pure data set for modeling, Downing would have to purchase a sample (or the entire file), solicit the businesses, and model the results. Because many of Downing's customers were on the list, the decision was made to build a *propensity* model. A *propensity* model is a model that predicts the propensity to take an action. In this case, I want to build a model that predicts the propensity to respond to an offer to buy products from Downing.

To create the modeling data set, the Downing customer file was matched to the purchased list of business prospects. For the names that matched, 12-month sales figures were overlaid onto the file of business names. For Downing Office Products, a response is defined as someone who buys office products.

The first step is to specifically define the dependent variable as someone with 12-month sales (*sales12mo*) greater than zero:

```
data ch09.downing;
 set ch09.downing;
 if sale12mo > 0 then respond = 1; else respond = 0;
run;
```

Table 9.1 displays the result of the file overlay. Downing has already benefited from prior sales to over half of the business list. Its goal is to leverage those relationships as well as develop new ones.

All Responders Are Not Created Equal

While I am interested in predicting who will respond, all responders are not alike. Some responders may spend less than $100 a year while others spend many thousand of dollars. My real goal is to predict dollar sales, but that would require using linear regression. Linear regression works best if the dependent variable, or the variable I am trying to predict, is normally distributed. In our

Table 9.1 Downing Business List Frequency and Weights

GROUP	LIST	PERCENT	WEIGHT
Responders	26,306	51.5%	f(12-month sales)
Nonresponders	24,761	48.5%	1
Total	51,067	100%	

case, all the nonresponders have 12-monthe sales of zero. This would make it difficult to fit a model using linear regression.

Instead, I can improve the results by using a weight to cause the model to favor the high spenders. It is important to note that the use of weights in this case will distort the population. So the resulting model will not yield an accurate point estimate. In other words, the resulting probability will not be an accurate estimate, but the file will still rank properly. If the model is built using weights, the highest spending responders should rank near the top. This will become clearer as we work through the case study.

Because I am dealing with a binary outcome (response) with a meaningful continuous component (sales), I want to look at the distribution of sales. The variable that represents 12-month sales is *sale12mo*. The following code produces the univariate output seen in Figure 9.1.

```
proc univariate data = ch09.downing plot;
where sale12mo > 0;
var sale12mo;
run;
```

The output in Figure 9.1 shows that over 50% of Downing's customers have 12-month sales of less than $100. And over 25% have 12-month sales of less than $50. To help the model target the higher-dollar customers, I will use a function of the sales amount as a weight.

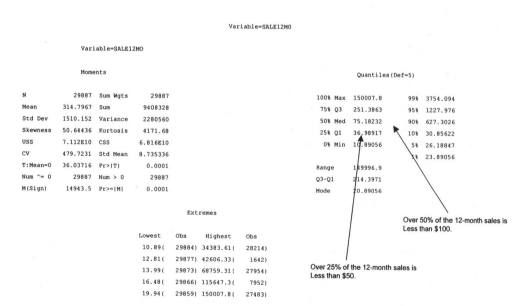

Figure 9.1 Univariate analysis of dependent variable.

As I mentioned previously, for responders I will define the weight as a function of the 12-month sales. The weights work exactly as they did when I took a sample in the case study in part 2. The higher the weight, the more that observation is represented in the file. It makes sense that if I use a function of the 12-month sales amount as a weight, the model prediction will lean toward the higher-sales responders.

To create the weight for the responders, I am going to take the 12-month sales value divided by the average 12-month sales value for all responders. By using this fraction, I can create higher representation among the big spenders without inflating the overall numbers in the sample. This will help to keep the coefficients in the normal range. The weight for nonresponders is 1. The weight that is used to favor big spenders is called *boostwgt*. The following code creates *boostwght:*

```
proc univariate data=ch09.downing noprint;
var sale12mo;
output out=wgtdata mean=s12mmean;
run;

data ch09.downing;
  set ch09.downing;
if (_n_ = 1) then set wgtdata;
if respond = 1 then boostwgt = sale12mo/s12mmean;
else boostwgt = 1;
run;
```

I will use the weight *boostwgt* to assist in transforming the variables. This will help me find the form of the variable that fits a model to target big spenders.

Preparing the Variables

As in our case study, the first step is to prepare the variables for entry into the model. The business data that was purchased has more than 250 predictive variables. The first step is to perform some simple procedure to eliminate weaker variables.

Continuous Variables

Many of these variables are numeric or continuous. Before I spend a lot of time looking at each variable individually, I am going to put them all through a stepwise logistic with only one step. (This is the same technique I used in chapter 4.) The first step defines the intercept. With the *details* option, I can look at the *list of variables not in the model*. This lists the univariate chi-square or individual predictive power of each variable. The following code, with an abbreviated variable list, is used to produce the univariate chi-square values:

```
proc logistic data=ch09.downing descending;
weight boostwgt;
model respond = p1prshh p2prshh p3prshh pamsy -- pzafflu peduca pzincom
pzsesi /selection=stepwise maxstep=1 details;
run;
```

The output in Figure 9.2 shows the list of univariate chi-square values for each variable. Because I am using the weight, all the chi-square values are inflated. Of the 221 continuous variables examined, I select 33 of the most significant. These variables will be examined more closely.

The next step is to look for missing values and outliers. Because of the high number of variables, I use PROC MEANS:

```
proc means data=ch09.downing n nmiss min mean max maxdec = 2;
weight boostwgt;
var pamsy pid80c4 pid80c8 plor2_5 pmobile — pzsesi
;
run;
```

In Figure 9.3, the output from PROC MEANS shows two variables with missing values. In chapter 4 I discussed a number of ways to handle missing values. Because that is not the emphasis of this chapter, I will just use mean substitution. For each variable, I also create a new variable to identify which records have missing values. The following code replaces the missing values for *pid80c4* and ppbluec and creates four new variables, *pid80crn*, *pc4_miss*, *ppbluecn*, and *pec_miss*. (Note: I'm using the first and last two letters to create a three-character reference to each variable.)

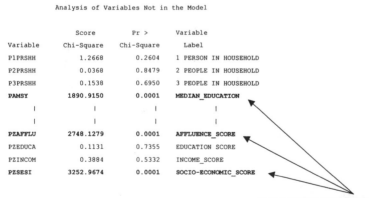

```
                Analysis of Variables Not in the Model


              Score        Pr >      Variable
Variable     Chi-Square   Chi-Square   Label
P1PRSHH        1.2668       0.2604    1 PERSON IN HOUSEHOLD
P2PRSHH        0.0368       0.8479    2 PEOPLE IN HOUSEHOLD
P3PRSHH        0.1538       0.6950    3 PEOPLE IN HOUSEHOLD
PAMSY       1890.9150       0.0001    MEDIAN_EDUCATION
   |            |            |           |
   |            |            |           |
PZAFFLU     2748.1279       0.0001    AFFLUENCE_SCORE
PZEDUCA        0.1131       0.7355    EDUCATION SCORE
PZINCOM        0.3884       0.5332    INCOME_SCORE
PZSESI      3252.9674       0.0001    SOCIO-ECONOMIC_SCORE
```

The chi-square values are inflated by the weights. So only the variables with very high chi-square values are selected for further consideration.

Figure 9.2 Univariate chi-square.

Variable	Label	N	Nmiss	Minimum	Mean	Maximum
PAMSY	MEDIAN_EDUCATION	51067	0	8.00	12.91	18.00
PID80C4	**P_HHS:_WITH_INCOME_$15K-<$25K**	**51027**	**40**	**0.00**	**16.07**	**58.30**
PID80C8	P_HHS:_WITH_INCOME_$75K_OR_MORE	51067	0	0.00	12.77	92.50
PLOR2_5	P_HSU:_TOT_OCC-LENG_RESIDENCE_2_TO_5_YRS	51067	0	0.00	26.87	63.40
PMOBILE	P_HSU:_MOBILE_HOMES_OR_TRAILERS	51067	0	0.00	4.05	94.10
PMVOOU	MEDIAN_VALUE_OF_OWNER_OCCUPIED_UNITS($)	51067	0	14999.00	133281.96	500001.00
PPAED3	P_POP:_ADULTS_25+-H_S_GRADUATES_ONLY	51067	0	0.00	16.99	100.00
PPAED5	P_POP:_ADULTS_25+-CLLEGE_GRAD_+_POSTGRAD	51067	0	0.00	18.57	66.70
PPBLUEC	**P_POP:_EMPL_16+-BLUE_COLLAR_OCCUP**	**50942**	**125**	**0.00**	**11.01**	**56.10**
PPC0509	P_POP:_CHILDREN-5_TO_9	51067	0	0.00	6.23	22.30
PPC1014	P_POP:_CHILDREN-10_TO_14	51067	0	0.00	5.73	37.40
PPC1517	P_POP:_CHILDREN-15_TO_17	51067	0	0.00	3.46	32.20
PPIPRO	P_POP:_EMPL_16+-INDUSTRY-O_PROF-REL_SVCS	51067	0	0.00	4.28	27.40
PPMTCP	P_POP:_16+-TRANS-CAR,TRUCK,VAN_CARPOOL	51067	0	0.00	5.52	25.60
PPOCCR	P_POP:_EMPL_16+-OCC-PRECSN_PRODCRAFT_RPR	51067	0	0.00	4.43	35.30
PPOOU1	P_HSU:_OWN_OCC_UNITS-VALUE_<$30K	51067	0	0.00	2.60	73.50
PPOOU2	P_HSU:_OWN_OCC_UNITS-VALUE_$30K-$50K	51067	0	0.00	5.18	83.30
PPOP1	P_POP:_00-18_YEARS_OLD	51067	0	0.00	23.37	65.60
PPOURE	P_HSU:_OCCUPIED-FUEL-OTHER_SOURCES	51067	0	0.00	6.07	100.00
PPPA2	P_POP:_06-17_YEARS_OLD	51067	0	0.00	14.12	53.10
PPPO1	P_POP:_EMPL_PERS_16+-PROFESSIONALS	51067	0	0.00	8.40	50.00
PPPO2	P_POP:_EMPL_PERS_16+-MANAGERIAL/ADMIN	51067	0	0.00	7.64	30.10
PPRMGR	P_POP:_EMPL_PERS_16+-PROF_+_MANAGERS	51067	0	0.00	16.04	50.70
PPROU6	P_HSU:_RENTAL_UNITS-RENT_$500+	51067	0	0.00	16.80	85.30
PPSAAM	P_POP:_SINGLE_ANCESTRY-U_S_AMERICAN	51067	0	0.00	4.13	53.20
PPSSEP	P_HSU:_SEWAGE_SEPTIC-CESSPOOL_SYSTEM	51067	0	0.00	13.39	100.00
PPTIM4	P_POP:_16+-TIME_LV_HOME_FOR_WK-8-8:30AM	51067	0	0.00	6.42	46.50
PPTIM5	P_POP:_16+-TIME_LV_HM_FOR_WK-8:30AM-12PM	51067	0	0.00	7.90	52.40
PPUM3	P_HSU:_NUMBER_OF_ROOMS-4-6	51067	0	0.00	52.41	100.00
PPURB	P_POP:_URBAN	51067	0	0.00	87.61	100.00
PWHITEC	P_POP:_EMPL_16+-WHITE_COLLAR_OCCUP	51067	0	0.00	32.22	100.00
PZAFFLU	AFFLUENCE_SCORE	51067	0	1.00	4.11	20.00
PZSESI	SOCIO-ECONOMIC_SCORE	51067	0	1.00	4.14	20.00

Figure 9.3 Means analysis of continuous variables.

```
    data ch09.downing;
     set ch09.downing;
    if pid80c4 = . then do;
            pid80c4n = 16.07;
            pc4_miss = 1;
    end;
    else do;
            pid80c4n = pid80c4;
            pc4_miss = 0;
    end;
    if ppbluec = . then do;
            ppbluecn = 11.01;
            pec_miss = 1;
    end;
    else do;
```

```
        ppbluecn = ppbluec;
        pec_miss = 0;
    end;
    run;
```

There do not appear to be any outliers, so I will begin transforming the variables. Recall the method in chapter 4. The first step is to segment the continuous variables into 10 equal buckets. Then I look at a frequency analysis to see if there are any obvious ways to segment the variable to create indicator (0/1) variables. The following code creates the buckets and produces the frequency for the variable for median education, *pamsy*:

```
proc univariate data=ch09.downing noprint;
weight boostwgt;
var pamsy;
output out=psydata pctlpts= 10 20 30 40 50 60 70 80 90 100 pctlpre=psy;
run;

data freqs;
setch09.downing;
if (_n_ eq 1) then set psydata;
retain psy10 psy20 psy30 psy40 psy50 psy60 psy70 psy80 psy90 psy100;
run;

data freqs;
 set freqs;
if pamsy < psy10 then psygrp10 = 1; else
if pamsy < psy20 then psygrp10 = 2; else
if pamsy < psy30 then psygrp10 = 3; else
if pamsy < psy40 then psygrp10 = 4; else
if pamsy < psy50 then psygrp10 = 5; else
if pamsy < psy60 then psygrp10 = 6; else
if pamsy < psy70 then psygrp10 = 7; else
if pamsy < psy80 then psygrp10 = 8; else
if pamsy < psy90 then psygrp10 = 9; else
psygrp10 = 10;
run;

proc freq data= freqs;
weight boostwgt;
table respond*psygrp10;
run;
```

In Figure 9.4, I see that the output gave us only 4 groups. I was expecting 10 groups. This is probably due to the limited number of values for *pamsy*. In the next step, I print out the values for the different deciles of *pamsy* to see why I have only 4 groups:

```
proc print data=psydata;
run;
```

The following output validates my suspicions. The groupings in Figure 9.3 *will* work for our segmentation.

```
OBS   PSY10  PSY20  PSY30  PSY40  PSY50  PSY60  PSY70  PSY80  PSY90
PSY100

 1    12     12     12     12     12     13     13     14     16     18
```

Based on the response rates for the groups in Figure 9.3, I will create two binary variables by segmenting pamsy at the values for PSY60 and PSY90. When you look at the column percent for respond = 1, you'll notice that as the values for pamsy increase, the response percents have a nice upward linear trend, so the continuous form may be more powerful. We will look at that in the next step.

```
data ch09.downing;
 set ch09.downing;
if pamsy < 13 then pamsy13 = 1; else pamsy13 = 0;
if pamsy < 16 then pamsy16 = 1; else pamsy16 = 0;
run;
```

TABLE OF RESPOND BY PAMGRP10

Notice there are only 4 groups when there should be 10 groups.

RESPOND	PAMGRP10				
Frequency					
Percent					
Row Pct					
Col Pct	1	6	9	10	Total
0	977	12003	5969	2231	21180
	1.35	16.61	8.26	3.09	29.32
	4.61	56.67	28.18	10.53	
	36.66	36.51	25.78	16.46	
1	1688.2	20870	17184	11324	51067
	2.34	28.89	23.79	15.67	70.68
	3.31	40.87	33.65	22.18	
	63.34	63.49	74.22	83.54	
Total	2665.25	32873.4	23153	13555.4	72247
	3.69	45.50	32.05	18.76	100.00

Figure 9.4 Segmentation analysis.

Again going back to the techniques in chapter 4, I use a quick method to determine the best transformation for the continuous variables. First, I transform pamsy using a variety of functions. Then I use logistic regression with the *selection=stepwise maxstep = 2* options to find the best fitting transformation:

```
data ch09.downing;
 set ch09.downing;

psy_sq   = pamsy**2;                               /*squared*/
psy_cu   = pamsy**3;                               /*cubed*/
psy_sqrt = sqrt(pamsy);                            /*square root*/
psy_curt = pamsy**.3333;                           /*cube root*/
psy_log  = log(max(.0001,pamsy));                  /*log*/
psy_exp  = exp(max(.0001,pamsy));                  /*exponent*/

psy_tan  = tan(pamsy);                             /*tangent*/
psy_sin  = sin(pamsy);                             /*sine*/
psy_cos  = cos(pamsy);                             /*cosine*/

psy_inv  = 1/max(.0001,pamsy);                     /*inverse*/
psy_sqi  = 1/max(.0001,pamsy**2);                  /*squared inverse*/
psy_cui  = 1/max(.0001,pamsy**3);                  /*cubed inverse*/
psy_sqri = 1/max(.0001,sqrt(pamsy));               /*square root inv*/
psy_curi = 1/max(.0001,pamsy**.3333);              /*cube root inverse*/

psy_logi = 1/max(.0001,log(max(.0001,pamsy))); /*log inverse*/
psy_expi = 1/max(.0001,exp(max(.0001,pamsy))); /*exponent inv*/

psy_tani = 1/max(.0001,tan(pamsy));                /*tangent inverse*/
psy_sini = 1/max(.0001,sin(pamsy));                /*sine inverse*/
psy_cosi = 1/max(.0001,cos(pamsy));                /*cosine inverse*/

run;

proc logistic data=ch09.downing descending;
weight boostwgt;
model respond = pamsy pamsy13 pamsy16 psy_sq psy_cu psy_sqrt psy_curt
psy_log psy_exp psy_tan psy_sin psy_cos psy_inv psy_sqi psy_cui psy_sqri
psy_curi psy_logi psy_expi psy_tani psy_sini psy_cosi /selection = step-
wise maxstep=2 details;
run;
```

In Figure 9.5, we see the results of the stepwise logistic on *pamsy*. The two strongest forms are the natural form, *psy_sq* and *pamsy13* (pamsy < 13). These two forms will be candidates for the final model.

This process is repeated for the remaining 32 variables. The winning transformations for each continuous variable are combined into a new data set called *acqmod.down_mod*;

```
                           The LOGISTIC Procedure

                      Analysis of Maximum Likelihood Estimates


                Parameter   Standard    Wald      Pr >      Standardized   Odds    Variable
   Variable  DF  Estimate    Error    Chi-Square  Chi-Square  Estimate     Ratio   Label


   INTERCPT   1   -0.3881    0.0646    36.0962     0.0001                          Intercept

   PAMSY13    1   -0.3274    0.0223    215.0965    0.0001     -0.110462    0.721

   PAM_SQ     1    0.00787   0.000337  545.1140    0.0001      0.200542    1.008



                Association of Predicted Probabilities and Observed Responses


                      Concordant = 34.3%     Somers' D = 0.076

                      Discordant = 26.7%     Gamma     = 0.125

                      Tied       = 39.0%     Tau-a     = 0.038

                      (651362866 pairs)      c         = 0.538

NOTE: The stepwise model building process has reached the MAXSTEP= 2 limit.



                           Summary of Stepwise Procedure


               Variable          Number    Score      Wald       Pr >     Variable
   Step    Entered   Removed      In     Chi-Square  Chi-Square  Chi-Square  Label


     1     PAM_SQ                  1       2249.5       .         0.0001
     2     PAMSY13                 2        215.6       .         0.0001
```

Figure 9.5 Variable transformation selection.

Table 9.2 is a summary of the continuous variables and the transformations that best fit the objective function.

The next step is to analyze and prepare the categorical variables.

Table 9.2 Summary of Continuous Variable Transformations

VARIABLE	PREFIX	SEGMENTS	TRANSFORMATION 1	TRANSFORMATION 2	DESCRIPTION
pamsy	psy	"< 12, 13,14,16"	sq	pamsy13	Median Education
pid80c4	pc4		sqrt	cui	Income $15K–<$25K
pid80c8	pc8	<5.1	sqrt	logi	Income $75K+
plor2_5	p_5		as is	tan	Length of Residence 2-5 Years

VARIABLE	PREFIX	SEGMENTS	TRANSFORMATION 1	TRANSFORMATION 2	DESCRIPTION
pmobile	ple	<.5	curt	cu	Mobile Homes in Area
pmvoou	pou	<65600	sqrt	cui	Median Value of Home
ppaed3	pd3	<21.3	as is	low	% 25+ Years & High School Grad
ppaed5	pd5		sqrt	curt	% 25+ Years & College Grad
ppbluec	pec	<9.4	as is	low	% 16+ Years Blue Collar
ppc0509	p09	< 6.9 & < 7.3	as is	cu	% w/Children 5–9
ppc1014	p14		as is	cu	% w/Children 10–14
ppc1517	p17	< 4.1	as is	cu	% w/Children 15–17
ppipro	pro		curt	cosi	% Empl 16+ Years Industry Services
ppmtcp	pcp	< 7.3	sqrt	curi	"% Trans: Car, Van Truck, Carpool"
ppoccr	pcr	< 4.9	sqrt	tani	% Empl 16+ Years Product Craft
ppoou1	pu1		curt	tan	% Homes Valued < $30K
ppoou2	pu2	< 14.1	curt	tan	% Homes Valued $30K–$50K
ppop1	pp1		as is	cu	% 0–18 Years Old
ppoure	pre	< 2.1 >18.9	med	sqrt	% Occupied Full– Other Sources
pppa2	pa2		as is	cu	% 6–17 Years Old
pppo1	po1	< 4.8	sqrt	logi	% Empl 16+ Years Professional
pppo2	po2		as is	logi	% Empl 16+ Years Managerial

continues

(Continued)

VARIABLE	PREFIX	SEGMENTS	TRANSFORMATION 1	TRANSFORMATION 2	DESCRIPTION
pprmgr	pgr	< 10.3	as is	logi	% Empl 16+ Years Prof & Managerial
pprou6	pu6		curt	logi	% Rental Units w/ Rent $500+
ppsaam	pam	< 6.8	as is	cosi	% Single Ancestry - US American
ppssep	pep		curt	cui	% Sewage/ Cesspool/ Septic System
pptim4	pm4		as is	sin	% Pop Leave for Work 8–8:30 AM
pptim5	pm5	< 4.3	curt	logi	% Pop Leave for Work 8–12:00 AM
ppum3	pm3		sq	cu	% Number of Rooms 4–6
ppurb	prb		cu	cos	% Urban
pwhitec	ptc	< 19.6	log	sq	% Employee 16+ White Collar
pzafflu	plu	< 7	low	sqrt	Affluence Score
pzsesi	psi		sqrt	cosi	Socio-Economic Score

Categorical Variables

As discussed in Chapter 4, logistic regression uses only numeric variables. And it sees all variables as continuous. In order to use categorical variables, I must create indicator, or binary, variables to state whether a given situation is true or false.

I have 15 categorical variables. The first step is to run a frequency against the weighted response variable. I also request the missing option and a chi-square test of significance:

```
proc freq data=ch09.down_mod;
weight boostwgt;
table respond*(buslevel subsidcd heircode strucode afflcode poprange
```

```
geogarea emplsize indscode mfglocal legalsta mktbilty offequip whitcoll
printer)/ chisq missing;
run;
```

Figure 9.6 displays the output for the first variable, *buslevel*. It shows that each value for *buslevel* has a significantly different response rate.

The values for this variable represent the status of the business. The following list details the values: 0 = Single Entity; 1 = Headquarters; 2 = Branch. To capture the values, I create two indicator variables, *bus_sgle* and *bus_hdqt*, each

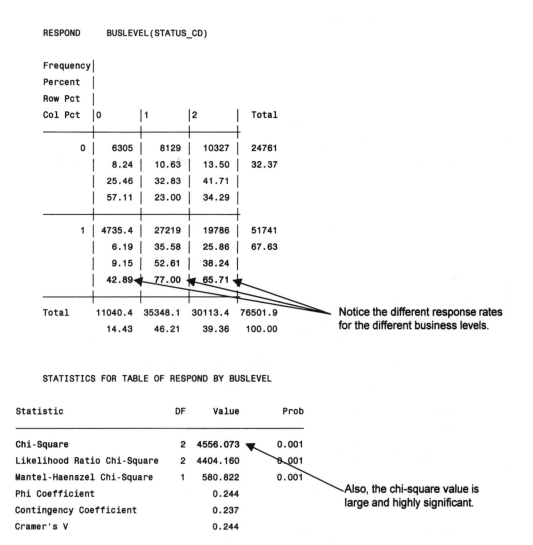

Figure 9.6 Frequency of business level by weighted response.

having the values of 0 and 1. If they are both equal to 0, then the value = 2 or Branch.

I run frequencies for all categorical variables and analyze the results. I create indicator variables for each categorical variable to capture the difference in weighted response. The following code creates indicator (0/1) variables for all categorical variables in the final model:

```
data ch09.down_mod;
  set ch09.down_mod;

bus_sgle = (buslevel = '0');
bus_hdqt = (buslevel = '1');

subsudz  = (subsidcd = '3');

heir_mis = (heircode = ' ');

autonent = (strucode = 'AE');
branch =   (strucode = 'BR');
sub_head =   (strucode = 'SH');
subsid =   (strucode = 'SU');

multaffl = (afflcode = '0');

pop_high = (poprange in (' ', '0'));
pop_num  = max(0, poprange);

geog_low = (geogarea in ('04','07','10'));

empl_100 = (emplsize = 'A');
empl_500 = (emplsize = 'E');
empl1000 = (emplsize = 'R');

ind_high = (indscode in ('A','B','C','L','N','U','Y'));
ind_low  = (indscode in ('D','J','T','Z'));

mfgloc_y = (mfglocal = 'Y');
mfgloc_n = (mfglocal = 'N');

offequ_y = (offequip = 'Y');

whiteco1 = (whitcoll in (' ','A'));
whiteco2 = (whitcoll in ('B','C'));

print_h  = (printer = 'C');
run;
```

Processing the Model

I now have a full list of candidate variables. As I did in part 2, I am running logistic regression with three different selection options. First, I will run the backward and stepwise selection on all variables. I will then take the combination of winning variables from both methods and put it into a logistic regression using the score selection. I will begin looking at models with about 20 variables and find where the score increase begins to diminish with each new variable.

The following code processes the backward selection procedure. The first section of code splits the file into modeling and validation data sets. Due to the large number of variables, I used the option *sls=.0001*. This keeps only the variables whose level of significance is very high. In other words, the probability that the variable is not truly predictive is less than .0001:

```
data ch09.down_mod;
  set ch09.down_mod;
if ranuni(5555) < .5 then splitwgt = 1;
  else splitwgt = .;
modwgt = splitwgt*boostwgt;
records=1;
run;


proc logistic data=ch09.down_mod descending;
weight modwgt;
model respond =   AUTONENT BUS_HDQT BUS_SGLE EMPL1000 EMPL_100 EMPL_500
GEOG_LOW HEIR_MIS IND_HIGH IND_LOW   MFGLOC_N MFGLOC_Y MULTAFFL OFFEQU_Y
P09_CU   P14_CU   P17_CU   PA2_CU    PAMSY13  PSY_SQ   PC4_CUI  PC4_SQRT
PC8_LOGI PC8_SQRT PCR_SQRT PCR_TANI  PD3_LOW  PD5_CURT PD5_SQRT PEC_LOW
PEP_CUI  PEP_CURT PGR_LOGI PID80C4   PID80C8  PLE_CU   PLE_CURT PLOR2_5
PLU_LOW  PLU_SQRT PM3_CU   PM4_SIN   PM5_CURT PM5_LOGI PMOBILE  PMVOOU
PO1_LOGI PO1_SQRT PO2_LOGI POP_HIGH  POP_NUM  POU_CUI  POU_SQRT PP1_CU
PPAED3   PPAED5   PPBLUEC  PPC0509   PPC1014  PPC1517  PPIPRO   PPMTCP
PPOCCR   PPOOU1   PPOOU2   PPOP1     PPOURE   PPPA2    PPPO1    PPPO2
PPRMGR   PPROU6   PPSAAM   PPSSEP    PPTIM4   PPTIM5   PPUM3    PPURB
PRB_COS  PRB_CU   PRE_MED  PRE_SQRT  PRINT_H  PRO_COSI PRO_CURT PSI_COSI
PSI_SQRT PTC_LOG  PTC_SQ   PU1_CURT  PU1_TAN  PU2_CURT PU2_TAN  PU6_CURT
PU6_LOGI PWHITEC  PZAFFLU  PZSESI    P_5_TAN  SUBSUDZ  WHITECO1 WHITECO2
/selection=backward sls=.0001;
run;
```

The next code performs a logistic regression on the same variables with the *selection=stepwise* option. In this model, I used the options, *sle=.0001* and *sls=.0001*. These options specify the level of significance to enter and stay in the model.

```
proc logistic data=ch09.down_mod descending;
weight modwgt;
model respond =    AUTONENT BRANCH    BUS_HDQT   EMPL1000 EMPL_100
EMPL_500
          |         |         |         |         |         |         |
          |         |         |         |         |         |         |
PU6_LOGI  P_5_TAN   SUBSUDZ   WHITECO1  WHITECO2
/selection=stepwise sle=.0001 sls=.0001;
run;
```

As I expect, the backward selection has many more variables. But the stepwise selection has five variables that were not selected by the backward selection method, *ppipro, pm3_cu, pppa2, ptc_sq*, and *pu1_curt*. I add these five variables to the list and run the logistic regression using the score selection. I want the best model based on the highest score so I use the option, *best=1;*

```
proc logistic data=ch09.down_mod descending;
weight modwgt;
model respond =   AUTONENT BUS_HDQT EMPL1000 EMPL_100 EMPL_500 GEOG_LOW
IND_HIGH IND_LOW   MFGLOC_N MFGLOC_Y MULTAFFL PA2_CU    PAM_SQ PC8_SQRT
PD3_LOW   PD5_CURT PD5_SQRT PEC_LOW   PEP_CUI   PGR_LOGI PLE_CU PLE_CURT
PLU_LOW   PM3_CU    PPIPRO    PPPA2     PTC_SQ   PU1_CURT PM5_CURT PM5_LOGI
PMOBILE   PMVOOU    PO2_LOGI POP_HIGH POP_NUM    POU_CUI   POU_SQRT PP1_CU
PPAED3    PPAED5    PPBLUEC   PPC1517   PPMTCP    PPOCCR    PPOOU1 PPOP1
PPPO1     PPRMGR    PPROU6    PPURB     PRB_COS   PRB_CU    PRE_MED PRE_SQRT
PRINT_H   PSI_SQRT PU2_CURT PU6_CURT PU6_LOGI  PZAFFLU   PZSESI SUBSUDZ
WHITECO1 WHITECO2   /selection = score best=1;
run;
```

Figure 9.7 shows an abbreviated output from the logistic with *selection=score*. I look for a point where the amount of increase in score starts to diminish. I end up selecting a model with 30 variables. I rerun these variables in a regular logistic to create an output data set that contains the predicted values. My goal is to create a gains table so that I can evaluate the model's ability to rank responders and 12-month sales. The following code runs the logistic regression, creates an output scoring file (*ch09.coeff*), creates deciles, and builds a gains table. Notice that I do *not* use the weight in the validation gains table:

```
proc logistic data=ch09.down_mod descending outest=ch09.coeff;
weight modwgt;
model respond = AUTONENT BUS_HDQT EMPL1000 EMPL_100 IND_HIGH IND_LOW
MFGLOC_N MFGLOC_Y MULTAFFL PA2_CU PC8_SQRT PD5_SQRT PEC_LOW PEP_CUI
PLU_LOW PM5_CURT PM5_LOGI PO2_LOGI POP_HIGH POP_NUM PPC1517 PPMTCP
PPOOU1 PPPA2 PRB_COS PRE_MED PRINT_H PU6_LOGI PZAFFLU SUBSUDZ WHITECO1
WHITECO2
output out=ch09.scored(where=(splitwgt=.)) p=pred;
run;

proc sort data=ch09.scored;
```

Regression Models Selected by Score Criterion

Number of Variables	Score Value	Variables Included in Model
1	3243.2012	PRINT_H
2	4673.6717	IND_HIGH PRINT_H
3	5615.9997	AUTONENT IND_HIGH PRINT_H
⋮	⋮	⋮
32	7900.7171	AUTONENT BUS_HDQT EMPL1000 EMPL_100 IND_HIGH IND_LOW MFGLOC_N MFGLOC_Y MULTAFFL PA2_CU PC8_SQRT PD5_SQRT PEC_LOW PEP_CUI PLU_LOW PM5_CURT PM5_LOGI PO2_LOGI POP_HIGH POP_NUM PPC1517 PPMTCP PPOOU1 PPPA2 PRB_COS PRE_MED PRINT_H PU6_LOGI PZAFFLU SUBSUDZ WHITECO1 WHITECO2
33	7903.6487	AUTONENT BUS_HDQT EMPL1000 EMPL_100 IND_HIGH IND_LOW MFGLOC_N MFGLOC_Y MULTAFFL PA2_CU PC8_SQRT PD5_SQRT PEC_LOW PEP_CUI PLU_LOW PM5_CURT PM5_LOGI PO2_LOGI POP_HIGH PPC1517 PPMTCP PPOOU1 PPPA2 PRB_COS PRE_MED PPROU6 PRINT_H PU6_CURT PU6_LOGI PZAFFLU SUBSUDZ WHITECO1 WHITECO2
34	7908.7531	AUTONENT BUS_HDQT EMPL1000 EMPL_100 IND_HIGH IND_LOW MFGLOC_N MFGLOC_Y MULTAFFL PA2_CU PC8_SQRT PD5_SQRT PEC_LOW PEP_CUI PLU_LOW PM5_CURT PM5_LOGI PO2_LOGI POP_HIGH POP_NUM PPC1517 PPMTCP PPOOU1 PPPA2 PRB_COS PRE_MED PPROU6 PRINT_H PU6_CURT PU6_LOGI PZAFFLU SUBSUDZ WHITECO1 WHITECO2

Figure 9.7 Logistic regression using score selection.

```
by descending pred;
run;

proc univariate data=ch09.scored noprint;
var records;
output out=preddata sum=totrec;
run;

data ch09.scored;
 set ch09.scored;
if (_n_ eq 1) then set preddata;
retain totrec;
number+1;
if number < .1*totrec then val_dec = 0; else
if number < .2*totrec then val_dec = 1; else
if number < .3*totrec then val_dec = 2; else
if number < .4*totrec then val_dec = 3; else
if number < .5*totrec then val_dec = 4; else
```

```
if number < .6*totrec then val_dec = 5; else
if number < .7*totrec then val_dec = 6; else
if number < .8*totrec then val_dec = 7; else
if number < .9*totrec then val_dec = 8; else
val_dec = 9;
run;

proc tabulate data=ch09.scored;
class val_dec;
var respond sale12mo pred records;
table val_dec='Decile' all='Total',
      records='Prospects'*sum=' '*f=comma10.
      pred='Predicted Probability'*mean=' '*f=11.5
      respond='Percent Respond'*mean=' '*f=11.5
      sale12mo='Sales'*sum=' '*f=dollar11. /rts = 9 row=float;
run;
```

Figure 9.8 shows the listing of parameter estimates for the final model. The most predictive variables are shown in bold. These can be used to assist in solicitation design and other marketing decisions. The validation gains table created in proc tabulate can be seen in Figure 9.9. These values are expanded into a spreadsheet that can be seen in Figure 9.10. This table calculates cumulative values for *response, 12-month sale,* and *lift.* Notice how the lift is much greater for *12-months sales* than it is for *lift.* Again, this is a direct result of the weighting used to attract big-spending responders.

In Figure 9.9 the model shows good rank ordering of prospects by response and sales. The deciles are all monotonically decreasing with a strong decline, especially in 12-month sales. In Figure 9.10 the cumulative values and lift measures show the true power of this model. Notice how the lift for sales is so much better than the lift for response. This is a result of the weighting.

Figure 9.10 also provides a wealth of information for making marketing decisions. As we did in chapter 7, we can use this table to decide how many deciles we want to solicit. For example, if we want target businesses with greater than $100 in sales, we would solicit through decile 5.

Figure 9.11 provides a visual account of the power of the model. Notice how the curve for 12-month sales is higher than the curve for response. This reflects the higher lift in the prediction of 12-month sales.

Validation Using Boostrapping

As I discussed in chapter 6, an excellent method for determining the robustness of your model is to create bootstrap samples and calculate confidence inter-

INTERCPT	1	0.7506	0.2611	8.2617	0.0040	.	.
AUTONENT	1	-0.2052	0.0633	10.5035	0.0012	-0.042573	0.814
BUS_HDQT	1	0.7762	0.0571	184.8936	0.0001	0.260119	2.173
EMPL1000	1	-1.4812	0.0970	233.3090	0.0001	-0.150708	0.227
EMPL_100	1	-0.9169	0.0601	232.8111	0.0001	-0.307432	0.400
IND_HIGH	**1**	**0.8740**	**0.0337**	**672.9275**	**0.0001**	**0.258750**	**2.396**
IND_LOW	1	-0.3534	0.0443	63.5675	0.0001	-0.065232	0.702
MFGLOC_N	1	0.5288	0.1000	27.9327	0.0001	0.054606	1.697
MFGLOC_Y	1	0.1821	0.0369	24.3494	0.0001	0.052091	1.200
MULTAFFL	1	-0.6808	0.1113	37.4442	0.0001	-0.059536	0.506
PA2_CU	1	-0.00002	8.058E-6	4.3566	0.0369	-0.038430	1.000
PC8_SQRT	1	-0.1234	0.0174	50.3146	0.0001	-0.125239	0.884
PD5_SQRT	1	0.2936	0.0235	156.5460	0.0001	0.275932	1.341
PEC_LOW	1	0.2948	0.0547	29.0877	0.0001	0.057662	1.343
PEP_CUI	1	0.000024	5.516E-6	19.0609	0.0001	0.051284	1.000
PLU_LOW	1	-0.2113	0.0508	17.2870	0.0001	-0.056275	0.810
PM5_CURT	1	-0.5363	0.0770	48.5132	0.0001	-0.124341	0.585
PM5_LOGI	1	-0.00015	0.000027	29.7264	0.0001	-0.050774	1.000
PO2_LOGI	1	0.00009	0.000013	51.8228	0.0001	0.069064	1.000
POP_HIGH	1	0.4787	0.1301	13.5354	0.0002	0.039682	1.614
POP_NUM	1	0.0320	0.0116	7.6027	0.0058	0.037302	1.032
PPC1517	1	0.1259	0.0241	27.1977	0.0001	0.112867	1.134
PPMTCP	1	-0.0357	0.00722	24.4660	0.0001	-0.049065	0.965
PPOOU1	1	-0.0194	0.00320	36.7982	0.0001	-0.062399	0.981
PPPA2	1	-0.0358	0.00847	17.8508	0.0001	-0.125015	0.965
PRB_COS	1	0.0823	0.0218	14.2576	0.0002	0.032876	1.086
PRE_MED	1	-0.2186	0.0564	15.0476	0.0001	-0.036912	0.804
PRINT_H	**1**	**1.1677**	**0.0282**	**1717.9214**	**0.0001**	**0.393023**	**3.215**
PU6_LOGI	1	-0.00002	6.788E-6	6.8735	0.0087	-0.024915	1.000
PZAFFLU	1	-0.0488	0.00837	34.0529	0.0001	-0.099705	0.952
SUBSUDZ	1	0.4180	0.0412	102.7551	0.0001	0.110608	1.519
WHITECO1	1	0.9920	0.0876	128.2056	0.0001	0.312601	2.697
WHITECO2	1	0.5755	0.0838	47.2052	0.0001	0.177885	1.778

The two highest predictors are *Heavy Printer Product Sales* and *High Ranking Industry Code*

Figure 9.8 Parameter estimates.

vals. The following code is a variation on the code in chapter 6. It calculates confidence intervals for *response, 12-month sales,* and *lift* for *12-month sales.* The program uses some macro language to reduce the amount of code. The first step creates a small sample to speed processing. Since my sample weight is artificial, I need to create a false sample weight equal to 1. This prevents having to change the program:

```
data ch09.bs_all;
set ch09.scored(keep= pred respond splitwgt records sale12mo val_dec);
smp_wgt=1;
run;
```

I use PROC UNIVARIATE to get the overall mean values for *respond (rspmean)* and *12-month sales (salmean).*

```
proc univariate data=ch09.bs_all noprint;
weight smp_wgt;
var respond sale12mo;
output out=preddata sumwgt=sumwgt mean= rspmean salmean;
run;
```

Decile	Prospects	Predicted Probability	Percent Respond	12-Month Sales Total	Average
0	2,557	0.90528	0.70473	$1,630,750	$638
1	2,558	0.82408	0.63409	$743,639	$291
2	2,558	0.76395	0.61181	$561,656	$220
3	2,557	0.70040	0.57567	$528,006	$206
4	2,558	0.62898	0.55004	$355,307	$139
5	2,558	0.56060	0.48045	$301,687	$118
6	2,557	0.49619	0.47086	$244,662	$96
7	2,558	0.42468	0.44488	$194,676	$76
8	2,558	0.33066	0.39210	$141,585	$55
9	2,558	0.19231	0.28186	$79,500	$31
Total	25,577	0.58270	0.51464	$4,781,469	$187

The ranking for both 'Percent Respond and 'Sales' is strong. Notice how the values monotonically decrease from decile 0 to decile 9.

Figure 9.9 Validation decile analysis.

Decile	Prospects	Cum % of Mailing	Probability of Response	Percent of Responders	Cumulative % Respond	Number of Resp	% of Total Responders	Cum # of Responders	Cum % of Total Response	Responders Lift	Cum Lift	Total 12-Month Sales	Cum 12-Month Sales	Cumulative % of Sales	Average Sales	Lift	Cum Lift
0	2,557	10%	90.53%	70.473%	70.473%	1,802	13.69%	1,802	13.69%	137	137	$1,630,750	$1,630,750	34.1%	$638	341	341
1	2,558	20%	82.41%	63.409%	66.940%	1,622	12.32%	3,424	26.01%	123	130	$743,639	$2,374,389	49.7%	$291	156	248
2	2,558	30%	76.40%	61.181%	65.020%	1,565	11.89%	4,989	37.90%	119	126	$561,656	$2,936,045	61.4%	$220	118	205
3	2,557	40%	70.04%	57.567%	63.157%	1,472	11.18%	6,461	49.08%	112	123	$528,006	$3,464,051	72.4%	$206	110	181
4	2,558	50%	62.90%	55.004%	61.526%	1,407	10.69%	7,868	59.77%	107	120	$355,307	$3,819,358	79.9%	$139	74	160
5	2,558	60%	56.06%	48.045%	59.279%	1,229	9.34%	9,097	69.11%	93	115	$301,687	$4,121,045	86.2%	$118	63	144
6	2,557	70%	49.62%	47.086%	57.538%	1,204	9.15%	10,301	78.26%	91	112	$244,662	$4,365,707	91.3%	$96	51	130
7	2,558	80%	42.47%	44.488%	55.906%	1,138	8.65%	11,439	86.90%	86	109	$194,676	$4,560,383	95.4%	$76	41	119
8	2,558	90%	33.07%	39.210%	54.051%	1,003	7.62%	12,442	94.52%	76	105	$141,585	$4,701,968	98.3%	$55	29	109
9	2,558	100%	19.23%	28.186%	51.464%	721	5.48%	13,163	100.00%	55	100	$79,500	$4,781,468	100.0%	$31	17	100
TOTAL	25,577		58.27%	51.465%		13,163	100.00%					$4,781,468			$187		

Compare the lift for responders and sales.

Figure 9.10 Validation gains table with lift.

226

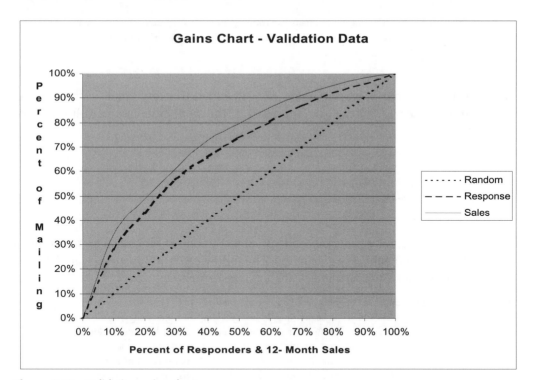

Figure 9.11 Validation gains chart.

The following data step appends the overall mean values to every record:

```
data ch09.bs_all;
 set ch09.bs_all;
if (_n_ eq 1) then set preddata;
retain sumwgt rspmean salmean;
run;
```

PROC SUMMARY creates mean values of *respond (rspmnf)* and *12-month sales (salmnf)* for each *decile (val_dec):*

```
proc summary data=ch09.bs_all;
var respond sale12mo;
class val_dec;
output out=ch09.fullmean  mean= rspmnf salmnf;
run;
```

The next data step uses the output from PROC SUMMARY to create a separate data set (salfmean) with the two overall mean values renamed. The overall mean values are stored in the observation where *val_dec* has a missing value (*val_dec* = .). These will be used in the final bootstrap calculation:

```
data salfmean(rename=(salmnf=salomn_g rspmnf=rspomn_g) drop=val_dec);
 set ch09.fullmean(where=(val_dec=.) keep=salmnf rspmnf val_dec);
smp_wgt=1;
run;
```

In the next data step, the means are appended to every value of the data set
ch09.fullmean. This will be accessed in the final calculations following the
macro.

```
data ch09.fullmean;
 set ch09.fullmean;
if (_n_ eq 1) then set salfmean;
retain salomn_g rspomn_g;
run;
```

The bootstrapping program is identical to the one in chapter 6 up to the point
where the estimates are calculated. The following data step merges all the bootstrap samples and calculates the bootstrap estimates:

```
data ch09.bs_sum(keep=liftf bsest_r rspmnf lci_r uci_r bsest_s salmnf
lci_s uci_s bsest_l lftmbs lci_l uci_l val_dec salomn_g);
 merge  ch09.bsmns1 ch09.bsmns2 ch09.bsmns3 ch09.bsmns4 ch09.bsmns5
ch09.bsmns6 ch09.bsmns7 ch09.bsmns8 ch09.bsmns9 ch09.bsmns10
ch09.bsmns11 ch09.bsmns12 ch09.bsmns13 ch09.bsmns14 ch09.bsmns15
ch09.bsmns16 ch09.bsmns17 ch09.bsmns18 ch09.bsmns19 ch09.bsmns20
ch09.bsmns21 ch09.bsmns22 ch09.bsmns23 ch09.bsmns24 ch09.bsmns25
ch09.fullmean;
by val_dec;
rspmbs  = mean(of rspmn1-rspmn25);      /* mean of response */
rspsdbs =  std(of rspmn1-rspmn25);      /* st dev of response */

salmbs  = mean(of salmn1-salmn25);      /* mean of sales */
salsdbs =  std(of salmn1-salmn25);      /* st dev of sales */

lftmbs  = mean(of liftd1-liftd25);      /* mean of lift */
lftsdbs =  std(of liftd1-liftd25);      /* st dev of lift */


liftf = 100*salmnf/salomn_g;            /* overall lift for sales */

bsest_r = 2*rspmnf - rspmbs;            /* boostrap est - response */
lci_r   = bsest_r - 1.96*rspsdbs;       /* lower conf interval */
uci_r   = bsest_r + 1.96*rspsdbs;       /* upper conf interval */

bsest_s = 2*salmnf - salmbs;            /* boostrap est - sales */
lci_s   = bsest_s - 1.96*salsdbs;       /* lower conf interval */
uci_s   = bsest_s + 1.96*salsdbs;       /* upper conf interval */

bsest_l = 2*liftf - lftmbs;             /* boostrap est - lift */
lci_l   = bsest_l - 1.96*lftsdbs;       /* lower conf interval */
uci_l   = bsest_l + 1.96*lftsdbs;       /* upper conf interval */
run;
```

Finally, I use PROC TABULATE to display the bootstrap and confidence interval values by decile.

```
proc tabulate data=ch09.bs_sum;
var liftf bsest_r rspmnf lci_r uci_r bsest_s salmnf
lci_s uci_s bsest_l lftmbs lci_l uci_l;
class val_dec;
table (val_dec='Decile' all='Total'),
(rspmnf='Actual Resp'*mean=' '*f=percent6.
bsest_r='BS Est Resp'*mean=' '*f=percent6.
lci_r  ='BS Lower CI Resp'*mean=' '*f=percent6.
uci_r  ='BS Upper CI Resp'*mean=' '*f=percent6.

salmnf ='12-Month Sales'*mean=' '*f=dollar8.
bsest_s='BS Est Sales'*mean=' '*f=dollar8.
lci_s  ='BS Lower CI Sales'*mean=' '*f=dollar8.
uci_s  ='BS Upper CI Sales'*mean=' '*f=dollar8.

liftf ='Sales Lift'*mean=' '*f=6.
bsest_l='BS Est Lift'*mean=' '*f=6.
lci_l  ='BS Lower CI Lift'*mean=' '*f=6.
uci_l  ='BS Upper CI Lift'*mean=' '*f=6.)
/rts=10 row=float;
run;
```

Decile	Actual Resp	BS Est Resp	BS Lower CI Resp	BS Upper CI Resp	12-Month Sales	BS Est Sales	BS Lower CI Sales	BS Upper CI Sales	Sales Lift	BS Est Lift	BS Lower CI Lift	BS Upper CI Lift
0	70%	71%	69%	72%	$638	$661	$557	$766	341	347	307	387
1	63%	63%	61%	65%	$291	$288	$249	$327	156	150	126	175
2	61%	61%	60%	63%	$220	$218	$197	$239	117	114	100	128
3	58%	58%	56%	59%	$206	$223	$155	$291	110	117	82	152
4	55%	55%	53%	57%	$139	$141	$127	$154	74	74	67	80
5	48%	48%	46%	50%	$118	$117	$91	$143	63	61	47	76
6	47%	47%	45%	49%	$96	$96	$81	$110	51	50	41	59
7	44%	45%	43%	47%	$76	$76	$60	$91	41	39	31	48
8	39%	39%	37%	41%	$55	$56	$48	$63	30	29	25	34
9	28%	28%	27%	30%	$31	$31	$27	$36	17	16	14	19
Total	51%	52%	50%	53%	$187	$191	$159	$222	100	100	84	116

Bootstrap confidence intervals (CI) are good indicators of the model's stability. You can bet 95% that the response and sales propensity and lift are within these ranges.

Figure 9.12 Bootstrap analysis.

The results of the bootstrap analysis give me confidence that the model is stable. Notice how the confidence intervals are fairly tight even in the best decile. And the bootstrap estimates are very close to the actual value, providing additional security. Keep in mind that these estimates are not based on actual behavior but rather a propensity toward a type of behavior. They will, however, provide a substantial improvement over random selection.

Implementing the Model

In this case, the same file containing the score will be used for marketing. The marketing manager at Downing Office Products now has a robust model that can be used to solicit businesses that have the highest propensity to buy the company's products.

The ability to rank the entire business list also creates other opportunities for Downing. It is now prepared to prioritize sales efforts to maximize its marketing dollar. The top scoring businesses (deciles 7–9) are targeted to receive a personal sales call. The middle group (4–8) is targeted to receive several telemarketing solicitations. And the lowest group (deciles 0–3) will receive a postcard directing potential customers to the company's Web site. This is expected to provide a substantial improvement in yearly sales.

Summary

Isn't it amazing how the creative use of weights can cause those high spenders to rise to the top? This case study is an excellent example of how well this weighting technique works. You just have to remember that the estimated probabilities are not accurate predictors. But the ability of the model to rank the file from most profitable to least profitable prospects is superior to modeling without weights. In addition, the mechanics of working with business data are identical to those of working with individual and household data.

Response models are the most widely used and work for almost any industry. From banks and insurance companies selling their products to phone companies and resorts selling their services, the simplest response model can improve targeting and cut costs. Whether you're targeting individuals, families, or business, the rules are the same: clear objective, proper data preparation, linear predictors, rigorous processing, and thorough validation. In our next chapter, we try another recipe. We're going to predict which prospects are more likely to be financially risky.

CHAPTER 10

Avoiding High-Risk Customers: Modeling Risk

Most businesses are interested in knowing who will respond, activate, purchase, or use their services. As we saw in our case study in part 2, many companies need to manage another major component of the profitability equation, one that does not involve purchasing or using products or services. These businesses are concerned with the amount of risk they are taking by accepting someone as a customer. Our case study in part 2 incorporated the effect of risk on overall profitability for life insurance. Banks assume risk through loans and credit cards, but other business such as utilities and telcos also assume risk by providing products and services on credit. Virtually any company delivering a product or service with the promise of future payment takes a financial risk.

In this chapter, I start off with a description of credit scoring, its origin, and how it has evolved into risk modeling. Then I begin the case study in which I build a model that predicts risk by targeting failure to pay on a credit-based purchase for the telecommunications or telco industry. (This is also known as an approval model.) As in chapter 9, I define the objective, prepare the variables, and process and validate the model. You will see some similarities in the processes, but there are also some notable differences due to the nature of the data. Finally, I wrap up the chapter with a brief discussion of fraud modeling and how it's being used to reduce losses in many industries.

Credit Scoring and Risk Modeling

If you've ever applied for a loan, I'm sure you're familiar with questions like, "Do you own or rent?" "How long have you lived at your current address?" and "How many years have you been with your current employer?" The answers to these questions—and more—are used to calculate your credit score. Based on your answers (each of which is assigned a value), your score is summed and evaluated. Historically, this method has been very effective in helping companies determine credit worthiness.

Credit scoring began in the early sixties when Fair, Isaac and Company developed the first simple scoring algorithm based on a few key factors. Until that time, decisions to grant credit were primarily based on judgment. Some companies were resistant to embrace a score to determine credit worthiness. As the scores proved to be predictive, more and more companies began to use them.

As a result of increased computer power, more available data, and advances in technology, tools for predicting credit risk have become much more sophisticated. This has led to complex credit scoring algorithms that have the ability to consider and utilize many different factors. Through these advances, risk scoring has evolved from a simple scoring algorithm based on a few factors to the sophisticated scoring algorithms we see today.

Over the years, Fair, Isaac scores have become a standard in the industry. While its methodology has been closely guarded, it recently published the components of its credit-scoring algorithm. Its score is based on the following elements:

Past payment history

- Account payment information on specific types of accounts (e.g., credit cards, retail accounts, installment loans, finance company accounts, mortgage)
- Presence of adverse public records (e.g., bankruptcy, judgments, suits, liens, wage attachments), collection items, and/or delinquency (past due items)
- Severity of delinquency (how long past due)
- Amount past due on delinquent accounts or collection items
- Time since (recency of) past due items (delinquency), adverse public records (if any), or collection items (if any)
- Number of past due items on file

- Number of accounts paid as agreed

Amount of credit owing

- Amount owing on accounts
- Amount owing on specific types of accounts
- Lack of a specific type of balance, in some cases
- Number of accounts with balances
- Proportion of credit lines used (proportion of balances to total credit limits on certain types of revolving accounts)
- Proportion of installment loan amounts still owing (proportion of balance to original loan amount on certain types of installment loans)

Length of time credit established

- Time since accounts opened
- Time since accounts opened, by specific type of account
- Time since account activity

Search for and acquisition of new credit

- Number of recently opened accounts, and proportion of accounts that are recently opened, by type of account
- Number of recent credit inquiries
- Time since recent account opening(s), by type of account
- Time since credit inquiry(s)
- Reestablishment of positive credit history following past payment problems

Types of credit established

- Number of (presence, prevalence, and recent information on) various types of accounts (credit cards, retail accounts, installment loans, mortgage, consumer finance accounts, etc.)

Over the past decade, numerous companies have begun developing their own risk scores to sell or for personal use. In this case study, I will develop a risk score that is very similar to those available on the market. I will test the final scoring algorithm against a generic risk score that I obtained from the credit bureau.

Defining the Objective

Eastern Telecom has just formed an alliance with First Reserve Bank to sell products and services. Initially, Eastern wishes to offer cellular phones and phone services to First Reserve's customer base. Eastern plans to use statement inserts to promote its products and services, so marketing costs are relatively small. Its main concern at this point is managing risk.

Since payment behavior for a loan product is highly correlated with payment behavior for a product or service, Eastern plans to use the bank's data to predict financial risk over a three-year period. To determine the level of risk for each customer, Eastern Telecom has decided to develop a model that predicts the probability of a customer becoming 90+ days past due or defaulting on a loan within a three-year period.

To develop a modeling data set, Eastern took a sample of First Reserve's loan customers. From the customers that were current 36 months ago, Eastern selected all the customers now considered high risk or in default and a sample of those customers who were still current and considered low risk. A high-risk customer was defined as any customer who was 90 days or more behind on a loan with First Reserve Bank. This included all bankruptcies and charge-offs. Eastern created three data fields to define a high-risk customer: *bkruptcy* to denote if they were bankrupt, *chargoff* to denote if they were charged off, and *dayspdue*, a numeric field detailing the days past due.

A file containing name, address, social security number, and a match key (*idnum*) was sent to the credit bureau for a data overlay. Eastern requested that the bureau pull 300+ variables from an archive of 36 months ago and append the information to the customer file. It also purchased a generic risk score that was developed by an outside source.

The file was returned and matched to the original extract to combine the 300+ predictive variables with the three data fields. The following code takes the combined file and creates the modeling data set. The first step defines the independent variable, *highrisk*. The second step samples and defines the weight, *smp_wgt*. This step creates two temporary data sets, *hr* and *lr*, that are brought together in the final step to create the data set *ch10.telco*:

```
data ch10.creddata;
  set ch10.creddata;
  if bkruptcy = 1 or chargoff = 1 or dayspdue => 90 then highrisk = 1;
  else highrisk = 0;
  run;

  data hr lr(where=(ranuni(5555) < .14));
   set ch10.creddata;
```

```
if highrisk = 1 then do;
        smp_wgt=1;
        output hr;
end;
else do;
        smp_wgt=7;
        output lr;
end;
run;

data ch10.telco;
set hr lr;
run;
```

Table 10.1 displays the original population size and percents, the sample size, and the weights:

Table 10.1 Population and Sample Frequencies and Weights

GROUP	POPULATION	POPULATION PERCENT	SAMPLE	WEIGHT
High Risk	10,875	3.48%	10,875	1
Low Risk	301,665	96.5%	43,095	7
TOTAL	312,540	100%	53,970	

The overall rate of high-risk customers is 3.48%. This is kept intact by the use of weights in the modeling process. The next step is to prepare the predictive variables.

Preparing the Variables

This data set is unusual in that all the predictive variables are continuous except one, *gender*. Because there are so many (300+) variables, I have decided to do things a little differently. I know that when data is sent to an outside source for data overlay that there will be missing values. The first thing I want to do is determine which variables have a high number of missing values. I begin by running PROC MEANS with an option to calculate the number of missing values, *nmiss*. To avoid having to type in the entire list of variable names, I run a PROC CONTENTS with a *short* option. This creates a variable list (in all caps) without any numbers or extraneous information. This can be cut and pasted into open code:

```
proc contents data=ch10.telco short;
run;

proc means data=ch10.telco n nmiss mean min max maxdec=1;
```

```
var AFADBM AFMAXB AFMAXH AFMINB AFMINH AOPEN AFPDBAL AFR29 AFR39 . . .
 . .
 . . . . . . . . . . . . . . . . UTR4524 UTR7924 UTRATE1 UTRATE2 UTRATE3;
run;
```

Figure 10.1 displays a portion of the results of PROC MEANS. Remember, there are 300+ variables in total, so my first goal is to look for an effective way to reduce the number of variables. I decide to look for variables with good coverage of the data by selecting variables with less than 1,000 missing values. There are 61 variables that meet this criterion.

With 61 variables, I am going to streamline my techniques for faster processing. The first step is to check the quality of the data. I look for outliers and handle the missing values. Rather than look at each variable individually, I run another PROC MEANS on the 61 variables that I have chosen for consideration. Figure 10.2 shows part of the output.

Variable	Label	N	Nmiss	Mean	Minimum	Maximum
AFADBM	MAX OPEN AUTO FINANCE UTILIZATION RAT	6110	47860	0.7	0.0	4.4
AFMAXB	MAX OPEN AUTO FINANCE BAL	6110	47860	10970.8	0.0	47808.0
AFMAXH	MAX OPEN AUTO FINANCE HIGH CREDIT	6110	47860	15523.3	106.0	49430.0
AFMINB	MIN OPEN AUTO FINANCE BAL > 0	6110	47860	10347.7	0.0	47808.0
AFMINH	MIN OPEN AUTO FINANCE HIGH CREDIT > 0	6110	47860	14885.0	79.0	49430.0
AFOPEN	# OF "OPEN"/ AUTO FIN ACCTS	10766	43204	0.6	0.0	5.0
AFRATE45	# OF AUTO FIN ACCTS/EVER 90+ DAYS	10375	43595	0.0	0.0	3.0
AFRATE79	# OF AUTO FIN ACCTS/EVER BAD DEBT	11159	42811	0.1	0.0	4.0
AFTRADES	**# OF AUTO FIN ACCTS**	**49516**	**4454**	**0.3**	**0.0**	**11.0**
AGE	**ACTUAL AGE OF SUBJECT**	**46214**	**7756**	**34.8**	**1.0**	**92.0**
AMTPD	**AMOUNT OF/PAST DUE BALANCES**	**48958**	**5012**	**904.3**	**0.0**	**7407450.0**
ATRATE3	# OF AUTO ACCTS/EVER 60 DAYS	3632	50338	0.0	0.0	2.0
ATRATE45	# OF AUTO ACCTS/EVER 90+ DAYS	3632	50338	0.0	0.0	3.0
ATRATE79	# OF AUTO ACCTS/EVER BAD DEBT	4062	49908	0.2	0.0	4.0
ATTRADES	**# OF AUTO ACCTS**	**49516**	**4454**	**0.1**	**0.0**	**7.0**
AVGMOS	**AVERAGE # OF/MONTHS OPEN**	**49326**	**4644**	**50.9**	**1.0**	**427.0**
BADPR1	**# OF 90-120 BAD DBT/PUB REC DEROG IN 24**	**51666**	**2304**	**1.8**	**0.0**	**54.0**
BADPR2	**# OF BAD DEBT /PUB REC DEROG W/I 24**	**51666**	**2304**	**1.6**	**0.0**	**54.0**
UTR4524	# OF UTILITY ACCT RATED 4-5 W/IN 24 MNTH	2598	51372	0.1	0.0	7.0
UTR7924	# OF UTILITY ACCT RATED 7-9 W/IN 24 MNTH	2987	50983	0.1	0.0	3.0
UTRATE1	# OF UTILITY ACCOUNTS EVER SATISFACTORY	2600	51370	0.7	0.0	4.0
UTRATE2	NUMBER OF UTILITY ACCOUNTS EVER 30 DAYS	2600	51370	0.0	0.0	3.0
UTRATE3	NUMBER OF UTILITY ACCOUNTS EVER 60 DAYS	2600	51370	0.0	0.0	2.0

Figure 10.1   Means of continuous variables.

At this point, the only problem I see is with the variable *age*. The minimum age does not seem correct because we have no customers under the age of 18. In Figure 10.3, the univariate analysis of *age* shows that less than 1% of the values for age are below 18, so I will treat any value of *age* below 18 as missing.

As I said, I am going to do things a bit differently this time to speed the processing. I have decided that because the number of missing values for each variable is relatively small, I am going to use *mean* substitution to replace the values. Before I replace the missing values with the mean, I want to create a set of duplicate variables. This allows me to keep the original values intact.

To streamline the code, I use an *array* to create a set of duplicate variables. An *array* is a handy SAS option that allows you to assign a name to a group of variables. Each of the 61 variables is duplicated with the variable names rvar1, rvar2, rvar3, though rvar61. This allows me to perform the same calculations on every variable just by naming the *array*. In fact, I am going to use several

Variable	Label	N	Mean	Std Dev	Minimum	Maximum
COLLS	# OF/COLLECTION ITEMS	52009	1.23	3.10	0.00	53.00
LOCINQS	# OF LOCAL INQ/IN PAST 6 MO	43212	1.45	1.81	0.00	43.00
INQAGE	AGE OF MOST/RECENT INQUIRY	43212	5.76	5.90	0.00	24.00
CRDPTH	AGE OF OLDEST TRADE	49328	103.33	89.01	1.00	846.00
TMINAGE	AGE OF YOUNGEST TRADE	49328	16.58	21.67	0.00	427.00
TOPEN3	# OF ACCTS OPENED/IN LAST 3 MO	49326	0.23	0.55	0.00	8.00
TOPEN6	# OF ACCTS OPENED/IN LAST 6 MO	49326	0.55	0.90	0.00	11.00
TOPEN12	# OF ACCTS OPENED/IN LAST 12 MO	49326	1.27	1.55	0.00	18.00
TOPEN24	# OF ACCTS OPENED/IN LAST 24 MO	49326	2.61	2.59	0.00	24.00
TRADES	# OF ACCTS ON FILE	53968	9.42	8.75	0.00	77.00
TOPEN	# OF "OPEN" ACCTS/ ON FILE	48925	5.08	4.20	0.00	43.00
TSBAL	TOTAL / OPEN BALANCES	47959	10577.02	13941.68	0.00	243751.00
TSHIC	TOTAL/ OPEN HIGH CREDITS	47942	19846.38	22641.56	0.00	322261.00
LAAGE	AGE OF/LAST ACTIVITY	53970	1.45	1.82	0.00	24.00
TOPENB50	# OF "OPEN" ACCTS WITH/BAL >50% HI CRED	45573	2.38	2.43	0.00	33.00
BRTRADES	# OF BANK REV ACCTS	49516	3.17	3.64	0.00	49.00
DCTRADES	# OF DEPT STORE ACCTS	49516	1.73	2.09	0.00	22.00
FFTRADES	# OF CON FIN CO ACCTS	49516	0.17	0.59	0.00	20.00
ORTRADES	# OF OTHER RETAIL ACCTS	49516	0.87	1.35	0.00	14.00
ATTRADES	# OF AUTO ACCTS	49516	0.09	0.34	0.00	7.00
AFTRADES	# OF AUTO FIN ACCTS	49516	0.33	0.74	0.00	11.00
CUTRADES	# OF CRED UNION ACCTS	49516	0.86	1.76	0.00	51.00
PFTRADES	# OF PRSL FIN ACCTS	49516	1.14	2.17	0.00	33.00
OITRADES	# OF OIL CO ACCTS	49516	0.07	0.32	0.00	6.00
TETRADES	# OF T&E ACCTS	49516	0.11	0.37	0.00	5.00
AGE	**ACTUAL AGE OF SUBJECT**	**46214**	**34.77**	**13.49**	**1.00**	**92.00**
TADB	TOTAL/AVERAGE DEBT BURDEN	47942	0.56	0.38	0.00	10.00
TPCTSAT	% OF SATS /TO TOTAL TRADES	47044	0.51	0.31	0.00	1.00

Figure 10.2 Means of selected variables.

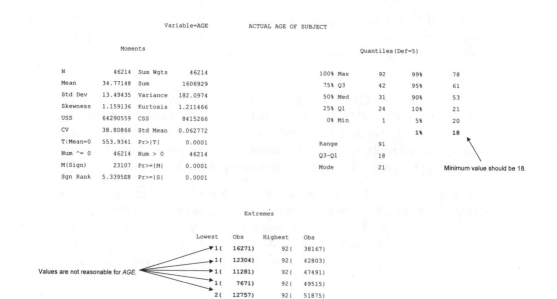

Variable=AGE   ACTUAL AGE OF SUBJECT

Moments

N	46214	Sum Wgts	46214
Mean	34.77148	Sum	1606929
Std Dev	13.49435	Variance	182.0974
Skewness	1.159136	Kurtosis	1.211466
USS	64290559	CSS	8415266
CV	38.80866	Std Mean	0.062772
T:Mean=0	553.9341	Pr>|T|	0.0001
Num ^= 0	46214	Num > 0	46214
M(Sign)	23107	Pr>=|M|	0.0001
Sgn Rank	5.3395E8	Pr>=|S|	0.0001

Quantiles(Def=5)

100% Max	92	99%	78
75% Q3	42	95%	61
50% Med	31	90%	53
25% Q1	24	10%	21
0% Min	1	5%	20
		1%	18

Range	91
Q3-Q1	18
Mode	21

Minimum value should be 18.

Extremes

Lowest	Obs	Highest	Obs
1(	16271)	92(	38167)
1(	12304)	92(	42803)
1(	11281)	92(	47491)
1(	7671)	92(	49515)
2(	12757)	92(	51875)

Values are not reasonable for *AGE*.

Missing Value	.
Count	7756
% Count/Nobs	14.37

Figure 10.3 Univariate analysis of age.

arrays. This will make it much easier to follow the code because I won't get bogged down in variable names.

In the following data step, I create an *array* called *riskvars*. This represents the 61 variables that I've selected as preliminary candidates. I also create an *array* called *rvar*. This represents the group of renamed variables, *rvar1–rvar61*. The "do loop" following the array names takes each of the 61 variables and renames it to rvar1-rvar61.

```
data riskmean;
  set ch10.telco;
array riskvars (61)
COLLS  LOCINQS  INQAGE . . . . . . . . . .  TADB25  TUTRADES  TLTRADES;
array rvar (61) rvar1-rvar61;
do count = 1 to 61;
        rvar(count) = riskvars(count);
end;
run;
```

NOTE: An array is active only during the data step and must be declared by name for each new data step.

The next step calculates the means for each of the 61 variables and creates an output data set called *outmns* with the mean values *mrvar1-mrvar61*.

```
proc summary data=riskmean;
weight smp_wgt;
var rvar1-rvar61;
output out=outmns mean = mrvar1-mrvar61;
run;
```

In this next data step, I append the mean values from outmns to each record in my original data set *ch10.telco*. Next, I assign the same array name, *rvars*, to *rvars1–rvars61*. I also assign two more arrays: *mrvars* represents the means for each variable; and *rvarmiss* indicates (0/1) if a customer has a missing value for each variable. The "do loop" creates the variables in the *array*, *rvarmiss*, represented by *rvarm1-rvarm6*. These are variables with the value 0/1 to indicate which customers had missing values for each variable. Then it assigns each mean value in the array, *mrvars*, to replace each missing value for *rvar1–rvar61*. The last line in the data step replaces the values for *age*, *rvar44*, that are below 18 with the mean for *age*, *mrvar44*:

```
data ch10.telco;
 set ch10.telco;
if (_n_ eq 1) then set outmns;
retain mrvar1-mrvar61;

array rvars (61) rvar1-rvar61;
array mrvars (61) mrvar1-mrvar61;
array rvarmiss (61) rvarm1-rvarm61;
do count = 1 to 61;
        rvarmiss(count) = (rvars(count) = .);
        if rvars(count) = . then rvars(count) = mrvars(count);
end;
if rvar44 < 18 then rvar44 = mrvar44; /* Age */
run;
```

The next step finds the best transformation for each continuous variable. The steps are the same as I demonstrated in part 2, chapter 4. I now have variables with the names *rvar1–rvar61*. I can use a macro to completely automate the transformation process. I use a macro "do loop" to begin the processing. The first step uses PROC UNIVARIATE to calculate the decile values. The next data step appends those values to the original data set, ch10.telco, and creates indicator (0/1) variables, *v1_10 – v61_10, v1_20 – v61_20, . . . v1_90 – v61*_90 to indicate whether the value is above or below each decile value. The final portion of the data step takes each of the 61 variables through the whole set of possible transformations:

```
%macro cont;
%do i = 1 %to 61;

title "Evaluation of var&i";
proc univariate data=ch10.telco noprint;
weight smp_wgt;
var rvar&i;
output out=svardata pctlpts= 10 20 30 40 50 60 70 80 90 pctlpre=svar;
run;

data freqs&i;
set ch10.telco(keep= smp_wgt highrisk rvar&i rvarm&i obsnum);
if (_n_ eq 1) then set svardata;
retain svar10 svar20 svar30 svar40 svar50 svar60 svar70 svar80 svar90;
v&i._10 = (rvar&i < svar10);
v&i._20 = (rvar&i < svar20);
v&i._30 = (rvar&i < svar30);
v&i._40 = (rvar&i < svar40);
v&i._50 = (rvar&i < svar50);
v&i._60 = (rvar&i < svar60);
v&i._70 = (rvar&i < svar70);
v&i._80 = (rvar&i < svar80);
v&i._90 = (rvar&i < svar90);

v&i._sq   = rvar&i**2;                    /* squared */
v&i._cu   = rvar&i**3;                    /* cube root */
v&i._sqrt = sqrt(rvar&i);                 /* square root */
         |       |       |       |       |       |
         |       |       |       |       |       |
v&i._cosi = 1/max(.0001,cos(rvar&i));     /* cosine inverse */
run
```

While we're still in the macro, a logistic regression is used to select the best-fitting variables. I use *maxstep=3* because the missing indicator variables, *rvarm1–rvarm61*, may turn out to be predictive for many variables. And I know that groups of variables have the exact same customers with missing values. For certain groups of variables, the missing value indicator variable will be redundant.

```
proc logistic data=freqs&i descending;
weight smp_wgt;
model highrisk = v&i._10 v&i._20 v&i._30 v&i._40 v&i._50 v&i._60 v&i._70
v&i._80 v&i._90 rvar&i rvarm&i v&i._sq v&i._cu v&i._sqrt v&i._curt
v&i._log v&i._tan v&i._sin v&i._cos v&i._inv v&i._sqi v&i._cui v&i._sqri
v&i._curi v&i._logi v&i._tani v&i._sini v&i._cosi
/ selection = stepwise maxstep=3;
title "Logistic for var&i";
run;
```

The final step sorts the data so that it can be remerged after the final candidate variables are selected.

```
proc sort data=freqs&i;
by obsnum;
run;
%end;
%mend;
%cont;
```

At this point, I have 61 logistic regression outputs from which to select the final variables. Table 10.2 displays the winning transformation for each variable. Notice how many have the missing identifier as a strong predictor.

To avoid selecting a missing value indicator that will be redundant for several variables, I run a means on the 61 missing indicator variables, *rvarm1–rvarm61*, and look for similar means. In Figure 10.4, notice how adjacent variables have similar means rates. This implies that they probably matched to the same customers.

After the top two transformations are selected for each of the 61 variables, the data sets are merged back to the original data set, *ch10.telco*, to create a modeling data set *ch10, telco2*. Finally, an indicator variable called *male* is created from the lone categorical variable, *gender*.

Table 10.2 Final List of Candidate Variables

RVAR	DESCRIPTION	TRANS 1	TRANS 2	TRANS 3
1	# of collection items	v1_curt	v1_70	rvarm1
2	# local inq/last 6 mos	rvarm2	v2_sq	v2_cu
3	age of most recent inquiry	rvarm3	v3_tani	v3_cu
4	age of oldest trade	rvarm4	v4_curt	v4_60
5	age of youngest trade	rvarm5	v5_sqrt	v5_70
6	# accts open in last 3 mos	rvarm6	v6_sqrt	
7	# accts open in last 6 mos	rvarm7	v7_curt	
8	# accts open in last 12 mos	rvarm8	v8_curt	v8_cos
9	# accts open in last 324 mos	rvarm9	v9_curt	v9_60
10	# of accts on file	v10_curt	v10_90	v10_40

continues

(Continued)

RVAR	DESCRIPTION	TRANS 1	TRANS 2	TRANS 3
11	# of open accts on file	rvarm11	v11_curt	v11_30
12	total open balances	rvarm12	v12_curt	v12_tan
13	total open high credits	rvarm13	v13_curt	rvar13
14	age of last activity	v14_logi	v14_80	rvar14
15	# accts with past due bal	v15_70	v15_80	
16	amount of past due balances	rvarm16	v16_curt	v16_log
17	# of accts currently satisfactory	rvarm17	v17_log	v17_10
18	# of accts currently 30 days	rvarm18	v18_sini	
19	# of accts currently 60 days	rvarm19	v19_sini	
20	# of accts currently 90+ days	v20_sini	rvarm20	v20_90
21	# of accts currently bad debt	v21_70	rvarm21	v21_90
22	# of accts piad satisfactorily	vrvarm22	v22_log	v22_10
23	# of accts 30 days late	rvarm23	v23_sin	v23_cosi
24	# of accts 60 days late	rvarm24	v24_tani	
25	# of accts 90+ days late	v25_90	rvarm25	v25_sqri
26	# of accts bad debt	v26_70	rvarm26	v26_90
27	# of accts sat in past 24 mos	rvarm27	v27_curt	v27_logi
28	# of accts 30 days in past 24 mos	v28_70	rvarm28	v28_cos
29	# of accts 60 days in past 24 mos	v29_80	rvarm29	v29_cosi
30	total # of open accts with bal > 0	v30_30	rvarm30	v30_logi
31	average number of months open	v31_70	rvarm31	v31_log
32	# of open accts w/bal > 75% utilization	v32_30	v32_80	rvarm32
33	# of open accts w/bal > 50% utilization	v33_20	rvarm33	v33_sini
34	# of bank revolving accts	v34_curt	rvarm34	v34_sq
35	# of dept store accts	rvarm35	v35_curt	v35_cosi
36	# of con finance co accts	rvarm36	rvar36	
37	# of other retail accts	rvarm37	v37_curt	v37_90

RVAR	DESCRIPTION	TRANS 1	TRANS 2	TRANS 3
38	# of auto accts	rvarm38		
39	# of auto finance accts	rvarm39	v39_tan	v39_cos
40	# of credit union accts	rvarm40	v40_log	v40_tani
41	# of personal fin accts	rvarm41		
42	# of oil co accts	rvarm42	v42_sqrt	
43	# of t&e accts	rvarm43	v43_sin	
44	actual age of customer	v44_10	rvarm44	v44_90
45	total average debt burden	rvarm45	v45_90	v45_cos
46	% of satisfactories to total trades	rvarm46	v46_curt	v46_90
47	# of 90+ bad debt accts in 24 mos	v47_70	v47_80	v47_90
48	% of all accts that are open	rvarm48	v48_cui	v48_90
49	# of 90-120 bad debt/pub rec derog in 24 mos	v49_log	v49_70	v49_sini
50	# of bad debt/pub rec derog w/i 24 mos	v50_70	v50_log	
51	# of accts curr sat with bal > $0	rvarm51	v51_log	v51_logi
52	months open for all trades	rvarm52	v52_log	v52_curi
53	# of open trades inc/closed narratives	rvarm53	v53_sqri	v53_10
54	% of open trades in 24 mos to tot open trades	rvarm54	v54_tani	v54_80
55	% of open accts open in last 12 months	rvarm55	v55_tani	v55_sin
56	% of open accts open in last 6 months	rvarm56	v56_tani	v56_sin
57	% of open accts open in last 3 months	rvar57	rvarm57	v57_tani
58	# of inq in last 12 mos	rvarm58	rvar58	v58_cos
59	# of trades with bal < 25% utilization	rvarm59	v59_curt	v59_50
60	number of telco/utility accts	rvarm60	rvar60	v60_cos
61	number of telco accts	rvarm61	v61_cu	

Variable	N	Nmiss	Mean	Minimum	Maximum
RVARM1	53970	0	0.0363350	0	1.0000000
RVARM2	53970	0	0.1993330	0	1.0000000
RVARM3	53970	0	0.1993330	0	1.0000000
RVARM4	53970	0	0.0860107	0	1.0000000
RVARM5	53970	0	0.0860107	0	1.0000000
RVARM6	53970	0	0.0860478	0	1.0000000
RVARM7	53970	0	0.0860478	0	1.0000000
RVARM8	53970	0	0.0860478	0	1.0000000
RVARM9	53970	0	0.0860478	0	1.0000000

Notice that several groups have the exact same missing rate

Figure 10.4 Similar mean values.

```
data ch10.telco2;
merge ch10.telco(keep=obsnum gender highrisk smp_wgt)
freqs1(keep=obsnum v1_curt v1_70)
freqs2(keep=obsnum rvarm2 v2_sq)
    |   |   |   |   |   |   |   |
    |   |   |   |   |   |   |   |
freqs59(keep=obsnum rvarm59 v59_curt)
freqs60(keep=obsnum rvarm60 rvar60)
freqs61(keep=obsnum rvarm61 v61_cu)
;
by obsnum;
male = (gender = 'M');
run;
```

I now have a data set that contains all the candidate variables. The next step is to process the model.

Processing the Model

I again use PROC CONTENTS with the *short* option to create a list of all the variables. I cut and paste the results into my logistic code. As in every previous model, the first step is to split the population into a model and development sample. Recall that this is done using a weight with half missing values. This will force the modeling process to ignore the records with weight = . (missing).

```
proc contents data=ch10.telco2 short;
run;


data ch10.telco2;
```

```
  set ch10.telco2;
if ranuni(5555) < .5 then splitwgt = 1;
  else splitwgt = .;
modwgt = splitwgt*smp_wgt;
records=1;
run;
```

The nest step is to run all 61 variables through a *backward* logistic and a *step-wise* logistic regression. The combination of winning variables is run through the *score* selection process.

```
proc logistic data=ch10.telco2(keep=modwgt splitwgt smp_wgt highrisk
MALE RVAR13 . . . . . V61_CU  V6_SQRT  V7_CURT  V8_CURT  V9_CURT)
descending;
weight modwgt;
model highrisk =
MALE RVAR13 . . . . . V61_CU V6_SQRT  V7_CURT  V8_CURT  V9_CURT
 /selection=backward;
run;

proc logistic data=ch10.telco2(keep=modwgt splitwgt smp_wgt highrisk
MALE RVAR13 . . . . .V61_CU V6_SQRT  V7_CURT  V8_CURT  V9_CURT)
descending;
weight modwgt;
model highrisk =
MALE  RVAR13 . . . . . V61_CU  V6_SQRT  V7_CURT  V8_CURT  V9_CURT
/selection=stepwise;
run;

proc logistic data=ch10.telco2(keep=modwgt splitwgt smp_wgt highrisk
MALE RVAR13 . . .  V61_CU V9_CURT)
descending;
weight modwgt;
model highrisk = MALE RVAR13 RVAR36 RVAR58 RVARM11 RVARM21 RVARM27
RVARM33 RVARM34 RVARM51 RVARM59 V10_CURT V12_CURT V12_TAN V15_70 V15_80
V1_CURT V20_SINI V22_LOG V25_90 V25_SQRI V32_30 V34_CURT V40_LOG V44_10
V45_90 V48_CUI V49_LOG V50_70 V52_LOG V53_10 V53_SQRI V54_TANI V56_SIN
V58_COS V59_CURT V61_CU V9_CURT
/selection=score best=1;
```

Figure 10.5 displays a portion of the output from the logistic regression with the *score* selection process. To select the final model, I run a logistic regression with 35 variables and produce a gains table. I then select a 20 variable model and repeat the process. The difference is so minimal that I decide to stick with the 20-variable model.

The following code is used to produce the final model. The *keep=* statement in the first line is used to reduce the number of variables that are brought into the processing. This allows the program to run much faster. While only half the

Number of Variables	Score Value	Variables Included in Model
1	1448.1695	V1_CURT
2	1999.8518	RVARM51 V1_CURT
3	2299.2717	RVARM27 V1_CURT V22_LOG
|	|	| | |
20	2887.9011	**MALE RVAR58 RVARM21 RVARM34 RVARM51 V10_CURT V12_TAN V15_70 V1_CURT V20_SINI V22_LOG V25_90 V34_CURT V44_10 V45_90 V53_SQRI V54_TANI V58_COS V61_CU V9_CURT**
21	2895.8333	RVAR58 RVARM21 RVARM27 RVARM34 RVARM51 V10_CURT V12_TAN V15_70 V1_CURT V20_SINI V22_LOG V25_90 V25_SQRI V34_CURT V44_10 V45_90 V53_SQRI V54_TANI V58_COS V61_CU V9_CURT
22	2902.7115	MALE RVAR58 RVARM21 RVARM27 RVARM34 RVARM51 V10_CURT V12_TAN V15_70 V1_CURT V20_SINI V22_LOG V25_90 V25_SQRI V34_CURT V44_10 V45_90 V53_SQRI V54_TANI V58_COS V61_CU V9_CURT
23	2909.4073	MALE RVAR58 RVARM21 RVARM27 RVARM34 RVARM51 V10_CURT V12_TAN V15_70 V1_CURT V20_SINI V22_LOG V25_90 V25_SQRI V34_CURT V44_10 V45_90 V53_10 V53_SQRI V54_TANI V58_COS V61_CU V9_CURT

Figure 10.5 Score logistic regression.

customers were used in processing, the *out=ch10.scored* data set contains all the customers. This is the advantage of using missing values for half the weights. Every record is scored with the final predictive value. I use the *(where=(splitwgt=.))* option to allow validation on those customers not used to build the model:

```
proc logistic data=ch10.telco2(keep= records modwgt splitwgt smp_wgt
highrisk MALE RVAR58 RVARM21 RVARM34 RVARM51 V10_CURT V12_TAN V15_70
V1_CURT V20_SINI V22_LOG V25_90 V34_CURT V44_10 V45_90 V53_SQRI V54_TANI
V58_COS V61_CU V9_CURT) descending;
weight modwgt;
model highrisk = MALE RVAR58 RVARM21 RVARM34 RVARM51 V10_CURT V12_TAN
V15_70 V1_CURT V20_SINI V22_LOG V25_90 V34_CURT V44_10 V45_90 V53_SQRI
V54_TANI V58_COS V61_CU V9_CURT;
output out=ch10.scored(where=(splitwgt=.)) p=pred;
run;
proc sort data=ch10.scored;
by descending pred;
run;
```

The remaining code creates the deciles and produces the gains table.

```
proc univariate data=ch10.scored noprint;
weight smp_wgt;
var pred;
output out=preddata sumwgt=sumwgt;
run;

data ch10.scored;
 set ch10.scored;
if (_n_ eq 1) then set preddata;
retain sumwgt;
number+smp_wgt;
if number < .1*sumwgt then val_dec = 0; else
if number < .2*sumwgt then val_dec = 1; else
if number < .3*sumwgt then val_dec = 2; else
if number < .4*sumwgt then val_dec = 3; else
if number < .5*sumwgt then val_dec = 4; else
if number < .6*sumwgt then val_dec = 5; else
if number < .7*sumwgt then val_dec = 6; else
if number < .8*sumwgt then val_dec = 7; else
if number < .9*sumwgt then val_dec = 8; else
val_dec = 9;
run;

proc tabulate data=ch10.scored;
weight smp_wgt;
class val_dec;
var highrisk pred records;
table val_dec='Decile' all='Total',
        records='Customers'*sum=' '*f=comma11.
        pred='Predicted Probability'*mean=' '*f=11.5
        highrisk='Percent Highrisk'*mean=' '*f=11.5
         /rts = 9 row=float;
run;
```

The parameter estimates and model statistics are displayed in Figure 10.6. Notice the variable with the highest Wald chi-square value is v1_curt. Looking back at Table 10.2, we see that this is a function of the *number of collection items*. This is the strongest predictor when considered in combination with all other predictors.

The decile analysis in Figure 10.7 shows both strong rank ordering and good predictive power. The next step is to validate the final model.

Variable	DF	Parameter Estimate	Standard Error	Wald Chi-Square	Pr > Chi-Square	Standardized Estimate	Odds Ratio
INTERCPT	1	-4.0628	0.1849	482.6861	0.0001		
MALE	1	0.0781	0.0280	7.7752	0.0053	0.051779	1.081
RVAR58	1	0.0310	0.00517	35.9768	0.0001	0.094855	1.032
RVARM21	1	-1.6180	0.1933	70.0817	0.0001	-0.562263	0.198
RVARM34	1	2.5010	0.2486	101.1964	0.0001	0.825148	12.195
RVARM51	1	0.3798	0.0880	18.6376	0.0001	0.152227	1.462
V10_CURT	1	0.2848	0.0624	20.8370	0.0001	0.292700	1.330
V12_TAN	1	0.000132	0.000061	4.6897	0.0303	0.022188	1.000
V15_70	1	-0.4120	0.0403	104.5103	0.0001	-0.255859	0.662
V1_CURT	1	0.2568	0.0225	130.2639	0.0001	0.227166	1.293
V20_SINI	1	-0.00002	6.016E-6	14.8561	0.0001	-0.120443	1.000
V22_LOG	1	-0.0290	0.00508	32.4825	0.0001	-0.115431	0.971
V25_90	1	0.0947	0.0526	3.2371	0.0720	0.048798	1.099
V34_CURT	1	-0.3176	0.0311	104.1042	0.0001	-0.291687	0.728
V44_10	1	0.2319	0.0524	19.5591	0.0001	0.076499	1.261
V45_90	1	-0.2636	0.0434	36.8467	0.0001	-0.098443	0.768
V53_SQRI	1	0.9954	0.1388	51.4302	0.0001	0.298189	2.706
V54_TANI	1	0.000017	5.276E-6	10.9466	0.0009	0.092067	1.000
V58_COS	1	0.0645	0.0207	9.7397	0.0018	0.059654	1.067
V61_CU	1	0.0154	0.00544	7.9998	0.0047	0.029856	1.015
V9_CURT	1	0.2347	0.0411	32.6719	0.0001	0.189143	1.264

Association of Predicted Probabilities and Observed Responses

Concordant = 67.0%		Somers' D = 0.373
Discordant = 29.6%		Gamma	= 0.386
Tied	= 3.4%	Tau-a	= 0.121
(117345240 pairs)		c	= 0.687

Figure 10.6 Final model output.

Validating the Model

Recall that in the beginning of the chapter, I said that in addition to the 300+ predictive variables, I also purchased a generic risk score from the credit bureau. To validate my model scores, I compare the rank ordering ability of my score to that of the generic score. Figure 10.8 compares the actual percentages in the best deciles. Also the lift is superior for the model I developed. This can also be seen in the gains chart in Figure 10.9. It is not unusual to do better with your own data. The real test will be in the implementation.

To complete the validation process, I will calculate bootstrap estimates for my predictive model.

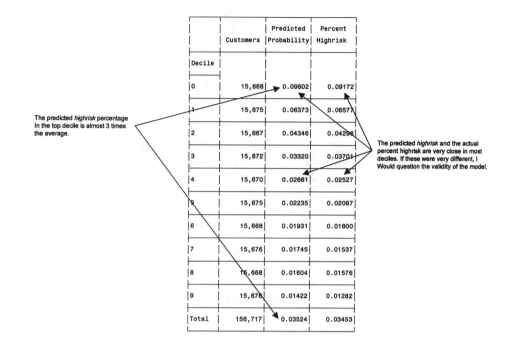

The predicted *highrisk* percentage In the top decile is almost 3 times the average.

The predicted *highrisk* and the actual percent highrisk are very close in most deciles. If these were very different, I Would question the validity of the model.

Decile	Customers	Predicted Probability	Percent Highrisk
0	15,668	0.09602	0.09172
1	15,675	0.06373	0.06577
2	15,667	0.04346	0.04296
3	15,672	0.03320	0.03701
4	15,670	0.02661	0.02527
5	15,675	0.02235	0.02067
6	15,668	0.01931	0.01800
7	15,676	0.01745	0.01537
8	15,668	0.01604	0.01576
9	15,678	0.01422	0.01282
Total	156,717	0.03524	0.03453

Figure 10.7   Validation decile analysis.

Bootstrapping

The program for creating the bootstrap estimates is similar to the program in chapter 9. The main difference is that in chapter 9, I had three variables, *response*, *12-month sales*, and *lift for 12-month sales*. Here I want two bootstrap estimates: predicted value (*pred*) of *highrisk* (*bsest_h*) and the *lift* (*bsest_l*) for *highrisk*. The following represents the final stage of the bootstrap program. This tabulate code creates the output in Figure 10.10.

```
proc tabulate data=ch10.bs_sum;
weight smp_wgt;
var liftf bsest_h hrmnf lci_h uci_h bsest_l lftmbs lci_l uci_l;
class val_dec;
table (val_dec='Decile' all='Total'),
(hrmnf='Predicted High Risk'*mean=' '*f=percent6.
bsest_h='BS Est High Risk'*mean=' '*f=percent6.
lci_h ='BS Lower CI Resp'*mean=' '*f=percent6.
uci_h ='BS Upper CI Resp'*mean=' '*f=percent6.
liftf ='High Risk Lift'*mean=' '*f=6.
bsest_l='BS Est Lift'*mean=' '*f=6.
lci_l ='BS Lower CI Lift'*mean=' '*f=6.
uci_l ='BS Upper CI Lift'*mean=' '*f=6.)
/rts=10 row=float;
run;
```

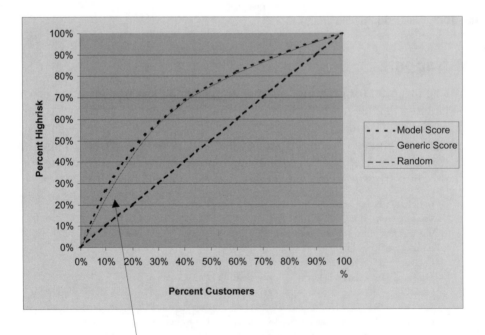

MODEL SCORE GAINS TABLE

Decile	Customers	Generic % of Highrisk	Cumulative % Highrisk	# of Highrisk	% of Total Highrisk	Cum # of Highrisk	Cum % of Highrisk	Lift	Cum Lift
0	15,668	9.172%	9.172%	1,437	26.55%	1,437	26.55%	266	266
1	15,670	6.577%	7.874%	1,031	19.04%	2,468	45.60%	190	228
2	15,671	4.296%	6.682%	673	12.44%	3,141	58.04%	124	193
3	15,674	3.701%	5.936%	580	10.72%	3,721	68.76%	107	172
4	15,674	2.527%	5.254%	396	7.32%	4,117	76.08%	73	152
5	15,669	2.067%	4.723%	324	5.98%	4,441	82.06%	60	137
6	15,669	1.800%	4.306%	282	5.21%	4,723	87.27%	52	125
7	15,677	1.537%	3.959%	241	4.45%	4,964	91.72%	45	115
8	15,669	1.576%	3.695%	247	4.56%	5,211	96.29%	46	107
9	15,676	1.282%	3.453%	201	3.71%	5,412	100.00%	37	100
TOTAL	156,717	3.454%		5,412	100.00%				

GENERIC SCORE GAINS TABLE

Decile	Customers	Generic % of Highrisk	Cumulative % Highrisk	# of Highrisk	% of Total Highrisk	Cum # of Highrisk	Cum % of Highrisk	Lift	Cum Lift
0	15,668	7.843%	7.843%	1,229	22.71%	1,229	22.71%	227	227
1	15,670	7.012%	7.427%	1,099	20.30%	2,328	43.01%	203	215
2	15,671	5.055%	6.637%	792	14.64%	3,120	57.65%	146	192
3	15,674	3.573%	5.871%	560	10.35%	3,680	68.00%	103	170
4	15,674	2.558%	5.208%	401	7.41%	4,081	75.41%	74	151
5	15,669	2.138%	4.696%	335	6.19%	4,416	81.60%	62	136
6	15,669	1.717%	4.271%	269	4.97%	4,685	86.57%	50	124
7	15,677	1.672%	3.946%	262	4.84%	4,947	91.41%	48	114
8	15,669	1.537%	3.678%	241	4.45%	5,188	95.86%	45	107
9	15,676	1.429%	3.453%	224	4.14%	5,412	100.00%	41	100
TOTAL	156,717	3.453%		5,412	100.00%				

Compare the percents and the cumulative percents

The cumulative lift for the custom model is much higher in the best deciles

Figure 10.8 Comparison of model score to generic score.

The gains chart shows a slight difference in the lower deciles

Figure 10.9 Gains chart for score comparison.

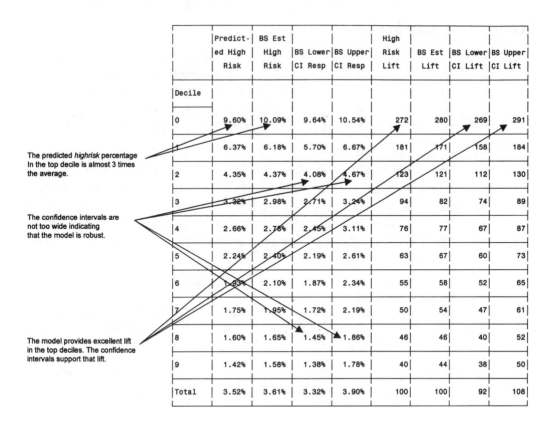

Decile	Predict- ed High Risk	BS Est High Risk	BS Lower CI Resp	BS Upper CI Resp	High Risk Lift	BS Est Lift	BS Lower CI Lift	BS Upper CI Lift
0	9.60%	10.09%	9.64%	10.54%	272	280	269	291
1	6.37%	6.18%	5.70%	6.67%	181	171	158	184
2	4.35%	4.37%	4.08%	4.67%	123	121	112	130
3	3.32%	2.98%	2.71%	3.24%	94	82	74	89
4	2.66%	2.78%	2.45%	3.11%	76	77	67	87
5	2.24%	2.40%	2.19%	2.61%	63	67	60	73
6	1.93%	2.10%	1.87%	2.34%	55	58	52	65
7	1.75%	1.95%	1.72%	2.19%	50	54	47	61
8	1.60%	1.65%	1.45%	1.86%	46	46	40	52
9	1.42%	1.58%	1.38%	1.78%	40	44	38	50
Total	3.52%	3.61%	3.32%	3.90%	100	100	92	108

The predicted *highrisk* percentage In the top decile is almost 3 times the average.

The confidence intervals are not too wide indicating that the model is robust.

The model provides excellent lift in the top deciles. The confidence intervals support that lift.

Figure 10.10 Model score bootstrap estimates and confidence intervals.

The overall model performance validates well with the top decile capturing almost three times the average. The tight width of the confidence intervals shows that the model is robust.

Implementing the Model

Risk scores are used in many phases of customer relationship management. As we saw in part 2, a risk adjustment was used to determine the lifetime value of prospects. This was based on a three-way matrix of gender, age, and marital status. It easily could have been derived from a risk model. In chapter 8, we saw how risk scores are used to segment customers and prospects. The model we just completed is being used to score First Reserve's banking customer for Eastern Telecom. Those banking customers who are low risk will receive a great offer for cellular products and services in their next monthly statement.

Scaling the Risk Score

To make risk comparison more user friendly, most risk scores are translated into a scale ranging from 450 to 850. This is accomplished by selecting a base value that equates to a 50/50 chance of some negative risk action, i.e., your objective. The scale is designed in such a way that the risk decreases as the score increases—the highest scoring customers are the lowest risk.

For the case study, I want to derive a formula to translate the probability of *highrisk* to a number between 450 and 850. Let's say I want to base the score at 480. The base equates to a probability of default of 50% or an odds of 50/50. Because the parameter estimates in logistic regression are linear in the log of the odds, the output can simply be rescaled so any desired number of score points doubles the odds. For example, the formula below doubles the odds every 40 points:

$$\text{Score} = 480 + 57.706 * \log((1 - p)/p)$$

Notice that I use (1-p)/p because I want "good to bad" odds for this formula. Table 10.3 shows the levels of probability along with the steps to translate it into the scaled risk score.

For Eastern Telco, the following code translates the predicted values into scores and creates the table in Figure 10.11:

```
data ch10.scored;
  set ch10.scored;
riskscor = 480 + 57.706*(log((1-pred)/pred));
run;

proc format;
value score
  450-<500 = '450 - 500'
  500-<550 = '500 - 550'
  550-<600 = '550 - 600'
  600-<650 = '600 - 650'
  650-<700 = '650 - 700'
  700-<750 = '700 - 750'
;
run;

proc tabulate;
weight smp_wgt;
format riskscor score.;
class riskscor;
var pred records;
table riskscor=' ' all='Total',
      (records='Customers'*sum=' '*f=comma12.
       pred='Predicted Probability'*mean=' '*f=percent12.2)
```

Table 10.3 Relationship of Odds to Scaled Risk Scores

PROBABILITY OF BAD	GOOD TO BAD ODDS	LOG OF ODDS	DERIVED RISK SCORE
50.00%	1/1	0.000	480
33.33%	2/1	0.693	520
26.12%	2.83/1	1.040	540
20.00%	4/1	1.386	560
15.02%	5.66/1	1.733	580
11.11%	8/1	2.079	600
8.12%	11.32/1	2.426	620
5.88%	16/1	2.773	640
4.23%	22.64/1	3.120	660
3.03%	32/1	3.466	680
2.16%	45.26/1	3.813	700
1.54%	64/1	4.161	720
1.09%	90.74/1	4.508	740
0.78%	128/1	4.846	760
0.55%	180.82/1	5.197	780
0.39%	256/1	5.545	800

```
/rts=20 row=float box='Risk Score';
run;
```

Figure 10.11 depicts good news for Eastern Telco. Most of First Reserve's customers have a relatively low risk level. If Eastern selects all names with a score of 650 or above, it will have almost 125,000 low-risk First Reserve customers to solicit.

A Different Kind of Risk: Fraud

The main focus of this chapter has been on predicting risk for default on a payment. And the methodology translates very well to predicting the risk of claims for insurance. There is another type of risk that also erodes profits: the risk of fraud. Losses due to fraud cost companies and ultimately consumers millions of dollars a year. And the threat is increasing as more and more consumers use credit cards, telecommunications, and the Internet for personal and business transactions.

Risk Score	Customers	Predicted Probability
450 - 500	7	42.01%
500 - 550	9	25.86%
550 - 600	2,636	13.37%
600 - 650	29,653	7.40%
650 - 700	56,860	3.20%
700 - 750	67,552	1.71%
Total	156,717	3.52%

Figure 10.11 Tabulation of risk scores.

Jaya Kolhatkar, Director of Fraud Management for Amazon.com, discusses the mechanics of developing fraud models and the importance of proper implementation:

Fraud in the e-tailing world has increased rapidly over the past two years. Being a virtual marketplace, most of the fraud checks in the physical retail world do not apply. Primarily, fraud is committed through the use of credit cards. There are several effective fraud management tools available from the credit card associations like address verification system, fraud scores, etc.; however, these are not enough for a rigorous fraud management system.

As Amazon.com moved from selling just books to books, music, video, consumer electronics, etc., fraud losses increased. In order to control these losses a two-pronged approach was developed. The two components were data analysis/model building and operations/investigations.

The data analysis component is the backbone of the fraud system. It is important to underscore that because fraud rates within the population are so low, a blend of two or more modeling techniques seems to work best at isolating fraud orders within the smallest percentage of the population. We have used logistic regression, decision trees, etc., in combination to create effective fraud models. Low fraud rates also impact data preparation/analysis. It is easy to misjudge spurious data for a new fraud trend.

Another important issue to keep in mind at this stage of model development is model implementation. Because we function in a real-time environment and cannot allow the scoring process to be a bottleneck in our order fulfillment process, we need to be very parsimonious in our data selection. While, at first, this seems to be very limiting from a variable selection point of view, we have found that using a series of scorecards built on progressively larger set of variables and implemented on a progressively smaller populations is very effective.

Given the "customer-centric" philosophy of Amazon.com, no order (except perhaps the most blatant fraud order) is cancelled without manual intervention. Even the best predictive system is inherently prone to misclassification. We use data analysis and optimization techniques to help the investigations staff hone in on the right set of orders.

To be effective in reducing fraud losses over a long period of time, the fraud models need to be constantly updated to capture any new patterns in fraud behavior.

Summary

Did you notice a lot of similarities between the risk modeling process and the response modeling process? While the goals and company focus are very different, the mechanics are quite similar. Sure, there were a few variations in the use of weights and the streamlined variable processing, but the main goal was achieved. We were able to determine which characteristics or variables are best at identifying risky customers.

This methodology works well for any industry seeking to limit risk. If you've ordered a new Internet service, the company probably looked at your credit report. They may have even evaluated your application based on a risk score similar to the one we just developed. The same methodology works well to predict the risk of claims. You would substitute claims data for risk data and gather predictive variables from the customer database and overlay data.

I hope you're not too stuffed. We have a couple more recipes to go. In the next chapter, I demonstrate how to build a churn model. Bon appetit!

CHAPTER 11

Retaining Profitable Customers: Modeling Churn

Have you ever been interrupted by a phone call during dinner with an invitation to switch your long-distance service? Or how about those low-rate balance transfer credit card offers that keep filling your mailbox? Many companies are finding it harder and harder to attract new customers. As a result, the cost of acquiring new customers is on the rise. This has created a major shift in marketing. Many companies are focusing more on retention because it costs much less to keep a current customer than to acquire a new one. And one way to improve retention is to take action before the customer churns. That's where churn models can help!

Churn models, also known as retention or attrition models, predict the probability of customer attrition. Because attrition has such a powerful impact on profitability, many companies are making these models the main focus of their customer loyalty program. In this chapter, I begin with a discussion of the importance of customer loyalty and its effect on profits in a number of industries. The remainder of the chapter details the development of a churn model that predicts the effect of a rate increase on credit card balances. The steps are familiar. I begin by defining the objective. Then I prepare the variables, process the model, and validate. I wrap up the chapter with some options for implementing a churn model and the effect on overall customer profitability.

Customer Loyalty

As I just mentioned, the main advantage of a retention program is economics. If you have $1 to spend on marketing, you would be much better off spending it on customer retention than customer acquisition. Why? It's much more expensive to attract a new customer than to retain a current one. Also, loyal customers tend to be less price-sensitive.

The airline industry is very adept at building customer loyalty. The more you fly with one airline, the more benefits you receive. Many other industries have followed the pattern with loyalty cards and incentives for repeat business. The gambling industry has embraced customer profiling and target modeling to identify and provide benefits for their most profitable customers. Credit card banks have affinity cards with everything from schools to pet clubs. These added benefits and incentives are essential for survival since most companies are learning that it is difficult to survive by competing on price alone. Building customer loyalty by creating additional value is becoming the norm in many industries.

Defining the Objective

For many industries, defining the objective is simple. You can have only one long-distance provider. If you switch, it's a complete gain for one company and a complete loss for the other. This is also true for energy providers; you have one source for your electrical power. Insurance customers generally patronize one company for certain types, if not all, of their insurance. For some industries, though, it's not so simple. For example, a catalog company may hope you are a loyal customer, but it doesn't really know what you are spending with its competitors. This is true for most retailers.

Credit card banks have exceptional challenges in this area due to the combination of stiff competition and industry dynamics. For the most part, the only profitable customers are the "revolvers" or those customers that carry a balance. "Silent attrition" occurs when customers pay down their balances without closing their accounts. Pure transactors, or customers that pay their balance every month, are profitable only if their monthly purchases are above a certain amount.

This chapter's recipe details the steps for building a model to predict attrition or churn for credit card customers following a rate increase. Rowan Royal Bank has a modest portfolio of 1.2 million customers. Its interest rates or APRs (annual percentage rates) are lower than the industry average, especially on its high-risk customers. But before it increases rates on the entire group of high-risk customers, the bank wants to predict which customers are highly rate-sensitive. In other words, they want to determine which customers have a high probability of shifting balances away following a rate increase. For these customers, the increase in interest revenue may be offset by losses due to balances attrition.

By definition, the opposite of customer retention or loyalty is customer attrition or churn. Measuring attrition is easy. Defining an attritor is the challenging part. There are many factors to consider. For example, how many months do you want to consider? Or do you compare lost balances to a beginning balance in a given month or the average of several months? Do you take a straight percentage drop in balances? If so, is this meaningful for someone with a very low beginning balance? In other words, the definition should not just describe some arbitrary action that ensures a strong model. The definition should be actionable and meaningful to the business goals. See the accompanying sidebar for Shree Pragada's discussion on the significance of this definition.

Defining Attrition to Optimize Profits

Shree Pragada, Vice President of Customer Acquisition at Fleet Credit Card Bank, discusses the effect of the definition of attritors on profitability.

The emphasis in model development is usually just on the model performance measures and not much on the model usage. In addition to building a statistically sound model, an analyst should focus on the business application of the model.

The following is an example from the financial services industry. A business manager requests for a model to identify balance attritors. If the analyst were to build a model just to suffice the request, he or she would define the objective to identify just balance attritors. But further inquiry into the application of the model reveals that the attrition probabilities will be applied to customers' account balances to estimate the level of balance at attrition risk—and eventually in a customer profitability system for targeting for a marketing promotion. The analyst would now change the objective to predicting balance attritors with the emphasis on attritors with significant account balances. As the financial impact of attrition is the final goal, such a change in the definition of the dependent variable will improve the effectiveness of the model in the business strategies.

The logical choice in this modeling exercise was to build a logistic model to predict the likelihood of attrition. The exercise also involved comparing several definitions of the dependent variable. For simplicity, we will focus on only two dependent variable definitions—one with the balance cut-off and the other without.

Definition: % Reprice Balance Attrition, the dependent variable, is the percent reduction in balance:

% Balance Attrition = 1 – Fraction of Pre-Event Balances Remaining

Business analysis reveals that most accounts tend to be unprofitable when more than 75% of the pre-reprice balances were paid off. Therefore, a binary variable is defined using this 75% balance attrition cutoff:

Dependent Variable: = 1 If % of Balance Attrition GT 75% = 0 otherwise

Fraction of balances left is defined as Average of the Three-Month Balances Post-Event over Average Annual Balance Pre-Event.

As the goal of this model is to predict the probability of "balance" attrition, the definition of the dependent variable has been altered to focus on the magnitude (or dollar amount) of balance attrition in addition to the likelihood of attrition. By doing this, customers with a high percent of attrition but with marginal amount of balance attrition (dollar amount) will be treated as nonattritors. As a result we can be more confident that we are modeling deliberate and significant balance attrition and not just swings in balance level that may not be related to reprice. The modified definition is:

Dependent Variable: = 1 If % of Balance Attrition GT 75% and Dollar Amount GT $1,000 = 0 Otherwise

Table 11.1 summarizes the model measurement statistics and percent of attritors in the top 10 of 20 segments of the Cumulative Gains tables:

Table 11.1   Comparison of Dependent Variable Definition—Minimum Percentage

MODEL DESCRIPTION	# / % OF ACCOUNTS CATEGORIZED AS ATTRITORS OF THE TOTAL SAMPLE OF 53,877 A/CS	RANK OF MAX. SEPARATION (OF 20)	KS	CLASSIFICATION @ MAX. SEPARATION	% OF ACCOUNT SEPARATED IN THE TOP 50% OF THE POP
(1) Dependent Variable Definition with a $1,000 Cut-off	12,231 / 22%	7	35.0%	70.49%	75%
(1) Dependent Variable Definition without $1,000 Cut-off	15,438 / 29%	7	39.9%	72.47%	76%

To the surprise of the Implementation/Targeting groups, Model 1 was recommended despite its lesser strength in identifying attritors. Because the model is used to understand the financial impact as a result of attrition, the dependent variable in Model 1 was changed to focus on attritors with significant account balances (over $1,000 in this case). This lowered the ability of the model to identify the likelihood of attrition, but it significantly improved the rank ordering of attritors with significant account balances, as evident in Table 11.2.

Table 11.2 Comparison of Dependent Variable Definition—Minimum Cut-off

MODEL DESCRIPTION	# / % OF ACCOUNTS CATEGORIZED AS ATTRITORS OF THE TOTAL SAMPLE OF 53,877 A/CS	RANK OF MAX. SEPARATION (OF 20)	KS	CLASSIFICATION @ MAX. SEPARATION	% OF ACCOUNT SEPARATED IN THE TOP 50% OF THE POP	% OF TOTAL LOST DOLLARS SEPARATED IN THE TOP 50% OF THE POP
(1) Dependent Variable Definition with a $1,000 Cut-off	12,231 / 22%	7	35.0%	70.49%	75%	**72%**
(1) Dependent Variable Definition without $1,000 Cut-off	15,438 / 29%	7	39.9%	72.47%	76%	**62%**

The data for modeling was randomly selected from the high-risk section of Rowan Royal Bank's customer portfolio. The attrition rate is almost 24%, so further sampling wasn't necessary. Prior work with attrition modeling had narrowed the field of eligible variables. In fact, a couple of the variables are actually scores from other models. Figure 11.1 shows the list of variables. Note: The term *FRUT* is commonly used in the credit card industry and stands for *Financial Revolving Unsecured Trade*.

I am defining an attritor using the definition developed by Shree Pragada in the above sidebar. The variable *pre3moav* equals the average balance for the three months prior to the rate increase. The variable *pst3moav* equals the average balance for the three-month period beginning the *fourth* month following the rate increase.

```
data ch11.rowan;
 set ch11.rowan;
pre3moav = mean(prebal3,prebal2,prebal1);
pst3moav = mean(pstbal4,pstbal5,pstbal6);

dollattr = (pre3moav - pst3moav)/pre3moav;
```

```
          -----Alphabetic List of Variables and Attributes-----
    #    Variable    Type    Len    Pos    Label

-----------------------------------------------------------------------------

   28    AGE_LT25    Char     1     132    Age < 25 Years

   13    ATTRITE     Num      8      96    Attrition 1=Yes 0=No

   21    AUTOLOAN    Char     1     118    Auto Loan

    1    AVBALFRU    Num      8       0    Avgerage Balalance on FRUTs

    5    AVPURINC    Num      8      32    Average Purchase Income

   24    CHILD       Char     1     128    Presence of Children

   20    DONATE      Char     1     117    Donates to Charities

   18    GENDER      Char     1     115    Gender

   17    HH_IND      Char     1     114    Head of Household Y/N

    4    HIBAL12M    Num      8      24    High Balance - 12 Months

   14    HOMEOWN     Char     1     104    Home Owner

   22    HOM_EQU     Num      8     119    Home Equity

   16    INCOME      Num      8     106    Household Income

    9    INTRATIN    Num      8      64    Interest Rate Increase

   15    MAILORD     Char     1     105    Mail Order Buyer

   25    MARITAL     Char     1     129    Marital Status

   30    MORTGAGE    Char     1     134    Mortgage Trade

   10    NCCBLGT0    Num      8      72    Number of Cards with Bal > $0

    3    NUMNEWAC    Num      8      16    Number of New Accts - 6 Months

   34    OBSNUM      Num      8     158    Customer Locator Number

    2    OPNTOBUY    Num      8       8    Open to Buy

    8    PACCT0BL    Num      8      56    Percent of Accounts w/$0 Balance

   11    PBALSHAR    Num      8      80    Percent of Tot Balances with Us

   27    POPDENS     Char     1     131    Populations Density

   32    PRE3MOAV    Num      8     142    Pre Reprice 3-Month Average Balance

    7    PROFSCOR    Num      8      48    Profitability Score

   33    PST3MOAV    Num      8     150    Post Reprice 3-Month Average Balance

   31    REGION      Char     7     135    Region of Country

   26    RETIRED     Char     1     130    Retired

   12    RISKSCOR    Num      8      88    Custom Risk Score

   29    SGLE_FAM    Char     1     133    Single Family Home

   23    SOMECOLL    Char     1     127    Education After HS

   19    SSN_IND     Char     1     116    Soc Sec No on FIle

    6    TIMTLFBT    Num      8      40    Time to First Balance Transfer
```

Figure 11.1 List of variables.

```
        if dollattr > 1000 and dollattr/pre3moav  > .75 then attrite = 1;
        else attrite = 0;
        run;
```

Preparing the Variables

This turns out to be one of the easiest recipes because I have relatively few variables. I begin by looking at the continuous variables using a program similar to the one I used in chapter 10. I'll follow up with the categorical variables using standard frequencies.

Continuous Variables

I begin with PROC MEANS to see if the continuous variables have missing or extreme values (outliers). Figure 11.2 displays the output.

```
        proc means data=ch11.rowan maxdec=2;
        run;
```

Variable	Label	N	Mean	Std Dev	Minimum	Maximum
AVBALFRU	Avgerage Balance on FRUTs	39674	788.29	653.43	-585.00	2722.00
OPNTOBUY	Open to Buy	39674	3529.09	1151.37	1303.00	7253.00
NUMNEWAC	Number of New Accts - 6 Months	39674	1.20	0.60	0.00	2.66
HIBAL12M	High Balance - 12 Months	39674	4065.96	898.00	1630.00	5795.00
AVPURINC	Average Purchase Income	39674	251.39	78.69	83.00	489.00
TIMTLFBT	Time to First Balance Transfer	39674	3.74	3.84	0.00	12.00
PROFSCOR	**Profitability Score**	39674	0.72	0.34	0.00	1.00
PACCT0BL	Percent of Accounts w/$0 Balance	39674	0.44	0.40	0.00	1.00
INTRATIN	Interest Rate Increase	39674	740.48	88.29	436.00	920.00
NCCBLGT0	Number of Cards with Bal > $0	39674	3.66	1.08	2.00	8.00
PBALSHAR	Percent of Tot Balances with Us	39674	37.23	12.00	0.00	57.40
RISKSCOR	**Custom Risk Score**	39674	513.40	59.16	481.00	632.00
ATTRITE	Attrition 1=Yes 0=No	39674	0.24	0.43	0.00	1.00
INCOME	Household Income	39674	51.45	21.13	0.00	235.00
HOM_EQU	Home Equity	39674	83287.96	6705.63	0.00	3741824.00
PRE3MOAV	Pre Reprice 3-Month Average Balance	39674	4066.47	1377.53	-399.00	10194.00
PST3MOAV	Post Reprice 3-Month Average Balance	39674	1199.35	954.08	-108.00	8050.00

All the variable seem to be within range with no missing values.   Two variables are scores from other models.

Figure 11.2   Means on continuous variables.

FAll the variables seem to be within range with no missing values. The next step is to look for segmentation opportunities and find the best form of each continuous variable. The following macro is a slight variation on the macro in chapter 10. It processes all continuous variables (listed at the bottom of the macro). The *var* calls the full variable name and *svar* calls a three-letter nickname for the variable used to create prefixes throughout the program. The %INCLUDE command accesses the program that creates the transformations run the logistic regression to determine the best final variable formations. That program is named *transf*:

```
%macro cont (var, svar);

title "Evaluation of &var";
proc univariate data=ch11.rowan noprint;
var &var;
output out=ch11.&svar.data pctlpts= 10 20 30 40 50 60 70 80 90 99 100
pctlpre=&svar;
run;


<<CODE IN THIS SECTION IS SIMILAR TO TRANSFORMATION CODE IN CHAPTER 10>>

proc freq data=&svar.dset;
table attrite*&svar.grp10/chisq;
run;

%INCLUDE transf;

%mend;
%cont(avbalfru, avb);
%cont(opntobuy, opn);
%cont(numnewac, num);
%cont(avpurinc, avp);
%cont(hibal12m, hib);
%cont(hom_equ,  hom);
%cont(income,   inc);
%cont(timtlfbt, tim);
%cont(nccblgt0, ncc);
%cont(pacct0bl, pac);
%cont(pbalshar, pba);
%cont(intratin, int);
%cont(riskscor, ris);
%cont(profscor, pro);
```

Similar to the program in chapter 10, this program automates the segmentation by creating segments at each decile. The segment variables are binary variables that split the file at each decile. The segment variables are tested along with the transformations in a stepwise logistic to determine the best two transformations.

Figure 11.3 shows the decile segmentation for the variable *avbalfru*. Notice how the attrition rate flattens out in deciles 3 through 5. This is a likely place for

```
ATTRITE(Attrition 1=Yes 0=No)     AVBGRP10
```

```
Frequency|
Percent  |
Row Pct  |
Col Pct  |     1|     2|     3|     4|     5|     6|     7|     8|     9|    10| Total
---------+------+------+------+------+------+------+------+------+------+------+
       0 | 3461 | 3320 | 3148 | 3101 | 3169 | 3068 | 3003 | 3035 | 2911 | 2029 | 30245
         | 8.72 | 8.37 | 7.93 | 7.82 | 7.99 | 7.73 | 7.57 | 7.65 | 7.34 | 5.11 | 76.23
         |11.44 |10.98 |10.41 |10.25 |10.48 |10.14 | 9.93 |10.03 | 9.62 | 6.71 |
         |86.92 |83.80 |79.29 |78.39 |79.54 |77.47 |75.80 |76.45 |73.27 |51.30 |
---------+------+------+------+------+------+------+------+------+------+------+
       1 |  521 |  642 |  822 |  855 |  815 |  892 |  959 |  935 | 1062 | 1926 | 9429
         | 1.31 | 1.62 | 2.07 | 2.16 | 2.05 | 2.25 | 2.42 | 2.36 | 2.68 | 4.85 | 23.77
         | 5.53 | 6.81 | 8.72 | 9.07 | 8.64 | 9.46 |10.17 | 9.92 |11.26 |20.43 |
         |13.08 |16.20 |20.71 |21.61 |20.46 |22.53 |24.20 |23.55 |26.73 |48.70 |
---------+------+------+------+------+------+------+------+------+------+------+
Total      3982   3962   3970   3956   3984   3960   3962   3970   3973   3955   39674
           10.04   9.99  10.01   9.97  10.04   9.98   9.99  10.01  10.01   9.97  100.00
```

Attrition percentage flattens in deciles 3 through 5.

Figure 11.3 Decile segmentation for average balance on FRUTs.

a binary split to create a segmentation variable. In Figure 11.4, notice how the variable *avb_20* was selected as the second best-fitting transformation.

Table 11.3 lists all the continuous variables and their top two transformations. These will be used in the final model processing.

Categorical Variables

The following frequency calculates the attrition rate for every level of each categorical variable.

```
proc freq data=ch11.rowan;
table attrite*(age_lt25 autoloan child donate gender hh_ind
      homeown mailord marital mortgage popdens region retired sgle_fam
      somecoll ssn_ind)/ chisq missing;
run;
```

Figure 11.5 displays the output for *population density (popdens)*. The attrition rates are very different for each level, so I will create indicator variables for three of the four levels and allow the fourth level to be the default. I repeat this process for every categorical variable. The following code transforms the categorical variables into numeric form for use in the model.

Summary of Stepwise Procedure

Step	Variable Entered	Removed	Number In	Score Chi-Square	Wald Chi-Square	Pr > Chi-Square	Variable Label
1	AVB_CU		1	2025.7		0.0001	
2	AVB_20		2	99.3571		0.0001	

Analysis of Maximum Likelihood Estimates

Variable	DF	Parameter Estimate	Standard Error	Wald Chi-Square	Pr > Chi-Square	Standardized Estimate	Odds Ratio	Variable Label
INTERCPT	1	-1.4039	0.0168	6962.4006	0.0001	.	.	Intercept
AVB_20	1	-0.3574	0.0360	98.6461	0.0001	-0.078772	0.699	
AVB_CU	1	1.7E-10	4.81E-12	1247.7074	0.0001	0.236011	1.000	

Association of Predicted Probabilities and Observed Responses

Concordant = 59.9%		Somers' D = 0.236
Discordant = 36.3%		Gamma = 0.245
Tied = 3.8%		Tau-a = 0.085
(285180105 pairs)		c = 0.618

The cube of avbalfru and the binary split at the 20% decile were selected as the best fitting transformations.

Figure 11.4 Logistic output for average balance on FRUTs.

```
data ch11.rowan;
 set ch11.rowan;

city = (popdens = 'C');
suburb = (popdens = 'S');
rural = (popdens = 'R');
if gender = 'I' then gender = 'U';
west = (region in ('west', ' '));
married = (marital = 'M');
single  = (marital = 'S');
unkngend = (gender = 'U');
if age_lt25 = 'Y' then age_d = 1;
else age_d = 0;
if autoloan = 'Y' then auto_d = 1;
else auto_d = 0;
if donate = 'Y' then donat_d = 1;
else donat_d = 0;
```

Table 11.3 List of Continuous Variable Transformations

VARIABLE NAME	DESCRIPTION	TRANS 1	TRANS 2
avbalfru	Average Balance on FRUTs	avb_20	avb_cu
opntobuy	Open to Buy	opn_30	opn_cu
numnewac	Number of New Accts in Last 6 Months	num_sq	num_exp
avpurinc	Average Purchase Income	avp_50	avp_cu
hibal12m	High Balance in Last 12 Months	hib_20	hib_sqrt
hom_eq	Home Equity	hom_90	hom_exp
income	Income	inc_30	inc_90
timtlfbt	Time to First BT	tim_sqrt	tim_sin
nccblgt0	Number of Cards with Bal > $0	ncc_90	ncc_curi
pacctobl	Percent of Accts with $0 Balance	pac_90	pac_sini
pbalshar	Percent of Total Balances with Us	pba_10	pba_cu
intratin	Interest Rate Increase	int_20	int_sqrt
riskscor	Custom Risk Score	ris_60	ris_cui
profscor	Profitability Score	pro_60	pro_sqri

```
if hh_ind = 'H' then hhind_d = 1;
else hhind_d = 0;
if homeown = 'Y' then home_d = 1;
else home_d = 0;
if mailord = 'Y' then mail_d = 1;
else mail_d = 0;
if mortgage = 'Y' then mort_d = 1;
else mort_d = 0;
if retired = 'Y' then ret_d = 1;
else ret_d = 0;
if sgle_fam = 'Y' then sgle_d = 1;
else sgle_d = 0;
if somecoll = 'Y' then coll_d = 1;
else coll_d = 0;
run;
```

ATTRITE(Attrition 1=Yes 0=No)   POPDENS(Populations Density)

```
Frequency|
Percent  |
Row Pct  |
Col Pct  |C        |R        |S        |U        | Total
         +---------+---------+---------+---------+
       0 |  16283  |   2529  |   7231  |   4202  |  30245
         |  41.04  |   6.37  |  18.23  |  10.59  |  76.23
         |  53.84  |   8.36  |  23.91  |  13.89  |
         |  74.64  |  87.45  |  80.93  |  69.65  |
         +---------+---------+---------+---------+
       1 |   5531  |    363  |   1704  |   1831  |   9429
         |  13.94  |   0.91  |   4.30  |   4.62  |  23.77
         |  58.66  |   3.85  |  18.07  |  19.42  |
         |  25.36  |  12.55  |  19.07  |  30.35  |
         +---------+---------+---------+---------+
 Total      21814      2892      8935      6033     39674
            54.98      7.29     22.52     15.21    100.00
```

Figure 11.5 Frequency analysis of population density.

Now that we have our full list of powerful candidate variables, it is time to process the full model.

Processing the Model

These steps are similar to past recipes. I begin with the backward and stepwise and throw the winners from both into a score selection model. In this case, the results from the backward and stepwise were identical, so I took the 22 chosen variables and ran logistic regression with the *selection = score, best = 2* options. Figure 11.6 displays an excerpt of the results. The scores change minimally, so I am going to test a couple of different model sizes to see if it makes a difference. This is usually a worthwhile exercise if the scores are close.

The code for processing the 15-variable model is shown here:

```
proc logistic data=ch11.rowan(keep= modwgt records smp_wgt splitwgt
attrite AVB_CU AVPURINC AVP_50 NCCBLGT0 NCC_CURI NUMNEWAC OPNTOBUY
OPN_30 PACCT0BL PAC_90 PBALSHAR PBA_CU PROFSCOR PRO_60 TIMTLFBT)
descending;
```

```
Number of        Score
Variables        Value    Variables Included in Model
       1      3252.6851   OPNTOBUY
-----------------------------------
       2      5508.0169   OPNTOBUY TIM_SQRT
-------------------------------------------
       3      6181.3733   OPNTOBUY PBALSHAR TIMTLFBT
----------------------------------------------------
            |            |            |            |
-------------------------------------------------------------------------------
      14      6546.0745   AVB_CU AVPURINC AVP_50 NCCBLGTO NCC_CURI NUMNEWAC OPNTOBUY OPN_30 PACCTOBL
                          PBALSHAR PBA_CU PROFSCOR PRO_60 TIMTLFBT
-------------------------------------------------------------------------------
      15      6552.3964   AVB_CU AVPURINC AVP_50 NCCBLGTO NCC_CURI NUMNEWAC OPNTOBUY OPN_30 PACCTOBL
                          PAC_90 PBALSHAR PBA_CU PROFSCOR PRO_60 TIMTLFBT
-------------------------------------------------------------------------------
            |            |            |            |            |            |
-------------------------------------------------------------------------------
      20      6575.3677   AVB_CU AVPURINC AVP_50 INT_20 MORT_D NCCBLGTO NCC_90 NCC_CURI NUMNEWAC OPNTOBUY
                          OPN_30 PACCTOBL PAC_90 PBALSHAR PBA_CU PROFSCOR PRO_60 RISKSCOR RIS_CUI
                          TIMTLFBT
-------------------------------------------------------------------------------
      21      6578.6541   AVB_CU AVPURINC AVP_50 INT_20 MORT_D NCCBLGTO NCC_90 NCC_CURI NUMNEWAC NUM_SQ
                          OPNTOBUY OPN_30 PACCTOBL PAC_90 PBALSHAR PBA_CU PROFSCOR PRO_60 RISKSCOR
                          RIS_CUI TIMTLFBT
-------------------------------------------------------------------------------
      22      6580.6165   AVB_CU AVPURINC AVP_50 INT_20 MORT_D NCCBLGTO NCC_90 NCC_CURI NUMNEWAC NUM_SQ
                          OPNTOBUY OPN_30 PACCTOBL PAC_90 PBALSHAR PBA_CU PROFSCOR PRO_60 RISKSCOR
                          RIS_CUI TIMTLFBT TIM_SQRT
-------------------------------------------------------------------------------
```

Figure 11.6 Score output.

```
weight modwgt;
model attrite =
  AVB_CU AVPURINC AVP_50 NCCBLGTO NCC_CURI NUMNEWAC OPNTOBUY OPN_30
PACCTOBL PAC_90 PBALSHAR PBA_CU PROFSCOR PRO_60 TIMTLFBT;
output out=ch11.scored(where=(splitwgt=.)) p=pred;
run;
```

The steps down to PROC TABULATE, are identical to those in chapter 10.

```
title "15 Variable Model";
proc tabulate data=ch11.scored;
weight smp_wgt;
class val_dec;
var attrite pred records;
table val_dec='Decile' all='Total',
        records='Customers'*sum=' '*f=comma9.
        pred='Predicted Probability'*mean=' '*f=11.5
```

```
            attrite='Percent Attritors'*mean=' '*f=percent9.2
            /rts = 8 row=float;
    run;
```

This process is repeated for the 10- and 22-variable models. The results are compared in Figure 11.7. You can see that there really isn't a significant difference in performance, so you might select the number of variables based on other criteria such as model stability or explanability.

Validating the Model

By now you've probably noticed that I like to calculate bootstrap estimates on all my models. It gives me the comfort that I have a robust model that doesn't over-fit the data. But before I calculate bootstrap estimates, I am going to compare the ability of the generic attrition score, *gen_attr*, to the model's ability to rank the true attriters. Figure 11.8 shows a gains table comparison of the three models and the generic score.

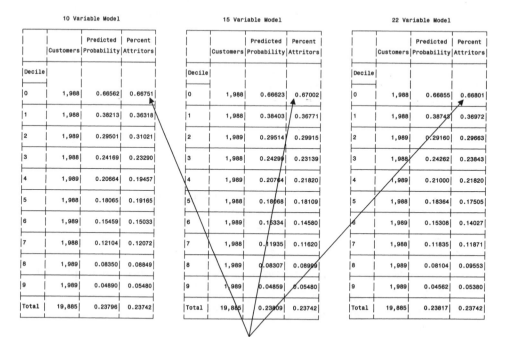

Figure 11.7 Model comparison for number of variables.

The 15-variable model is slightly better in the top deciles.

Decile	Customers	10 Variable Model			15 Variable Model			22 Variable Model			Generic Score		
		% of Attritors	Lift	Cum Lift	% of Attritors	Lift	Cum Lift	% of Attritors	Lift	Cum Lift	% of Attritors	Lift	Cum Lift
0	1,988	66.75%	281	281	67.00%	282	282	66.80%	281	281	62.226%	273	273
1	1,988	36.32%	153	217	36.77%	155	219	36.97%	156	219	37.214%	163	218
2	1,988	31.02%	131	188	29.92%	126	188	29.66%	125	187	28.566%	125	187
3	1,988	23.29%	98	166	23.14%	97	165	23.84%	100	166	23.675%	104	166
4	1,988	19.46%	82	149	21.82%	92	150	21.82%	92	151	19.797%	87	150
5	1,988	19.17%	81	138	18.11%	76	138	17.51%	74	138	17.620%	77	138
6	1,988	15.03%	63	127	14.58%	61	127	14.03%	59	127	14.983%	66	128
7	1,988	12.07%	51	117	11.62%	49	117	11.87%	50	117	11.289%	49	118
8	1,988	8.85%	37	109	9.00%	38	109	9.55%	40	109	7.140%	31	108
9	1,988	5.48%	23	100	5.48%	23	100	5.38%	23	100	5.570%	24	100
TOTAL	19,880	23.74%			23.74%			23.74%			22.81%		

Notice how the cumulative lift values for the three models are identical in the last 5 deciles.

Figure 11.8   Score comparison gains table.

The differences or similarities are easy to see in Figure 11.9, which is a gains chart comparing all four model scores. This also shows that there is hardly any difference in the performance of the three models.

Bootstrapping

The following code is excerpted from the bootstrapping macro in chapter 10. It is identical except for the dependent variable and the variable prefixes and suffixes. Recall that the data set, *ch11.scored*, is an output data set from PROC LOGISITIC, shown previously.

```
data ch11.scored;
set ch11.scored(keep= pred attrite splitwgt records val_dec smp_wgt);
run;

proc univariate data=ch11.scored noprint;
weight smp_wgt;
var attrite;
output out=preddata sumwgt=sumwgt mean=atmean;
run;
```

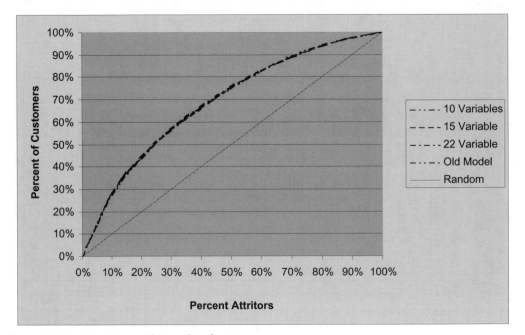

Figure 11.9   Score comparison gains chart.

```
proc sort data=ch11.scored;
by descending pred;
run;

data ch11.scored;
 set ch11.scored;
if (_n_ eq 1) then set preddata;
retain sumwgt atmean;
run;

proc summary data=ch11.scored;
weight smp_wgt;
var pred;
class val_dec;
output out=ch11.fullmean mean=atmnf;
id smp_wgt;
run;

data atfmean(rename=(atmnf=atomn_g) drop=val_dec);
 set ch11.fullmean(where=(val_dec=.) keep=atmnf val_dec);
run;

data ch11.fullmean;
 set ch11.fullmean;
if (_n_ eq 1) then set atfmean;
retain atomn_g;
run;
```

```
%macro bootst25;
%do samp = 1 %to 25;
```

<< THE REMAINDER OF THE CODE IN THIS SECTION IS SIMILAR TO THE BOOT-STRAPPING CODE IN CHAPTER 6 >>

The following PROC TABULATE creates the table seen in Figure 11.10.

```
proc tabulate data=ch11.bs_sum;
weight smp_wgt;
var liftf bsest_a atmnf lci_a uci_a bsest_l lftmbs lci_l uci_l;
class val_dec;
table (val_dec='Decile' all='Total'),
(atmnf='Predicted Attrition'*mean=' '*f=percent10.2
bsest_a='BS Est Attritors'*mean=' '*f=percent10.2
lci_a ='BS Lower CI Resp'*mean=' '*f=percent10.2
uci_a ='BS Upper CI Resp'*mean=' '*f=percent10.2

liftf ='Actual Lift'*mean=' '*f=8.
bsest_l='BS Est Lift'*mean=' '*f=8.
lci_l ='BS Lower CI Lift'*mean=' '*f=8.
uci_l ='BS Upper CI Lift'*mean=' '*f=8.)
/rts=10 row=float;
run;
```

In figure 11.10, we can see the bootstrap estimates and confidence intervals for the probability of attrition or churn. The tight range of the confidence interval give me confidence that the model is robust.

Implementing the Model

Now that we have a probability of churn, we can use it in a couple of ways. First, we can use it to gain a deeper understanding of our customers. This is achieved through customer profiling. Using a decile analysis of churn score across some key drivers of attrition or churn, we can begin to understand the characteristics of a loyal or disloyal customer.

Creating Attrition Profiles

Rowan Royal Bank is interested in knowing how the key drivers of the 15-variable model behave within each decile. With this information, it can create profiles of its customers based on their probability to move balances following a rate increase. The following code, similar to the code used in chapter 7, used PROC TABULATE to create the gains table in Figure 11.11.

	Predicted Attrition	BS Est Attritors	BS Lower CI Resp	BS Upper CI Resp	Actual Lift	BS Est Lift	BS Lower CI Lift	BS Upper CI Lift
Decile								
0	66.56%	66.28%	64.15%	68.40%	280	277	270	285
1	38.21%	40.09%	38.20%	41.99%	161	168	161	175
2	29.50%	27.95%	25.80%	30.09%	124	117	108	125
3	24.17%	25.35%	23.45%	27.24%	102	106	99	114
4	20.66%	22.04%	20.16%	23.93%	87	92	85	99
5	18.07%	17.30%	16.07%	18.53%	76	72	67	78
6	15.46%	15.64%	14.12%	17.17%	65	65	59	72
7	12.10%	12.10%	10.22%	13.97%	51	51	43	58
8	8.35%	7.99%	6.64%	9.34%	35	33	28	39
9	4.89%	4.19%	3.30%	5.07%	21	18	14	21
Total	23.80%	23.89%	22.21%	25.57%	100	100	93	107

Figure 11.10 Bootstrap estimates of 15-variable attrition model.

```
proc tabulate data=ch11.scored;
weight smp_wgt;
class val_dec ;
var  AVPURINC NCCBLGT0 NUMNEWAC OPNTOBUY PACCT0BL
 PBALSHAR PROFSCOR TIMTLFBT;
table val_dec=' ' all='Total',
        AVPURINC*mean=' '*f=dollar8.
        NCCBLGT0*mean=' '*f=comma8.
        NUMNEWAC*mean=' '*f=comma8.
        OPNTOBUY*mean=' '*f=dollar8.
        PACCT0BL*mean=' '*f=percent8.
        PBALSHAR*mean=' '*f=percent8.
        PROFSCOR*mean=' '*f=8.2
        TIMTLFBT*mean=' '*f=8.2
```

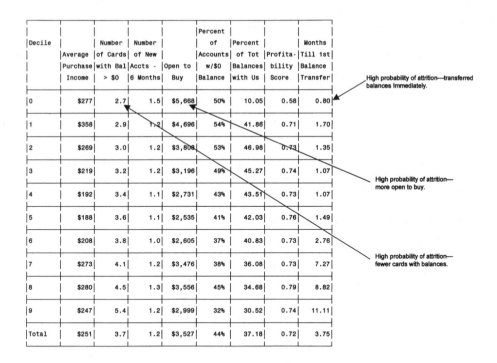

Decile	Average Purchase Income	Number of Cards with Bal > $0	Number of New Accts - 6 Months	Open to Buy	Percent of Accounts w/$0 Balance	Percent of Tot Balances with Us	Profita-bility Score	Months Till 1st Balance Transfer
0	$277	2.7	1.5	$5,668	50%	10.05	0.58	0.80
1	$358	2.9	1.2	$4,696	54%	41.86	0.71	1.70
2	$269	3.0	1.2	$3,808	53%	46.98	0.73	1.35
3	$219	3.2	1.2	$3,196	49%	45.27	0.74	1.07
4	$192	3.4	1.1	$2,731	43%	43.51	0.73	1.07
5	$188	3.6	1.1	$2,535	41%	42.03	0.76	1.49
6	$208	3.8	1.0	$2,605	37%	40.83	0.73	2.76
7	$273	4.1	1.2	$3,476	38%	36.08	0.73	7.27
8	$280	4.5	1.3	$3,556	45%	34.68	0.79	8.82
9	$247	5.4	1.2	$2,999	32%	30.52	0.74	11.11
Total	$251	3.7	1.2	$3,527	44%	37.18	0.72	3.75

High probability of attrition—transferred balances immediately.

High probability of attrition—more open to buy.

High probability of attrition—fewer cards with balances.

This table provides a profile of customers with a high or low likelihood of attriting.

Figure 11.11 Customer profile by decile.

```
        /rts = 10 row=float box = '              Decile';
run;
```

Figure 11.11 displays the average values by decile. Notice how some variables have definite trends while others are less variable. You could say that a person who is likely to churn has the following characteristics:

- Fewer cards with balances
- More new accounts with competitors
- More "open to buy" or room on their existing cards
- Higher percentage of accounts with $0 balance
- Low percentage of balances with Rowan
- Low profitability score (based on prior model)
- Moved balances to Rowan quickly following prior balance transfer offer

This information is quite useful in helping Rowan understand how its customers think and what might be motivating their behavior. This can lead to smarter marketing decisions, greater customer loyalty, and higher profits.

Optimizing Customer Profitability

Many factors influence credit card profitability. Most revolvers are profitable, but so are some transactors. The following formula details one method for calculating 12-month credit card profitability:

Assumptions

- Behavior for next 12 months will mimic behavior for past 12 months.
- Risk adjustment is a function of current status and historical trends.
- Attrition adjustment is independent of market pressures.

Values Needed for Calculation

1. Average daily balance.
2. Net purchases (purchases – returns).
3. Finance charges.
4. Late, over-limit, cash advance, annual, and miscellaneous fees.
5. Attrition probability based on churn model score.
6. Charge-off probability based on risk score.

Components of Profit and Loss

- Fee Income (#4)—Sum of fees for prior 12 months. Value assumes similar behavior for next 12 months.
- Finance charges (#3)—Not a straight function of balance as all balances may not be at same rate.
- Interchange income ($1.44\% \times$ #2)—Fee charged to retailer or point of sale vendor for use of card.
- Cost of Funds ($5.42\% \times$ #1)—Reflects market prices and bank's borrowing power.
- Attrition adjustment (#5 $\times$ #3)—Probability of attrition from model is based on rate increase. Customer typically moves entire balance resulting in lost finance charges.
- Charge-off provision (#6 $\times$ #1)—Probability of charge-off based on risk model. Customer typically defaults on entire balance.
- Rebates and royalties (rate $\times$ #2 and/or #3)—Percent of balance or finance charges promised to customer or affinity partner.
- Operating expense ($45 annually)—Cost of annual account processing.
- Taxes ($38\% \times (A + B + C - D - E - F - G - H)$)—For Uncle Sam.

The final equation is this: One-Year Risk Adjusted Profit = A + B + C – D – E – F – G – H – I. This formula establishes a profit value for each customer based on variable costs and revenue. When using this value to make marketing decisions, it is important to remember that it does not consider fixed costs such as salaries and overhead.

This is an excellent formula for calculating one-year risk adjusted profit for credit card customers. One effective use of this formula is to determine if raising interest rates will increase or decrease customer profitability. One advantage of this formula is that it will determine the answer to this question on each individual customer. The results, however, are more meaningful on an aggregate basis. To clarify, let's work through an example.

Let's say Jane Smith has the following profile: Average balance – $5,252; Net purchases $1,876; Finance charges – $731; Fees – $29; Attrition probability following reprice – 38%; Charge-off probability prior to reprice – 2.2%; Rebate – 1%. Table 11.4 details the net profit calculation for Jane Smith. The second column shows that prior to a 4% increase in APR, one-year risk adjusted profit for Jane Smith is $179.36. Now let's recalculate it after the rate increase. First we must make the following assumptions:

- Fees and purchases remain the same.
- Balances decrease by probability of attrition. This is not precise on an individual basis but accurately reflects group behavior.

Table 11.4 Effects of Reprice on Profitibility

	PRE REPRICE	POST REPRICE – 38% CHURN RATE	POST REPRICE – 43% CHURN RATE	POST REPRICE – 39.5% CHURN RATE
Average balance	$5,252.00	$3,256.24	$2,993.64	$3,177.46
Net purchases	$1,876.00	$1,876.00	$1,876.00	$1,876.00
Finance charge	$ 731.00	$ 583.47	$ 536.42	$ 569.35
Fee income	$ 29.00	$ 29.00	$ 29.00	$ 29.00
Attrition probability	0%	38%	43%	39.5%
Charge-off provision	2.2%	2.8%	2.8%	2.8%
Rebate	1%	1%	1%	1%
Pretax profit	$ 289.29	$ 295.89	$ 272.91	$ 288.99
Taxes	$ 109.93	$ 112.44	$ 103.71	$ 109.82
Net profit	$ 179.36	$ 183.45	$ 169.21	$ 179.18

- Probability of charge-off increases by 25% following reprice.
- Customers that are in financial trouble will usually let their higher rates cards go into default first.

The third column shows the profits following the reprice. At a 38% probability of churn, it would be marginally profitable to increase Jane's interest rate by 4%. The fourth column, however, tells a different story. If the probability of churn is 43%, the reprice would make Jane less profitable. In fact, we find the exact probability of churn at which the reprice will not affect profits for Jane Smith is approximately 39.5%. This measure can be calculated for each customer giving Rowan Royal the ability to enact one-to-one customer relationship management that optimizes profits for the entire customer portfolio.

Retaining Customers Proactively

The same techniques that are used to increase profits with rate increases can be used to improve customer loyalty. Consider the previous example where we determined how to increase profits by predicting which customers would be profitable following a rate increase. We can use the same formula to evaluate incentives for customers to build balances. For example, we could develop a model that predicts which customers will increase balances following a rate decrease or some other incentives like higher rebates or air miles. The techniques for calculating profit and managing name selection are the same.

Many of the automated campaign management tools are designed to score a customer with various embedded models each time new information is received on a customer. This creates many opportunities to take immediate action when a change is detected. For example, if a customer suddenly decreases their balance, their risk decreases along with their profits. This might be a good time to offer them a lower rate along with some balance transfer incentives. Or if their risk score suddenly drops into a risky range, you can increase their rate or limit their access to more credit. The possibilities are endless. And the advances in technology that allow us to integrate and automate these analytic tools are rapidly changing the way we manage our customers. It is becoming impossible to survive without them.

Summary

Did you notice how the mechanics of the attrition or churn model are similar to those of many of the other recipes? Again, the main distinction between the models is the objective. I was able to use many of the same processing steps. I feel these models truly emphasize the importance of a clearly defined objective, not just from a modeling point of view, but also from a business point of view.

Attrition or churn models are increasing in popularity as companies in all industries struggle to understand and retain their most profitable customers. Along with response and risk models, churn models are becoming an integral part of campaign management both manual and automated. With only slight modification, these techniques will work well for companies in all areas of financial services as well as utilities, telcos, high-tech, retail, publishing, catalog, gaming, and travel.

Before we begin the next recipe, take a break and work up an appetite. In the next chapter, I build a lifetime value model. It's a high calorie treat!

CHAPTER 12

Targeting Profitable Customers: Modeling Lifetime Value

I n the early years of direct marketing, much of the growth in revenue took place through the acquisition of new customers. Today, however, markets are more saturated. New customers are gained mainly at the expense of competitors. This makes it more difficult and expensive to acquire new customers. To compensate, many companies are relying on their current customer base to generate the bulk of their profits. They are staying competitive by placing more emphasis on developing new products and services to offer to their existing customers. This not only affects the value of existing customers, but it changes the value of a potential customer or prospect.

As a result, companies are willing to spend more to attract new customers by focusing on long range or lifetime value (LTV). In this chapter, I introduce the basic concepts of lifetime value. I introduce several formulas for calculating lifetime value with applications in a variety of industries. In the last half of the chapter, I expand the net present value (NPV) model developed in part 2. Recall that NPV assigns profits based on a single product. In this chapter, I expand the NPV model to predict lifetime value by incorporating cross-sell and up-sell potential for each prospect through a series of predictive models. These models are incorporated into a lifetime value calculation for our insurance prospect base. The benefits of using lifetime value modeling are quantified by comparing the predicted profits to those in the net present value model in chapter 7.

What Is Lifetime Value?

Lifetime value is the expected value of a prospect or customer over a specified period of time, measured in today's dollars. Lifetime value is measured in various ways, depending on the industry, but basically represents future revenues less overhead and expenses. This valuation allows companies to allocate resources based on customer value or potential customer value.

Historically, marketing strategies were driven by the financial benefits of a single campaign. Customer profitability was optimized by the net profits of the initial sale. But with the increased cost of acquiring customers and the expansion of products and services to existing customers, companies are expanding their marketing strategies to consider the lifetime value of a potential customer.

Lifetime value measurements on a customer portfolio can quantify the long-term financial health of a company or business. In the following sidebar, William Burns, Adjunct Professor of Business Administration at San Diego State University, explains the holistic importance of the lifetime value measure.

Uses of Lifetime Value

Lifetime value measurements are useful for both acquiring customers and managing customer relationships. For new customer acquisition, the increased expected value allows companies to increase marketing expenditures. This can broaden the universe of profitable prospects. Later on in this chapter, I will show how this is carried out in our life insurance case study.

For customer relationship management, the uses of a lifetime value measurement are numerous. Once an LTV is assigned to each customer, the customer database can be segmented for a variety of purposes. In many cases, the 80/20 rule applies—that is, 20% of the customer base is generating 80% of the profits.

Armed with this information, your company is able to take actions or avoid an action based on the long-term benefit to the company. Marketing programs can be tailored to different levels of profitability. For example, banks and finance companies use LTV to determine risk actions such as rate increases or line adjustments. Multiline companies use LTV to sequence product offers. Many companies offer premium customer service, such as an 800 number, to their high-value customers. Whatever the action or treatment, many companies are using LTV to optimize their customer relationship management.

Why Is Lifetime Value Important for Marketing Decisions?

Economists have long argued that business decisions should seek to maximize value for shareholders and that all projects can and should be systematically examined in this light. Consistent with this perspective, marketers must recognize that their efforts should be guided by value maximization as well. Ideally, the practice of value optimization should begin during the market segmentation stage. Experience has shown that customers vary widely in their value to a business due to differing spending patterns, loyalty, and tendency to generate referrals. Hence, segmentation should include considerations of customer lifetime worth. Similar arguments can be made for other marketing activities. As it turns out, the lifetime value (LTV) of a customer represents an attractive metric for marketing managers for the following reasons:

- All factors being equal, increasing the LTV of customers increases the value of the firm.

- Customer LTV can be directly linked to important marketing goals such as sales targets and customer retention.

- LTV calculations require the marketer to take a long and comprehensive view of the customer.

- LTV accounts for differences in risk level and timing of customer profit streams.

The economic logic behind maximizing customer value is based on the notion that every marketing action has an opportunity cost. That is, investors who help capitalize a business can earn returns from a number of sources both within and outside the company. To cultivate loyal investors, it is not enough to simply have revenues exceed costs and call this a profitable marketing venture. A simple example illustrates this point.

Suppose I am considering a promotion designed to acquire new customers. This program may at first appear justified because total revenues are projected to soon exceed total costs based on some break-even analysis. After forecasting the likely return on investment (adjusted for risk), though, I may discover that the long-term economic impact of, say, increasing retention of our most valuable customers is much higher. Had I gone ahead with the promotion, I might have destroyed rather than improved economic value. How many marketing managers think in these terms? It's not a trivial question, given that the most economically viable firms will attract the best customers, employees, and investors over time and thereby will outdistance their competitors.

Components of Lifetime Value

Lifetime value can be calculated for almost any business. In its simplest form, it has the following base components:

Duration. The expected length of the customer relationship. This value is one of the most critical to the results and difficult to determine. And like many aspects of modeling, there are no hard-and-fast rules for assigning duration. You might think that a long duration would be better for the business, but there are two drawbacks. First, the longer the duration, the lower the accuracy. And second, a long duration delays final validation. See the accompanying sidebar, for a discussion by Shree Pragada on assigning duration.

Time period. The length of the incremental LTV measure. This is generally one year, but it can reflect different renewal periods or product cycles.

Revenue. The income from the sale of a product or service.

Costs. Marketing expense or direct cost of product.

Discount rate. Adjustment to convert future dollars to today's value.

Some additional components, depending on the industry, may include the following:

Renewal rate. The probability of renewal or retention rate.

Referral rate. The incremental revenue generated.

Risk factor. The potential losses related to risk.

Assigning Duration

Shree Pragada, Vice President of Customer Acquisition for Fleet Credit Card Bank, discusses some considerations for assigning duration in the credit card industry.

With customer relationship management (CRM) becoming such a buzzword and with the availability of a variety of customer information, CRM systems have become quite widespread. In estimating customer or prospect profitability in CRM systems, the duration for the window of financial evaluation appears to be fuzzy. Should it be six months, one year, three years, six years, or longer? Even within an organization, it can be noticed that different durations are being used across different departments for practically the same marketing campaign. The finance department may want to have CRM systems configured to estimate profitability for as much as six or seven years, assuming that a portfolio with 15–20% account attrition will continue to yield value for about six to seven years. The risk management department may be interested in three- to four-years' duration as credit losses take about three years to stabilize. Some marketing departments would be comfortable executing million-dollar campaigns with just response predictions that span just over three to four months. Everyone has a different duration for evaluating expected profitability and for the logical explanations why that duration could be better. So, how long should I aim to evaluate customer profitability and why?

For starters, there is no cookie-cutter solution for the best duration across all customer profitability systems. For instance, the mortgage industry should develop profitability systems that span over several years while the credit card industry might benefit from shorter and much more focused duration. And, within an industry different marketing campaigns will need different durations depending on the campaign goals and the profit drivers. I will look at the credit card industry to elaborate on this point.

Consider two marketing campaigns:

- Rate Sale Offer for six months to improve purchase activity by giving a promotional annual percentage rate for a short period of time.

- Balance Transfer Offer for two years to increase card receivables by enticing customers to transfer balances from competitors through low-rate balance transfer offers.

The difference that I wish to show between these marketing offers is that Offer 1 is good for only six months while Offer 2 is good for two years. Studying the performance of these marketing offers will show that customer behavior stabilizes or regresses to its norm sooner for Offer 1 than for Offer 2. The reasons are quite obvious.

Let me digress a little into what constitutes a success or failure in a marketing campaign. Every marketing campaign will alter the normal customer behavior by a certain degree. When customers respond to marketing offers, say a balance transfer offer, they will bring additional balances, pay more finance charges, probably even use their cards more. They will digress from their norm for a "duration" after which they will regress to their normal account behavior. The more they digress, the more profitable they tend to be. (The case of negative behavior has been discounted for simplicity.) The success of a marketing program depends on how much customers have digressed from their norm and how many—in short, the "positive incremental value." Because CRM systems are primarily put to task to configure/identify marketing programs to maximize

continues

(Continued)
profitability, attention should be paid to this "duration" for which the marketing programs tend to alter overall customer behavior.

To summarize, as profitability is estimated by modeling the many customer behaviors, the "duration" should not be more than the duration for which any of the underlying behaviors can be modeled comfortably. For instance, credit losses can be estimated fairly for over 3 years, but account balance fluctuations can hardly be modeled past 18 months to 2 years. So this would limit the duration for a CRM system in the Card Industry to about 2 years. An alternative to trying to model difficult behavior past the comfortable duration is to estimate a terminal value to extend the duration to suit traditional financial reporting.

Applications of Lifetime Value

As mentioned previously, the formulas for calculating lifetime value vary greatly depending on the product and industry. In the following cases, Arthur Middleton Hughes, Director of Strategic Planning at M\S Database Marketing, illustrates some unique calculations. In addition, he shows how to calculate the discount rate for a particular business.

Lifetime Value Case Studies

Lifetime value has become a highly useful method for directing marketing strategies that increase customer lifetime value, retain customers that have high lifetime value, and reprice or discard customers with negative lifetime value. The following cases highlight some uses of LTV calculations.

Business-to-Business Marketing

Lifetime value tables for business-to-business customers are easy to develop. To show how this is done, let's develop the lifetime value of customers of an artificial business, the Weldon Scientific Company, that sells high-tech equipment to factories and laboratories.

Let's explain some of the numbers in Table 12.1. Year 1 represents the year of acquisition, rather than a calendar year. Year 1 thus includes people acquired in several different years. Year 2 is everybody's second year with Weldon. I am

Table 12.1 Lifetime Value Table for Business to Business

	YEAR 1	YEAR 2	YEAR 3
Customers	20,000	12,000	7,800
Retention Rate	60.00%	65.00%	70.00%
Orders/year	1.8	2.6	3.6
Avg. Order Size	$2,980	$5,589	$9,106
Total Revenue	$107,280,000	$174,376,800	$255,696,480
Direct Cost %	70.00%	65.00%	63.00%
Costs	$75,096,000	$113,344,920	$161,088,782
Acquisition Costs $630	$87,696,000	$113,344,920	$161,088,782
Total Costs	$87,696,000	$113,344,920	$161,088,782
Gross Profit	$19,584,000	$61,031,880	$94,607,698
Discount Rate	1.13	1.81	2.53
Net Present Value Profit	$17,330,973	$33,719,271	$37,394,347
Cumulative NPV Profit	$17,330,973	$51,050,244	$88,4444,591
Customer Lifetime Value	$867	$2,553	$4,422

assuming that Weldon has acquired 20,000 business customers, including a number of independent distributors. A year later, only 12,000 of these customers are still buying. That means that Weldon's retention rate is 60%. Over time, the retention rate of the loyal Weldon customers who are still buying goes up.

The average customer placed an average of 1.8 orders in their year of acquisition, with an average order value of $2,980. As customers became more loyal, they placed more orders per year, of increasing size.

The acquisition cost was $630 per customer. The cost of servicing customers came down substantially after the first year. Most interesting in this chart is the discount rate, which is developed in a separate table. The discount rate is needed because to compute lifetime value I will have to add together profit received in several different years. Money to be received in a future year is not as valuable as money in hand today. I have to discount it if I want to compare and add it to current dollars. That is the purpose of the discount rate summarized in Table 12.2.

Table 12.2 Discount Rate by Year

	YEAR 1	YEAR 2	YEAR 3
Year	0	1	2
Risk Factor	1.8	1.5	1.4
Interest Rate	8.00%	8.00%	8.00%
A/R Days	65	85	90
Discount Rate	1.13	1.81	2.53

The formula for the discount rate is this:

Discount rate $= ((1 + \text{interest rate}) \times (\text{risk factor}))^{\text{Year} + \text{AR}/365}$

It includes the interest rate, a risk factor, and a payment factor. In the first year, Weldon tries to get new customers to pay up front, relaxing to a 60-day policy with subsequent orders. For established customers, 90-day payment is customary. The risk factor drops substantially with long-term customers. The combination of all of these factors gives Weldon a sophisticated discount rate that is responsive to the business situation that it faces.

When the Repurchase Cycle Is Not Annual

The retention rate is typically calculated on an annual basis. A 60% retention rate means that of 10,000 customers acquired in Year 1, there will be only 6,000 customers remaining as active customers in Year 2. This is easy to compute if customers buy every month or once a year. But what is the annual retention rate if 50% of the customers buy a product only every four years? This is true in many business-to-business situations. Here a formula is necessary. The formula is this:

$RR = (RPR)^{(1/Y)}$

RR is the annual retention rate, RPR is the repurchase rate, and Y is the number of years between purchases. The following two examples illustrate the use of this formula for automobile purchases.

Automobile Purchase by One Segment

A segment of Buick owners buys a new car every four years. About 35% of them buy a Buick, and the balance buys some other make of car. What is their annual retention rate?

$RR = (RPR)^{(1/Y)}$

$RR = (0.35)^{(1/4)}$

$RR = 76.9\%$

Automobile Purchase by Several Segments

Buick owners can be divided into four segments: those who buy a new car every one year, two years, three years, and four years. Their respective repurchase rates are shown in Table 12.3.

Table 12.3 Table Repurchase Rates by Segment

SEGMENT	YEARS BETWEEN PURCHASE	REPURCHASE RATE	ANNUAL RETENTION	ACQUIRED CUSTOMERS	RETAINED CUSTOMERS
A	1	55.00%	55.00%	90,346	49,690
B	2	45.00%	67.08%	170,882	114,631
C	3	40.00%	73.68%	387,223	285,308
D	4	35.00%	76.92%	553,001	425,347
Total			72.83%	1,201,452	874,976

Table 12.3 provides some interesting information. The repurchase rate of those who buy a Buick every year seems much higher than that of those who wait four years between automobile purchase. Their annual retention rate, however, is far lower.

Restaurant Patrons by Week

A business-area restaurant had a regular clientele of patrons who ate there almost every day. The restaurant decided to try database marketing. Its staff set up a system to gather the names of their customers and gave points for each meal. They discovered that they were losing about 1% of their clients every week. What was their annual retention rate? The formula is the same:

$$RR = (RPR)^{(1/Y)}$$

In this case, the repurchase rate is 99%, and the period involved is 1/52 of a year, so the formula becomes:

$$RR = (.99)^{(1/(1/52))}$$

$$RR = 59.3\%$$

This tells us that the restaurant's annual retention rate is 59.3%.

Calculating Lifetime Value for a Renewable Product or Service

William Burns contributed the following simple formula for calculating lifetime value for a renewable product or service.

1. Forecast after-tax profits over the lifetime of the customer group. Begin with determining the possible lifespan of a customer and the typical billing cycle. Useful forecasts must be based on a sound theory of customers in your organization.

2. Determine the expected rate of return (r) for the marketing project in mind. The firm's finance group is the best source of help, but outside financial expertise can also be used.

3. Calculate the net present value (NPV) of the CFt over the lifetime of the customer group. The general formula to do this calculation is as follows:

$$PV = CF_1/(1 + r)^1 + CF_2/(1 + r)^2 + \ldots + CF_t/(1 + r)^t$$

Where subscript t is the number of time periods composing the lifetime of the customer group (time period should correspond to billing cycle). PV represents the upper limit of what should be paid to acquire a customer group.

$$NPV = PV - CF_0$$

Where CF_0 represents the after-tax cost of acquiring the customer group. NPV represents the actual worth of the customer group after acquisition.

$$LTV = NPV/C$$

Where C is the total number of customers initially acquired. LTV represents the worth of a typical customer to the company at the time of acquisition.

Calculating Lifetime Value: A Case Study

As I expand the case study in Part 2 to calculate lifetime value, I will leverage knowledge gained through years of practice by experts in the direct marketing industry. Donald R. Jackson, author of *151 Secrets of Insurance Direct Marketing Practices Revealed* (Nopoly Press, 1989), defines "Policy Holder Lifetime Value":

> Policy Holder Lifetime Value is the present value of a future stream of net contributions to overhead and profit expected from the policyholder.

He goes on to list some key opportunities available to companies that use lifetime value for insurance marketing:

> Policy Holder LTV provides a financial foundation for key management decisions:
>
> 1. Developing rates for insurance products
>
> 2. Assigning allowance for policyholder acquisition
>
> 3. Setting selection criteria for policyholder marketing
>
> 4. Choosing media for initial policyholder acquisition
>
> 5. Investing in reactivation of old policyholders
>
> 6. Assigning an asset value to your policyholder base

As I discussed earlier, prospects may be marginally profitable or even unprofitable when they first become customers. They *have* expressed an interest in doing business with you, so the hard work is done. You now have an opportunity to develop a profitable long-term relationship within which you can sell them different products (cross-sell) or more of the same product (up-sell). To cross-sell a life insurance customer, you might try to sell the customer health or accident insurance. An up-sell is typically an offer to increase the coverage on the customer's current policy.

In chapter 7, I calculated the net present value of a single product for a group of prospects. This produced the expected profits for a single policy over three years. It accounted for risk and cost of mailing for the single product. In this chapter, I incorporate the value of additional net revenue to prospects, which allows me to calculate their lifetime value. The first step is to develop models to estimate the probability of incremental net revenue for each prospect. For clarity, I'll call this model our Cross-Sell Up-Sell Revenues (CRUPS) model.

Case Study: Year One Net Revenues

To develop the incremental net revenue models, I take a sample of customers, both current and lapsed, that were booked between three and four years ago. I use their prospect information to develop three models, one model to predict incremental net revenues for each of the first three years.

Because this is a model using customer information, I pull data from the data warehouse. Customers that were booked between three and four years ago are identified. I extract 2,230 customers along with their information at the time of acquisition for modeling. Additional sales, claims, and policy lapse information for the following three years are appended from the customer files. This data has been corrected for missing values and outliers.

The following code calculates the net revenues for each incremental year by summing the total sales reduced by the percent of claims. The variables names are *crupsyr1*, *crupsyr2*, and *crupsyr3* for each of the three years:

```
acqmod.crossell;
acqmod.crossell;
crupsyr1 = sum(of sale01Y1-sale12Y1)*(1-claimpct);
crupsyr2    sum(of sale01Y2-sale12Y2)*(1-claimpct);
crupsyr3    sum(of sale01Y3-sale12Y3)*(1-claimpct);
run;
```

The following code begins by randomly assigning a missing weight to half of the data set. Because I am planning to use linear regression to predict additional net revenues, I must get all variables into a numeric, continuous form. The remaining code creates indicator variables by assigning numeric values to n − 1 levels of each categorical variable. For example, the variable *pop_den* has four levels: A, B, C, and missing. The three indicator variables, *pop_denA*, *pop_denB*, and *pop_denC*, have values of 0 and 1. The missing level is represented when the values for the other three indicator variables equals 0:

```
data acqmod.crossell;
  set acqmod.crossell;
if ranuni(5555) < .5 then splitwgt = 1; else splitwgt = .;

pop_denA = (pop_den = 'A');
pop_denB = (pop_den = 'B');
pop_denC = (pop_den = 'C');
trav_cdd = (trav_cd = '1');
bankcrdd = (bankcrd = 'Y');
deptcrdd = (deptcrd = 'Y');
fin_cod  = (fin_co  = 'Y');
pre_crdd = (pre_crd = 'Y');
upsccrdd = (upsccrd = 'Y');
apt_indd = (apt_ind = 'Y');
sgle_ind = (sgle_in = 'Y');
finl_idm = (finl_id = 'M');
finl_idn = (finl_id = 'N');
hh_indd  = (hh_ind =  'H');
gend_m   = (gender = 'M');
driv_inA = (driv_in = 'A');
driv_inN = (driv_in = 'N');
mob_indN = (mob_ind = 'N');
mob_indY = (mob_ind = 'Y');
mortin1M = (mortin1 = 'M');
mortin1N = (mortin1 = 'N');
mortin1Y = (mortin1 = 'Y');
autoin1M = (autoin1 = 'M');
autoin1N = (autoin1 = 'N');
autoin1Y = (autoin1 = 'Y');
childind = (childin = 'Y');
run;
```

Similar to the processing in chapter 5, the following code finds the best transformation for each continuous variable. I create predictors for the first-year model using the following code. The second- and third-year models are created using the same techniques:

```
data acqmod.agedset;
set acqmod.crossell(keep=pros_id infd_age crupsyr1);

age_sq   = infd_age**2;
age_cu   = infd_age**3;
age_sqrt = sqrt(infd_age);
age_curt = infd_age**.3333;
age_log  = log(max(.0001,infd_age));
   |       |     |     |     |
   |       |     |     |     |
age_tani = 1/max(.0001,tan(infd_age));
age_sini = 1/max(.0001,sin(infd_age));
age_cosi = 1/max(.0001,cos(infd_age));

run;
```

Because I am using continuous values to predict a continuous value, I use linear regression. In SAS the procedure is called PROC REG:

```
title "Regression on Inferred Age";
proc reg data=acqmod.agedset;
model crupsyr1 = infd_age
age_sq age_cu age_sqrt age_curt age_log
age_tan age_sin age_cos age_inv age_sqi
age_cui age_sqri age_curi age_logi
age_tani age_sini age_cosi
/ selection = stepwise stop = 2 details;
run;
```

In Figure 12.1, I see that the best form of the variable Inferred Age is the inverse cube root (*age_cui*). This will be a candidate in the final model. This step is repeated for all the continuous variables. The following code sorts and combines the data sets with the best transformation of each continuous variable:

```
%macro srt(svar);
proc sort data = acqmod.&svar.dset;
by pros_id;
run;

%mend;
%srt(age)
%srt(inc)
%srt(hom)
%srt(toa)
%srt(tob)
```

```
%srt(inq)
%srt(top)
%srt(crl)

proc sort data = acqmod.crossell;
by pros_id;
run;

data acqmod.crs_vars;
merge
acqmod.crossell
acqmod.agedset(keep = pros_id age_cui infd_agf)
acqmod.incdset(keep = pros_id inc_curt inc_estf)
acqmod.homdset(keep = pros_id hom_log hom_equf )
```

Evaluation of Inferred Age

Stepwise Procedure for Dependent Variable CRUPSYR1

Step 1   Variable AGE_CUI Entered   R-square = 0.01948362   C(p) =   2.58075135

	DF	Sum of Squares	Mean Square	F	Prob>F
Regression	1	22899.00042250	22899.00042250	44.27	0.0001
Error	2228	1152396.1116851	517.23344331		
Total	2229	1175295.1121076			

Variable	Parameter Estimate	Standard Error	Type II Sum of Squares	F	Prob>F
INTERCEP	31.26086000	0.77670788	837863.00781190	1619.89	0.0001
AGE_CUI	-210779.0793435	31678.34903207	22899.00042250	44.27	0.0001

Bounds on condition number: 1,   1

All variables left in the model are significant at the 0.1500 level.

No other variable met the 0.1500 significance level for entry into the model.

Summary of Stepwise Procedure for Dependent Variable CRUPSYR1

Step	Variable Entered Removed	Number In	Partial R**2	Model R**2	C(p)	F	Prob>F
1	AGE_CUI	1	0.0195	0.0195	2.5808	44.2721	0.0001

Figure 12.1 Regression output for Inferred Age.

```
acqmod.toadset(keep = pros_id toa_sqrt tot_accf)
acqmod.tobdset(keep = pros_id tob_curt tot_balf)
acqmod.inqdset(keep = pros_id inq_log inql6mof)
acqmod.topdset(keep = pros_id top_sqrt tot_opaf)
acqmod.crldset(keep = pros_id crl_log credlinf);
by pros_id;
run;
```

The following code uses linear regression to find the best predictors for First Year Cross-Sell Up-Sell Revenues (*crupsyr1*).

```
proc reg data=acqmod.crs_vars;
weight splitwgt;
model crupsyr1 = actop16 age_fil amtpdue hom_equ inc_est infd_ag inql6m
no30day no90eve nobkrpt totopac tot_acc tot_bal pop_denA pop_denB
pop_denC trav_cdd bankcrdd deptcrdd pre_crdd upsccrdd apt_indd sgle_ind
finl_idm finl_idn hh_indd gend_m driv_inA driv_inN mob_indN mob_indY
mortin1M mortin1N mortin1Y autoin1M autoin1N autoin1Y childind age_cui
inc_curt  hom_log toa_sqrt tob_curt inq_log top_sqrt crl_log
/selection=rsquare best=2 stop=20;
run;
```

In Figure 12.2, see how the score selection process in logistic regression, the selection=rsquare option calculates the best models for every possible number of variables. Best=2 was used to produce two models for each number of variables. Stop=20 was used to limit the number of possible models. The 15-variable model with the highest r-square was selected as the final model. The following code reruns the regression to create an output data set that is used for validation:

```
proc reg data=acqmod.crs_vars outest=acqmod.regcoef1;
weight splitwgt;
model crupsyr1 = AGE_FIL BANKCRDD DEPTCRDD UPSCCRDD APT_INDD GEND_M
DRIV_INA DRIV_INN MORTIN1M MORTIN1Y AGE_CUI TOA_SQRT INQ_LOG TOP_SQRT
CRL_LOG;
output out=acqmod.out_reg1 p=pred r=resid;
run;
```

Next, I sort and create deciles to see how well the model predicts Year One Net Revenue:

```
proc sort data=acqmod.out_reg1;
by descending pred;
run;

proc univariate data=acqmod.out_reg1(where=(splitwgt = .)) noprint;;
var pred;
output out=preddata nobs=nobs;
run;
```

```
data acqmod.val_dec;
 set acqmod.out_reg1;
if (_n_ eq 1) then set preddata;
if _N_ < .1*nobs then val_dec = 0; else
if _N_ < .2*nobs then val_dec = 1; else
if _N_ < .3*nobs then val_dec = 2; else
if _N_ < .4*nobs then val_dec = 3; else
if _N_ < .5*nobs then val_dec = 4; else
if _N_ < .6*nobs then val_dec = 5; else
if _N_ < .7*nobs then val_dec = 6; else
if _N_ < .8*nobs then val_dec = 7; else
if _N_ < .9*nobs then val_dec = 8; else
val_dec = 9;
records=1;
run;

title1 "Gains Table - Year One Cross Sell / Up Sell Revenues";

PROC tabulate data=acqmod.val_dec;
class val_dec;
var  pred records crupsyr1;
table val_dec='Decile' all='Total',
        records='Prospects'*sum=' '*f=comma10.
```

```
Number in    R-square   Variables in Model
  Model


-------------------------------------------------------------------------------
    13    0.63639406   AGE_FIL DEPTCRDD UPSCCRDD APT_INDD GEND_M DRIV_INA MORTIN1M MORTIN1Y AGE_CUI
                       TOA_SQRT INQ_LOG TOP_SQRT CRL_LOG
    13    0.63636162   AGE_FIL INQL6M DEPTCRDD UPSCCRDD APT_INDD GEND_M DRIV_INA MORTIN1M MORTIN1Y
                       AGE_CUI TOA_SQRT TOP_SQRT CRL_LOG
-------------------------------------------------------------------------------
    14    0.63717590   AGE_FIL TOT_ACC BANKCRDD DEPTCRDD UPSCCRDD APT_INDD GEND_M DRIV_INA MORTIN1M
                       MORTIN1Y AGE_CUI INQ_LOG TOP_SQRT CRL_LOG
    14    0.63716286   AGE_FIL BANKCRDD DEPTCRDD UPSCCRDD APT_INDD GEND_M DRIV_INA MORTIN1M MORTIN1Y
                       AGE_CUI TOA_SQRT INQ_LOG TOP_SQRT CRL_LOG
-------------------------------------------------------------------------------
    15    0.63780291   AGE_FIL BANKCRDD DEPTCRDD UPSCCRDD APT_INDD GEND_M DRIV_INA DRIV_INN MORTIN1M
                       MORTIN1Y AGE_CUI TOA_SQRT INQ_LOG TOP_SQRT CRL_LOG
    15    0.63778600   AGE_FIL INQL6M TOTOPAC TOT_ACC DEPTCRDD UPSCCRDD APT_INDD GEND_M DRIV_INA
                       DRIV_INN MORTIN1M MORTIN1Y AGE_CUI TOP_SQRT CRL_LOG
-------------------------------------------------------------------------------
    16    0.63844129   AGE_FIL TOTOPAC TOT_ACC BANKCRDD DEPTCRDD UPSCCRDD APT_INDD GEND_M DRIV_INA
                       DRIV_INN MORTIN1M MORTIN1Y AGE_CUI INQ_LOG TOP_SQRT CRL_LOG
```

Figure 12.2 Linear regression output for selection=rsquare.

```
        pred='Predicted Revenues Year 1'*(mean=' '*f=dollar11.2)
        crupsyr1 ='Actual Revenues Year 1'*(mean=' '*f=dollar11.2)
         /rts = 9 row=float;
run;
```

See in Figure 12.3 that the model produces strong rank-ordering of names by 1st Year Net Revenues. The following code plots the predicted values against the actual values.

```
proc summary data=acqmod.val_dec;
var pred crupsyr1;
class val_dec;
output out=acqmod.valplot mean=predmean crupmean;
run;
```

```
Decile Analysis - Year One Cross Sell / Up Sell Profits
```

		Predicted Revenues Year 1	Actual Revenues Year 1
Decile	Prospects		
0	114	$571.54	$620.35
1	114	$471.09	$487.72
2	114	$410.03	$392.98
3	114	$361.51	$359.65
4	114	$310.48	$267.54
5	114	$257.82	$233.33
6	114	$198.78	$159.65
7	114	$128.30	$118.42
8	114	$55.39	$49.12
9	114	$-39.47	$11.30
Total	1,140	$272.01	$269.47

The deciles show strong rank ordering.

Figure 12.3   Decile analysis of Year One Cross-Sell Up-Sell Model.

```
proc plot data=acqmod.valplot;
plot predmean*crupmean;
run;
```

The results can be seen in Figure 12.4, which shows a plot of the average decile's values for the predicted and actual Net Revenue. The near diagonal plot shows strong predictive power.

The previous process is repeated for years 2 and 3. The final calculations are combined with the data set that was scored in chapter 7.

Lifetime Value Calculation

I'm now ready to apply our three new models to the campaign data from chapter 7. Recall that I had a data set, *acqmod.test*, consisting of a 5,000-record ran-

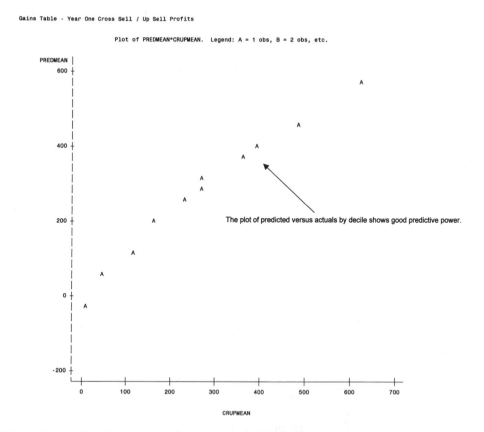

Figure 12.4 Plot of average predicted and actual by decile.

dom sample from the score file at the outside list company. The following code uses PROC SCORE to apply the three mode scores to the data sample:

```
proc score data=acqmod.test
        out=acqmod.crup1ys1 predict score=acqmod.regcoef1 type=parms;
id  pros_id records;
VAR AGE_FIL BANKCRDD DEPTCRDD UPSCCRDD APT_INDD GEND_M DRIV_INA DRIV_INN
MORTIN1M MORTIN1Y AGE_CUI TOA_SQRT INQ_LOG TOP_SQRT CRL_LOG;
run;


proc score data=acqmod.test
        out=acqmod.crup1ys2 predict score=acqmod.regcoef2 type=parms;
id  pros_id records;
VAR  ACTOPL6 INC_EST TOTOPAC TOT_ACC DEPTCRDD PRE_CRDD UPSCCRDD GEND_M
DRIV_INA DRIV_INN MOB_INDY AGE_CUI;
run;


proc score data=acqmod.test
        out=acqmod.crup1ys3 predict score=acqmod.regcoef3 type=parms;
id  pros_id records;
VAR ACTOPL6 INC_EST NO30DAY NO90EVE DEPTCRDD PRE_CRDD UPSCCRDD GEND_M
MOB_INDY AUTOIN1N HOM_TANI TOP_SQRT;
run;
```

The scoring programs create three separate files. The following code sorts the three data sets using *pros_id* as a match key.

```
%macro srt(dsn);
proc sort data = acqmod.&dsn;
by pros_id;

run;
%mend;
%srt(crup1ys1)
%srt(crup1ys2)
%srt(crup1ys3)
%srt(test)
```

Next I need to merge our three scored data sets with our main data set (*acqmod.test*). The variable, model1, is the default name for the Net Revenue predicted by each model. I need to rename the variable when I merge the results from the three models. I name them *crupsyr1, crupsyr2, crupsyr3* to match the original names:

```
data acqmod.ltv;
merge acqmod.crup1ys1(rename=(model1=crupsyr1))
acqmod.crup1ys2(rename=(model1=crupsyr2))
```

```
     acqmod.crup1ys3(rename=(model1=crupsyr3)) acqmod.test;
by pros_id;
```

The next step is to calculate the discounted profits for the next three years. This is a function of several factors. First, I have the cost of additional offers over the next three years. I have the variables *off_yr1*, *off_yr2*, *off_yr3* that represent the number of times each customer was mailed in each year. They are multiplied by the cost of a mailing, $.78. A yearly account maintenance fee of $20 is subtracted from each year's net revenues. And, finally, it is divided by the discount rate.

```
year1pr = (crupsyr1 -.78*off_yr1 - 20)/1.15;
year2pr = (crupsyr2 -.78*off_yr2 - 20)/(1.15*1.15);
year3pr = (crupsyr3 -.78*off_yr3 - 20)/(1.15*1.15*1.15);
```

Recall the risk matrix that assigns a risk adjustment based on a combination of gender, marital status, and age. The following code creates a variable called risk_adj to use in the LTV calculation:

```
if gender = 'M' then do;
     if marital = 'M' then do;
               if infd_ag2 < 40 then risk_adj = 1.09;
          else if infd_ag2 < 50 then risk_adj = 1.01;
          else if infd_ag2 < 60 then risk_adj = 0.89;
          else                       risk_adj = 0.75;
     end;
     else if marital = 'S' then do;
               if infd_ag2 < 40 then risk_adj = 1.06;
          |        |        |         |         |
          |        |        |         |         |
     else if marital = 'W' then do;
               if infd_ag2 < 40 then risk_adj = 1.05;
          else if infd_ag2 < 50 then risk_adj = 1.01;
          else if infd_ag2 < 60 then risk_adj = 0.92;
          else                       risk_adj = 0.78;
     end;
end;
```

Now I'm ready to calculate the lifetime value. From chapter 7, I know that the average net present value of the initial policy is $811.30. The lifetime value (*ltv_3yr*) is derived by multiplying the probability of becoming active (*pred_scr*) times the risk adjustment index (*risk_adj*) times the sum of the discounted profits from the initial policy (*prodprof*) and the expected profits for the following years minus the initial marketing expense:

```
prodprof = 811.30;
ltv_3yr= pred_scr*risk_adj*(prodprof + year1pr + year2pr + year3pr) -
.78;
run;
```

To create a gains table based on lifetime value, I sort and create deciles based on the newly derived variable, *ltv_3yr*.

```
proc sort data=acqmod.ltv;
by descending ltv_3yr;
run;

proc univariate data=acqmod.ltv noprint;
var ltv_3yr;
output out=preddata nobs=nobs;
run;

data acqmod.val_ltv;
 set acqmod.ltv;
if (_n_ eq 1) then set preddata;
if _N_ < .1*nobs then val_dec = 0; else
if _N_ < .2*nobs then val_dec = 1; else
if _N_ < .3*nobs then val_dec = 2; else
if _N_ < .4*nobs then val_dec = 3; else
if _N_ < .5*nobs then val_dec = 4; else
if _N_ < .6*nobs then val_dec = 5; else
if _N_ < .7*nobs then val_dec = 6; else
if _N_ < .8*nobs then val_dec = 7; else
if _N_ < .9*nobs then val_dec = 8; else
val_dec = 9;
records=1;
run;

PROC tabulate data=acqmod.val_ltv;
class val_dec;
var ltv_3yr pred_scr records crupsyr1 crupsyr2 crupsyr3 year1pr year2pr
year3pr risk_adj;
table val_dec='Decile' all='Total',
        records='Prospects'*sum=' '*f=comma9.
        pred_scr='Predicted Active Rate'*(mean=' '*f=9.5)
        (crupsyr1 ='Predicted Customer C/U Revenues Year 1'
        crupsyr2 ='Predicted Customer C/U Revenues Year 2'
        crupsyr3 ='Predicted Customer C/U Revenues Year 3')
          *(mean=' '*f=dollar11.5)
        risk_adj = 'Risk Index'*(mean=' '*f=6.2)
        (year1pr ='Discounted Customer C/U Profits Year 1'
        year2pr ='Discounted Customer C/U Profits Year 2'
        year3pr ='Discoutned Customer C/U Profits Year 3')
          *(mean=' '*f=dollar11.5)
        ltv_3yr = 'Total   3-Year Lifetime Value'
          *(mean=' '*f=dollar8.5)
         /rts = 8 row=float;
run;
```

The decile analysis in Figure 12.5 displays a wealth of information. Recall that in chapter 7 I calculated the average three-year net present value of a life insurance prospect based on the purchase of a single policy. In Figure 12.5, I have the same sample of names. But this time, I've included all expected customer profits for the three-year period following activation. Notice that the ranking of "active rate" is still monotonically decreasing, but the slope is not as strong. The average risk indices are also slightly different from those in Figure 7.6. But the far right column, Total 3-Year Lifetime Value, shows good profitability in the top deciles.

Notice that the lifetime value (LTV) is positive through decile 7. Compare this to Figure 7.6, where the net present value was positive only through decile 5. If name selection was simply based on mailing to prospects with positive value, using lifetime value could expand the names selection to capture two addi-

Decile	Prospects	Predicted Active Rate	Predicted Customer C/U Revenues Year 1	Predicted Customer C/U Revenues Year 2	Predicted Customer C/U Revenues Year 3	Risk Index	Discounted Customer C/U Profits Year 1	Discounted Customer C/U Profits Year 2	Discounted Customer C/U Profits Year 3	Total 3-Year Lifetime Value
0	500	0.00413	$349.21	$236.65	$101.85	1.06	$280.65	$160.76	$53.06	$4.75
1	500	0.00217	$359.85	$233.66	$88.69	1.04	$289.85	$158.54	$44.38	$2.03
2	500	0.00168	$351.04	$220.04	$79.95	1.03	$282.24	$148.34	$38.69	$1.31
3	500	0.00134	$364.00	$224.96	$78.35	1.01	$293.40	$151.99	$37.62	$0.88
4	500	0.00113	$359.34	$219.31	$75.61	1.00	$289.35	$147.75	$35.85	$0.60
5	500	0.00098	$356.67	$211.82	$71.08	0.99	$287.09	$142.16	$32.93	$0.39
6	500	0.00084	$352.78	$209.11	$66.44	0.98	$283.69	$140.06	$29.89	$0.21
7	500	0.00070	$354.59	$208.17	$64.58	0.97	$285.30	$139.40	$28.70	$0.04
8	500	0.00059	$332.19	$192.89	$56.84	0.96	$265.96	$127.94	$23.66	$-0.13
9	500	0.00039	$313.86	$159.02	$46.38	0.96	$250.13	$102.50	$16.91	$-0.37
Total	5,000	0.00139	$349.35	$211.55	$72.97	1.00	$280.76	$141.93	$34.16	$0.97

Figure 12.5 Decile analysis for lifetime value.

tional deciles. Let's say the company has a *hurdle rate* of $.80. In other words, the company requires $.80 in income to cover fixed expenses. The single policy NPV selection (Figure 7.6) could justify selecting only two deciles, but the LTV selection (Figure 12.6) could select four deciles and still be profitable.

Now that I have an expected lifetime value measurement for each prospect, I carry this through to calculate cumulative average lifetime value, sum of lifetime value per decile, and cumulative sum of lifetime value. These allow us to measure additional gains from the use of the lifetime value measurement in the prospect file. For example, by using lifetime value I can mail deeper into the file and capture additional expected profits. Again, comparing decile 7 to decile 5 as a cut-off point, I can expect an additional $88,616 in profits. If I want to consider the $.80 hurdle rate, I compare expected profits through decile 4 versus decile 2. These additional 2 deciles allow for a $323,446 increase in expected profits. Either way, predicting lifetime value is truly more powerful in selecting profitable names.

Figure 12.7 displays a visual account of the power of the lifetime value model. Notice the model's ability to concentrate the actives and high lifetime value prospects into the lower deciles. The active rate drops quickly in the first few deciles. Lifetime value increases steadily until it peaks in decile 8.

Summary

Well, I hope you didn't get burned! This was the most advanced recipe in the book. But what power! As you can see, lifetime value brings together many of the other measurements used in marketing and business decision making. By

Decile	Number	Predicted Active Rate	Risk Index	Average LTV	Cum LTV	Sum LTV	Sum Cum LTV	Lift	Cum Lift
1	147,692	0.413%	1.06	$4.75	$4.75	$701,538	$701,538	489	489
2	147,692	0.217%	1.04	$2.03	$3.39	$299,815	$1,001,353	209	349
3	147,692	0.168%	1.03	$1.31	$2.70	$193,477	$1,194,830	135	278
4	147,692	0.134%	1.01	$0.88	$2.24	$129,969	$1,324,799	91	231
5	147,692	0.113%	1.00	$0.60	$1.91	$88,615	$1,413,414	62	197
6	147,692	0.098%	0.99	$0.39	$1.66	$57,600	$1,471,014	40	171
7	147,692	0.084%	0.98	$0.21	$1.45	$31,015	$1,502,030	22	150
8	147,692	0.070%	0.97	$0.04	$1.28	$5,908	$1,507,937	4	131
9	147,692	0.059%	0.96	-$0.13	$1.12	-$19,200	$1,488,737	(13)	115
10	147,692	0.038%	0.96	-$0.37	$0.97	-$54,646	$1,434,091	(38)	100

Figure 12.6 Lifetime value gains table.

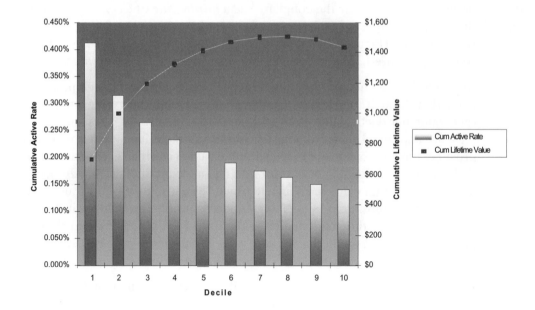

Figure 12.7 Lifetime value gains chart.

using a measure of lifetime value, no matter what the industry, you can gain accuracy at every level. You need to identify all the components carefully. And it requires a lot of planning and analysis. But it can be used in many areas of the business from marketing and name selection to pricing, risk action and analysis, and asset valuation of your customer base. No matter what industry you're in, it's worth calculating lifetime value and incorporating it into your business model.

CHAPTER 13

Fast Food: Modeling on the Web

W hy do you buy fast food? Speed? Convenience? Fast food restaurants are designed to handle large volumes of food in a quick and efficient manner. Think of this food as data, and you have a direct parallel to the Web. The volume of data captured from the Web is increasing exponentially. And speed is becoming a critical competitive factor. This creates many opportunities and challenges for modeling and analysis. The opportunities arise from the sheer volume of data. The challenges are due to the incredible speed at which the data is generated. This combination deems it necessary to use automated modeling software to be competitive.

All of the modeling techniques I've described in prior chapters require considerable time and management. To be effective and competitive on the Web, though, models need to be developed or available in real time. In other words, they need to be created and utilized immediately and automatically. This chapter is not a recipe per se. Instead, my goal is to share several ways that automated modeling and analysis software is being used to manage and redefine the customer experience on the Web.

In this chapter, I invited several contributors who I feel are leading the industry in Web mining and modeling to share their views. The chapter opens with a discussion of some common objectives in Web mining and modeling. The next section outlines the steps to the most common type of Web mining, Web usage mining. An overview is provided for several of the techniques. The remainder of the chapter describes some ways in which Web mining and e-commerce are changing the dynamics of marketing in the areas of branding and increasing customer loyalty.

Web Mining and Modeling

I would like to begin by distinguishing between Web mining and Web modeling. Web mining consists of analyzing Web traffic or usage behavior for customers and prospects. Web modeling involves using the results of Web analysis to define business rules that can be used to shape the customer experience. As you will see in the discussion that follows, some tools exist that allow certain types of modeling to be done in real time. In other words, certain models are built and implemented within the same user session. Other, more traditional models, such as predictive models, segmentation, and profiling, are built offline with the resulting scores or segments accessible during the online session.

The steps for mining Web data are familiar. As you might expect, *defining the objective* is the first step. The remaining steps are a slight variation of those discussed in part 2.

Defining the Objective

The Web is quickly becoming a major channel for managing customer relationships. Why? First, companies can now use packaged software to tailor a customer's Web site experience based on either the customer's actions during each visit or a database that contains prior Web behavior and other predictive and descriptive information such as segmentation and model scores. Second, the Web allows for interaction with the customer in real time. In other words, just like with a telephone call, a customer can carry on a conversation with a company representative through a live chat session.

The Web is also a low-cost channel for prospecting. Many companies are turning to broadcast advertising or mass mailing to drive prospects to their Web sites. Once they log onto the site, much of the process is accomplished in a few minutes at a fraction of the cost. In addition to buying many products and services, a customer can now apply for a credit card, a mortgage, a car loan, a personal loan, a business loan, or an insurance policy online.

A Credit Card Case Study

To give you an example, let's say a bank wants to process credit card applications online. The bank creates or adapts a database and links it to its Web site.

The database contains identifying information such as name, address, and social security number along with segment values and model scores. One score could be a risk score similar to the one I developed in chapter 10. Other scores might reflect propensity to revolve, price sensitivity, or profitability. As a prospect enters the Web site, he or she is prompted to complete an online application. The prospect enters his or her name, address, and social security number, along with some demographics such as income, length of residence, and number of dependents. The information is matched to the database to retrieve segment values and model scores. New scores may also be derived from information entered during the session. In the end, the bank is able to assess the credit worthiness and potential profitability of the prospect.

Some Web sites are set up to barter for terms in real time. For example, we can take the credit card application a step further. Let's say the bank has determined a minimum introductory interest rate and maximum term for an online prospect based on his or her risk score, segment values, and data collected during the session. If the prospect does not accept the terms offered, the bank can ask the prospect to name the introductory rate and counter with a shorter term and a higher long-term or "goto" rate. In other words, the possibilities for customized marketing and empowering the customer are endless.

Sources of Web Data

The power of the Web lies in its ability to use data in real time to affect a customer's online experience. Devyani Sadh, Ph.D., president of Data Square, LLC, provides a detailed explanation of the many Web site data sources.

Every click on a Web site combines to generate a pattern for the organization to use in its business planning. A Web server, when properly configured, can record every click that users make on a Web site. For each click in the so called "clickstream," the Web server appends a line to a text file called a server log, recording information such as the user's identity, the page clicked, and the time stamp. At a very minimum, all Web servers record access logs and error logs. Web servers can also be configured to append a type of file called the referrer log to the standard log file format. The following list details some valuable sources of Web site data:

A. Server logs

Access log. Each time a visitor to a Web site requests a file from the Web server an entry is placed in a special ASCII text file called an access log. The access log records hits (file requests) as well as the success or failure in fulfilling each request. Every transaction made during the connection is recorded chronologically on the access log, making it a key component in discovering who is visiting the Web site and what pages he or she is viewing.

Referrer log. The referrer log is a log file on the Web server that contains entries indicating the location from which a visitor came and the path and/or keywords that led to the Web site. The location (URL) might indicate a link from another page on the same Web site or a "hit" originating from a search engine such as Yahoo or Alta Vista. In the case of a search engine hit, the keywords used to locate your Web site or Web page will be indicated in the referrer log in addition to the URL of the search engine.

B. Cookie

A cookie is a small amount of information sent by a Web server to the user's computer when he or she visits the site. Cookies detail the locations where visitors go while on a Web site. When the visitor returns to the same Web site, cookies (which are stored in the user's own hard disk) enable the site to determine the visitor's identity and preferences. Although the use of cookies has stirred controversy over the issue of privacy on the Internet, Web sites and, in particular, e-commerce sites have utilized them as a key marketing component in the provision of personalized Web pages and product offerings.

C. Form or user registration data

Web sites can capture important data by prompting the user to register at the onset of a visit and provide personal information such as name and address, date of birth, gender, occupation, etc. This information generates valuable databases for subsequent mining and provides a foundation for the gathering of additional demographic and household data used in creating detailed user profiles.

D. E-mail inquiry or response data

Many Web sites include a "mail to" e-mail link so that visitors can instantly inquire about your products and services or provide vital feedback about your company's e-commerce site or products. Web data mining techniques can be performed on aggregate customer e-mail response data to generate valuable information on business trends and profitability analysis. The Web site might then utilize the resulting information to automate e-mail notification to a particular visitor or a targeted group of users concerning special offers or discounts on items of interest, and ultimately follow up with more promotional announcements depending on customers' responses to the initial e-mailings.

E. Web purchase data

Information gleaned from Web purchase records such as customer's name, address, zip code, demographic data, item(s) selected, and sale price(s), can be complemented and enhanced with data from non-Web information repositories such as accounting systems and sales-automation databases and then mined to provide valuable insights into current and potential marketing strategies. In addition to the above commonly used Web data available through the company Web site, compiled information detailing the online behavior of individuals at other sites can be purchased (at an aggregate level) from third party Internet data providers.

As mentioned earlier, non Web-based data sources like those discussed in chapter 2 are also used to support Web mining. Customer behavior, transaction, demographic, and traditional model scores are often integrated into the rules that help to shape the customer's Web site experience.

Preparing Web Data

Preparing Web data for analysis also presents unique challenges for the data miner or modeler. Devyani details some of the issues and methods for getting the Web data into a form that is useful for mining.

> True statistics can be derived only when the data in the server logs presents an accurate picture of site user-access patterns. Because a single "hit" generates a record of not only the HTML page but also of every graphic on that page, the data cleaning process eliminates redundant log entries with image file extensions such as gif, jpeg, GIF, JPEG, jpg, JPG, and map.
>
> Data cleaning also includes determining whether all visits have been recorded in the access log. Tools and methods used to speed up response time to file requests such as page caching and site mirroring can significantly reduce the number of measured hits a page receives because such accesses are not recorded in the central server's log files. To remedy the problematic grouping of many page hits into one hit, access records can be projected by using site topology or referrer logs along with temporal information to infer missing references.
>
> Proxy servers also make it difficult to accurately determine user identification because entire companies or online services often share "unique addresses" or machine names for all users, grouping many users under one or more IDs. To overcome the fact that user IDs are not unique in file requests that traverse proxy servers, algorithm checks can be conducted to identify user request patterns. Combining IP address, machine name, browser agent, and temporal information is another method to distinguish Web site visitors.
>
> Once the cleaning step is completed, the data needs to be processed in a comprehensive format, integrating data collected from multiple server logs such as referrer and access logs. The sequences of page references in the referrer log need to be grouped into logical units representing Web transactions or user sessions. Subsequently, log entries can be partitioned into logical clusters using one or a series of transaction identification modules.
>
> In general, a user session refers to all page references made by a client during a single visit to a site, with the size of a transaction ranging from a single page reference to every page referenced within that session. A clean server log can be considered in one

of two ways—either as a single transaction of many page references or as a set of many transactions, each consisting of a single page reference.

Transaction identification allows for the formation of meaningful clusters of references for each user. A transaction identification module can be defined either as a merge or a divide module; the latter module divides a large transaction into multiple smaller ones, whereas the former merges small transactions into larger ones. The merge or divide process can be repeated more times to create transactions appropriate for a given data mining task. Any number of modules could be combined to match input and output transaction formats.

Unlike traditional domains for data mining such as point-of-sale databases, there is no convenient method of clustering page references into transactions smaller than an entire user session. A given page reference can be classified as either navigational or content based on the total time the page was referenced. Two types of transactions are defined:

Navigation content. In this type of transaction, there is a single content reference. All the navigation references in the traversal path lead to the content reference. This type of transaction is generally used to derive the path traversal patterns in a Web site.

Content only. This type of transaction records all content references for a given user session and is useful in the discovery of relationships between the content pages of a site.

Once the varied data sources are combined and assembled, preliminary checks and audits need to be conducted to ensure data integrity. The next step involves deciding which attributes to exclude or retain and convert into usable formats.

Selecting the Methodology

Successful data mining and modeling of Web data is accomplished using a variety of tools. Some are the familiar offline tools. Others are being invented as the Web provides unique opportunities. Devyani describes some of the familiar and not-so-familiar tools for Web mining and modeling:

> While most techniques used in Web data mining originate from the fields of data mining, database marketing, and information retrieval, the methodology called path analysis was specifically designed for Web data mining. Current Web usage data mining studies use association rules, clustering, temporal sequences, predictive modeling, and path expressions. New Web data mining methods that integrate different types of data will be developed as Web usage continues to evolve.

Path Analysis

Path analysis techniques involve determining the path of each visitor by linking log file entries and sorting them by time. Graphs are typically used to represent path traversals through the pages of a Web site. In mapping the physical layout of a Web site, a graph's nodes can represent Web pages, and the directed edges can indicate hypertext links between pages. Graphs can be used to represent other navigational characteristics of a Web site; for example, edges can indicate the number of users that link to one page from another.

Alternatively, navigation-content transactions or user sessions can be used for path analysis. This type of analysis is helpful in determining the most frequently visited paths in a Web site. Because many visitors do not generally browse further than four pages into a Web site, the placement of important information within the first four pages of a site's common entry points is highly recommended.

Association Rules

Association rule techniques are generally applied to databases of transactions where each transaction consists of a set of items. It involves defining all associations and correlations among data items where the presence of one set of items in a transaction implies the presence of other items. In the context of Web data mining, association rules discover the relations among the various references made to the server files by a given client. The discovery of association rules in an organization's typically very large database of Web transactions can provide valuable input for site restructuring and targeted promotional activities.

Sequential Patterns

Sequential pattern analysis can be used to discover temporal relationships among data items as in, for example, similar time sequences for purchase transactions. Because a single user visit is recorded over a period of time in Web server transaction logs, sequential pattern analysis techniques can be implemented to determine the common characteristics of all clients that visited a particular page (or a sequence of pages) within a certain time period. E-retailers can then combine these results with information from traditional transactional databases to predict user-access patterns and future sales associated with specific site traversal patterns. With targeted advertisement campaigns aimed at specific users and specific areas within the site based on typical viewing sequences, companies can more effectively develop site structure and related features. This analysis can also be used to determine optimal after-market purchase offerings (along with offer and message strategy) for specific product groups and different customer segments as well as the optimal timing for various stages in the contact strategy.

Clustering

Clustering is the method by which a data set is divided into a number of smaller, more similar subgroups or clusters. The goal in cluster detection is to find previously unknown similarities in the data. Clustering data is a very good way to start analysis on the data because it can provide the starting point for discovering relationships among subgroups. An example of clustering is looking through a large number of initially undifferentiated e-commerce customers and trying to see if they fall into natural groupings. To build these groupings, you can use both transactional data and demographic information as input.

Jesus Mena, in his book entitled *Data Mining Your Website*, described clustering analysis on a sample data set of 10,000 records. Applying Kohonen neural network (a type of artificial intelligence) to the data, Mr. Mena discovered five distinct clusters, which were subsequently evaluated with a rule-generating algorithm. The results revealed that visitors referred to a particular Web site by the Infoseek search engine were much more likely to make multiple purchases than visitors coming through Yahoo. When household information was added to the data set of server log files, it was found that specific age groups were associated with a higher propensity to shop when they were referred to the e-retail site by other search engines. Clustering analysis can give companies a high-level view of relationships between products, transactional data, and demographic information and therefore can greatly contribute to the development of highly effective marketing strategies.

Market basket analysis is a clustering technique useful for finding groups of items that tend to occur together or in a particular sequence. The models that this type of clustering builds give the likelihood of different products being purchased together and can be expressed in conditions in the form of rules such as IF/THEN. The resulting information can be used for many purposes, such as designing a Web site, limiting specials to one of the products in a set that tend to occur together, bundling products, offering coupons for the other products when one of them is sold without the others, or other marketing strategies.

Predictive Modeling and Classification

Predictive Modeling and Classification analyses are used to project outcomes based on the existence of other available variables. For example, propensity to buy a certain product can be predicted based on referring URL, domain, site traversal patterns, number of visits, financial/credit information, demographics, psychographics, geo-demographics, and prior purchase and promotion history. For customers, all of the above data sources could be used as predictors. For registered users that are not customers, all but prior purchase history could be used and finally for non-registered visitors, only log file data could be used from a predictive standpoint.

Predictive Modeling plays a very significant role in acquisition, retention, cross-sell, reactivation and winback initiatives. It can be used to support marketing strategies for converting prospects to visitors, online shoppers to visitors, browsers to buyers, first timers to repeaters, low-enders to power-shoppers, and attritors to reactivators. Modeling and Classification can also be used to support ad and site content personalization and to design and execute targeted promotions, offers and incentives based on preferences and interests.

Collaborative Filtering

Collaborative filtering is a highly automated technique that uses association rules to shape the customer Web experience in real time. Bob McKim, president of M/S Database Marketing, discusses the power of collaborative filtering on the Web.

The *L.A. Times* called automated collaborative filtering "powerful software that collects and stores behavioral information making marketers privy to your private information." The DMA is calling for controls on Internet software that tracks Web site behavior and determines what Web site content is suitable for presentation."

Advocates of collaborative filtering systems state that "in one second collaborative filtering can turn a browser into a buyer, increase order size, and bring more buyers back more often. The key is making the right suggestion to the right buyer at the right time—and doing it in real time. This is called suggestive selling, and collaborative filtering is the gold standard for speed, accuracy, and ROI."

So who's right? Is Automated Collaborative Filtering (ACF) of information the anti-Christ or the savior for consumers and marketers?

Collaborative Filtering of Information

Technologically, ACF is an unprecedented system for the distribution of opinions and ideas and facilitation of contacts between people with similar interests. ACF automates and enhances existing mechanisms of knowledge distribution and dramatically increases their speed and efficiency

The system is nothing new. In fact, it's as old as humanity. We've known it as "recommendations of friends" and "word of mouth." Our circle of acquaintances makes our life easier by effectively filtering information each time they give us their opinion. Friends' recommendations give us confidence that a book is or isn't worth our time and money. When friends can't make a recommendation themselves, they usually know someone who can.

The only new wrinkle is that today, in this information-heavy Internet Age, reliance on human connections for finding exactly what you want has become insufficient. As smart as humankind is, our brains can store and share only so much information.

How Automated Collaborative Filtering Systems Work

We gain information from friends in two ways:

1. We ask them to let us know whenever they learn about something new, exciting, or relevant in our area of interests.

2. Friends who know our likes and dislikes and or needs and preferences give us information that they decide will be of benefit to us.

continues

(Continued)

ACFS works the same way by actively "pushing" information toward us.

Amazon.com and CDNOW already use this technology for marketing. If you've visited Amazon.com's site you've been asked to complete a personal record of your listening and reading history and enjoyments. You've read that Amazon.com promises if you complete this survey it will be able to provide you with suggestions on which books you might enjoy based on what people with similar interests and tastes would choose. Voila! You've enrolled in an Automated Collaborative Filtering System (ACFS). If you like Robert Ludlum and Ken Follett, Amazon.com's ACFS knows you're likely to enjoy Tom Clancy. Amazon.com goes further and recommends titles from all these authors. While you may have read many of the titles, chances are there are some you've been meaning to read. Thus, ACFS is helping you by bringing you information you need.

Trends in the Evolution of ACFS

Storing knowledge outside the human mind is nothing new either. Libraries have been a repository of knowledge for thousands of years. The emergence of computers as a data storage tool is simply an improvement—albeit an incredible one—over libraries. Computers have an amazing capacity for storage and retrieval, and with systems linked to the Internet, great prowess at filtering and retrieving information and knowledge quickly and efficiently. Until now, the stumbling block to retrieving useful information was the inability of computers to understand the meaning of the knowledge or judge what data is good and relevant.

ACFS provides the solution by performing information searches with human intelligence. It does this relatively simply by recording people's opinions on the importance and quality of the various pieces of knowledge and uses these records to improve the results of computer searches.

ACFS allows people to find others with similar opinions, discover experts in the field, analyze the structure of people's interests in various subjects and genres, facilitate creation of interest groups, decentralize mass communication media, improve targeting of announcements and advertisements, and do many other useful things that, together with other intelligent technologies, promise to raise the information economy to new levels.

Knowledge Management

The work here has already begun with pattern recognition and signal processing techniques and higher-end, common-sense information analysis tools. Real-time technology dynamically recommends the documents, data sources, FAQs, and mutual "interest groups" that can help individuals with whatever task is at hand. The benefit is that hard-won knowledge and experience get reinvested instead of reinvented.

Marketing Campaigns

ACFS can allow marketers to realize the full efficiencies of mail or e-mail in their communications by finding like-minded people who are in the window of making purchase decisions. With ACFS, marketers can realize results that will turn the two-percent response paradigm upside down and generate high ROIs.

Ad Targeting

ACFS can make target communications smarter, less intrusive, and more desired. Most of us ignore banner ads because they're not what we're looking for. But if ads became relevant—and personal—we'll pay attention and most likely buy. Web site ads in front of the right visitors equal enhanced click-through rates for advertisers and increased ad revenues.

E-commerce

The patented ACF techniques originally developed in 1995 are key to the amazing success of all of today's top Internet marketers. These techniques are what drives the personalized recommendations that turn site browsers into buyers, increase cross-sells and up-sells, and deepen customer loyalty with every purchase.

Call Centers

When an agent can view the personal interests of a party, it can quickly match it with the greater body of knowledge of other customers. This is the Lands' End approach taken to a higher level. It uses the same CF techniques that have transformed e-commerce, but with the personalized cross-sell and up-sell recommendations delivered through real-time prompts to each agent's screen. This personalization enhances the profitability of every inbound and outbound campaign.

ACFS Applications in the Near Future

Soon, ACF technology will be an established information retrieval tool and will make information retrieval systems more intelligent and adaptable for providing common-sense solutions to complex personal challenges.

Finding Like-Minded People

This is a key function of ACFS. Finding people who share interests is important to each of us in finding further directions in life, from starting social and economic activities to forming friendships and families, getting advice on important personal decisions, and feeling more confident and stable in our social environment. Many people abandon the idea of opening their own business because

continues

(Continued)

they lack expertise in a certain business aspect. Others never find new jobs because of mismatched experience or qualifications. ACFS can aid in these and social activities by helping people find the right chat room and bringing like-minded individuals together in interests from opera to business start-ups.

Managing Personal Resources

The first generation of software for managing personal resources is already on the market, mostly on large mainframe computers. Collaborative filtering software already exists to assist marketers. The next stage is expected to include elements of ACFS such as recorded opinions of human experts in various interest spheres and recommendations of like-minded people and object classification and information retrieval rules derived from their personal information-handling patterns of their own software agents. These could be PCs or mainframes.

With good information protection technologies, people will be able to trust the large servers to store personal data and ensure its security and accessibility from anywhere in the world. These tools will be able to provide the search for personal information on a global or company-wide basis, with consideration of access rights.

For privacy protection, much of the personal interest and occupation data could be stored on one's local computer. The information would spring to life only when the corresponding server recognized the return and started its matching processing on the demand of the user—not the marketer. This would ensure that an individual's interests remain private except when the individual chooses to share them with a friend or colleague.

Branding on the Web

With hundreds of thousands of Web sites directly available to consumers, the old approach to marketing is losing its effectiveness. Mark Van Clieaf, president of MVC International, describes the evolution of marketing into a new set of rules that work in the online world.

> The Internet has changed the playing field, and many of the old business models and their approaches to marketing, branding, and customers are being reinvented. Now customer data from Web page views to purchase and customer service data can be tracked on the Internet for such industries as packaged goods, pharmaceutical, and automotive. In some cases new Web-based business models are evolving and have at their core transactional customer information. This includes both business-to-consumer and business-to-business sectors. Marketing initiatives can now be tracked in real-time interactions with customers through Web and call center channels.
>
> Thus the 4 Ps of marketing (product, price, promotion, and place) are also being redefined into the killer Bs (branding, bonding, bundling, billing) for a digital world. Branding

becomes a complete customer experience (branding system) that is intentionally designed and integrated at each customer touch point (bonding), provides for a customizing and deepening of the customer relationship (bundling of multiple product offers), and reflects a preference for payment and bill presentment options (billing).

Branding may also be gaining importance as it becomes easier to monitor a company's behavior. Bob McKim describes some ways in which collaborative filtering can be used to further empower the consumer. Many people feel suspicious of plumbers and car mechanics because they tend to under-perform and over-charge. What if there was a system for monitoring the business behaviors of less-than-well-known companies by day-to-day customers that could be accessed by potential users? It stands to reason that the firms would have more incentive to act responsibly.

Direct references to a company and its product quality, coming from independent sources and tied to the interests of particular users, seems far superior to the current method of building product reputation through "branding." Consumers' familiarity with the "brand" now often depends more on the size of the company and its advertising budget than the quality of its products. The "socialization" of machines through ACFS seems a far more efficient method of providing direct product experiences and information than the inefficient use of, say, Super Bowl advertising.

Historically, the advantages of knowledge sharing among individuals and the benefits of groups working together have led to language, thinking, and the specialization of labor. Since the dawn of computers, machines—as knowledge carriers—have repeated the early stages of human information sharing. Now, taken to the next level—beyond marketing and selling of goods and services—ACFS offers society an opportunity to learn from the greater collective body of experiences.

Gaining Customer Insight in Real Time

Market research has traditionally been a primary method for gaining customer insight. As the Web facilitates customer interaction on a grand scale, new methods of conducting customer research are emerging. These methods are enabling companies to gather information, perform data mining and modeling, and design offers in real time, thus reaching the goal of true one-to-one marketing. Tom Kehler, president and CEO of Recipio, discusses a new approach to gaining customer insight and loyalty in real time on the Web.

New opportunities for gathering customer insight and initiating customer dialogue are enabled through emerging technologies (Web, interactive TV, WAP) for marketing and customer relationship management purposes. Real-time customer engagement is helping leading organizations in the packaged goods, automotive, software, financial services, and other industries to quickly adjust advertising and product offerings to online customers.

Traditional focus groups are qualitative in nature, expensive to execute, and prone to bias from either participants or the facilitator. Web-enabled focus groups collect customer insights and dialogue on a large scale (moving from qualitative to quantitative) in a self-organizing customer learning system, and a unique survey design and analysis process. Web-enabled focus groups engage customers in collaborative relationships that evoke quality customer input, drive customers to consensus around ideas, and, beyond customer permission, generate customer-welcomed offers.

First-generation Web-based marketing programs, even those that claimed to be one-to-one, were built on traditional approaches to marketing. Research was conducted to determine strategy for outbound campaigns. From the customer's perspective, the Web was no more interactive than television when it came to wanting to give feedback. Listening and participation are requisites to permission-based marketing programs that build trust and loyalty. Rather than use research to drive one-way marketing programs, interactive technologies offer the opportunity to make marketing two-way. Listening and participation change the fundamental nature of the interaction between the customer and the supplier.

Technologies are being developed that use both open-ended and closed customer research and feedback enabling a quantitative approach to what was previously qualitative customer insight. Through the use of these technologies, marketers can produce reports and collect customer insights (open and closed responses) that can even rank and sort the open-ended responses from customers. This mix of open-ended and closed survey design without the use of a moderator provides for ongoing continuous learning about the customer. The use of open-ended questions provides an opportunity to cost-effectively listen to customers and take their pulse. It also provides for a one-to-one opportunity to reciprocate and provide offers based on continuous customer feedback.

Customer feedback analysis from client sites or online panels can be input into a broad range of marketing needs including the following:

- Large-scale attitudinal segmentation linked to individual customer files
- Product concept testing
- Continuous product improvement
- Web site design and user interface feedback
- Customer community database management
- Customer management strategies
- Dynamic offer management and rapid cycle offer testing

The attitudinal, preference data integrated with usage data mining (customer database in financial services, telco, retail, utilities, etc.) are very powerful for segmentation, value proposition development, and targeting of customer with custom offers, thus creating real one-to-one marketing on a large scale.

Web Usage Mining—A Case Study

While this brief case study won't give you the techniques to perform Web analysis manually, it will give you a look at what statistics are commonly measured on Web sites. The results of these statistics can be used to alter the Web site, thereby altering the next customer's experience. The following list of measurements is commonly monitored to evaluate Web usage:

General Statistics

Most Requested Pages

Least Requested Pages

Top Entry Pages

Least Requested Entry Pages

Top Entry Requests

Least Requested Entry Requests

Top Exit Pages

Single Access Pages

Most Accessed Directories

Top Paths Through Site

Most Downloaded Files

Most Downloaded File Types

Dynamic Pages and Forms

Visitors by Number of Visits During Report Period

New versus Returning Visitors

Top Visitors

Top Geographic Regions

Most Active Countries

North American States and Provinces

Most Active Cities

Summary of Activity for Report Period

Summary of Activity by Time Increment

Activity Level by Day of the Week

Activity Level by Hour of the Day

Activity Level by Length of Visit

Number of Views per Visitor Session

Visitor Session Statistics

Technical Statistics and Analysis

Dynamic Pages & Forms Errors

Client Errors

Page Not Found

Server Errors

Top Referring Sites

Top Referring URLs

Top Search Engines

Top Search Phrases

Top Search Keywords

Most Used Browsers

Most Used Platforms

This is just a partial listing of statistics. Depending on the nature of the Web site, there could be many more. For example, a site that sells goods or services would want to capture shopping cart information. This includes statistics such as: In what order were the items selected? Did all items make it to the final checkout point or were some items removed? Was the sale consumated or was the shopping cart eventually abandoned? It's not surprising that shopping cart abandonment is highest at the point where a credit card number is requested. Information of this type has many implications for Web site design and functionality.

Typically, the first thing a company wants to know is the number of hits or visits that were received on the Web site. Table 13.1 displays some basic statistics that relate to the frequency, length, and origin of the visits.

In Figure 13.1 additional insights are gained with a breakdown of visitors by origin for each week. This behavior might reflect variation in activity related to regional holidays or other issues. Monitoring and understanding visitor behavior is the first step in evaluating and improving your Web site.

Another relevant measurement is how many pages are viewed. This can reflect content as well as navigability. If a majority of the visitors viewed only one page, it may imply that they did not find it easy to determine how to take the next step (see Table 13.2).

Table 13.1 Statistics on Web Site Visits

STATISTIC—REPORT RANGE: 02/20/1999 00:00:00–03/19/2000 23:55:47		
Hits	Entire Site (Successful)	4,390,421
	Average Per Day	156,800
	Home Page	315,622
Page Views	Page Views (Impressions)	22,847
	Average Per Day	11,530
	Document Views	341,288
Visitor Sessions	Visitor Sessions	122,948
	Average Per Day	4,391
	Average Visitor Session Length	00:31:44
	International Visitor Sessions	11.52%
	Visitor Sessions of Unknown Origin	32.49%
	Visitor Sessions from United States	55.99%
Visitors	Unique Visitors	59,660
	Visitors Who Visited Once	52,836
	Visitors Who Visited More Than Once	6,824

Figure 13.2 allows for a visual evaluation of the number of pages viewed per visit. This can be helpful in looking for plateaus, for example, at "3 pages" and "4 pages." This tells you that the navigation from page 3 is working well.

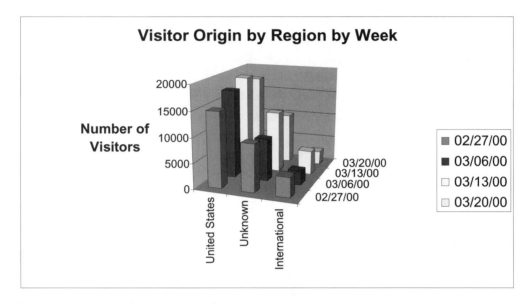

Figure 13.1 Origin of visitors by week.

Table 13.2 Number of Pages Viewed per Visit

NUMBER OF PAGES VIEWED	NUMBER OF VISITS	% OF TOTAL VISITS
1 page	44,930	50.31%
2 pages	15,075	16.88%
3 pages	9,038	10.12%
4 pages	5,680	6.36%
5 pages	5,277	5.91%
6 pages	2,492	2.79%
7 pages	1,920	2.15%
8 pages	1,223	1.37%
9 pages	1,054	1.18%
10 pages	1,000	1.12%
11 pages	822	0.92%
12 or more pages	777	0.87%
Totals	89,306	100%

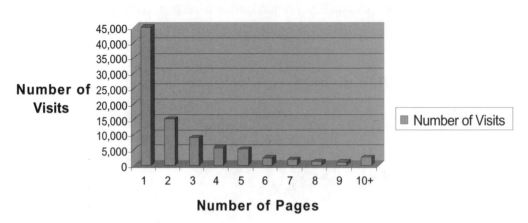

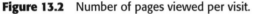

Figure 13.2 Number of pages viewed per visit.

Summary

These are exciting times! In this final chapter, I've tried to present a sample menu of some cutting-edge techniques and applications for mining and modeling on the Web today. Some techniques—like path analysis—were created specifically for monitoring activity on the Web. Others techniques are variations or adaptations of some of the familiar methods used in marketing for many years. As the medium continues to evolve, all these methods—old, new, and some not yet created—will be integrated into Web activities. And the results will support the rules that shape the Web experience of every prospect and customer.

Branding will grow in importance as company access is equalized through the Web. Word of mouth will gain importance as new tools are developed to gather instant consensus and recommendations. The Web offers prospecting and customer relationship management opportunities that are limited only by the imagination. The bigger the challenge, the bigger the opportunity! The trick is to think outside of the box.

As the Web equalizes the playing field for many industries, we begin to see that speed is becoming the ultimate competitive advantage. As you venture into the world of fast food, remember that convenience comes with a little higher price tag. But the increased efficiency is often worth it. Bon appetit!

Univariate Analysis for Continuous Variables

I n this appendix you will find univariate analysis of the continuous variables discussed in chapter 3.

Home Equity

Univariate Procedure

Variable=HOM_EQU2
Weight= SMP_WGT

Moments

N	85404	Sum Wgts	729228
Mean	99517.35	Sum	7.257E10
Std Dev	454749.4	Variance	2.068E11
Skewness	.	Kurtosis	.
USS	2.488E16	CSS	1.766E16
CV	456.9549	Std Mean	532.5255
T:Mean=0	186.8781	Pr>|T|	0.0001
Num ^= 0	55575	Num > 0	55575
M(Sign)	27787.5	Pr>=|M|	0.0001
Sgn Rank	7.7216E8	Pr>=|S|	0.0001

```
                         Quantiles(Def=5)

              100% Max    2322136      99%    580534
               75% Q3    141398.5      95%    296562
               50% Med      62520      90%    226625
               25% Q1           0      10%         0
                0% Min         0        5%         0
                                       1%         0

              Range       2322136
              Q3-Q1      141398.5
              Mode              0
```

```
                          Extremes

              Lowest    Obs      Highest     Obs
                   0( 85390)     2322136( 72630)
                   0( 85389)     2322136( 77880)
                   0( 85381)     2322136( 77883)
                   0( 85380)     2322136( 81343)
                   0( 85371)     2322136( 82750)
```

```
                      Univariate Procedure

Variable=HOM_EQU2
Weight=  SMP_WGT


              Histogram                          #       Boxplot
2350000+*                                        119        *
       .*                                          4        *
       .*                                          6        *
       .*                                          2        *
       .*                                          8        *
       .*                                          6        *
       .*                                         10        *
       .*                                         10        *
       .*                                         11        *
       .*                                         10        *
       .*                                         26        *
       .*                                         33        *
       .*                                         40        *
       .*                                         47        *
       .*                                         58        *
       .*                                         90        *
       .*                                        110        *
       .*                                        213        *
       .*                                        339        0
       .*                                        737        0
       .***                                     2269        0
       .*******                                 7248        |
       .******************                     20285     +-----+
 50000+*************************************** 53723     *--+--*
       +----+----+----+----+----+----+----+----+--
       * may represent up to 1120 counts
```

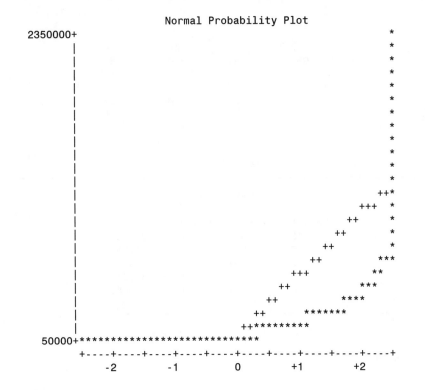

Normal Probability Plot

Inferred Age

Univariate Procedure

Variable=INFD_AG
Weight= SMP_WGT

Moments

N	85404	Sum Wgts	729228
Mean	42.83768	Sum	31238435
Std Dev	27.21078	Variance	740.4265
Skewness	.	Kurtosis	.
USS	1.4014E9	CSS	63234643
CV	63.52067	Std Mean	0.031865
T:Mean=0	1344.363	Pr>|T|	0.0001
Num ^= 0	85404	Num > 0	85404
M(Sign)	42702	Pr>=|M|	0.0001
Sgn Rank	1.8235E9	Pr>=|S|	0.0001

```
                      Quantiles(Def=5)

           100% Max      65       99%      64
            75% Q3       49       95%      59
            50% Med      42       90%      55
            25% Q1       36       10%      30
             0% Min      25        5%      27
                                   1%      25

           Range         40
           Q3-Q1         13
           Mode          39
```

```
                         Extremes

        Lowest     Obs      Highest     Obs
            25(    85399)        65(    84255)
            25(    85395)        65(    84326)
            25(    85390)        65(    84334)
            25(    85383)        65(    85187)
            25(    85372)        65(    85368)
```

```
                   Univariate Procedure

Variable=INFD_AG
Weight=  SMP_WGT


              Histogram                      #        Boxplot
   65+*******                              1020          |
     .*******                              1131          |
   61+************                         1781          |
     .***********                          1846          |
   57+***************                      2254          |
     .**********************               3523          |
   53+**************************           4101          |
     .*********************************    5451          |
   49+***********************************  5580        +--+
     .***********************************  5684        |  |
   45+***********************************  5689        |  |
     .****************************************  6296   *--+--*
   41+*************************************************  7118  |  |
     .**************************************************** 7477 |  |
   37+********************************************  6663     +--+
     .******************************       4681          |
   33+*************************            3979          |
     .**********************               3442          |
   29+*******************                  3090          |
     .******************                   2877          |
   25+************                         1721          |
     ----+----+----+----+----+----+----+----+----+---
      * may represent up to 156 counts
```

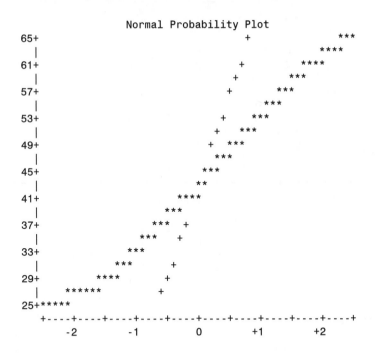

```
                        Normal Probability Plot
    65+                                   +              ***
      |                                                 ****
    61+                                   +           ****
      |                               +             ***
    57+                               +          ***
      |                                       ***
    53+                            +        ***
      |                         +       ***
    49+                      +    ***
      |                         ***
    45+                      ***
      |                     **
    41+                  ****
      |                 ***
    37+              ***    +
      |             ***   +
    33+           ***
      |         ***         +
    29+      ****         +
      |   ******        +
    25+*****
       +----+----+----+----+----+----+----+----+----+----+
          -2        -1         0        +1        +2
```

Total Accounts

Univariate Procedure

Variable=TOT_ACC
Weight= SMP_WGT

Moments

N	85404	Sum Wgts	729228
Mean	19.96658	Sum	14560189
Std Dev	32.37958	Variance	1048.437
Skewness	.	Kurtosis	.
USS	3.8026E8	CSS	89539683
CV	162.1689	Std Mean	0.037917
T:Mean=0	526.5797	Pr>|T|	0.0001
Num ^= 0	85404	Num > 0	85404
M(Sign)	42702	Pr>=|M|	0.0001
Sgn Rank	1.8235E9	Pr>=|S|	0.0001

```
                    Quantiles(Def=5)

            100% Max      87      99%      52
             75% Q3       27      95%      41
             50% Med      19      90%      35
             25% Q1       12      10%       6
              0% Min       1       5%       4
                                  1%       2

            Range         86
            Q3-Q1         15
            Mode          14
```

```
                         Extremes

            Lowest    Obs      Highest    Obs
                1(  76936)       76(     521)
                1(  75718)       77(   77634)
                1(  74479)       78(     684)
                1(  72540)       78(   69582)
                1(  72152)       87(   47533)
```

```
              Histogram                      #        Boxplot
   87.5+*                                     1           *
       .
       .*                                     4           *
       .*                                     7           0
       .*                                    40           0
       .*                                   284           0
       .*                                   305           0
       .**                                  628           0
       .****                               1241           |
       .********                           2359           |
       .************                       4246           |
       .*********************              6887           |
       .*******************************   10509         +--+
       .*********************************************  13711     |    |
       .*********************************************** 15120  *--+--*
       .*********************************************   14211    +--+
       .************************************           11271     |
    2.5+***************                                 4580     |
       ----+----+----+----+----+----+----+----+----+---
       * may represent up to 315 counts
```

Univariate Procedure

Variable=TOT_ACC
Weight= SMP_WGT

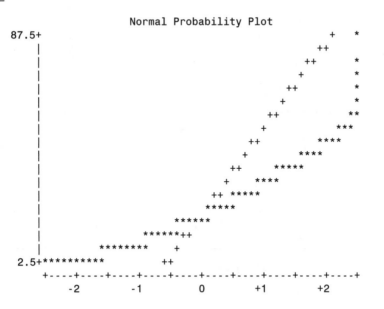

Normal Probability Plot

Accounts Open in Last 6 Months

Univariate Procedure

Variable=ACTOPL6
Weight= SMP_WGT

Moments

N	85404	Sum Wgts	729228
Mean	1.153018	Sum	840813
Std Dev	3.209506	Variance	10.30093
Skewness	.	Kurtosis	.
USS	1849203	CSS	879730.5
CV	278.357	Std Mean	0.003758
T:Mean=0	306.7817	Pr>|T|	0.0001
Num ^= 0	60711	Num > 0	60711
M(Sign)	30355.5	Pr>=|M|	0.0001
Sgn Rank	9.2147E8	Pr>=|S|	0.0001

Quantiles(Def=5)

100%	Max	16	99%	5
75%	Q3	2	95%	3
50%	Med	1	90%	3
25%	Q1	0	10%	0
0%	Min	0	5%	0
			1%	0

Range	16
Q3-Q1	2
Mode	1

Extremes

Lowest	Obs	Highest	Obs
0(	85404)	11(	41050)
0(	85401)	12(	56381)
0(	85394)	13(	64495)
0(	85388)	14(	23611)
0(	85384)	16(	18716)

```
            Histogram                                 #      Boxplot
16.5+*                                                1         *
    .
    .*                                                1         *
    .*                                                1         *
    .*                                                1         *
    .*                                                3         *
    .*                                                8         *
    .*                                               14         *
 8.5+*                                               29         0
    .*                                               93         0
    .*                                              271         0
    .*                                              702         |
    .***                                           2106        |
    .********                                      5945        |
    .*********************                        16464       +--+
    .**************************************************** 35072   *--+--*
 0.5+**********************************            24693       +--+
    ----+----+----+----+----+----+----+----+----+----+---
     * may represent up to 731 counts
```

Evaluation of actopl6

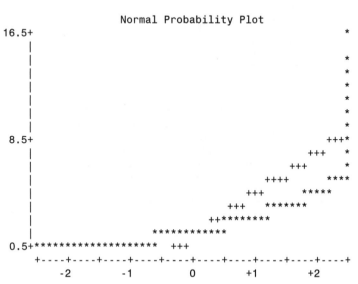

Univariate Procedure

Variable=ACTOPL6
Weight= SMP_WGT

Total Balances

Univariate Procedure

Variable=TOT_BAL
Weight= SMP_WGT

Moments

N	85404	Sum Wgts	729228
Mean	129490.5	Sum	9.443E10
Std Dev	504678.2	Variance	2.547E11
Skewness	.	Kurtosis	.
USS	3.398E16	CSS	2.175E16
CV	389.7416	Std Mean	590.9937
T:Mean=0	219.1063	Pr>|T|	0.0001
Num ^= 0	83616	Num > 0	83616
M(Sign)	41808	Pr>=|M|	0.0001
Sgn Rank	1.7479E9	Pr>=|S|	0.0001

```
                    Quantiles(Def=5)

            100% Max    5544774      99%     741006
             75% Q3      182987      95%     399898
             50% Med      79779      90%     298176
             25% Q1     10690.5      10%       1096
              0% Min          0       5%        261
                                      1%          0

            Range        5544774
            Q3-Q1      172296.5
            Mode               0
```

Extremes

```
            Lowest    Obs     Highest    Obs
                0(  85280)   3983490(  40154)
                0(  85133)   4102490(  23869)
                0(  84961)   4163294(  19189)
                0(  84873)   4701462(  69915)
                0(  84835)   5544774(  17281)
```

```
               Histogram                              #        Boxplot
5750000+*                                             1          *
       .
       .*                                             1          *
       .*                                             2          *
       .*                                             4          *
       .*                                             4          *
       .*                                            13          *
       .*                                            18          *
       .*                                            55          *
       .*                                           246          *
       .**                                         2096          0
 250000+*********************************************** 82964   +--0--+
       ----+----+----+----+----+----+----+----+----+---
        * may represent up to 1729 counts
```

Univariate Procedure

Variable=TOT_BAL
Weight= SMP_WGT

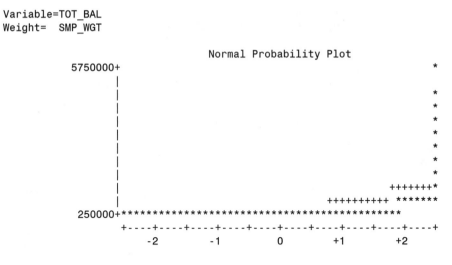

Normal Probability Plot

Number of Inquiries in Last 6 Months

Univariate Procedure

Variable=INQL6M
Weight= SMP_WGT

Moments

N	85404	Sum Wgts	729228
Mean	0.903981	Sum	659208
Std Dev	3.9358	Variance	15.49052
Skewness	.	Kurtosis	.
USS	1918848	CSS	1322937
CV	435.3854	Std Mean	0.004609
T:Mean=0	196.1362	Pr>|T|	0.0001
Num ^= 0	41183	Num > 0	41183
M(Sign)	20591.5	Pr>=|M|	0.0001
Sgn Rank	4.2402E8	Pr>=|S|	0.0001

Quantiles(Def=5)

100% Max	22		99%	6
75% Q3	1		95%	4
50% Med	0		90%	3
25% Q1	0		10%	0
0% Min	0		5%	0
			1%	0
Range	22			
Q3-Q1	1			
Mode	0			

```
                         Extremes

            Lowest     Obs     Highest     Obs
                0(   85402)        16(   28580)
                0(   85401)        17(   58346)
                0(   85400)        18(    9388)
                0(   85399)        18(   56381)
                0(   85398)        22(   41413)
```

```
                   Univariate Procedure

Variable=INQL6M
Weight=  SMP_WGT

                  Histogram                      #        Boxplot
      22.5+*                                      1           *
          .
          .
          .
          .*                                      2           *
          .*                                      1           *
          .*                                      1           *
          .*                                      2           *
          .*                                      3           *
          .*                                      5           *
          .*                                     12           *
      11.5+*                                     28           *
          .*                                     49           *
          .*                                     80           *
          .*                                    161           *
          .*                                    322           *
          .*                                    569           *
          .**                                  1134           *
          .***                                 2328           0
          .******                              4845           0
          .**********                          9974           |
          .**********************             21666         +--+
       0.5+*************************************** 44221   *--+--*
          ----+----+----+----+----+----+----+----+----+---
          * may represent up to 922 counts
```

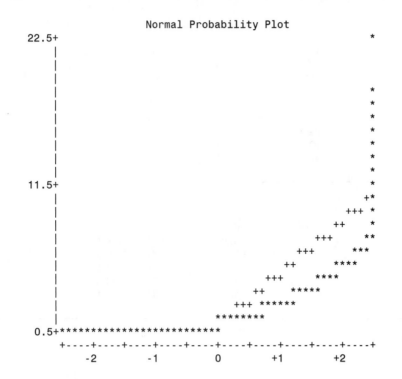

Normal Probability Plot

Total Open Accounts

Univariate Procedure

Variable=TOTOPAC
Weight= SMP_WGT

Moments

N	85404	Sum Wgts	729228
Mean	12.57202	Sum	9167868
Std Dev	20.34971	Variance	414.1109
Skewness	.	Kurtosis	.
USS	1.5062E8	CSS	35366311
CV	161.8651	Std Mean	0.02383
T:Mean=0	527.5679	Pr>|T|	0.0001
Num ^= 0	85404	Num > 0	85404
M(Sign)	42702	Pr>=|M|	0.0001
Sgn Rank	1.8235E9	Pr>=|S|	0.0001

Quantiles(Def=5)

100% Max	63	99%	34
75% Q3	17	95%	25
50% Med	12	90%	22
25% Q1	7	10%	4
0% Min	1	5%	3
		1%	2
Range	62		
Q3-Q1	10		
Mode	10		

Extremes

Lowest	Obs	Highest	Obs
1(	85290)	54(	56001)
1(	85068)	57(	25775)
1(	84622)	57(	56381)
1(	84417)	59(	69582)
1(	84246)	63(	684)

```
Histogram                          #           Boxplot
   62.5+*                                           1              *
      .*                                            3              *
      .*                                           19              *
      .*                                           50              0
      .*                                          180              0
      .*                                          454              0
   32.5+***                                      1181              0
      .******                                    3316              |
      .***************                           7733              |
      .*******************************          16218            +--+
      .************************************************* 24252   *--+--*
      .***********************************************  22915    +--+
    2.5+******************                           9082          |
      ----+----+----+----+----+----+----+----+----+---
       * may represent up to 506 counts
```

Univariate Procedure

Variable=TOTOPAC
Weight= SMP_WGT

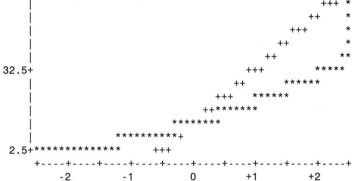

Normal Probability Plot

```
62.5+                                                        +*
    |                                                    +++ *
    |                                                 ++    *
    |                                              +++     *
    |                                           ++        *
    |                                        +++         *
    |                                     ++           **
32.5+                                  +++        *****
    |                               ++       ******
    |                            +++    ******
    |                         ++********
    |                    ********
    |               **********+
 2.5+**************            +++
    +----+----+----+----+----+----+----+----+----+----+
        -2        -1         0        +1        +2
```

Total Credit Lines

Univariate Procedure

Variable=CREDLIN
Weight= SMP_WGT

Moments

N	85404	Sum Wgts	729228
Mean	173929	Sum	1.268E11
Std Dev	581723.2	Variance	3.384E11
Skewness	.	Kurtosis	.
USS	5.096E16	CSS	2.89E16
CV	334.4601	Std Mean	681.2158
T:Mean=0	255.3215	Pr>|T|	0.0001
Num ^= 0	85366	Num > 0	85366
M(Sign)	42683	Pr>=|M|	0.0001
Sgn Rank	1.8219E9	Pr>=|S|	0.0001

Quantiles(Def=5)

100% Max	9250120	99%	867178
75% Q3	237600	95%	488500
50% Med	123900	90%	370506
25% Q1	35445	10%	14610
0% Min	0	5%	7500
		1%	1159
Range	9250120		
Q3-Q1	202155		
Mode	10000		

```
                           Extremes

            Lowest      Obs      Highest       Obs
                0(    84821)   4577900(    23869)
                0(    79629)   4828676(    19189)
                0(    74719)   5451884(    69915)
                0(    70318)   5745300(    17281)
                0(    59675)   9250120(    13742)
```

```
                Histogram                          #        Boxplot
9250000+*                                          1           *
        .
        .
        .
        .
        .
        .
        .*                                         1           *
        .*                                         1           *
4750000+*                                          2           *
        .*                                         5           *
        .*                                         4           *
        .*                                        10           *
        .*                                        11           *
        .*                                        30           *
        .*                                        86           *
        .*                                       394           *
        .***                                    3439           0
 250000+***************************************** 81420      +--+--+
        ----+----+----+----+----+----+----+----+---
         * may represent up to 1697 counts
```

Univariate Procedure

Variable=CREDLIN
Weight= SMP_WGT

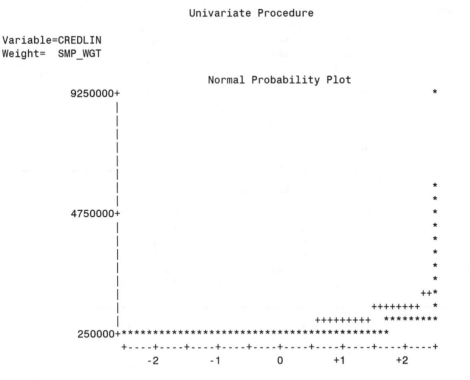

```
                      Normal Probability Plot
      9250000+                                              *
             |
             |
             |
             |
             |
             |
             |                                           *
             |                                           *
      4750000+                                           *
             |                                           *
             |                                           *
             |                                           *
             |                                           *
             |                                           *
             |                                         ++*
             |                              ++++++++  *
             |                     ++++++++ ********
       250000+*************************************************
             +----+----+----+----+----+----+----+----+----+----+
                 -2        -1         0        +1        +2
```

Age of File

Univariate Procedure

Variable=AGE_FIL
Weight= SMP_WGT

```
                         Moments
          N            85404   Sum Wgts     729228
          Mean      174.3028   Sum        1.2711E8
          Std Dev   254.3212   Variance   64679.28
          Skewness         .   Kurtosis          .
          USS       2.768E10   CSS        5.5238E9
          CV        145.9077   Std Mean   0.297818
          T:Mean=0  585.2661   Pr>|T|       0.0001
          Num ^= 0     85351   Num > 0       85351
          M(Sign)    42675.5   Pr>=|M|      0.0001
          Sgn Rank  1.8212E9   Pr>=|S|      0.0001
```

```
                    Quantiles(Def=5)

        100% Max      666        99%      347
         75% Q3       227        95%      329
         50% Med      169        90%      295
         25% Q1       108        10%       52
          0% Min        0         5%       31
                                  1%        5

        Range        666
        Q3-Q1        119
        Mode         214
```

```
                    Extremes

     Lowest      Obs      Highest     Obs
          0(  84242)         619(  84665)
          0(  81481)         625(  58765)
          0(  80706)         663(  38006)
          0(  80589)         666(  10497)
          0(  76936)         666(  71596)
```

```
              Histogram                     #        Boxplot
   675+*                                     3           *
      .*                                     2           *
      .*                                     1           *
      .*                                    12           0
      .*                                    26           0
      .*                                    96           0
      .**                                  663           |
      .*******************                7110           |
      .*******************                7651           |
      .*************************************************** 18394     +--+
      .*****************************************         15859    *--+--*
      .*********************************************    16906     +--+
      .**************************                       10678        |
    25+*********************                             8003        |
      ----+----+----+----+----+----+----+----+----+---
       * may represent up to 384 counts
```

Univariate Procedure

Variable=AGE_FIL
Weight= SMP_WGT

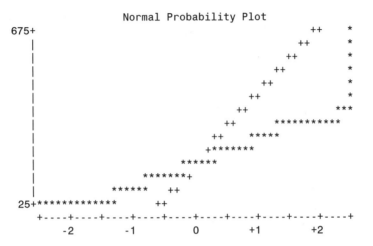

Normal Probability Plot

Number of 30-Day Delinquencies

Univariate Procedure

Variable=NO30DAY
Weight= SMP_WGT

Moments

N	85404	Sum Wgts	729228
Mean	0.718138	Sum	523686
Std Dev	5.898548	Variance	34.79287
Skewness	.	Kurtosis	.
USS	3347494	CSS	2971415
CV	821.3675	Std Mean	0.006907
T:Mean=0	103.9667	Pr>|T|	0.0001
Num ^= 0	22303	Num > 0	22303
M(Sign)	11151.5	Pr>=|M|	0.0001
Sgn Rank	1.2436E8	Pr>=|S|	0.0001

```
                    Quantiles(Def=5)

       100% Max      43       99%      10
        75% Q3        1       95%       4
        50% Med       0       90%       2
        25% Q1        0       10%       0
         0% Min       0        5%       0
                               1%       0

       Range         43
       Q3-Q1          1
       Mode           0
```

```
                      Extremes

      Lowest     Obs      Highest    Obs
           0(  85404)         37(  78590)
           0(  85403)         38(  44354)
           0(  85402)         38(  47412)
           0(  85401)         43(   7285)
           0(  85400)         43(  46812)
```

```
                 Univariate Procedure

Variable=NO30DAY
Weight=  SMP_WGT


                Histogram                           #        Boxplot
    43+*                                            2           *
      .
      .*                                            2           *
      .*                                            5           *
      .*                                            3           *
      .*                                            2           *
      .*                                            6           *
    29+*                                            7           *
      .*                                           10           *
      .*                                           12           *
      .*                                           28           *
      .*                                           48           *
      .*                                           58           *
      .*                                           82           *
    15+*                                          116           *
      .*                                          211           *
      .*                                          312           *
      .*                                          558           *
      .*                                         1070           *
      .**                                        2290           0
      .*****                                     6606           0
     1+******************************************* 73976      +--+--+
      ----+----+----+----+----+----+----+----+----+---
      * may represent up to 1542 counts
```

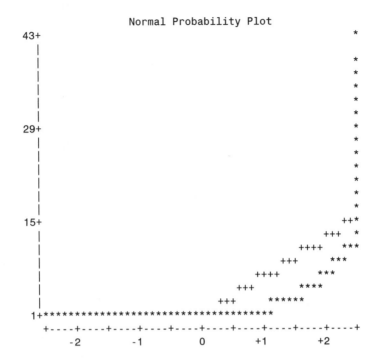

Normal Probability Plot

Replacing Missing Values for Income

The first frequency shows the distribution of HOME EQUITY. This is used to create the matrix that displays the mean INCOME by HOME EQUITY range and AGE Group.

HOMEQ_R	Frequency	Percent	Cumulative Frequency	Cumulative Percent
$0-$100K	53723	62.9	53723	62.9
$100-$20	20285	23.8	74008	86.7
$200-$30	7248	8.5	81256	95.1
$300-$40	2269	2.7	83525	97.8
$400-$50	737	0.9	84262	98.7
$500-$60	339	0.4	84601	99.1
$600-$70	213	0.2	84814	99.3
$700K+	590	0.7	85404	100.0

Mean INCOME by HOME EQUITY and AGE Group

	Age Group			
	25-34	35-44	45-54	55-65
Home Equity				
$0-$100K	$47	$55	$57	$55
$100-$20	$70	$73	$72	$68
$200-$30	$66	$73	$76	$68
$300-$40	$70	$80	$84	$76
$400-$50	$89	$93	$94	$93
$500-$60	$98	$101	$102	$97
$600-$70	$91	$105	$109	$104
$700K+	$71	$102	$111	$107

The following regression uses INFERRED AGE, HOME EQUITY, CREDIT LINE and TOTAL BALANCES to predict missing values for INCOME.

```
Step 0    All Variables Entered    R-square = 0.66962678   C(p) = 5.00000000
```

	DF	Sum of Squares	Mean Square	F	Prob>F
Regression	4	372912001.28200	93228000.320499	43230.8	0.0001
Error	85315	183983294.99609	2156.51755255		
Total	85319	556895296.27809			

Variable	Parameter Estimate	Standard Error	Type II Sum of Squares	F	Prob>F
INTERCEP	36.87607683	0.25721498	44325117.661102	20554.0	0.0001
INFD_AG2	0.11445815	0.00602800	777500.06857066	360.54	0.0001
HOM_EQU2	-0.00000343	0.00000040	158246.95496857	73.38	0.0001
CREDLIN2	0.00011957	0.00000120	21410199.091371	9928.14	0.0001
TOT_BAL2	-0.00000670	0.00000136	52180.72203473	24.20	0.0001

```
Bounds on condition number:    19.28444,     161.5108
---------------------------------------------------------
```

All variables left in the model are significant at the 0.1000 level.

OBS	_MODEL_	_TYPE_	_DEPVAR_	_RMSE_	INTERCEP	INFD_AG2
1	INC_REG	PARMS	INC_EST2	46.4383	36.8761	0.11446

OBS	HOM_EQU2	CREDLIN2	TOT_BAL2	INC_EST2
1	-.0000034348	.00011957	-.0000067044	-1

The following print output displays the values for INCOME after regression substitution.

OBS	INC_EST2	INC_EST3
436	.	43.3210
2027	.	44.5382
4662	.	40.2160
5074	.	43.5390
5256	.	41.6833
5552	.	43.1713
6816	.	41.4527
8663	.	62.8130
10832	.	42.3638
11052	.	42.4500
14500	.	41.6961
14809	.	41.2255
15132	.	63.4676
15917	.	41.2685
16382	.	41.8029
16788	.	40.8224
16832	.	34.2062
16903	.	42.0813
17201	.	43.5734
17419	.	42.8501
17540	.	43.9865
17700	.	40.3016
18045	.	42.4653
18147	.	43.5607
18254	.	41.3758
18296	.	41.3878
18362	.	41.5944
18597	.	40.7010
18931	.	51.3921
19058	.	42.4845
20419	.	42.0720
20640	.	40.1936
22749	.	42.1277
23201	.	42.6050
23334	.	42.4007
23651	.	41.7607
24227	.	34.0227
24764	.	39.8351
25759	.	42.0662

continues

(Continued)

OBS	INC_EST2	INC_EST3
26608	.	54.4467
30922	.	42.8928
31141	.	41.6508
32963	.	42.6343
32986	.	41.2255
34175	.	41.2114
34702	.	41.6541
35897	.	47.0708
36616	.	42.7077
42978	.	41.3285
44612	.	53.0752
45165	.	43.7436
45959	.	41.1110
46242	.	41.9122
46428	.	41.6833
46439	.	42.5990
47002	.	42.0267
47400	.	41.8678
48237	.	51.3944
49472	.	44.1610
50012	.	41.7293
50059	.	43.1998
50236	.	42.3850
50446	.	42.0642
51312	.	42.6312
52741	.	42.0676
53961	.	42.1993
53972	.	43.8084
54715	.	43.3766
55422	.	44.0192
57848	.	45.8676
59262	.	41.3399
59450	.	41.4544
59512	.	43.7946
59675	.	41.4544
60545	.	46.7328
64254	.	52.3536
66336	.	42.3752
69200	.	43.4159
70318	.	41.5689
72152	.	41.6255
72540	.	42.5443
74479	.	42.8142
75718	.	42.3963
76936	.	42.8469

Univariate Analysis of Categorical Variables

In this appendix you will find simple frequencies of the categorical variables discussed in chapter 3.

Categorical Variables

POP_DEN	Frequency	Percent	Cumulative Frequency	Cumulative Percent
	143889	19.7	143889	19.7
A	46934	6.4	190823	26.2
B	267947	36.7	458770	62.9
C	270458	37.1	729228	100.0

TRAV_CD	Frequency	Percent	Cumulative Frequency	Cumulative Percent
	220060	30.2	220060	30.2
1	509168	69.8	729228	100.0

BANKCRD	Frequency	Percent	Cumulative Frequency	Cumulative Percent
N	40817	5.6	40817	5.6
Y	688411	94.4	729228	100.0

APT_IND	Frequency	Percent	Cumulative Frequency	Cumulative Percent
N	600369	82.3	600369	82.3
Y	128859	17.7	729228	100.0

Categorical Variables

CLUSTR1	Frequency	Percent	Cumulative Frequency	Cumulative Percent
	594	0.1	594	0.1
A1	1854	0.3	2448	0.3
A2	947	0.1	3395	0.5
A3	2278	0.3	5673	0.8
A4	2269	0.3	7942	1.1
B1	1573	0.2	9515	1.3
B2	1306	0.2	10821	1.5
B3	1668	0.2	12489	1.7
B4	1120	0.2	13609	1.9
C1	2518	0.3	16127	2.2
C2	5759	0.8	21886	3.0
C3	404	0.1	22290	3.1
C4	1194	0.2	23484	3.2
D1	59097	8.1	82581	11.3
D2	7114	1.0	89695	12.3
D3	8268	1.1	97963	13.4
D4	14128	1.9	112091	15.4
E1	1614	0.2	113705	15.6
E2	1091	0.1	114796	15.7
E3	13479	1.8	128275	17.6
E4	7695	1.1	135970	18.6
E5	3808	0.5	139778	19.2
F1	878	0.1	140656	19.3
F2	1408	0.2	142064	19.5
F3	1272	0.2	143336	19.7
G1	5459	0.7	148795	20.4
G2	28935	4.0	177730	24.4
G3	33544	4.6	211274	29.0
G4	14517	2.0	225791	31.0
G5	3862	0.5	229653	31.5
H1	41	0.0	229694	31.5
H2	153	0.0	229847	31.5
H3	1550	0.2	231397	31.7
H4	1321	0.2	232718	31.9
H5	1757	0.2	234475	32.2
I1	121832	16.7	356307	48.9
I2	24836	3.4	381143	52.3
I3	29429	4.0	410572	56.3
I4	6902	0.9	417474	57.2
I5	65318	9.0	482792	66.2
J1	180767	24.8	663559	91.0
J2	65669	9.0	729228	100.0

Categorical Variables

INC_GRP	Frequency	Percent	Cumulative Frequency	Cumulative Percent
	750	0.1	750	0.1
A	566	0.1	1316	0.2
B	12040	1.7	13356	1.8
C	41007	5.6	54363	7.5
D	64095	8.8	118458	16.2
E	82088	11.3	200546	27.5
F	62449	8.6	262995	36.1
G	47412	6.5	310407	42.6
H	40136	5.5	350543	48.1
I	41641	5.7	392184	53.8
J	43885	6.0	436069	59.8
K	43091	5.9	479160	65.7
L	40647	5.6	519807	71.3
M	35647	4.9	555454	76.2
N	30169	4.1	585623	80.3
O	24702	3.4	610325	83.7
P	20056	2.8	630381	86.4
Q	17819	2.4	648200	88.9
R	81028	11.1	729228	100.0

SGLE_IN	Frequency	Percent	Cumulative Frequency	Cumulative Percent
N	627089	86.0	627089	86.0
Y	102139	14.0	729228	100.0

FINL_ID	Frequency	Percent	Cumulative Frequency	Cumulative Percent
A	24293	3.3	24293	3.3
M	11908	1.6	36201	5.0
N	693027	95.0	729228	100.0

HH_IND	Frequency	Percent	Cumulative Frequency	Cumulative Percent
	119833	16.4	119833	16.4
H	609395	83.6	729228	100.0

GENDER	Frequency	Percent	Cumulative Frequency	Cumulative Percent
F	293331	40.2	293331	40.2
I	124038	17.0	417369	57.2
M	311859	42.8	729228	100.0

Categorical Variables

SSN_IND	Frequency	Percent	Cumulative Frequency	Cumulative Percent
N	283	0.0	283	0.0
Y	728945	100.0	729228	100.0

DRIV_IN	Frequency	Percent	Cumulative Frequency	Cumulative Percent
A	338410	46.4	338410	46.4
N	333066	45.7	671476	92.1
O	57752	7.9	729228	100.0

MOB_IND	Frequency	Percent	Cumulative Frequency	Cumulative Percent
	437608	60.0	437608	60.0
N	246167	33.8	683775	93.8
Y	45453	6.2	729228	100.0

MORTIN1	Frequency	Percent	Cumulative Frequency	Cumulative Percent
	163498	22.4	163498	22.4
M	185182	25.4	348680	47.8
N	78226	10.7	426906	58.5
Y	302322	41.5	729228	100.0

MORTIN2	Frequency	Percent	Cumulative Frequency	Cumulative Percent
	322189	44.2	322189	44.2
M	87986	12.1	410175	56.2
N	175422	24.1	585597	80.3
Y	143631	19.7	729228	100.0

AUTOIN1	Frequency	Percent	Cumulative Frequency	Cumulative Percent
	261487	35.9	261487	35.9
A	135457	18.6	396944	54.4
N	127951	17.5	524895	72.0
Y	204333	28.0	729228	100.0

Categorical Variables

AUTOIN2	Frequency	Percent	Cumulative Frequency	Cumulative Percent
	386914	53.1	386914	53.1
A	57109	7.8	444023	60.9
N	206299	28.3	650322	89.2
Y	78906	10.8	729228	100.0

INFD_AG	Frequency	Percent	Cumulative Frequency	Cumulative Percent
25	13682	1.9	13682	1.9
26	11819	1.6	25501	3.5
27	11137	1.5	36638	5.0
28	12633	1.7	49271	6.8
29	12336	1.7	61607	8.4
30	12522	1.7	74129	10.2
31	15535	2.1	89664	12.3
32	15653	2.1	105317	14.4
33	17603	2.4	122920	16.9
34	18485	2.5	141405	19.4
35	20648	2.8	162053	22.2
36	27641	3.8	189694	26.0
37	29476	4.0	219170	30.1
38	30475	4.2	249645	34.2
39	33801	4.6	283446	38.9
40	32400	4.4	315846	43.3
41	28286	3.9	344132	47.2
42	27794	3.8	371926	51.0
43	26004	3.6	397930	54.6
44	26421	3.6	424351	58.2
45	21694	3.0	446045	61.2
46	24183	3.3	470228	64.5
47	24773	3.4	495001	67.9
48	24662	3.4	519663	71.3
49	24190	3.3	543853	74.6
50	25831	3.5	569684	78.1
51	22334	3.1	592018	81.2
52	19074	2.6	611092	83.8
53	16752	2.3	627844	86.1
54	16067	2.2	643911	88.3
55	15032	2.1	658943	90.4
56	10454	1.4	669397	91.8
57	9350	1.3	678747	93.1
58	8349	1.1	687096	94.2
59	7780	1.1	694876	95.3
60	8172	1.1	703048	96.4
61	7487	1.0	710535	97.4
62	5336	0.7	715871	98.2
63	4489	0.6	720360	98.8
64	4486	0.6	724846	99.4
65	4382	0.6	729228	100.0

AGE_IND	Frequency	Percent	Cumulative Frequency	Cumulative Percent
E	204132	28.0	204132	28.0
F	525096	72.0	729228	100.0

Categorical Variables

DOB_YR	Frequency	Percent	Cumulative Frequency	Cumulative Percent
0000	193460	26.5	193460	26.5
1900	10672	1.5	204132	28.0
1933	4382	0.6	208514	28.6
1934	4486	0.6	213000	29.2
1935	4489	0.6	217489	29.8
1936	5205	0.7	222694	30.5
1937	5074	0.7	227768	31.2
1938	5203	0.7	232971	31.9
1939	5264	0.7	238235	32.7
1940	5668	0.8	243903	33.4
1941	6100	0.8	250003	34.3
1942	7242	1.0	257245	35.3
1943	11260	1.5	268505	36.8
1944	12115	1.7	280620	38.5
1945	12240	1.7	292860	40.2
1946	14302	2.0	307162	42.1
1947	16127	2.2	323289	44.3
1948	15912	2.2	339201	46.5
1949	16367	2.2	355568	48.8
1950	16709	2.3	372277	51.1
1951	17097	2.3	389374	53.4
1952	16767	2.3	406141	55.7
1953	17725	2.4	423866	58.1
1954	18232	2.5	442098	60.6
1955	18541	2.5	460639	63.2
1956	18244	2.5	478883	65.7
1957	19008	2.6	497891	68.3
1958	19885	2.7	517776	71.0
1959	19833	2.7	537609	73.7
1960	18873	2.6	556482	76.3
1961	18967	2.6	575449	78.9
1962	18945	2.6	594394	81.5
1963	17876	2.5	612270	84.0
1964	16903	2.3	629173	86.3
1965	15641	2.1	644814	88.4
1966	14213	1.9	659027	90.4
1967	13757	1.9	672784	92.3
1968	11442	1.6	684226	93.8
1969	10731	1.5	694957	95.3
1970	10476	1.4	705433	96.7
1971	8726	1.2	714159	97.9
1972	7703	1.1	721862	99.0
1973	7366	1.0	729228	100.0

HOMEQ_R	Frequency	Percent	Cumulative Frequency	Cumulative Percent
$0-$100K	449255	61.6	449255	61.6
$100-$20	178739	24.5	627994	86.1
$200-$30	64218	8.8	692212	94.9
$300-$40	20089	2.8	712301	97.7
$400-$50	6650	0.9	718951	98.6
$500-$60	3003	0.4	721954	99.0
$600-$70	1932	0.3	723886	99.3
$700K+	5342	0.7	729228	100.0

Categorical Variables

CHILDIN	Frequency	Percent	Cumulative Frequency	Cumulative Percent
N	577499	79.2	577499	79.2
Y	151729	20.8	729228	100.0

HOMEVLR	Frequency	Percent	Cumulative Frequency	Cumulative Percent
	239556	32.9	239556	32.9
C	51	0.0	239607	32.9
D	2135	0.3	241742	33.2
E	12731	1.7	254473	34.9
F	30353	4.2	284826	39.1
G	45397	6.2	330223	45.3
H	52762	7.2	382985	52.5
I	53632	7.4	436617	59.9
J	48610	6.7	485227	66.5
K	42960	5.9	528187	72.4
L	35313	4.8	563500	77.3
M	53132	7.3	616632	84.6
N	34544	4.7	651176	89.3
O	21226	2.9	672402	92.2
P	14080	1.9	686482	94.1
Q	15300	2.1	701782	96.2
R	8364	1.1	710146	97.4
S	5114	0.7	715260	98.1
T	3317	0.5	718577	98.5
U	2340	0.3	720917	98.9
V	8311	1.1	729228	100.0

CLUSTR2	Frequency	Percent	Cumulative Frequency	Cumulative Percent
	698544	95.8	698544	95.8
1	2138	0.3	700682	96.1
2	1765	0.2	702447	96.3
3	795	0.1	703242	96.4
4	1999	0.3	705241	96.7
A	9784	1.3	715025	98.1
B	6651	0.9	721676	99.0
C	4710	0.6	726386	99.6
D	2842	0.4	729228	100.0

Berry, Michael J.A., and Gordon Linoff. 1997. *Data Mining Techniques*. New York: John Wiley & Sons.

Berry, Michael J.A., and Gordon Linoff. 1997. *Mastering Data Mining*. New York: John Wiley & Sons.

Hosmer, David W., and Stanley Lemeshow. 1989. *Applied Logistic Regression*. New York: John Wiley & Sons.

Hughes, Arthur M. 1994. *Strategic Database Marketing*. Chicago: Probus Publishing.

Journal of Targeting, Measurement and Analysis for Marketing. London: Henry Stewart Publications.

Tukey, John W. 1977. *Exploratory Data Analysis*. Reading, MA: Addison-Wesley.

The CD-ROM contains step-by-step instructions for developing the data models described in *Data Mining Cookbook*. Written in SAS code, you can use the contents as a template to create your own models. The content on the CD-ROM is equivalent to taking a three-day course in data modeling.

Within chapters 3 through 12 of this book are blocks of SAS code used to develop, validate, and implement the data models. By adapting this code and using some common sense, it is possible to build a model from the data preparation phase through model development and validation. However, this could take a considerable amount of time and introduce the possibility of coding errors. To simplify this task and make the code easily accessible for a variety of model types, a companion CD-ROM is available for purchase separately.

The CD-ROM includes full examples of all the code necessary to develop a variety of models including response, approval, attrition or churn, risk, and lifetime or net present value. Detailed code for developing the objective function includes examples from the credit cards, insurance, telecommunications, and catalog industries. The code is well documented and explains the goals and methodology for each step. The only software needed is BASE SAS and SAS/STAT. The spreadsheets used for creating gains tables and lift charts are also included. These can be used by plugging in the preliminary results from the analyses created in SAS. While the steps before and after the model processing can be used in conjunction with any data modeling software package, the code can also serve as a stand-alone modeling template. The model processing steps focus on variable preparation for use in logistic regression. Additional efficiencies in the form of SAS macros for variable processing and validation are included.

Hardware Requirements

To use this CD-ROM, your system must meet the following requirements:

Platform/processor/operating system: Windows® 95, NT 4.0 or higher; 200 MHz Pentium

RAM: 64 MB minimum; 128 MB recommended

Hard drive space: Nothing will install to the hard drive, but in order to make a local copy of all the files on the CD-ROM requires 5 MB of free space.

Peripherals: CD-ROM drive. You also will need to have the following applications to make full use of the CD-ROM: a running copy of SAS 6.12 or higher software to process SAS code provided; a browser such as Internet Explorer or Netscape Navigator to navigate the CD-ROM; Microsoft Excel 97/2000 or Microsoft Excel 5.0/95.

Installing the Software

Insert the CD-ROM and launch the readme.htm file in a web browser, or navigate using Windows Explorer to browse the contents of the CD. The model programs and output are in text format that can be opened in any editing software (including SAS) that reads ASCII files. Spreadsheets are in Microsoft Excel 97/2000 and Microsoft Excel 5.0/95. Launch the application (SAS 6.12 or higher) and open the file directly from the CD-ROM. If you wish to make changes, you can rename the files and save them to your local hard drive.

Using the Software

The CD is organized into folders that correspond to each chapter in *Data Mining Cookbook*. Within each folder are sub-folders containing SAS programs, SAS output, Excel spreadsheets. The programs can be used as templates. You just need to change the data set and variable names. More specific instructions on how to use the programs are included. The output is included to provide a more complete understanding of the recipes in *Data Mining Cookbook*. The spreadsheets contain all formulas used to create the tables and charts in *Data Mining Cookbook*.

Thank You for Buying
Data Mining Cookbook!

http://dataminingcookbook.wiley.com

We invite you to receive a series of "Data Modeling Tips" from Olivia Parr Rud. She will provide you with practical, actionable insights and ideas drawn from her vast experience as a data modeler.

- Fill out the registration form at **http://dataminingcookbook.wiley.com** to register for "Data Modeling Tips" e-mails.

- Submit your questions about data modeling, as well as any comments about the book, to askthechef@dataminingcookbook.com. The author will respond to selected questions and comments in her "Data Modeling Tips" e-mails.

Note: The "Data Modeling Tips" e-mails are the product of the author, Olivia Parr Rud. Wiley Computer Publishing holds no responsibility for their content and/or distribution.